STUDIES IN ANCIENT TECHNOLOGY

VOLUME VIII

STUDIES
IN ANCIENT TECHNOLOGY

BY

R. J. FORBES

VOLUME VIII

WITH 46 FIGURES, MAPS AND TABLES

LEIDEN
E. J. BRILL
1964

PRINTED IN THE NETHERLANDS

CONTENTS

LIST OF ABBREVIATIONS USED IN THE TEXT

AAA:	*Annals of Archaeology and Anthropology* (Liverpool)
AfO:	*Archiv für Orientforschung*
AJSL:	*American Journal of Semitic Languages and Literatures*
Ant. J.:	*Antiquaries Journal* (London)
AO:	*Der Alte Orient* (Leipzig)
APAW:	*Abhandlungen der Preussischen Akademie der Wissenschaften*
AR:	J. H. BREASTED, *Ancient Records of Egypt* (Chicago, Third Imp. 1927)
ARL:	D. D. LUCKENBILL, *Ancient Records of Assyria and Babylonia* (Chicago, 1926)
BA:	*Beiträge zur Assyriologie*
B.A. report:	*Report of the British Academy* (London)
BK:	see KB
Bab. Miz.:	F. H. WEISZBACH, *Babylonische Miszellen*
CAH:	*Cambridge Ancient History*
CT:	*Cuneiform texts from Babylonian tablets, etc. in the British Museum*
DP:	*Délégation en Perse*, edit. J. DE MORGAN
FALKENSTEIN:	A. FALKENSTEIN, *Archaïsche Texte aus Ur* (Leipzig, 1936)
HWB:	ERMAN-GRAPOW, *Handwörterbuch der aegyptischen Sprache*
ILN:	*Illustrated London News*
ITT:	*Inventaire des tablets de Tello*
JEA:	*Journal of Egyptian Archaeology* (London)
JEOL:	*Jaarbericht Ex Oriente Lux* (Leyden)
KAH:	*Keilschrifttexte aus Assur historischen Inhalts*
KAR:	*Keilschrifttexte aus Assur religiösen Inhalts*
KAVI:	*Keilschrifttexte aus Assur verschiedenen Inhalts*

KB: H. H. Figulla-E. F. Weidner, *Keilinschriften aus Boghazkoi*

OLZ: *Orientalische Literatur Zeitung* (Leipzig)

PW: Pauly-Wissowa, *Real-Encyclopädie der klassischen Altertumswissenschaft*

RA: *Revue d'Assyriologie* (Paris)

ŠL: Deimel, *Sumerisches Lexikon* (Rome)

Sethe, *Urk.*:   *Urkunden des ägyptischen Altertums*, edit. K. Sethe

VAB: *Vorderasiatische Bibliothek* (Leipzig)

YOS: *Yale Oriental Series, Babylonian texts*

PREFACE

When during the German occupation of our country the author sat down to write his METALLURGY IN ANTIQUITY, little could he know that there would be many years between the completion of the manuscript (1942) and its final publication (1950). If this book appeared without references to essays and books published during the intervening period this was entirely due to the impossibility of obtaining such literature in this country during the early post-war years. The surprisingly favourable reception of this book has now called for a reprint which led to a complete recasting and rewriting of a large part of the original text, at the same time bringing its references up to date.

This new edition of Metallurgy in Antiquity will embrace the vols. VIII and IX of my Studies in Ancient Technology. Vol. VIII will be devoted to the discussion of early metallurgy, the smith and his tools, gold, silver and lead, zinc and brass. Vol. IX will contain the chapters on copper, tin and bronze and iron. The friendly suggestions of my critics have been a great help in recasting the original, and I still hope that I will do a service to archaeologists and technologists by explaining something of the tools and methods of ancient metallurgy, and the background of the ancient smith. Again I would like to say with Livy in the Preface to his Ab Urbe Condita:

"I, on the other hand, shall look for a further reward of my labours in being able to close my eyes to the evils which our generation has witnessed for so many years; so long, at least, as I am devoting all my thoughts to retracing these pristine records, free from all the anxiety which can disturb the historian of his own times even if it cannot warp him from the truth".

Amsterdam, April 1963   R. J. FORBES.

CHAPTER ONE

SYNOPSIS OF EARLY METALLURGY

"We cannot but marvel at the fact that fire is necessary
for almost every operation. By fire minerals are dis-
integrated and copper produced, in fire is iron born
and by fire it is subdued, by fire gold is purified!"
(Pliny, *Nat. History* 36.200)

Before we start our discussion of the most important metals and
their alloys in the pre-classical and classical world it would seem
necessary to sketch briefly the main lines along which these metals
were conquered by mankind. This will also give us an opportunity
to discuss some of the basic technical points which will crop up again
and again in our story. Armed with these definitions we will be able
to see the limits which Nature set beyond which Man could not proceed
and which determine to a large part the use man made of metals.

1. *The traditional Metal Ages*

In tradition and in reality the *Metal Ages* play a large part. The idea
of dividing the history of the world in different periods named after
metals is probably of Iranian origin. The same sequence of "Metal
Ages" as given in Dan. 2.31—45 is found in the Avesta and it recurs
in Buddhist doctrines. Greek poets and philosophers have taken up
the idea, Hesiod mentions it in his *Works and Days* (1) though he
inserts a Heroic Age between the Bronze and the Iron Age. But generally the series consists of a Golden, Silver, Bronze and Iron Age from
Plato's *Republic* onwards upto Claudianos (400 A.D.). Still often one
of the metals is missing, as in the writings of Aratos, Cicero, Juvenal,
Festus or Ovid (2). But in these writings the Metal Ages are used to
depict the progress or often the decline of mankind, they are used to
illustrate the loss of primeval simplicity and bliss by the achievements
of material civilisation and the moral sins of mankind.

The prophet Daniel gives the sequence gold-silver-copper(bronze)-
iron, the Persian tradition has gold-silver-steel-an iron alloy of unknown composition. In the Near East this tradition formed part of

the later Babylonian planetary lore which supposed a bond between planets and metal and thus expressed the influence which certain planets had during the history of mankind. Hesiod's scheme may belong to the Oriental tradition which reached Greece from Babylon and Iran (3).

Gradually as Christian writers take over this idea they use it to describe the coming of the Last Judgement. Slowly the division of the history of mankind into four Metal Ages is given up and we find a division into four World Empires, which idea is to dominate medieval historiography and even philosophy of history for many more centuries.

But the idea of the four Metal Ages as the progress of material civilisation, each metal more or less characterizing the period called after it is a far later one though we find the earlier stages of this conception in Plato and Lucretius (4). The latter's scheme is stone-wood-copper and bronze-iron.

2.   The archaeological Metal Ages

The creator of the archaeological terms "Stone Age, Bronze Age", etc. was Christian Jurgensen Thomsen, who became curator of the Danish National Museum in 1816, which post he held until his death in 1865. In 1813 he had already read in a work by Vedel-Simonsen, that the oldest inhabitants of Scandinavia had first made their weapons and implements of stone and wood, subsequently of copper and bronze and finally of iron. This inspired him to arrange his collections by classifying them into three Ages of Stone, Bronze and Iron and from 1819 onwards the visitors of the museum listened to this classification as expounded in his guide lectures. In 1836 this classification appeared in print in his guide-book of the Museum.

In 1876 this scheme, which had finally survived many attacks, was expanded by the proposal made by Francois von Pulski at the International Congress of Archaeology at Budapest to insert a Copper Age between Stone and Bronze Age. Von Pulski was inspired by the many copper implements found in Hungary and he put his ideas in writing in his book on the Copper Age of Hungary in 1884.

These divisions of the history of mankind have been used since in archaeology as convenient labels, for it was gradually realized the rise of metallurgy was not the prime factor in the transition from Stone to Metal Age.

For the rise of metallurgy forms only part of that "prelude to urban revolution" as Gordon Childe has so aptly called the transition of Stone to Metal Age. The moving force of this revolution is the invention of the plough and the great change from food-gathering to food-production and the enlargment of diet which accompany it. In the wake of this raising of the standard of living and the production of surplus food to feed a minority of the population no longer bound to agriculture follow many achievements that belong to the necessities of modern life. There are the invention of the wheel with its consequences, wheeled carriages and wheel-turned pottery. The invention of the sun-dried and the baked brick and the production of quarried natural stone lead to architecture. Wheeled cart and sailing craft go to establish long-distance communications. For many ages already semi-precious and precious stones and native metals had been sought for their magical properties and in other branches of mining we can also prove that there were centres of production in the Neolithic or Stone Age whose products were the objects of international trade if perhaps only passed from tribe to tribe. But the new means of communication break down the isolation of settled groups, they establish lasting contacts with the nomads and the direct transmission of trade goods over long distances. The growing knowledge of the physical and chemical properties of metals and ores, the conquest of new smelting and working processes stimulate this trade. As most ores are far from common their demand leads to a revolution of neolithic economy. The surplus of agricultural products of the peasant civilisations in the river-valleys is bartered for the mineral products of the mountain dwellers. Already the small region of the Aunjetitz civilisation has yielded more than 600 Kgrs. of metal finds which surely represent only a fraction of what existed in this era formerly!

The centres of production are either the mining districts, the metallurgical centres (smelting sites and forges) but the itinerant smiths must also have played a part. Once the magical transsubstantiation of copper ores with carbon and fire was achieved and had become common knowledge, similar experiments with other stones led to the discover of more metals.

The smith more and and more becomes an important factor in international trade. In the earlier stages of the history of metallurgy mainly finished products were exported from the great producing centres but by the Iron Age either raw materials or semi-manufactured articles become the trade stock and the itinerant smith became more important to local needs than the producer. Since the Bronze Age ever growing specialisation leads to the formation of different types of smiths, the growth of a factory system of manufacture is already noticeable in the period of the New Kingdom of Egypt when standard types of metal objects become more common at the cost of style. Still this process cannot be stopped and it is developed by the Roman capitalists to something very near our factory-systems.

It would be important to study the routes of early metal trade. Very valuable material would be got by the study of the depot finds. From the four types of depots of metal objects two are of no use to this subjects for either domestic or votive hoards have nothing to do with metal trade, but founder's hoards (made up of old implements, broken objects, cakes and ingots) and commercial hoards (raw and half-finished tools, weapons, and ingots, but often very like the show-collection of a commercial traveller!) would certainly yield valuable clues as to the variety and extent of metal trade (5). Thus Coghlan has demonstrated contacts between the Beaker people who started metallurgy in Ireland, the Saale region and Brittany.

Fig. 1.
The oak sample-case of a Bronze Age itinerant smith found in Pomerania,
Germany (after Franz)

Again one must not exaggerate the importance of metallurgy in these early societies. The progress of metallurgy was slow, for no doubt not all metals were better than stone and it took a long schooling of generations of smiths and smelters to produce something like bronze which was definitely better than flint or polished stone. Still in the long run metallurgy had profound influence on early economy. For metallurgy accompanies the rise of urban civilisation and the formation of the first empires in history. Many of these empires were imposed on the original peasant civilisation of Neolithic times by invading warrior tribes and the rise of metallurgy enabled the dominating classes of assembling riches in the form of metal rings, bars, etc. What had been hardly possible in Neolithic times, the formation of social classes based on relative riches, became a possibility now. Metals traded by the weight, served as the earliest form of money after corn, cattle or hides had failed as a means of barter for long-distance trade. We find that ingots of metals acquire standard shapes and weights though only many centuries afterwards the bankers of Lydia hit on the idea of coining precious metals, that is to say to ensure the user constant value by purity of metal, constant weight and a hall-mark stamped on the coin. Still the lumps of metal served

Fig. 2.
A typical Bronze Age hoard found in Brandenburg (Germany)
(After Franz)

well in international trade and the rôle of metals as a means of the accumulation of wealth in the hands of few cannot be denied by any serious student of Antiquity. And indeed much of ancient history could be rewritten as a struggle for the domination of quarries and ore-deposits or metal-supplies!

But as we have pointed out, important as it may be, metallurgy was neither the prime nor the most important factor in the rise of urban civilisation. It is also accompanied and stimulated by the evolution of the calendar, writing, calculus and measurement, which guided and controlled by the primitive mind and its belief in the harmonious cosmos, formed the foundations of modern science. The doctrines of pre-Greek science had a profound influence on everything which we call applied science, and therefore on the evolution of mining and metallurgy too. It accounts for the eagerness of the early Sumerians to study nature and its products, to apply the "firetest" and many other experimental means of discrimination to ores, etc. and to arrange the results in their lists with the clear nomenclature which is such a help to our understanding of these ancient texts.

The Greeks and Romans have done little to understand the structure of metals better. Aristotle in the third and fourth book of his Meteorologica describes their external features and properties, but his theory that they consist of varying mixtures of the elements earth and water does not yield a real solution of the problem of their varying plasticity, hardness, etc. Pliny, who provides us with most of our information about metals in the classical world, is very matter of fact and does not venture to give any theory of metals (6).

Thus metallurgy can be said to be one of the important factors in the rise of urban civilisation, which in its turn profoundly affected it. The historian of metallurgy cannot afford to ignore the social, economic, religious and material aspects of the civilisation in which metallurgy played a part of growing importance. He will then find that these factors account for the seemingly illogical developments of metal technique which are strewn on his path and that they impart a sudden and unexpected meaning to seemingly dull facts.

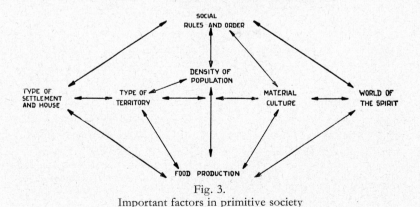

Fig. 3.
Important factors in primitive society

If then the use of such terms as "Bronze Age" and "Iron Age" has become common among archaeologists and others, we must realize that they were nothing but names for certain contexts of archaeological finds, prompted by the impression which metal objects make over pottery and other excavated objects. Indeed, these terms as applied to certain periods of civilisation have become paradoxes as our knowledge of Antiquity grew. For one can truly say that at present the Bronze Age is the period in which bronze gradually ousts copper from its prominent place in metallurgy and when at the end of the Bronze Age bronze has come into general use, the first signs of its younger rival, iron, are found. Thus the poet's words that "each age is a dream that is dying or one that is coming to birth" is made true even in the story of the material equipment of mankind. It has been correctly pointed out (7) that only by considering both the chemical-technological aspects as well as the typological ones we can build up chronological series and find out the traderoutes of metals.

Even their sequence did not prove to hold good everywhere in the world. The series Copper Age, Bronze Age and Iron Age was originally built up on the evidence of European prehistory and as the excavations of the Near East yielded their masses of material this idea was found to hold good there too. We now know that this was because we are quite near the original centre of metallurgy here and that the theoretical sequence holds good for primary and secondary centres and some of the further ones, but that we must be very careful of pitfalls. African metallurgy remained a puzzle until it was realised that there the Iron Age preceeded the Bronze Age. Again in other parts of the world there was no Bronze Age at all. Neolithic tribes of Assam and Burma came into contact with our modern Steel Age before they had known any copper or bronze, and it would be easy to multiply these examples. We will discuss two such cases later on.

3. *The stages of metallurgy*

As long as we remember well that these terms are only convenient names for certain aspects of civilisation characterised by many more things than just the use of bronze or iron, we may go on using them for the lack of better ones.

But we must also remember that they are no indication of the evolution of metallurgy in that particular region or anywhere because they do not represent the true *stages of metallurgy*. These stages are characterised not by any particular metal but by many processes and methods going hand in hand, by a complex of discoveries and inventions guided by some leading ideas.

I   Native metal as stones

II   Native metal stage (hammering cutting.etc.)
      (copper gold. silver. meteoric iron)

III   Ore stage (from ore to metal. alloys
             composition as primary factor)
      (lead. silver copper antimony. tin. bronze. brass)

IV   Iron stage (processing as primary factor)
      (cast iron wrought iron steel)

Fig. 4.
Evolution of Metallurgy

The earliest metals collected by man were native metals (copper, gold, silver and meteoric iron) which occur as such in nature. During a long time they were not recognised as a special kind of stone, but simply treated as the common stock of raw materials then used, viz. stone, bone or wood. By and by it was realised that these "strange stones" had some very individual properties, that they could be reshaped by heating and hold their shape when cooled. Some of the earlier processes applied to native metals remained in use, others were modified to suit the new way of treating them. Thus arose a complex of which hammering, tempering, cutting and grinding are typical methods. This must be considered to be the earliest stage of metallurgy which we might call the *native metal stage*. As we will have occasion to prove a new step was the discovery of the reduction of ores followed by the discovery that metals could be melted and cast. This led to a total change of the methods of metallurgy and the rise of what we should like to call the *ore stage*. Its methods are casting, welding, soldering and many other new processes together with the reduction of ores and the manufacture of alloys. At this stage mining and metallurgy go their own way and are no longer in one hand. Now a series of new metals are discovered (lead, silver, antimony, etc.) and the manufacture of alloys are taken in hand either by working ores or smelting a metal with an ore, later on by mixing two metals. In the latter case a distinct improvement was achieved, as it was now possible to make alloys of a composition wavering only within close limits, which advantage was, however, to become valuable only as the use of certain alloys for certain very specific purposes came to the fore. In earlier times bronze in general was already sufficient an improvement on copper, and keeping the composition of bronze within certain limits would not have impressed itself as a necessity. Generally speaking the alloys and their manufacture are characteristic for this "ore stage".

The next stage is the "iron stage" which practically coincides with the "Iron Age" of tradition. But though the wrought iron and steel (and perhaps also the chance cast iron!) were in reality alloys of iron and carbon their properties were much less dependent on their composition but generally speaking determined by their treatment. Here hammering, tempering, quenching and annealing were far more important than variations in the composition. Therefore the "iron stage" means the discovery and mastering of quite a new complex of processes and treatments, the details of which will be discussed later on. Once we start using the metal technique of a certain period as a criterion and no longer the kind of metal or alloy, we see that the development in every region becomes a succession of stages of phases each of which are complete in themselves. Seeing that each of these stages has its own complex of processes and techniques we need not wonder that the transition from one period to another is much less smooth than generally supposed.

The older histories of metallurgy (8) have not always realised this very clearly, but the post-war books on the history of metallurgy have learnt from the past (9) and some of the recent regional histories (10) have been very careful on this point.

Before we go on discussing discoveries and inventions and the *evolution of material culture* we must state quite clearly what we mean by these terms which are often so loosely employed. To this end we can do no better than reproduce the gist of Harrison's brilliant essay on this subject (11). By the aid of *methods*, often dependent upon extraneous *means*, man employs *materials* for the achievement of *results*, many but by no means all of which persist as artefacts or other products. Food was the only material which man had always to seek, but apart from this only the obtrusive materials attracted him, being under no compulsion to consider them. Therefore metal made its first impression as a fascinating luxury, from which evolved a need.

Now the idea of human progress is a fairly recent one, it became popular in the XVIIIth century only. But in reality man's progress is hardly that slowly rising line which lurks in the back of our mind when we talk of it. Man invents his ways as well as his means, but means are far older than man; they may be called "pure methods" indeed. Substance is the static warp, method the dynamic woof of man's material culture. But aims and ends as well as ways and means were and are the product of evolution.

Now we can define evolution as due to action and reaction in a developing brain and versatile hands in an expanding environment if we do not forget that this is just a statement but not an explanation!

For unconditioned foresight does not happen and directed research is apt to be overrun by invention, though the inventor only appears to be looking ahead! Artefacts then arose out of the rough and tumble of environment growing with knowledge and the accumulation of knowledge and artefacts. Chemically speaking the endproduct of the reaction is a catalyst, which enhances the speed of reaction and causes the formation of still more endproduct. In other words once the process of manufacture of artefacts started, the ball went on rolling quicker and quicker. The invention of script and the use of human speech have greatly enhanced the process by linking up the future and the past. In many cases we do not know how certain inventions took place. For instance there is still a gap between the discoveries of two properties of clay (plasticity and baking properties) and the production of the first earthenware pot, which is only more or less bridged by our "plastered pot" theory. In treating discovery very seriously we are often prone to forget that human mind is very prone to skid on trifles. Products of *discovery* are all artificially extracted, prepared and compounded materials which have no significant form impressed on them but which are merely the raw materials for future production. But *inventions* are all shaped or constructed artefacts. Many simple types therefore are mere products of discovery, a subjective event which may be applied to objective application. But invention which is really applied discovery is always objective.

In metallurgy we often have quite a series of discoveries. For instance the use of bronze for tools and weapons starts with the discovery of the hammering of copper and ends at the discovery of the casting of bronze. The discovery of the new alloy is followed by the directional effort towards repetition, then a search is made for the ameliorating impurity in the copper, once this cause has been established, which again provides the basis for experimental smelting or directed research.

Then the transfer of ideas in technique is analogous to cross-mutation. The discovery of the cire-perdue process of casting bronze not only presupposes knowledge of bronze and casting methods but also the behaviour of waxes and fats when melted and cooled again.

This brings up the old question of diffusion of achievements of material culture or the possibility of invention of the same process in different kinds of the world. Simple primary discoveries such as plasticity and malleability may be repeated but every artefact that consists of a series of discoveries is more likely to have been diffused than reinvented! We must not forget that not need but prosperity is the mother of invention and that the early metal worker was not pushed along the path of progress because he had no idea that it was a path at all. Such an achievement as the production of bronze is already sufficiently marvellous and if we would be led to suppose that it evolved independently in the New and the Old World our wonderment would be simply doubled!

Thus there is no progress by small changes but a rather spasmodic evolution directed by creative invention, by the presence of the motives of intention and insight in the utilisation of the material world. Even the word metal still holds something of this directed research. Though older philologists like Renan and Riedenauer have looked for a Semitic root for this word, Curtius and Bezzenberger have searched rather for an Indo-European root, though Schrader believed in neither. It is now, however, held with Liddell-Scott that this word is connected with the Greek *metallao*: to search (after other things), thence *metalleia*: searching for metals, mining and *metallon*: mine, quarry (originally probably meaning "place of searching"). It is curious to notice that Homer never uses the word *metallon* but always *metallao* instead! When speaking of gold ores, Pliny has a somewhat similar explanation of the word, saying (12): "Wherever one vein is found another is not far to seek." This is the case also with many other ores and seems to be the source of the Greek name *metalla* thus giving this word (*met'alla*) the literal meaning "one after another".

Herodotus still uses the word metallon for "mine" (13) and it is applied in this sense in the documents pertaining to the silver mines of Laureion (14). The meaning "metal" is seldom attached to the word in Greek but this was the principal meaning of the Latin "metallum".

4. *Metallurgy in Africa and the New World*

We have already referred to the fact that the sequence Stone-, Bronze-, Iron-Age holds good only for the continuum Near East and Western Europe. This story of metallurgy does not fit *Africa* (15). Here the Iron Age follows the Stone Age, for the earliest metal-workers used iron. The earliest iron-smiths of western Africa were Negroes who presumably acquired the art from the Meroitic Kingdom of the Upper Nile in the centuries immediately prior to the beginning of our Christian era. The "whites" (Hamites) probably brought the art to the Negro tribes of the interior. The Negroes of the Western Sudan certainly learnt it from the camel-riding Berbers, the more western tribes may be across the Sahara but certainly not later than 400 A.D. However the art of smelting did not reach the forested coastlands of Guinea until comparatively late. Over most of the Negro area the technique is the same: wrought iron is produced under a hand-forced draught in a simple pit or hearth. Sometimes the yield is increased by building over the pit a small clay chimney charged with alternate layers of charcoal and ore, the bellows being worked during the smelting.

Thus we see the strange "Siderolithic" of the Nok culture of the last few centuries B.C., when tuyères and other evidences of iron-working are associated with stone axes and even pottery sculpture picturing a man handling a hafted stone axe! Here copper and bronze were still some centuries in the future! Iron reached the Bushongo about the sixth century A.D., the Baganda about 1000 A.D. and Angola not earlier than 1475! In Cameroun the Bikom smiths still resmelt the old slagheaps of earlier inhabitants with their superior "Catalan forge" type of furnace, but on the other hand still use stone hammers and a granite anvil.

In south-central Africa the first metal-workers seem to have been basically of the same stock as the Bush-Hottentot people (but with Negroid admixture) north of the Zambesi. After their stay in Northern Rhodesia in the first century A.D. they seem to have crossed the Zambesi before 700 A.D. (since the site of Zimbabwe was occupied by that time) and the Limpopo about 1055. They formed communities of mixed farmers who worked iron and native copper and also (where these metals occured) tin and gold. The natives of the south-east coast seem to have learnt of iron from Arab or Indian traders about 600 A.D., but by this time a flourishing gold trade began with the Arabs at Kilwa (tenth century) and Sofala. The knowledge of metalworking was introduced into Southern Africa via the Horn, on the one hand, and across the Sahara, on the other. At the beginning of the fifteenth century the hunting groups among the farming tribes had disappeared under the stress of the immigration of the later Iron Age people, they turned partly to food-production and to metal-working. Iron had been the trade object for the silent trade against gold with inland tribes, but the quest for gold from all sides was followed by the quest for tin. In Nigeria the exported tin met the incoming brass and copper brought across the Sahara to West Africa, there gradually producing a casting art reaching its culmination in the bronzes of Benin.

Another picture different from that of Western metallurgy can be taken from the *New World* where metallurgy developed completely independently on entirely different lines (16).

Native gold is found in great quantities in Colombia, Ecuador, Peru and Bolivia, almost entirely in the beds of mountain streams. This gold often contained as much as 20% of silver. Native silver and silver ores are abundant only in Peru and Bolivia, native platinum in southern Colombia and Ecuador. Possibly the first working of native metal took place on the Peruvian coast or in the adjacent highlands and spread northwards to Colombia and Central America and southwards to Bolivia. This took place early in the Christian era, perhaps even a few centuries earlier. The nuggets of native gold were hammered into thin sheets to be cut into small rectangles sewn to clothing, head ornaments, etc. The gold was often embossed with raised lines and dots and heated to a dull heat (annealed) to relieve it from strains.

Somewhat about 700 A.D. came the discovery of melting, casting, soldering and gilding in the Chimu region of the Peruvian coast, these techniques spread slowly to Ecuador in the north and to Nazca in the south. About the same time the Colombians discovered the copper-gold alloys called "tumbago" and colouring by the "mise en couleur" technique, which process spread as far south as Peru. The metals used included (a) nearly pure gold (0—5% silver), (b) silver-rich gold (15—30% silver) and (c) a gold-silver alloy with 35—50% silver, this being an artificial alloy, the two former ones native metals. The silver used in other ornaments was either fairly pure (0—20% copper) or a silver-copper alloy with over 20% of copper. The silver itself was mostly taken as a native metal, only in few cases do slight amounts of lead point to the extraction of plumbiferous silver ores. The native copper probably came from the highlands.

At a slightly later date (about 1100 A.D.) the smelting of copper and tin ores and the production of bronze were discovered in the Bolivian highlands, spreading south to the coast and thence carried slowly northwards by the Inca. By the time of the conquest (A.D. 1530) the knowledge of bronze had not yet reached Colombia.

By 1200 A.D. fairly large quantities of gold, silver and copper became available to the Chimu inhabitants of the south coast of Peru. Now large objects of more varied size could be made such as cuffs, armlets, large decorated discs and masks. The methods remained the same and during the next two centuries the smiths managed to hammer out large dishes, beakers and cups from single sheets of metal. The alloy of gold and silver was increasingly used. Both geometrical patterns or the old-fashioned series of dots were used to decorate such vessels. The Inca conquest of this region about 1400 modified but did not fundamentally change the metallurgy, though new forms and ornaments were sometimes used. Still no casting of gold or bronze was attempted here until the Spaniards put an end to the operations in 1534.

The knowledge of the Chimu metallurgy reached Mexico by sea during the thirteenth century, Colombian metallurgy became known there somewhat later. The metal objects, which are found in late Mexican sites only, differ in character from those in the southern hemisphere. The Mexicans chose their own forms and styles and they became masters in casting metal objects, using a copper-lead alloy for bells and making superior jewelry by the time of the landing of Cortez (1519). From these few lines it is clear that the course of metallurgy in pre-Columbian America was entirely different from that in the Old World or in Africa.

5. What is a Copper Age?

The loose way of thinking in the past led to many a difficulty. Once a certain term like Copper Age or Bronze Age is used forgetful of the fact that it is (or at least should be) used to denote a specified complex of metal techniques, but not just the common use of a certain metal, inconsistencies are apt to occur. The use of a specific set of techniques such as casting, annealing, embossing, etc. is more specific of a particular archaeological period than the native metal, extracted metal and alloy that happens to be favoured during a certain period.

For instance the term *Copper Age or Chalcolithic* is often used to denote the period between Neolithic Age and the "advent of Bronze", or if a true neolithic is absent, the gap between Mesolithic and the "Bronze Age". But the term Copper Age is also very often used in cases where the influence of the knowledge of metal is suspected only from the other archaeological remains of the period. Just as Peake complained more than thirty years ago, the Neolithic seemed to grow to be a Metal Age without metal. Even areas into which metal objects have been carried by trade need not themselves be in the Metal Age. Unless smiths are imported to work there, the Stone Age must be said to continue.

Metallurgically speaking there is no gap between Copper and Bronze Age, for ore-extracted copper is to bronze what iron is to steel. They represent sequent phases of one stage of metallurgy. Bronze, that is an alloy of copper with over 2% of tin (the maximum one can expect as a natural impurity in copper), can be obtained by "refining" crude copper with tin ore or by alloying the two metals, each separately reduced from their ores. But to the ancient inventive metallurgist this was a new "artificially improved copper", though it merely represents a succesful sideline in the development of copper metallurgy, which again forms part of the "ore stage" of metallurgy.

Now Montelius suggested long ago to drop the terms Copper Age and Bronze Age and to adopt the word "Erzzeitalter", but as the word "Erz" can not be replaced by a similar term in English or any other language, it might be better to use the term *Metal Age* for the period between mesolithic (and/or neolithic) and the Iron Age, in which the regional civilisation shows the existence and influence of copper metallurgy or any other non-ferrous metal. If necessary a "Chalcolithic" could be intercalated. This "Metal Age" would show, metallurgically speaking, all the aspects we have ascribed to the "ore stage" discussed above, being the stage between the use of native metal and the introduction of iron metallurgy.

But whatever term we use, whether we say "Metal Age" or continue to use the older "Bronze Age" we must never forget that the alloy bronze is only part-aspect of a type of civilisation which we try to describe with this term. The archaeological complex which we call Bronze Age is not defined when we know where and when copper and tin were mined and worked or whether bronze was in general use. For a long time during this period the use of bronze was not, as Spengler aptly remarked, common practice. Only the rich and the craftsmen would possess bronze and copper tools and weapons, the majority of the population being quite content with stone or wooden tools and implements which as the result of a long series of experiments were often quite good. A few tons of copper must have been quite sufficient to meet the world's demand every year. Copper implements are not always decidedly better than stone ones and only bronze is decidedly superior but it had to prove its worth first, before it was universally accepted it was tested in the hands of several critical generations. The older Neolithic materials survived for quite a long time and copper remained like gold and silver an object of trade in luxuries. Its rarity in the earlier periods may even account for its rapid spread in small quantities. As Spengler put it: "If a chieftain in Spain possessed a copper sword or dagger, this would be the talk of ten villages!" Again as technique improved the older copper and bronze objects may have been recast and reworked as many obsolete and broken pieces in depot finds (founder's hoards) prove. Therefore as de Morgan says, many chalcolithic stations have been classed as neolithic simply because copper was absent, as the metal was extremely precious and handled with the greatest care. The features of a Bronze (or Metal) Age are thus not marked by the presence of metal only; many other characteristics may be found in the type and form of the pottery, architecture, etc.

6.   *The birthplace of Old World metallurgy*

We have already mentioned that metallurgy can not be spread by trade only but that the possibilities of diffusion are associated with the spread of the craftsmen themselves. We have also brought forward strong arguments for the diffusion of metallurgy and this brings us to the question whether we can fix or at any rate guess the original centre, the *birthplace of metallurgy*, with some reasonable certainty.

For the Near East this problem has often been discussed and many suggestions have been made. Montelius ascribed the invention of copper metallurgy to the Sumerians, Naville to the Hamites of Southern Arabia, O'Leary to the Armenoid race round Mount Ararat, whence it spread to Mesopotamia and Egypt. Hall suggested that copper came from Asia and reached Egypt and Cyprus by the Syrian coast, but Elliot Smith claimed that Egypt knew copper far earlier than Cyprus, that it was in fact invented in Egypt in Wadi Alaqi and that all the stages of its evolution can be found in Egypt. Sidney Smith thinks that both Egypt and Mesopotamia derived their knowledge of copper metallurgy from Cappadocia but that each developed it independently. Rostovtzev pointed out the importance of the Transcaucasian mines both for Sumer and Caucasia. He considers copper industry to have arisen simultaneously in Turkestan, Elam, Caucasia, Mesopotamia and Egypt and maintains that the "animal decoration" was characteristic for this early metallurgical period.

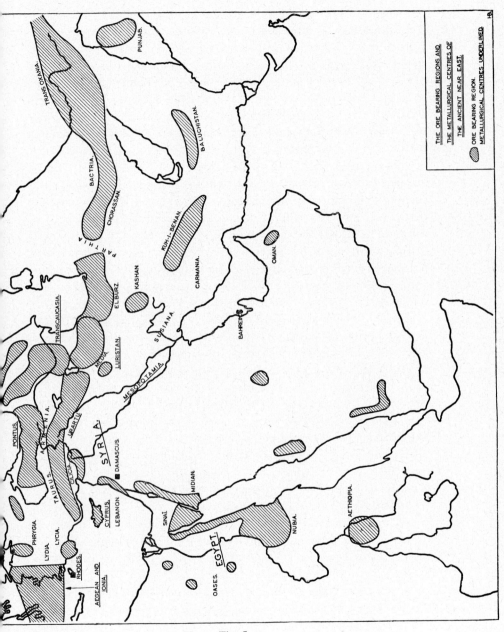

Fig. 5.
The orebearing regions and metallurgical centres of the Ancient Near East

Frankfort was one of the most fervent exponents of the "Armenian-Transcaucasian" centre, whence the early copper types spread to Europe over Hissarlik II or occasionally by the way of the Russian steppes. He was even inclined to see its influence radiating by the way of south-western Persia to China following the "painted pottery" belt. In a later publication he says: "All stylistic evidence suggest quite clearly that there existed already an important centre of metallurgy well before 3000 B.C. somewhere south of the Caucasian mountains with which the Sumerians were in contact. (To Frankfort the bearers of the highland civilisation were Sumerians.) Childe rightly distinguished between reactive regions where discoveries were made and shapes evolved and the mining regions in later use. The first movement from Asia to bring copper to the Aegean started in South-West Asia Minor. The Caucasian region or at least some region of the southern or eastern littoral of the Black Sea was exporting copper objects and not metal only. Forms found in China suggest that the knowledge of copper working spread from the Persian-Caucasian province".

Childe also believed in this ancient centre in the highlands of Armenia, Transcaucasia and Persia. As the river-valleys lack the necessary ores, the early invention of the production of copper, etc. led to trade relation with the löss regions and river valleys. Incidentally this trade led to urban civilisation in Asia Minor, Anatolia and Cyprus being drawn into the process around 3000 B.C., then somewhat later Troy I, the Cyclades and Crete. But by 3000 B.C. Egypt and Mesopotamia already possessed separate schools of metallurgy, the early Sumerian school being certainly superior to the Egyptian as it knew bronze and used core casting! Again the majority of European metal forms go back to early prehistoric or Sumerian models which numerical preponderence of diffused Sumerian types considerably weakens the theory of Egyptian origin of metallurgy (Elliot Smith, Perry, etc.).

The main evidence on the original centre of metallurgy, however, depends on the prehistoric relations of Egypt and Mesopotamia and their relative dates. At any rate the barbarians north of the Balkans do not start to use metals much before 2000 B.C.

On the other hand a specialist on Caucasian archaeology, Hančar, is of the opinion that copper industry in these regions is not as old as supposed by Frankfort and others. He considers the Copper Age of Kuban, Egypt and Mesopotamia individual growths on a common base, but connects Kuban with Tureng Tepe and more closely with Tepe Hissar III. He admits that Frankfort's metallurgical centre in

Armenia and Transcaucasia is proved by weapons, ornaments and other influences in Sumer, Northern Syria, Crete, Egypt and even Europe for early dynastic times (2900—2500 B.C.) but at the same time we should not forget that we must look east for the sources of Sumerian copper!

And this is what de Morgan said already many years earlier: "Only Chaldea, Susa, Egypt and the Aegean islands are entitled by their antiquity to harbour the country of the origin of copper. But only Elam and the Iranian plateau have yielded traces of pure neolithic civilisation (at that time!) not Mesopotamia. Neither in Chaldea nor Iran were the first metallurgical essays made, nevertheless, it is highly probable that Western Asia is at least one of the principal secondary centres where the knowledge of metal was propagated.

But early metal traffic was not effected by caravans but the metal went from hand to hand. This trade was very active from Mesopotamia to the Phoenician coast. The earliest settlers in Crete and Cyprus were metallurgists introducing copper in the fourth millennium B.C. and bronze in the third.

Even Witter, who stoutly upholds his theory of a separate Middle European metallurgical school of independent growth and even one of the same date as those in the Ancient East, points to the east for the sources of Sumerian metallurgy and stressess the necessity of further excavations in Baluchistan and the Makran to investigate the common source of Sumerian and Indus civilisation.

Post-war Near Eastern archaeology seems to confirm the hypothesis that we must look for the birthplace of Old World metallurgy in the mountain region stretching from Anatolia through the Armenian Mountains eastwards into Afghanistan. The eastern flank is notably rich in native metals and ores but apart from a few excavations at Anau and in Baluchistan little is yet known on the earlier prehistory of this region (17). Here too the Chalcolithic period is the era when awareness of "metal" is seeping into an otherwise lithic culture. When the early settlements at Jarmo, Jericho and other sites were discovered and their very early date was established beyond doubt, this changed the entire face of early Near Eastern history. We now know that the hill-folk, first living in the fertile regions along the foothills of the Elburz, Taurus and towards the Caspian Sea began to descend between 6000 B.C. and 3700 B.C. slowly occupying the river-valleys and the Fertile Cresent.

About 5000 B.C. they had begun gathering native gold and copper already and had just discovered annealing as is proved by finds at Sialk and Hassuna. The first settlers in the Mesopotamian plain came from Iran and some have called the Ubaid-period "debased Persian." But they already used smelted copper, which became more general in the subsequent Uruk period. By 2500 B.C. the Royal Tombs of Ur show us a profusion of gold, electrum, silver copper and various types of bronzes.

The use of smelted copper and its manufacture had spread to Western Asia by 4000 B.C. (e.g. to the Ghassulian sites in Palestine) and though the prehistoric Egyptians used native copper during the Amratian period, the knowledge of smelting it from ores seems to date from the last phase of this period (3800—3700 B.C.) or may be from the early Gerzean phase. By 3500 B.C. metallurgy had been absorbed by the civilisation in Mesopotamia, metals like gold and copper are as characteristic of this culture as are its typical weapons, tools, ceramics, textiles and funerary customs. This stage is reached in Egypt some three hundred years later and by 2500 B.C. the entire region between the Nile cataracts and Indus is metal-minded. By this time metallurgy seems to have started in China, but the Chinese did not become true metallurgists until the Lungshan stage (1800—1500 B.C.). In the northern steppes of continental Asia the first metal artifacts appear about 1800—1500 B.C. (the Glaskovo period) in the Baikal regions. In Europe the earliest metal objects are hardly earlier than 2000 B.C. and the new finds have now definitely upset theories, we believe, like the independent rise of metallurgy in Central Europe, for here too the manufacture of metals and their alloys from local ores can not be separated from the entire archaeological-typological context of the cultures in which the metals are found. However, as there are still some who believe in this *origin of Central European metallurgy* a few words should be said about it.

This problem often put forward under the guise of the priority of Asia over Europe or vice-versa is a chronological problem. Only too often authors forget that European prehistorical chronology which must be used to arrange the metallurgical data, is a framework of relative dates, some of which can be linked up with absolute or relative dates of the chronological frame of the Ancient Near East. It is absolutely impossible to separate these European and Near Eastern chronologies, which are interdependent and it is also impossible to antedate events of cultures in Europe without taking any notice of the links with Near Eastern dates! We can not discus the question here as it

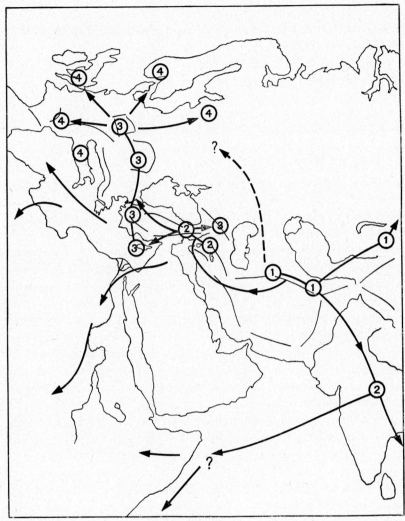

Fig. 6.
The diffusion of early metallurgy

falls outside the scope of this book, but we should like to give a few remarks for the benefit of the reader.

Witter has proved in a series of brilliant analyses that Central European metallurgy grew up independently and found its own methods in working its specific ores. His collaborators have tried to fix the date of the origin of this Central European metallurgy in the period of "the Copper Age in the Near East" and to prove that this industry was an original growth not founded by knowledge diffused from the Near East. But many of his countrymen (Franz, Quiring, and many others) do not believe in this antedating fixed on the dates given by Kossinna and they agree with the many publications by Gordon Childe deriving this Central European industry from the Near East. There is no doubt as Childe proved repeatedly that at least five of the earliest European metal types go back to Sumerian originals and Witter has not succeeded in proving that no trade routes could have been used from the Near East to Central Europe either by the way of the south, west or south-east, because he uses the inflated dates of Kossina's chronology which stand without proof. The archaeological arguments for early Near Eastern and European chronology have again been expounded by Gordon Childe in a masterly essay on the Orient and Europe (18). The fact of imports of early metal types from the East and such secondary arguments as the existence of an Aryan word for copper derived from the Sumerian URUDU (a substance known very early to the Sumerians as they wrote it with a simple ideogram!) go to prove Childe's contention that Central European metallurgy was founded somewhat before 2000 B.C., by influences penetrating by the way of Anatolia, Troy II and the Danube valley and occasionally by the way of the Russian steppes from Caucasia. The Central European bronze industry of Elbe and Saale starts in Danubian IV and though Aunjetitz traditions form its base, Britannico-Hibernian models from the West and perhaps even immigration of Irish craftsmen played their part. The bell-beaker folk were tradesmen and craftsmen who as bands of armed merchants and prospectors did much to spread metallurgical knowledge in Europe. Though there is a general but far from exact correlation between the distribution of metals and the foci of megalithic architecture the extreme rarity of metals in megalithic tombs is a fatal objection to the theory of Perry and the Manchester school that these megalith-building people were Egyptian metallurgists spreading the knowledge when prospecting in prehistoric Europe. Though the details are not yet absolutely certain, yet it can no longer be doubted that metallurgy, at least its elements, was brought to Central Europe along the lines sketched by Childe. That Central Europe subsequently formed an independent centre with its own growth can no longer be doubted either after reading Witter's books and papers. If he doubts Childe's results because he doubts the results of the typological method in general, he falls in the same pit and uses typological proofs with a wrong frame of relative dates, drawing in such arguments as the antiquated theory of the similarity of early European axes and Egyptian axes once put forward by Flinders Petrie, but never accepted by other archaeologists. Again he has not proved his contention that Childe's arguments would hold for simple ores only but not for the complex ores of Central Europe.

7. *Evolution of the production of metals*

Though this volume and its sequel will discuss the story of each metal such as gold, silver, copper and iron in detail, we feel that it would be profitable to show that metallurgically speaking the three "metal stages" briefly outlined above each represent a complex of techniques, tools and instruments and above all ideas and skill of the smiths. Such methods and ideas may be transferred from one metal to the other or applied to an alloy, etc. and hence there are a number of techniques which are basic in a wide sector of metallurgy.

The "native metal stage" is a most interesting phase which has drawn much attention during the last decade.

The advantages of metal over stone were obvious. There were not only the colour and gloss, more important to primitive man than to us, but also its malleability, its permanency as compared with stone or wood or bone and the faculty of keeping its sharp edge better. Its malleability when hot was an important factor and when its fusibility was discovered and the subsequent solidification after cooling the metal acquired some of the merits of potter's clay, there was no longer any restriction to shape or size and it could be remelted for reuse.

But casting was an achievement of the true metallurgy of the "ore stage". This phase meant a widening range and better utilisation of the four essential elements of metallurgy: 1) ores, 2) fuel and fire-making, 3) the production of draught by blast air and 4) the necessary tools, furnaces and crucibles. All of these elements wanted careful adapting to the new conditions or discovery if still unknown. Only then could the discovery of the smelting of ores and the smelting of metals be followed up. Only then could the discoveries of new metals and alloys be achieved. Even the most important technique of these days, casting, is so intricate a process that we may well wonder at its early inception. With this technique which uses the most typical characteristic of metals true metallurgy is born. Then the alloys were inventions which possessed some outstanding feature. Not only was their gloss generally more constant but they had a lower melting point than the components which meant easier casting, especially valuable in regions like the Ancient Near East where fuel was expensive from the earliest times onwards at least in the rivervalleys. Again the extreme hardness of bronze was constant as it was not achieved by hammering of the cutting edge as in the case of copper and therefore was not a property that was lost during use of the implement. As soon as the composition of the alloys was well controlled by the smelter he could count on a range of constant properties just as in the case of pure metals, but very often this was not an essential as long as the variation was limited.

But the characteristics of the "native metal stage" and the "ore stage" can be far better illustrated in discussing the early metallurgy of copper, though the details are not yet always clear. We choose copper for though gold is the earliest metal discovered and used by mankind in many countries as far as evidence goes, its production entails so little difficulties that we can not expect that it had any stimulating effects on the development of the very earliest metallurgical methods. For gold occurs either as nuggets of native metal in the detritus of gold-bearing rocks or else gold-bearing minerals enclose these small particles of comparatively pure metal and not compounds of gold to be smelted. The production of gold, therefore, boils down to the collection of this gold-bearing ore, its crushing, separation of the gold particles from the fragments of enclosing rocky material by washing or panning and melting the gold dust or nuggets together into a workable lump. Gold production could never lead to that most important discovery in metallurgy, the working of ores for the production of metals!

But copper apart from comparatively widely scattered deposits of native copper, occurs mainly in the form of ores, e.g. of compounds of copper and other substances, partly chemically bound, partly a physical mixture. We can divide the copper ores into two groups. First of all come the easily reducible oxyde and carbonate ores (including the silicate chrysocolla) then the more complex ores of the sulphide type, all compounds of sulphur and copper mixed with varying quantities of sulphides of such other metals as iron, antimony, arsenic, etc., the working of which entails more manipulations than the first group demands (19).

We distinguish the following phases of copper metallurgy:

    I Shaping native copper.

    II Annealing native copper.

III Smelting oxyde and carbonate ores.
IV Melting and refining copper.
V Smelting sulphide ores.

Technical details of the processes will be discussed when we deal with the metallurgy of copper in the Ancient Near East (Vol. IX). We must, therefore, leave the proofs until later and content ourselves with a summary of the more important features of these phases.

I—Copper metallurgy started when primitive man noticed large lumps of dark stone in the gold-bearing river-beds which when hammered looked like gold. He soon tried to work the malleable metal by hammering, cutting, bending, grinding and polishing, e.g. by applying all those processes which he used when working bone, stone or fibres. This phase which can not be called more than an introductory phase of copper metallurgy, entails no special ingenuity, it simply is the discovery of a new natural material. This phase was never left behind by the pre-Columbian Indians, who though working and knowing copper must be said to be truly Neolithic people. There is no sense in talking of a Copper Age in North America, as long as the specific qualities of copper are not shown to have been appreciated and used by the Indians before their contact with the whites. It seems that this discovery of copper was made among the cattle-raising inhabitants of the plains and mountain ranges east of the Caspian, who perhaps also dominated Turkestan and Tibet. Menghin gave a tentative date, the sixth and fifth millennium B.C., which must remain until further excavations in these regions have proved this hypothesis and furnished a closer date. It should be remembered that these regions are rich in mineral deposits and that native gold, silver, copper and iron are known to occur rather frequently.

II—The phase of annealing native copper was the first phase of true metallurgy. Witter and others have supposed that this new property of copper was discovered when copper borers were heated in a fire to facilitate penetration or by the accidental dropping of a lump of copper in a fire by a primitive smith. It then appeared to him that copper when hot was much more malleable and easy to shape and thenceforwards tempering or annealing of copper followed by hammering was common practice. It had the advantage over hammering without heating, that the copper remained tough and did not become brittle. Also more forms of native copper, which hitherto resisted working because of their natural brittleness, could be worked with good results.

This discovery must have been made around 5000 B.C. for the technique was common knowledge of the peasant culture that had spread over South-Western Asia and North Africa by the fourth millennium B.C. After studying the early copper axes of these regions Marples states expressily that the early agricultural squatters had trifling quantities of copper but did not know how to fuse or melt them.

III—Recent experiments by Coghlan have proved that the discovery of the melting of copper was preceded by the discovery of the production of copper from oxyde ores. Until recently most authors, even Witter, thought that melting and with it the knowledge of casting came first. Putting the reduction of copper ores first might seem an illogical link in the chain of reasoning. Coghlan, however, proved that the favourite camp fire, which was thought to be linked so intimately with the discovery of casting copper and the reduction of copper ores, could not possibly be used for any production or melting of copper on a larger scale. The temperature of a wood fire is hardly higher than 600—700° C, whilst oxydes and carbonates of copper can not be reduced below 700—800° C and copper does not melt below 1085° C. The only thing that could be achieved in a camp fire would be the heating of copper lumps before hammering or the heating of several smaller nuggets to be forged together into a larger piece. Primitive pot-bowl or "hole-in-the-ground" furnaces of the type advocated by Gowland for Bronze Age copper smiths will not give the necessary high temperatures unless aided by the blowpipe or bellows, natural draught being insufficient. Coghlan made it most probable that the reduction of copper ores was discovered by the reduction of blue copper frit or glaze in a pottery kiln, the only primitive furnace, which yields the requisite high temperatures as experiments proved. Afterwards the pottery furnace was used to melt copper. Both technical conditions and kiln constructions suitable to produce the reducing atmosphere point towards the pottery kiln as the instrument in which the first ores were smelted and the first copper melted. These two steps (phases III and IV) must have been taken in rapid succession for the earliest copper objects from excavations like Sialk (Iran) show that the art of casting this metal had already been mastered. A large variety of theories have been brought forward to explain the first reduction experiments of copper ores. It is often said that malachite was a pigment used in Neolithic times long before even native copper into came use. Witter claimed that the presence of blue and green stones was noticed near the native copper and some early smith hit on the idea of submitting these brightly coloured stones to the "fire test". Elliot Smith and many others located this invention in the eastern desert of Egypt (where no early copper mining was ever proved!) and he supposed that a lump of malachite chanced to fall into a camp-fire and was reduced to the glittering red metal! Apart from the infrequency of such occurences as Rickard already noticed from the observations of ethnologists studying African metallurgy, we have had occasion to point out the extreme improbability of this theory,

Fig. 7.
Seal from Susa said to depict smiths using the blowpipe to smelt metals
(after Scheil)

seeing that the technical conditions for the reduction of ores are hardly ever reached in camp-fires. Spielmann who holds with Petrie that the ancient Egyptians came from a region in the Caucasus between the rivers Iora and Kura and that they brought their knowledge of copper with them, thinks that it was discovered by the natural action of burning petroleum or petroleum gases!

Gsell, quoting Much (20) tried to prove that copper was discovered when pyrites were heated to make gold in early times. It is true that under special conditions copper pyrites mixed with charcoal may when heated in an air blast give copper in one stage only, but this does not seem to be a natural result as such a smelting will usually yield a crude copper still rich in sulphur, which has to be retreated. Indeed it is considered most probable that the primitive smiths were not able to smelt sulphides in one stage, no single example of such smelting having been even found. Therefore, Gsell's further claim that crucible melting and casting were used as soon as pottery making was discovered is false too. As long as no counterproof is brought forward, it would seem to us that Coghlan's experiments and exact temperature measurements have proved beyond doubt that the reduction of copper ores of the oxidic type was discovered in the pottery kiln when applying the blue frits of copper ore and that the idea of casting copper followed rapidly.

Childe has very aptly called this discovery of the transmutation of the blue, green, red or grey ores to tough red metal one of the most dramatic leaps in history. Now the primitive smith who had discovered the annealing of native copper was confronted with a complex of processes connected with the reduction of ores and the production of copper in a molten form. Had annealing copper allowed him to fashion this metal better than by the application of neolithic methods, now he found in casting a process that relieved him of a large part of this fashioning job. Again it allowed him to evolve forms that were more natural to metal, that used the inherent properties of the metal more efficiently and deviated from the earlier shapes of metal objects which were hardly more than crude imitations in metal of Neolithic stone implements and weapons.

Again Witter pointed out that the discovery of reduction and casting is intimately linked with the evolution of smithing as a job, the earliest craft in human history that became a full time job and led to the recognition of the smith as the earliest craftsman, as we shall see. It is important to remember the intimate connection between this phase of metallurgy and the pottery kiln. Only a civilisation that made well-baked pottery requiring a high baking temperature would possess the technical equipment that made the reduction of ores possible. We find the people of Al 'Ubeid and kindred cultures in possession of this knowledge and even in the earlier Anau I culture not only a coarse type of pottery akin to that on earlier generations of inventors of this craft occurs, but also a well-baked, finely decorated type which shows that the Anau people possessed from the first good pottery kilns. Among these early agriculturists the earliest clans of smiths must have grown out of the earlier workers of native copper, as free men honoured and feared as the master-magicians on a new craft gradually acquiring that peculiar social and religious state which we shall have occasion to discuss later on. The intricacy of their craft forced them to devote their entire time to their job, depending for their food and clothes on their kinsman, indeed a significant departure from the ordinary life of a neolithic self-supporting peasantry, which goes far to explain their peculiar social status in later ages (chapter three).

IV—The reduction of oxyde and carbonate ores like malachite, lazurite and the like had been the discovery of a new process, a new way of obtaining a substance already known. The knowledge of melting copper which followed it so closely being linked to the same technical apparatus, proved a new way of fashioning metal objects. Molten copper could be cast into forms hitherto undreamt of and practical tests very soon led to those specific "metal" types which contrast very much with the earlier metal imitations of stone tools. Henceforwards the way of the smith deviated from that of the flint-worker and stonecutter. His became a new dramatic and mysterious cycle of melting, casting and solidifying. This art not only required a high temperature like the reduction of ores but also a knowledge and ability to manufacture crucibles, tongs and means of developing blast air (Blowpipe, bellows).

When we study archaeology we find that both stages had already been reached in early Near Eastern prehistory (about 4300 B.C.), the first traces having been found in the Al'Ubeid culture of Ur, full development was certainly reached at the Uruk stage in Mesopotamia (3500 B.C.).

V—The last stage, the reduction of sulphide ores, certainly falls in historic times, though its exact beginning is still obscure. It is quite possible, as Witter suggested, that the early metallurgists were started in this line because the blue and green copper ores which they worked until then occured in close association with the yellow, grey and black sulphides, which generally occupy the deeper strata in the same mines. Submitting them to the "fire test" would be a logical consequence of their curiosity of the secrets of nature. Heating experiments figure largely in the "chemical" texts of the Assyrians for instance. Heating these sulphides would yield a black glassy "matte", that was fusible, contained small particles of copper and turned green when attacked by humidity. A second smelting with charcoal would yield copper. The two stages of roasting and smelting could not be combined in ancient technology, though a similar result might be reached under very special circumstances as discussed above. However, the two-stage way of producing copper in the different types of furnaces each suited to one of the stages was the common smelting practice of the ancient metallurgists. Finds of such specialised furnaces and lumps of semi-refined and pure copper both in the Near East and such European metallurgical centres as Mitterberg, etc. prove this.

The easily workable oxyde ores gradually gave out and though we must reckon with many widely distributed small deposits of poor quality ore, many of them must have been finished early in historical times so that we can no longer locate them. The difficulty of fixing the period of transition of oxyde to sulphide ores lies in the lack of proper analytical data of ancient copper objects. Rickard very correctly remarked that each copper relic should be subjected to microscopic (and we would add spectrographic) examination to ascertain its texture and to conclude from the inclusion of particles of oxyde or slag whether the metal has gone through the fire or whether it is native metal. Thus not only the transition from phase II to III could be fixed correctly for every region and the results linked up chronologically to prove the spread of this new technique, but we would be able to fix the transition from phase III to V too. Now we can only say for certain that the Romans treated sulphide ores as in their times the simpler ores had given out, but as far as the scanty evidence goes the transition of phase III to V must be pushed back to the Late Bronze Age and perhaps earlier. Technical skill and equipment of the Amarna Age would certainly permit the working of copper pyrites.

Quiring connected the working of pyrites with the invention of bellows, which he dates around 1580 B.C., as that is the date of the earliest picture (on Egyptian monuments). His conclusions are, however, based on the analyses of early copper objects and they too lead him to fix a date around 1500 B.C. for this transition.

The *iron stage of metallurgy* is another important revolution. The Iron Age of the Near East is rung in by the migrations of about 1200 B.C. accompanied by the rise of the prices of corn and general articles. Gradually, however, the prices fall back as the cheaper and better iron implements are used more generally. Iron ores are widely distributed and as soon as they could be smelted and the iron produced showed properties at least equal to those of bronze, everybody could afford and would buy iron tools. Economically speaking iron-smelting first made metal tools so cheap that they could be universally used for clearing forests and draining marshes and other heavy work. It is certain that the advent of iron changed the face of the world not only as a new material for arms but also by equiping man better in his struggle with nature.

It may seem strange that copper should be the oldest metal produced from ores for though the melting point of copper is only 1085° and that of pure iron is 1530° C, the reduction temperature of copper oxides is higher than that of iron oxides, which means in plain language that it is easier in principle to produce fron from iron ores than copper from its ores when smelting with charcoal as the primitive smelters did.

For this reason many archaeologists and even technologists like Beck have supposed that iron was produced and known earlier than copper but for several reasons did not become popular and had to wait its turn. However, we now have overwhelming archaeological and other evidence that iron came later than copper in the Near East and in prehistoric Europe, though in Africa iron preceded both copper and bronze. The smithing (and mostly the smelting too!) of iron is found nearly everywhere in the Old World among both agricultural and pastoral peoples, but it lacks among those in the New World and in Oceania. Its production and working spread far beyond the region in which copper and bronze were used when iron was invented and it ousted these two as the main material of the metal worker.

At first sight there seems no reason for the developments of copper metallurgy. Iron ores are more abundant and more widespread than copper ores and far more so than tin ores. Iron, at least its "steely" form, has many obvious advantages over bronze, it is stronger and more elastic and will both take and keep a finer cutting edge. The reason is undoubtedly that the working of iron awaited a quite new series of experiments and discoveries generally distinct from those habitually employed in the smelting of copper and tin. To understand this it is imperative to view the process of iron-smelting from the point of view of a copper-smith, thus Forde, whose excellent reasoning we follow in these lines.

Throughout two or more millennia the burning of certain kinds of coloured stones in a furnace to produce a flow of reddish metal had become a fixed pattern. Experiments with other stones must have been made, but they yielded no flow of metal. From the point of view of a copper-smith the smelting of iron ore would appear a complete failure, it would result in a bloom, a spongy mass of fused stone full of air-holes and as unmetallic a product as can be imagined, for the pasty small globules of iron would be embedded and concealed in the mass of slag and cinders. When hammered cold the bloom would be of no use, when hammered hot it would give no quick result, that could be appreciated!

The great centres of the bronze working of the Ancient East with their specialized smelting and smithing methods offered neither good chances for lucky accidents with iron ore, nor rewards to deliberate experiments along traditional lines. Nevertheless iron objects were made and used during these times. The number may be quite small, but it is definite! Nearly all the early objects that were recovered were ornaments not tools! Both the rarity and the ornamental use indicates fairly clearly that there was not at this time any established technique for smelting the abundant ores of iron. The meteoric origin of these early finds has been established beyond doubt in most of these cases.

Fig. 8.
A Batak goldsmith using the blowpipe
(Inst. v.d. Tropen, Amsterdam)

But from the fourteenth century onwards iron rapidly becomes more abundant throughout the Ancient East, more especially between 1200 and 1000 B.C. Tools and weapons are now made of it and within a few centuries important centres of manufacturing spring up in many cities. Shortly before this time the essential discovery must, therefore, have been made. It does not demand a hotter furnace but it does require a larger and more continuous body of heat and a suitable flux with which the impurities of the ore can combine. A larger furnace and a more powerful blast are therefore essential to maintain the smelting process. Furthermore the product must be subjected to a far more prolonged hammering at red-heat than was customary among copper workers in order to beat out the slag and cinders and to consolidate the metallic mass. Greek traditions coincide with the fact that iron working was invented in the mountains between Taurus and Black Sea, or as the legends have it, by the Chalybes. By 1200 local smelting was developed in Anatolia, Phrygia, Syria and perhaps Cyprus. By 800 it had reached Assyria, Persia, India, Egypt, Crete, Greece and Central Europe and Italy. It had remained inferior to bronze as long as the furnaces were not hot enough or the forging and reheating was not intense enough to cause some of the carbon of the charcoal to combine with the iron and produce a low carbon steel which could be hardened by forging and quenching in water. Quenching alone would have had no effect unless the iron had been carburised (or forced to take up carbon) in the forge-fire. Though this seems to have been understood by some primitive smiths since about 1400 B.C., the device was often used with ordinary wrought iron, such as was produced directly from the ore, without any effect of course. Even in the Dark Ages this principle of carburizing does not seem to have been generally understood and swords often bent in battle and had to be straightened underfoot! To produce iron (read: steel!) objects as tough as bronze required either knowledge of the carburizing-quenching technique or an ore, that contained certain impurities, which might give the iron the properties of steel such as a manganiferous ore. This was the main advantage of the ores of Noricum, which yielded a "natural steel" and thus made the Hallstatt civilisation famous!

Though some have tried to prove the opposite, iron is certainly not an original African invention. The earlier iron-workings of the Egyptian provincial town of Meroë in Nubia are hardly older than 700 B.C. From this point the craft of the African smith seems to have spread slowly southwards to the Sudan and further. The use of copper and bronze appears never to have crossed the Sahara in pre-iron days.

Thus the iron production of Africa and the Old World almost certainly derive from a single Near Eastern centre, in which the essential discoveries and inventions were made during the period of 1400—1200 B.C. Essential for the development of the Iron Age were the following technical achievements, each of which embraces a number of methods and receipes:

a) The correct slagging of the iron ore. Every ore contains *gangue*, that is the ore contains non-metalliferous or non-valuable metalliferous minerals, which endanger the efficiency of the smelting and the purity of the iron produced. For ores are always *smelted*, that is they are radically transformed by means of heat, air and charcoal and produce a (fairly pure) metal from a metallic compound, the ore. This process should never be called *melting* which is just liquefaction and nothing else. Therefore, we *melt* metals if we want to cast them, but we *smelt* ores (even though we could melt them in some cases) if we want to obtain the metals enclosed therein (21). But to smelt ores efficiently we must get rid of the gangue. This may be done in some cases by pounding and washing the ore, but generally the mixture is so intimate,

Fig. 9.
Primitive iron smelters at Bijapath (India).
Note the furnace with the hole for withdrawing the slag. The old smith works the bellows and supports himself on a stick, in front of him is a diggingstick, near the bellows two pairs of tongs, behind him a fourth man is breaking up lumps of ore with a hammer. To the right of the furnace a pan used for filling the furnace, a hack used in digging ore and a basket full of charcoal

that we must add a substance that binds the gangue in some way to form the slag. Sometimes the gangue slags easily, that is it separates from the metal produced and the main part is liquified and drops away from the metal and the rest of the slag and cinders which together form the mass we call a *bloom*. But often the molten slag is too viscuous to separate readily from the metal and this would endanger the economy or even the succes of the process. This is why a proper *flux* is selected that is a salt or other mineral added in smelting to assist fusion of the gangue by forming more fusible compounds. Thus for instance we add lime to iron ores containing siliceous gangue. The flux differs with the gangue of the ore and as there are a large variety of iron ores, each ore differing in gangue according to the deposit, the selection of the correct flux is an important item in iron-working. It is true that the ancients often smelted iron ore without a flux at the expense of a large part of the iron, so that later generations could be quite content to resmelt the old slags! But a large part of the ancient iron-smelters did use a flux and this selection entailed a good deal of skill and experience.

b) The handling of the bloom. The bloom had to be reheated and

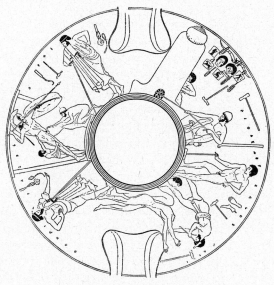

Fig. 10.
The Greek smith at work (after Blümner)

rehammered to get rid of the enclosed slag and cinders and to consolidate the mass of iron globules. This was not only a tedious work and cost a lot of fuel, but it meant the development of tools to handle such large, heavy and red-hot masses, tools which were entirely different from those used for copper or bronze, where casting was the most important way of turning out finished products.

c) The technique of carburising, quenching and tempering. To turn the soft ductile wrought iron into the hard, tough steel, which alone was really superior to bronze, the iron had to be reheated and reforged, followed by quenching. The first operation, reheating and reforging, led involuntarily to carburising. It is still an open question whether the ancients really grasped what happened, but the practical result could be achieved and was achieved first by chance, then by experience, until carburising and giving the wrought iron a widely varying carbon content was a common technique. Then quenching was discovered, the importance grasped of cooling quickly (and not very slowly in the air) after carburising at high temperatures. Then in Roman times a further nicety was added to the list of discoveries, the effect of annealing or tempering, which enabled the smith to soften the hardening effects of quenching, to take away some of the brittleness (and some of the hardness!) of hard steel and to give it some of the toughness required for its work. The regulation and the interplay of the three techniques determined the succes of the ancient smith and devoid as he was of modern apparatus and above all of modern temperature control, we need not wonder that he often failed.

It is, however, clear that iron-working embraced three groups of technical niceties, which demanded a new set of experiments before they were sufficiently appreciated and a different skill and experience than that which the ancient copper smiths had accumulated in the course of age. The Iron Age is a new metallurgical stage, a technical world of its own. In the Copper Age the stress lies on the *composition* of alloy (or impurities in the metal) but in the Iron Age the properties of the iron are much less determined by its carbon content or accidental or natural impurities but far more by its *handling*, by the temperature to which it has been heated, by the way and speed of quenching, the time and temperature of tempering or annealing. It is the true age of the smith!

In studying the processes and operations used by the ancient smiths we have a number of pictures on classical vases, tombs and reliefs but very little from earlier times. Thus in Egyptian metal-working scenes there is no single instance of the smelting of metals from its ores, but only the melting, alloying and working of metals (22). Fortunately we possess later handbooks by metallurgists, mostly among the early printed books from the sixteenth century onwards (23) which are only too often neglected by archaeologists seeking information about ancient technology. The XIth century priest Theophilus, the XVIth century doctor Agricola and his contemporary Biringuccio when describing the metallurgical methods of their days very often refer to classical methods, quote methods of long standing and, what is most important to us, often add illustrations to these descriptions. In view of the conservatism of technologists in these early periods it is perfectly admissible to regard many of these later methods as slightly improved survivals of older methods, whose principles have remained unchanged. (24)

But we must avoid getting ahead of our story and enter here into details of the particular metals, lest our reader should cry out like the companion of a long-winded smelter on an old Egyptian relief:

"Air for my brother and beer for Sokaris, o, King!"

BIBLIOGRAPHY

1. HESIOD, *Works and Days* 109—201
2. OVID, *Metamorphoses* I, 89—150
3. GRIFFITHS, J. GWYN, *Archaeology and Hesiod's Five Ages* (J. Hist. Ideas XVII, 1956, 109—119)
4. PLATO, *Protagoras* 322; Lucretius, de rerum natura V.925
5. BRUNN, W. A. VON, *Die Schatzfunde der Bronzezeit als wirtschaftsgeschichtliche Quellen* (Forschungen und Fortschritte 21/23, 1947, 257—260)
   COGHLAN, H. H. and CASE, H., *Early metallurgy of Copper in Ireland and Britain* (Proc. Preh. Soc. XXIII, 1957, 91—123)
   FRANZ, L., *Vorgeschichtliches Leben in den Alpen* (Wien, 1929)
   FRANZ, L., *Jäger, Bauern, Händler* (Leipzig, 1939)
   OTTO, H., *Analyse der Metallbeigaben aus schnurkeramischen Gräbern von Niederkaina, Kreis Bautzen* (Arb. Forsch. Ber. Sächsischen Bodendenkmalpflege, 1951, II, 40—47)
   OTTO, H., *Die chemische Zusammensetzung einiger Hortfunde aus der halleschen Gegend* (Jhrsschr. Mitteld. Vorgeschichte 34, 1950, 90—100)
   OLDEBERG, A., *Bronsskölden från Nackhalle i Halland* (Var Bygd 1953, 14—28)
   OLDEBERG, A., *Koppar och Därmed legerade metaller und forhistorisk tid* (Nordisk Kultur XIV, 1953, 125—154)
   WITTER, W., *Neues zu den Barrenring-Hortfunden im Vorlande der Ostalpen* (Praeh. Z. XXXIV/V, 1953, 179—190)
6. KRAWCZUK, A. and PIASKOWSKI, J., *Metallurgy in the published works of Aristotle* (Kwart. Hist. Kultury Materialnej VI, 1958, 3, 323—342)
   PIASKOWSKI, J., *La métallurgie dans l'Histoire Naturelle de Pline* (Archaeologia IX, 1957, 99—122)
7. CHILDE, V. GORDON, *Archaeological Ages as Technological Stages* (JRAI 74, 1944)
   OTTO, H., *Typologische und technologische Bronzezeit* (Forschungen und Fortschritte 25, 1949, 73—76)
8. AGRICOLA, G., *Zwölf Bücher vom Berg- und Hüttenwesen* (Berlin, 1929)
   ANDRÉE, J., *Bergbau in der Vorzeit* (Leipzig, 1922)
   BIRINGUCCIO, V., *Pirotechnia* (edit. JOHANNSEN, Braunschweig, 1925)
   CARPENTER, H. C. H., *Metals in the service of human life and industry* (London, 1933)
   CHILDE, V. GORDON, *New Light on the Most Ancient East* (London, 1934)
   CHILDE, V. GORDON, *Man makes himself* (London, 1936)

CHILDE, V. GORDON, *Dawn of European civilisation* (London, 1939)
CLINE, W., *Mining and metallurgy in Negro Africa* (Paris, 1937)
DAVIES, O., *Roman Mines in Europe* (London, 1936)
FORBES, R. J., *Materialen van 3300 jaren geleden* (Chem. Weekblad 37, 1940, pp. 371—375)
FORDE, C. DARYLL, *Habitat, economy and society* (London, 1934)
FRANKFORT, H., *Studies in the early pottery of the Near East* (London, 1927, vol. II)
GOWLAND, W., *The art of working metals in Japan* (J. Inst. Metals 4, 1910, 4)
—, *The early metallurgy of silver and lead* (London, 1901)
—, (Archaeologia, 57, 1901, 1)
—, *The Metallurgy of Non-Ferrous Metals* (London, 1914)
—, (Trans. Japan Soc. London, 13, 1915, 20)
—, *The metals in Antiquity* (R. Anthrop. Inst. London, 1912)
HADFIELD, R., *The rise of metallurgy* (2. edit, Sheffield, 1933)
HOERNES, M., *Die Metalle* (Wien, 1909)
HYMAN, H., *Old writers on metallurgy* (Metal Industry, vol. 25, 1924, pp. 388, 449, 510, 584; vol. 26, 1925, pp. 10, 200)
KÖSTER, W., *Der metallische Werkstoff* (Berlin, 1935)
LIPPMANN, E. O. VON, *Entstehung und Ausbreitung der Alchemie* (Berlin, 1919/1932, 2 vols.)
LUCAS, A., *Ancient Egyptian Materials and Industries* (London, 1962)
MANCHESTER, H. H., *An illustrated history of mining and metallurgy* (Engineering Mining Journal, vol. 115, 1923, p. 889; vol. 114, 1922, pp. 409, 449, 495, 545)
MEISSNER, BR., *Babylonien und Assyrien* (Heidelberg, 1920/25, 2 Bde)
NEUMANN, B., *Die Metalle, Geschichte, Vorkommen, Gewinnung* (Halle, 1904)
PARTINGTON, J. R., *Origins and development of applied chemistry* (London, 1935)
REITEMEYER, J. F., *Geschichte des Bergbaues und des Hüttenwesens bei den alten Völkern* (Göttingen, 1785)
RICKARD, T. A., *Man and Metals* (London, 1932, 2 vols)
RÖSSING, A., *Geschichte der Metalle* (Berlin, 1901)
ROSSIGNOL, J., *Les métaux dans l'antiquité* (Paris, 1863)
SAYCE, R. U., *Primitive arts and crafts* (London, 1933)
THEOBALD, W., *Des Theophilus Presbyter Diversarium Artium Schedula* (Berlin, 1933)
THOMPSON, R. C., *Dictionary of Assyrian chemistry and geology* (London, 1936)
THORNDIKE, L., *History of magic and experimental science* (London, 1929, 2 vols.; New York, 1934, vols. III & IV)
9. AITCHINSON, L. A., *History of Metals* (London, 1960, vol. I)
BEARZI, B., *La metallurgia nella antichità* (Metall. Ital.1951, no. 6, 3—8)
BINAGHI, R., *La metallurgia ai tempi dell'impero romano* (Roma, 1946)
CANEVA, *Miniere ed impianti metallurgici etruschi* (La fonderia italiana, 1957, April, 162ff)

GILLE, B., *Les origines de la grande industrie métallurgique en France* (Paris, 1949)

GRAY, D. H. F., *Metal-working in Homer* (JHS LXXIV, 1954, 1—15)

SQUARZINA, *Industria e legislazione mineraria in Italia* (I. Età antica) (Industria Miner. 1952/53)

10. NEEDHAM, J., *The development of iron and steel in China* (London, 1958)

OLDEBERG, A., *Metallteknik under Förhistorisk Tid* (Lund, 1942/3, 2 vols.)

PLEINER, R., *Alteuropäisches Schmiedehandwerk* (Prague 1962)

TYLECOTE, R. F., *Metallurgy in Archaeology* (a prehistory of metallurgy in the British Isles) (London, 1962)

11. HARRISON, R., *Report Brit. Assoc. Adv. Sci.* (1930, 137—159)

12. PLINY, *Nat. Hist.* XXXIII, 96

13. HERODOTUS III.57

14. HOPPER, R. J., *The Attic silver mines in the fourth century B.C.* (ABSA XLVIII, 1953, 200—254)

15. BRENTZ, P. L., *Metallurgy in Africa* (Iscor News 15, 1950, 771—775)

CARL, L., and PETIT, J., *Une technique archaïque de la fabrication du fer dans le mourdi* (Sahara Oriental) (Ethnographie (Fr.) 50, 1955, 60—81)

CLARK, J. DESMOND, *Pre-European copper working in south central Africa* (Rhodesian Mining and Eng. Review, Sept. 1957, 35—41)

CLINE, W., *Mining and Metallurgy in Negro Africa* (Paris, 1937)

FAGG, W., *Ironworking with a stone hammer among the Tula of Nigeria* (Man, 1952, no. 76)

GILLE, B., *Etudes sur la métallurgie du fer à Madagascar* (Techniques et Civilisations IV, 1955, 144—147)

GUGGENHEIM, H., *Smiths of the Sudan* (Natural History 70, 1961, 8—19)

HUARD, P., *Contribution à l'étude du cheval, du fer et du chameau au Sahara oriental* (Bull. Inst. Franc. Afrique Noir (Dakar) 22, sér. B, 1960, 134—178)

JEFFREYS, M. D. W., *Some notes on the Bikom blacksmiths* (Man, 1952, no. 75)

LECLANT, J., *Le fer dans l'Egypte ancienne, le Soudan et l'Afrique* (Le Fer à travers les Ages, Nancy, 1956, 83—91)

WAINWRIGHT, G. A., *The coming of iron to some African peoples* (Man XLII, 1942, 61, 103—108)

16. BARRADAS, J. P. DE, *Viejas y nuevas teorías sobre el origen de la Orfebrería Prehispánica en Colombia* (Bogota, 1956)

BARGALLO, M. *La mineraria y la metalurgia en la America espanola durante le epoca colonial* (Mexico, 1955)

BERGSØE, P., *The metallurgy and technology of gold and platinum among the Precolumbian Indians* (Kopenhagen, 1937)

BERGSØE, P., *The gilding process and the metallurgy of copper and lead among the Precolumbian Indians* (Kopenhagen, 1938)

FESTER, G. A., *Copper and copper alloys in ancient Argentina* (Chymia 8, 1962, 21—31)

KROEBER, A. L., *Quantitative analyses of ancient Peruvian metal* (Amer. Ant. XX, 1954, 160—162)

RIVER, P. and ASANDAUX, H., *La métallurgie en Amérique précolombienne* (Paris, 1946)

ROOT, W. C., *The Metallurgy of the Southern Coast of Peru* (Amer. Ant. XV, 1949, 10—37)

ROOT, W. C., *Metallurgy* (In: Handbook of the South American Indians, vol. 5, 1949, 205—225)

ROOT, W. C., *Gold-copper alloys in ancient America* (J. Chem. Educ. 28, 1951, 76—78)

17. BRAIDWOOD, R. J., and WILLEY, G. R., (edit.), *Courses toward Urban Life* (Edinburgh Univ. Press, 1962)

BRAIDWOOD, R. J., BURKE, J. E., and NACHTRIEB, N. H., *Ancient Syrian copper and bronzes* (J. Chem. Educ. 28, 1951, 87—96)

PALLOTTINO, M., *Gli scavi di Karmir-Blur in Armenia e il problema delle connessioni tra l'Urartu, la Grecia e l'Etruria* (Archaeol. Class. VII, 1955, 109—123)

PIGGOT, ST., *The dawn of Civilisation* (London, 1961)

18. CHILDE, V. GORDON, *Report Brit. Assoc. Adv. Science* 1938, 182

19. COGHLAN, H. H., *Native copper in relation to prehistory* (Man 1951, 156)

OTTO, H., *Die chemische Zusammensetzung von bronzezeitlichen Bronzen* (Naturw. Rundschau II, 1949, 106—110)

20. MUCH, *Die Kupferzeit*, 298

21. READ, TH., *Metallurgical fallacies in archaeological literature* (AJA 38, 1934, 382)

22. WAINWRIGHT, G. A., *Rekhmire's metal workers* (Man XLIV, 1944, 75, 94—98)

23. GILLE, B., *Les traités de métallurgie du XVIe au XVIIIe siècle* (Techniques et Civilisations IV, 1954, 181—186)

24. SISCO, A. G., and SMITH, C. S., *Bergwerk- und Probierbüchlein* (New York, 1949)

AGRICOLA, *De Re Metallica* (German Edit. V.D.I. Verlag, Berlin, 1928) (Engl. edit. H. C. and L. H. HOOVER, New York, 1950)

ERCKER, LAZARUS, *Beschreibung allerfürnemsten mineralischen Ertzt- und Berckwercksarten* (Engl. Transl. Sisco, A. G. and SMITH, C. S., Chicago, 1951)

SMITH, C. S. and GNUDI, M. T., *Biringuccio, De la Pirotechnie libri X* (New York, 1943)

BARBA, A. A., *El Arte de los Metales* (Engl. transl. R. E. DOUGLASS and E. P. MATHEWSON, New York, 1923)

PEDER MANSSONS *Schriften über technische Chemie und Hüttenwesen* (trans. O. JOHANNSEN, Berlin, 1941)

RÉAUMUR, R. A. FERCHAULT DE, *L'art de convertir le fer forgé en acier et l'art d'adoucir le fer fondu* (Engl. trans. A. G. SISCO, Chicago, 1956)

THEOBALD, W., *Des Theophilus Presbyter Diversarium artium schedula* (Berlin, 1933)

CHAPTER TWO

OLD TOOLS AND NEW METHODS

And, strange to tell, among that Earthen Lot
Some could articulate, while others not.
(Omar Khayyâm, Rubaiyat)

Before plunging into the details of the history of metallurgy it seems
fitting to devote a few pages to the assistence which modern research
can give to our subject. The history of the various metals given in the
course of the next chapters will be based on historical, philological
and archaeological data and finds. Modern analytical methods are
most valuable to derive pertinent information from the metal objects
excavated from various sites or stored in our museums.

In the past many of these metal objects, though carefully registered
and inspected at the time of their excavation, disappeared from sight
in the museum storerooms or lingered in museum showcases. Only
the most striking ones were illustrated in catalogues or handbooks
on archaeology and art. However, in order to provide us with the
maximum possible information they should at least be cleaned and
properly conserved for future generations to study. During the last
twenty years the art of conservation has become a most valuable field
of applied research and we now possess a series of excellent handbooks
on the preservation and restoration of museum objects (1), an art
sponsored with succes by the International Institute for Conservation
of Historic and Artistic Works. The latest methods in this field can
be found in IIC's Studies in Conservation.

Some people still object against the destruction of the patina on
many of the ancient metal objects, the aesthetic effect of which they
admire. However, they do not realize, that this layer of oxidized metal
does not belong to the metal and that there are many types of corrosion
products (patina) which are malignant and apt to destroy the entire
metal object within a few years or transform it into an unrecognizable
mass of corroded metal (2). Should we want to extract the maximum
information from such objects we must remember that this patina is

a foreign phenomenon and not an intrinsic part of the metal object. In ancient times when the metal object was made and used it would have formed part of the owner's task to keep it free from rust and oxidation and it is our task to restore its ancient appearance. The author has had the opportunity to examine several cleaned objects which did not only profit by their cleaning, but which yielded important inscriptions on cleaning and thus became more useful to the archaeologist. Whenever the object is not hopelessly broken or destroyed by oxidation it should be cleaned and its life lengthened by the appropriate treatments to be found in the handbooks mentioned. The electrolytic treatment has been developed by many scientists to become a safe routine method even in the hands of those who are not fully acquainted with this kind of work (15) and a long and safe life can now be guaranteed to properly treated metal finds.

Proper cleaning and restauration can also in many cases lead to the correct identification and recognition of the materials used in making these ancient objects. The proper description of the material and the correct labelling of museum objects are still subjects which leave much to be desired and especially the smaller museums do not pay much attention to them. The author once came across the oxidised remains of a tin ring described as "ivory" and the material from which the famous statue of Pepi I, so important in the history of metallurgy, was fashioned, was once described as bronze and at the same time as copper in contemporaneous handbooks. The terms bronze and copper and even brass are still used so loosely in catalogues and handbooks that any attempt to establish a chronological spread of the alloy bronze is greatly imperilled by these statements and only very careful authors can avoid slips in this important matter.

This often very loose identification of the material may be partly due to the fact that many archaeologists are not fully aware of the possibilities of new methods of analysis of metals and still think that the *chemical analysis* is the one and only panacea of all ills. This is of course far from true. The chemical analysis of metal objects reveals their compositions and identifies the constituents of metals and alloys and their quantitative relation, but nothing else! Its great disadvantage is that it destroys part of the object at least, though modern methods of microanalysis allow full figures when using a minute fraction only, but this destruction of archaeological matter has witheld many to use it. In fact, there is a great ressemblance between forensic and archaeological investigations in that the matter to be analysed can be produced only once and if possibly should not be destroyed in the course of analysis as it will be lost irretrievably.

We will have occasion to show that the essential information which we look for in ancient metallurgical products is not only the chemical composition and impurities in the metal, but also the treatment to which they were subjected during their manufacture, their "metallurgical history". This can not been obtained by chemical analysis, but we can apply *non-destructive methods* which yield far more information than the destructive chemical analysis would.

One of the most important groups of tests in use in the metal industry is *metallography*, the study of the structure or constitution of metals and alloys in relation to their physical and mechanical properties. We can learn from the routine examination and interpretation of the gross structural details of such metal objects as applied in industry for they can be applied to ancient metal objects too with profit, but even more information can be obtained from the study of the structure of metals with the help of the (optical or electron) microscope and this is what is usually understood by metallographic study of ancient objects. The method is non-destructive. By polishing, etching and observing a very small part of the object we can draw conclusion on the treatment who which the metal was subjected before its use or discovery and at the same time we get a rough idea of its chemical composition and the main impurities of the metal. We must remember that we are often misled by the accuracy of modern chemical analysis and attach too much importance to precision and the determination of very low percentages of impurities without remembering that such impurities might be due to the crude metallurgical methods of the ancients and that they were not intentional additions as they might be in modern metal objects, because now we know the effect of these impurities. It is too often forgotten that the ancients did not appreciate the ins and outs of metallurgy as they were unable to correlate the special properties of metals and alloys with the amounts of different constituents for the lack of proper analytical methods. What they achieved was knowledge by trial and error and though they mastered many of the main rules of metallurgy such niceties must have escaped them. Even for this reason chemical analysis is not always necessary as it may merely lead us on the wrong track if the figures obtained are not handled by persons who are well acquainted with ancient metallurgy and its achievements. As metallographical methods give us the details on the treatment of the metal and a rough insight into its composition and as they damage the object but slightly and cost very little money and time if applied to a series of objects they are greatly to be preferred to chemical methods, which should be applied, only (as a confirmation of the results obtained with the former methods) to broken and valueless metal finds of the same series.

Modern metallographic methods are very suitable for the examination of ancient metal objects (3), they are time- and labour-saving and give results which are far more important than figures on the chemical composition only as can be seen from the examples we have given in the bibliography (4). They have been more generally applied during the last twenty years and the further chapters of this book will show how informative this branch of research has been.

Another interesting metallographic test is *X-ray metallography* which depends on the impingement of an X-ray on suitable specimens of metals or alloys and the subsequent diffraction of the beam from the regularly spaced atomic planes in the metal. This method has been used more and more during the past fifteen years by Mme Weill and others (5).

A systematic qualitative and quantitative analysis of metals was based on spectrographical methods by Gerlach and it became a good tool when about 1925 it became possible to measure the intensity of the spectral lines. Hence it has often been used during the past fifteen years as it surpasses chemical analysis in speed, sensitivity and accuracy (6). The analytical errors are reduced to 1—2% of the amounts present in the metal and the observational data are collected within ten minutes. This method was the basis for Witter's survey of the Central European prehistoric bronzes and their ores (7).

In some cases very simple means can be used to obtain the information desired. Caley (8) showed that specific gravity measurements were sufficient to distinguish mint coins from faked or debased ones. In the case of gold coins with a high gold content this method is reliable and sufficiently accurate, for silver coins the silver content should be very high; it is not suitable for objects composed of alloys of base metals only. Thus he showed that the Persians had a good method of removing silver, copper and other impurities from gold. By repeated refining they approached the limits of possible purification with the methods then available and the weight variations of gold coins is only 1.3%.

The number of analyses at our disposal has increased vastly through the work of several committees, the oldest being the "Committee" appointed (by the Royal Anthropological Institute) to report on the probable source of the supply of copper used by the Sumerians, which worked on the belief, that the slight nickel content of Sumerian copper was sufficiently characteristic to indicate the ore from which the metal was smelted. Eight reports were presented to the section H of the British Association for the Advancement of Science (9). The first report had to admit failure to trace an ore containing the elements for which special search was being made. The second gave analyses of objects from Mohenjo Daro, Ur and Kish; the third incorporated figures on South African and Indian objects. The fourth report covered Mohenjo Daro and Luristan bronzes, the fifh and sixth from Tell Asmar and Khafaje, from Tell Duweir and Tell Ajjul. The seventh report concentrated on objects from Troy and gave some valuable analyses of early iron, the eigth on objects from Kusara. Most of these interim reports also contain short notes on other objects of importance. Though its original object was not achieved it was found so valuable that archaeologists disposed of facilities for the accurate analysis of ancient metallic objects that in 1939 the Ancient Metal Objects Committee was founded.

The war interfered and in 1945 a new Ancient Mining and Metallurgy Committee was founded which published a series of reports on native copper and ancient artifacts (10), on Bronze Age and Iron metal objects from Azarbaijan (11), on various copper and bronze artifacts (12) and on British and Irish celts (13).

Reports on the methods used by these Committees have been published (14) and experience has taught us that "because of day-to-day variations it is very difficult to use analyses to correlate ores with the final metal products" (15) and that since full quantitative figuring for individual trace elements is irrelevant for defining a special impurities pattern, a semi-quantitative method is quite sufficient. The symbols used for this purpose should be internationally fixed (16).

What we need most now is a thorough investigation of all the metal remains now buried in our museum storerooms. The analysis of a few metal finds may give us some valuable figures but there is always a chance that we are misled. Ancient metallurgy was far from foolproof and lack of proper temperature control and other modern apparatus often delivered the ancient smith in the hands of the fickle goddesses of Fortune and Chance. It may, therefore, be that some object analysed by us is just such a chance product, an unusual result produced unwittingly by the ancient smith, which might lead us to draw entirely wrong conclusions as to his skill and technique. To make sure we should apply statistical methods, that is we should analyse a series of objects belonging to the same kind and date and take the average result as a picture of the technique of that time, using the unusual, exceptional figures to complete this picture of the average. If these investigations are repeated with other series of dated finds, we will in due course gather the results of chronological statistical series of analysis of well-dated metal objects, which will permit us to draw certain conclusions on the development of metallurgical technique.

Though this be the only way of obtaining certainty it may seem a most expensive one to the reader, but this is not so, if these investigations are properly handled. For not only are modern analytical methods far less expensive that the old full chemical analysis, but if such work were concentrated in a central laboratory in each country these results could be achieved with relatively little money. In England we have a core of such a central laboratory in the Ancient Metal Objects Committee, the work of which could be done in any well equiped museum laboratory or at some university. It will not be difficult to achieve a similar concentration of work in any other country. A second advantage of this concentration of archaeological-chemical investigations is that it could be put in the hands of the few experts that should handle this kind of matter, that is in the hands of chemists and scientists who are at the same time interested in archaeology and have studied ancient metallurgy. Only these would know how to attack the problems and what to look for, they only would be able to draw all the hidden information from these metal objects which can not be replaced without losing any datum. Only too often the analysis of these objects was entrusted to experts, who however clever, were not interested or initiated in the mysteries of ancient metallurgy, and thus they have unwittingly destroyed valuable evidence. What remains to be done is, therefore, not only expert examination and re-examination of ancient furnaces, smelting sites, mines, etc. but also further information of ores and deposits in the Near East and chronological-statistical series of analyses of ancient ores, slags and metal objects.

Bibliography

1. E. T. HALL, *Analysis of archaeological specimens, a new method* (Times Science Review, Autumn 1953, 12)

   LUCAS, A., *Antiques, their restoration and preservation* (2 edit., London, 1932)

   PLENDERLEITH, H. J., *The preservation of antiquities* (London, 1934)

   PLENDERLEITH, H. J., *The conservation of antiquities and works of art* (London, 1956)

   SALIN, E., *Traitement au laboratoire des fer archéologiques* (Métaux et Civilisation I, 1945, 49—61)

   SCOTT, A., *Cleaning and restoration of museum exhibits* (London, 1926)

2. CIALDEA, U., *Restoration of antique bronzes* (Mouseion XVI, 1931, 57)

   COLLINS, W. F., *The corrosion of early Chinese bronzes* (J. Inst. Metals, 45, 1931, 23)

   FARNSWORTH, M., *The use of sodium metaphosphate in cleaning bronzes* (Techn. Studies Field Fine Arts IX, 1940, 21)

   FINK, G. and ELDRIDGE, C. H., *The restoration of ancient bronzes and other alloys* (Metrop. Museum, New York, 1925)

   GETTENS, R. J., *Mineralization, electrolytic treatment and radiographic examination of copper and bronze objects from Nuzi* (Techn. Stud. Field Fine Arts I, 1933, 119)

   GETTENS, R. J., *The corrosion products of an ancient Chinese bronze* (J. Chem. Educ. 28, 1951, 67—71)

   KENTLÄMAA, M., *Das elektrolytische Reinigungsverfahren von im Boden gefundenen Metallgegenständen* (Helsinki, 1939)

   MATSUNO, T., *Constituents of ancient bronze and the constitutional relations between the original alloy and the patina* (J. Chem. Ind. Japan, 24, 1921, 1369)

   MYERS, O. H., *Note on the treatment of a bronze weight* (JEA 25, 1939, 102)

   NICHOLLS, H. W., *Restoration of ancient bronzes and cure of malignant patina* (Field. Museum Nat. Hist. Chicago, Museum Technique Series, no. 3, 1930, 1)

   ROCCHI, F., *Per la conservazione e lo studio sperimentale dell monete e delle altre antichità* (Atii Mem. Ist. Numism. Ital. 1917, 1)

   ROCCHI, F., *Saggio di patologia degli argenti antichi* (Riv. Numism. Ital. 1918)

   ROSENBERG, G. A., *Antiquités en fer et en bronze; leur transformation dans la terre contenant de l'acide carbonique et des chlorures et leur conservation* (Copenhague, 1917)

3. FRANCE-LANORD, A., *Les techniques métallurgiques appliquées à l'archéologie* (Rev. Mét. 49, 1952, 411—422)

   FRANCE-LANORD, A., *Examens métallographiques non-destructifs* (Rev. Hist. Sidérurgie III, 1962/63, 253—270)

LEONI, M., *Archaeologia e metallografia* (Sibrium II, 1955, 35—42)

MILNER, G. W. C., *Non-ferrous metallurgical analysis* (Analyst 81, 1956, 619)

PETRIKOVITZ, H. VON, *Was erwartet der Archäologe von der Metallkunde* (Stahl und Eisen 77, 1957, 1 ff)

VOCE, E. *Scientific evidence concerning metal-working techniques* (Man, 61, 1961, 68—71)

WEILL, A., *Examens de surfaces par l'intermédiaire de répliques en vernis nitrocellulosique* (Bull. Lab. Musée du Louvre, 1959, sept., 4, 21—29)

COGHLAN, H. H., *Metallurgical Analysis of Archaeological Materials.* I. (Viking Fund Publications in Anthropology no. 28, 1—20, paper read at the Wenner-Gren Congress, Austria, 1959)

4. CARPENTER, H. C. H. and ROBERTSON, J. M., *The metallography of some ancient Egyptian implements* (J. Iron Steel Inst. 121, 1930, 417)

COMFORT, H., *A hoard of Greek Jewelry* (AJA 54, 1950, 121—126)

FINK, C. G. and POLUSHKIN, E. P., *Microscopic study of ancient bronze and copper* (Metals Technology III, 1936, Techn. Publ. no. 639)

GOORIECKX, D., *Méthode d'examen et de traitement de boucles en fer damasquinées d'argent* (Bull. Inst. R. Patr. Artist. Bruxelles, I. 1958, 125—131)

HAUTTMANN and MORTON, F., *Metallographic study of an iron horseshoe dagger from the Hallstatt graveyard* (Jahrb. oberösterr. Musealver. 100, 1955, 261—262)

LESMARIES, A., *Sur les analyses micrographiques des bronzes anciens* (REA 29, 1927, 52)

NEUMANN, B., *Römischer Damaststahl* (Arch. Eisenh. wesen III, 1927, 241)

PANSERI, C. e LEONI. M., *Sulla tecnica di fabbricazione degli specchi etruschi* (Fonderia ital. VI, 1957, 309—317)

PENNIMAN, T. K. and ALLEN, I. M., *A Metallurgical study of four Irish Early Bronze Age Ribbed Halberds in the Pitt Rivers Museum* (Man LX, 1960, no. 120)

STANLEY, G. H., *The composition of some prehistoric South African bronzes with notes on the methods of analysis* (S. Afr. J. Sci. 26, 1929, 44)

R. STREBINGER & R. NIEDERHUEMER, *The chemical study of an antique art object* (J. Chem. Educ. 30, 1953, 291—295)

WHARTON, C. L. and SAYRE, M., *Metallographic study of primitive copper work* (Amer. Antiquity I, 1935, 109)

SALIN, E., *Etude chimique et métallographique d'une épée de Luristan* (VIIe B.C.) (Rev. Hist. Sidérurgie III, 1961/62, 209—218)

5. WEILL, A. R., *Un problème de métallurgie archéologique: examen aux rayons X d'un objet égyptien en électrum* (Revue de Métall. XLVIII, 1951, 2, 97—104)

—, *Analyse aux rayons X de deux plaques d'or provenant de fouilles archéologiques* (La Metal. Ital. 1951, 12, 3—7)

—, *Etude aux rayons X d'objets égyptiens et romains à base d'or* (Rev. de Métall. XLIX, 1952, no. 4, 293—298)

6. DERKOSCH, J., MAYER, F. X. und NEUNINGER, H., *Spektralanaly-
tische Untersuchungen von urzeitlichen Kupferfunden* (Mikrochim.
Acta 1956, no. 11, 1649—1661)
   GERLACH, W., *Neue spektralanalytische Untersuchungen* (FuF XI,
1935, 86)
   GETTENS, R. J. and WARING, C. L., *The composition of some ancient
Persian and other Near Eastern silver objects* (Ars Orient. II, 1957,
83—90)
   HÜLLE, W., *Die Spektralanalyse im Dienste der Vorgeschichtsforschung*
(Nachrichtenbl. Dtsche Vorzeit, 9, 1933, 84)
   LEONARD, A. G. G. and WHEELER, P. F., *Spectrographic analysis of
Irish ringgold* (Sci. Proc. R. Dublin Soc. 19, 1929, 35)
   WINKLER, J. E. R., *Quantitative spektralanalytische Untersuchungen
an Kupferlegierungen zur Analyse vorgeschichtlicher Bronzen* (Landes-
anstalt f. Volkheitskunde, Halle, 1935)
7. W. WITTER, *Die älteste Erzgewinnung im nordisch-germanischen Le-
benskreis* (Leipzig, 1938, 2 vols.)
   WITTER, W., *Wie ich zum Erforscher vorgeschichtlicher Metallgewin-
nung wurde* (Jhsschr. Mitteld. Vorgeschichte 33, 1949, 98—107)
   OTTO, H., WILHELM WITTER, 1866—1949 (Jahresschr. Mitteld.
Vorgeschichte 34, 1950, 188—190)
   OTTO, H. und WITTER, W., *Handbuch der ältesten vorgeschichtlichen
Metallurgie in Mitteleuropa* (Leipzig, 1952)
8. CALEY, E. R., *The specific gravity and fineness of Persian Darics* (Numis-
matic Review II, 1944, July 21—23)
   —, *Methods of distinguishing cast from struck coins* (Numismatic
Review II, 1945, April/June, 21—24)
   —, *Validity of the specific gravity method for the determination of
the finesess of gold objects* (Ohio J. Sci. XLIX, 1949, 73—82)
   —, *Notes on the chemical composition of Parthian coins* (Ohio J. Sci.
50, 1950, 107—120)
   —, *Fineness of the gold coins of the Roman Empire* (Numismatist
63, 1950, 2, 66—70)
   —, *Estimation of Composition of Ancient Metal Objects, utility of spe-
cific gravity measurements* (Anal. Chem. 24, 1952, no. 4, 676—681)
   —, *Chemical dating of bronze coin blanks from the Athenian agora*
(Ohio J. Sci. 55, 1955, 44—47)
   —, and MCBRIDE, H. D., *Chemical composition of Antoniani of
Trajan, Decius, Trebonianus, Gallus and Valerian* (Ohio J. Sci. 56,
1956, 285—289)
   CONDAMIN, J., *Note technique* (Revue Numism. 6e sér. III, 1961
62—73)
   DAHL, O., *Die Arbeitsmethoden der antiken Münztechnik insbesondere
der Falschmünzerei* (Metallwirtschaft 10, 1931, 659)
   ELAM, C., *An investigation of the microstructure of fifteen silver Greek
coins and some forgeries* (J. Inst. Metals 45, 1931, 57)
   MILNE, J. G., *Greek and Roman coins and the study of history* (London,
1939)

9. 1928, 1930, 1930, 1932, 1933, 1935, 1936, 1938
10. MAN, 1948 nos. 3 & 17; MAN 50, 1950, 147—149
11. MAN, 1949, no. 178; MAN 1950 no. 4 & 49
12. MAN 1951 no. 234
13. MAN 1953 no. 150; MAN 1954 no. 21; Ores and Metals (R, Anthropological Instit. Ocean. Paper no. 17, London, 1963)
14. COGHLAN, H. H., *The Value of Analyses and Metallographic Study of Metal Artifacts* (Museums Journal 48, 1948, 79—81)
    —, *Report on Analytical Methods* (J.R.A.I. 92, 1962, i, 125—140)
15. THOMPSON, F. C., *The early metallurgy of copper and bronze* (Man 58, 1958, 1—7) (Man 1956, 1432)
16. PITTIONI, *Viking Fund Publications in Anthropology* 28, 1960, 24

New methods and case histories are regularly reported in "Studies in Conservation" and in the I.I.C. Abstracts of the Technical Literature on Archaeology and the Fine Arts published by the I.I.C., London.

CHAPTER THREE

THE EVOLUTION OF THE SMITH, HIS SOCIAL AND SACRED STATUS

"God gave them no sheep but cleverness instead
If they were rich, they would but lie a-bed"
(Suk saying)

Before turning to the tools of the metal-worker and the history of the separate metals we must pause a few moments on the figure of the smith. For since the first smiths started their craft in the Late Stone Age and since the first metals were used by mankind, this mysterious trade, which was so different from the other Neolithic arts and crafts, formed the centre of a wealth of myths and legends and the smith grew to form a special social type encumbered with religious rites and taboos, endowed by popular feeling with magical potencies in many directions.

A few attempts have been made (1), but the real story of the smith is not yet available. Andrée (2) has collected a lot of valuable ethnographical material but the archaeological and historical evidence was never published. May be the interlocking of technical, archaeological and philological factors has discouraged work in this line, but the few notes collected below will show the reader that a rich harvest awaits him, who will dare to attack the complicated question, which could easily form the subject of a separate monograph. We can do no more than glance over the "Promised Land", and while spying the land we hope to be as lucky as the smith's dog "so well used to the sparks that he'll not burn".

1. *Status of the smith*

Before discussing some of the factors that made the smith the important figure he is in primive societies, let us survey the *status of the smith with some tribes in Africa, Asia and Europe.*

As great differences are obvious in Africa, it is difficult to group the different complexes of social favours and taboos geographically. In the grass-lands of North-East Africa the caste of the smiths is generally despised, their work is not attended by any ritual. Guilds, magic, bonds with the secret societies and club-houses are features of the West African smith. In the Congo region and surrounding countries to the East and the South the smiths form no clans but guilds, they are considered the equals or sometimes identified with priests and chiefs, their work is regulated by a ponderous ceremonial, in which "medicines" and "spirits" play a large part. But on the other hand such features as trade-secrets, taboos, personification of the tools, transmission of the crafts from father to son are spread all over Africa and it is difficult to find their country of origin or even the way along which they penetrated Africa. Let us therefore take a few examples at random.

In North-East Africa the smiths of the Masai and the Bari are slaves and pariahs (3), often remnants of subjugated aboriginals. Thus the Tumalods are the slaves of the Somalis and the Watta are subjects of the Galla. Their status with the Nandi is somewhat better, here they are not forced to intermarry. But the Somali will never enter a smithy, does not shake hands with a smith or marries his daughter (4). Among the Tibbu (5) they form a pariah-caste with rigid taboos, their craft is handed from father to son, though they do not differ anthropologically from their tribesmen! The word "smith" is considered to be a term of abuse, though it is also unwise to curse or insult a smith. Even the fellahin of Eastern Egypt and the Oases hold the smith in awe, he is a tramp whom one respects but avoids and there are many similar cases (6).

Among the WaChagga (7) the smiths form a separate clan, which seems to have been adopted long ago by the tribe. The smith is honoured as the maker of deadly weapons, because he knows how to join iron and iron and because he possesses tools of great power. Though he is not considered to be a magician, it is dangerous to bleed him and it is unusual to marry his daughters. The smiths do not join the warriors, they make their weapons using iron, which is, however, taboo in many ceremonies.

Among other tribes in West Africa every familygroup has a smith, for whom corn and other agricultural products are cultivated and for whom the community builds a smithy. The tools of this smith have great power, they are considered to do the work, not the smith and they would kill the smith, who gave up his craft, or they would at least smite him with a fever lasting a year (8). The Fans make no difference between the chief, the medicineman and the smith, because the smithcraft is so higly honoured that only chiefs and their kin are allowed to ply it (9). In Benin a smith can be enobled, he is generally considered to be a magician (10). On the Loango coast the ritual nails are forged by a priest-smith (11). In the Congo or Ogowe regions, where there is no smith, bellows or smith-tools hang in the fetish-houses. In the Congo region and in West Africa the smith is generally a honoured and rich man, who inherits his craft. He is a potent ma-

Fig. 11.
Making the holy kris (Java)

gician, his fire is holy, his social position is high in proportion (12). This in great contrast to the pariah-smiths of the Masai, though this tribe acknowledges some magical power of the smith's products. Swords will spill blood, therefore they shall be cleaned before use with butter or fat. Among the Baghirmi Arabs of Lake Tchad (13) there are many groups and sub-groups, but the Ḥad-dâdîn, the smiths, form an undivided clear and a separate caste as with so many other African tribes. Neither are they Arabs, but probably of Hamitic-Negritic stock.

Cline (14) gives many other examples in detail and finally he draws this conclusion: "Hunting is ritualized as much as metal-working, both require considerable skill and occupation excluding most of the cattle-raising or agricultural population. The smith provides weapons and tools necessary for life but his trade asks for a long and arduous practice, tending to isolate him seasonally or throughout the year. It may affect his position with people who identify cattle-raising or agri-culture with everything that is noble or with people who despise manual labour. The smith has the most elevated position in the Congo

Fig. 12.
Javanese court goldsmith (Jokjakarta)

and West Africa where the arts and crafts were well developed. Both ritual and caste are conditioned by the cultural frame rather than by the wonderment of primitive man at processes which he failed to understand".

And we must add, that the present situation has of course been changed and often very drastically by imports of cheap European industrial products. For the Negro smiths are very ingenious crafts-men in inventing and using new tools, types of bellows, etc. but now they often work with imported iron (15).

Apart from the guilds or clans of smiths we find many itinerant smiths or tinkers, who are very specially considered to be powerful magicians (16). Africa is still a field in which the primitive smith can be studied from many aspects, as there is hardly another region in the world where we find such a well-developed smithcraft, which reached such a height before the advent of modern industrial products and here types and forms are far better developed than in Oceania or America (17).

In Asia the situation is far less clear, because many strata of higher civilisations overlie the more primitive strata and the archetypes break through only now and then.

The position of the smith in Java or Bali is most interesting. Under the empire of Modjopahit Java counted no less than 800 smith-families in the eleventh century. When this empire was dissolved four centuries later many of them flew to Bali. The ironsmith was honoured as a wise expert, but only he, for the Cheribon lawbook ruled the copper-, gold- and silver-smiths out of court and admits only the *pande* or iron-smith.

The armourer or *empu* is greatly honoured in Bali. He fulfils a very special duty in the kampong, for is not all metal 'charged' and there-fore dangerous to everyone but to him who knows how to handle it? He has the magical power to work the dangerous metal. But the close bond between the smith is not only formed by their trade-secrets, but also by the magical rites of their craft and the initiation of their pupils. Special mantra's are recited before the use of every tool. These *pande-wési* (ironsmiths or foremen) have a written tradition which claims their creation through the intercession of Brahma (who takes the place of the fire-god Agni!), who gave them their sakti or magical power. This guild embraces not only the iron-smiths but also the thinkers, gold- and silver-smiths, carpenters, draughtsmen and painters, it allows them certain rights, they are freed for certain imposts and communal tasks. This written tradition would make them part of the Triwangsa and therefore elevate them above the common people though the members of the Triwangsa doubt this (18). We shall revert to some aspects of the Javanese smith later on.

In others parts of the Indonesian Archipelago we find the same peculiar position of the smith. The Batak smith worships his tools in particular and gives them mysterious names (19). For the tools are supposed to do the work and the spirits of these tools protect the smith and his family. The smith himself is a priest, by whose power the weapons are imbued with a mighty spirit, but then this applies to the armourer or ironsmith only. The son shall take up the trade of his father lest "the tools lay snares for him". Most operations are preceded by an offering, whilst the tribesmen pour out libations in the smithy in case of illness thus using it as a temple! In general it seems that the smithy is regarded as a temple of the spirits of the earth, whose power resides in the tools and products of the smith. Among the Bahau and Kenya Dajaks every village has a smith or two, whose smithy stands

Fig. 13.
Smithy of the Papuas at Manokwari (New Guinea)

near the "long house" (20). This professional smith is imbued by a special spirit called "to̱ temne̱" (smith-spirit) without whom he would lack his expert knowledge. But a civilian can also call upon this spirit to possess him and to deliver him of his ailments. The smith must propitiate this spirit by regular offerings in the smithy. Many of these old customs have disappeared because the Dajak smiths now work imported iron and no longer smelt the ores themselves.

The smiths of Doré (New-Guinea) form a special caste, during their initiation they swallow special "medicines" and avoid pork. The Buginese have a smith-caste, that keeps its trade secret just like the smiths of the Igorotes of Central Luzon (21). In Madagascar the smiths occupy a position like those of Java, from whom they seem to have adopted tools and bellows, which differ entirely from the types used in the African continent.

On the continent of Asia the Baris live as pariah-smiths with the agricultural and pastoral Shiaposh of the Eastern Hindu-Kush (22). In Nepal too the smiths are pariahs, but they are highly honoured by the hill-tribes of Assam, where every village has a smith, who, however, only works scrap bronze from Tibet or iron bars from Assam (23). This degeneration of the craft of the smith is striking all over Asia. The Kazak tinkers are much less skilful and self-reliant than formerly, often they are itinerant smiths.

Kalmuck smiths no longer attempt to make any complicated implement. No Siberian smith smelts iron any longer, but the Tungus smiths forge iron tools from bars and scrap iron (24). Still Tartar and Siberian smiths produced iron from local ores when the Russians occupied the country, mostly working ores from rivers and mountain streams.

Around no craftsman in Japan has mythical legend and ancient story thrown such a halo as around the smith. In remote Antiquity his ancestors are numbered among the Gods of the Divine Age and in later times his astounding feats form the themes of innumerable tales. His profession, notwithstanding the manual labour it involved, was deemed an honourable one and men of noble birth were not debarred from pursuing it (25).

In America metallurgy was introduced either by the Aztecs and Incas or by the European, except perhaps with the pre-Columbian Indians of Colombia and Peru. But here again we lack proper information as hardly anything is known about pre-Columbian metallurgy and the position of the smith among Indian tribes. The Navajos seem to have possessed intinerant smiths, who not only worked iron, but also copper, silver, etc. (26).

The smith of prehistoric Europe occupied an honoured position. Had not the gods themselves forged metals according to the Voluspä? In Scandinavia and England the smiths were considered the equals of the bards or priests and no slave could profess their craft without seeking permission to do so. The famous smiths of Wales, who made their own iron, were by the laws of that country allowed to sit near the priest of the household in the king's presence (27). They had mysterious powers, for were not the maxims of Druids, smiths and wise women dreaded by the Celts? (28). And though we do not know much from direct tradition, the great part which the smith-craft plays in legend and myth (Wieland, Mimir), figures like the giants, dwarfs, elves and fairies, who forge metals and watch their accumulated treasures in mountain recesses, the "super-smiths" of the Kalewala, Kaweli-poeg and the myths of the Esthonians, these all tell us something about the lost glory of the prehistoric smith. But even in early historic days he was highly appreciated for his skill and the variety of things he produced. About 1000 A.D. Aelfric of Eynsham says (29): "How does the ploughman get his plough or his ploughshare, or his goad, but by my craft? How does the fisherman obtain his hook, or the shoemaker his awl, or the tailor his needle, but by my work?"

Sometimes we are allowed a glimpse of the status of the prehistoric smith from archaeology. Thus, for instance in the Transcaucasia of the Middle Kuban period when local metallurgy developed strongly on Mesopotamian and Anatolian lines, smiths were admitted to the ranks of the barrowbuilders, as is proved by the moulds and tools found in their tombs from that period onwards (30).

We shall revert to the gods and heroes of the smith later on.

2. *Diffusion of metallurgy and the smith*

But before discussing the characteristics of the primitive smith we must follow up this somewhat dry summary of ethnological and historical examples by a discussion of the *diffusion of metallurgy from the point of view of the smith*. Still we can not pretend to be "the little smith of Nottingham who doth the work that no man can", our evidence is far too meagre for that and we can give no more than a working hypothesis.

In discussing the archaeological material on the evolution of metallurgy we saw that metallurgy came to the Near East from the East and the North. The oldest metal objects have been found along the mountain range that reaches from the Caspian Sea and the Elburz to the Hindu Kush and the T'ien Shan mountains towards Lake Baikal. In these mountains there are many places where copper and iron ores occur, while the mountain streams contain alluvial gold, magnetite and cassiterite. There is an old practically forgotten suggestion of Lenormant, who contended that the discovery of metallurgy should be ascribed to the Turanians and Ugro-Finns. Andrée (31) has elaborated this thesis by saying that the northern slopes of these mountains were originally occupied by tribes akin to the Chudes or Chudaki, who had invented metallurgy and who were the ancestors of the Finns! Waitz (32) even proposed to consider the Finns as the aborigines of prehistoric Europe, who had brought metallurgy from their Asiatic home and transmitted this knowledge to the Indo-Europeans and other, tribes inhabiting Europe later on. Of course this no longer holds good in the light of modern archaeology, however strong the evidence of metallurgy may be in the Kalewala and the myths of the Letts and Esthonians.

It is highly improbable that these West-Finns came to Europe before the rise of the Danubian I civilisation which marks the rise of metallurgy in Central Europe.

Much more light could be thrown on the question by an exhaustive study of the primitive smiths of Asia, a subject that never received that same attention as the study of African metallurgy. Still here and there evidence crops up. Thus Ruben (33) published a remarkable study of the Asûr, a primitive tribes of smiths living in the mountains of Chota Nagpur in India. Nowadays they no longer smelt ores but forge iron bars which they buy. Originally they were half-nomads, who remained between a few months to three years on spots where there were ores and fuel until they had exhausted them. They formed a community of specialists, divided in totemclans, who hunted a little and kept cattle, though they did not raise them. They did not know agriculture and gathered fruits, nuts, etc. The single smith was honoured by the surrounding tribes, though he be from a totally different anthropological stock, but as a mass the smiths were despised and hated though feared. Ruben has proved that we have to do with a tribe that originally belonged to a cattle-raising culture, which tribe specialised in metallurgy and which was driven by the Aryan invaders from their original home to the hinterlands of Dekhan. The Asûr originally lived north of the mountains of the Punjab, where the cattle-raising culture is at home and where the earliest metal objects were found. This culture is certainly connected with early metallurgy also by the fact that they were the first to possess good pottery. We have already pointed out that metallurgy and the possession of proper furnaces are intimately linked and that it is impossible to smelt ores in a camp fire. Coghlan in his interesting experiments at the Borough Museum (Newbury) in 1938 proved beyond doubt that the only primitive furnace that would smelt ores was the pottery kiln, which later on led to special metallurgical furnaces as metal technique improved. But reverting to the ethnological evidence there are many signs that the iron workers of many jungle tribes of southern India are immigrants and form a sort of alien guild or craft, just as much of the practice of iron working in Africa has been spread by the guild of artisans (34). It would then seem from archaeological, mineralogical and ethnological evidence that the cattle-raising cultures of the northern slopes of the Altaï and Paropamisos discovered metallurgy after evolving the art of the potter, probably discovering native metals (gold, copper and meteoric iron) when tending their herds in their summerquarters on the mountain-slopes both in the hills and the mountain-streams. Possibly they had even discovered the working of some ores, for the smelting of copper is already in possession of the prehistoric peasant culture when it spreads from these quarters over the whole of the Near East and North-Africa. The oldest settlements of Anau yield quite good copper instruments made from copper ores! From this home of metallurgy the craft spread with the peasants to secondary centres like Caucasia, Elam, Armenia and Pontus, whence it migrated to tertiary centres like Phrygia, Lydia, Cyprus, the Balkans and the Danube valley to spread beyond.

With the coming of these primitive smiths there arose among the non-metalworking tribes around them the many legends and myths about gnomes, dwarfs, kobolds, Dactyloi, Kuretes, Korybantes, Telchines, Hephaistos and others that tell us of the smiths and their fire-god, their mysterious rites and their craft.

Even the history of iron, that late-comer among the metals, seems to point to the original working of magnetite and other iron ores of the mountain streams. The civilisations of the alluvial river-valleys, which possessed no ores worth mentioning always regarded metal-craft as a highly mysterious job, though the smiths living amongst them gradually lost their original traits and we find only smith-guilds with little or no special traditions or rites to remind us of their ancestors.

But "often a full dexterous smith forges a very weak knife" and the suggestions given above remain to be proved by excavations both in the Armenian highlands and the regions of Afghanistan and Baluchistan which are so desirable from many another point of view.

But whatever future excavations may tell, it has been proved beyond doubt that the smith occupied a special position in primitive society. He can but excercise his own craft, whereas the primitive potter would not be hindered in his agricultural occupations and many other crafts of prehistoric man simply filled up his spare time. We must admit that the smith must dispose of a formidable body of industrial lore. Craft traditions embodied the results of long experience and of many deliberate experiments. It may seem to us no more than applied science with a tangle of magic, but science it was that was handed down from generation to generation of smiths.

It is certain that the effective utilisation of metal discoveries involved the elaboration of a highly complicated technique through series of inventions. These form a range of discoveries and inventions so abstruse and complex that independent origin in parts of the Old World must be considered fantastically improbable, at least in the early millenia of the history of mankind. As to the links between Old and New World metallurgy no discussion is possible at the present stage as we possess insufficient data and analyses from the American continent. From what we know it seems that the foundations of metallurgy penetrated into the New World and there were developed on original lines best suited to local circumstances.

In the Old World, mining and metallurgy were originally practised by a caste or clan of few members, the membership of which implied initiation in the tangle of technical traditions, but which conferred upon the members some degree of immunity from the bondage of tribal customs and duties. We must never forget that the number of smiths in primitive society was small. A tribe of a few thousand members would not use more than 1 Ton of metal a year, that is less than the production of ten smiths, who even now produce with ease three to five Kgrs. of metal a day with very primitive means (35).

The diffusion of the special lore of these craftsmen is of course associated with the spread of the craftsmen themselves, for instance prospecting, sometimes not only in quest of ore but as perambulating smiths seeking fortunes by plying their trade among barbarians, sometimes as slaves captured in warfare, often as smiths who had secured initiation and returned home.

Naturally the pupils were not always as clever as the masters, those who had learnt a new technique were apt to apply it very clumsily, the proficiency of the trade was only acquired by generations of practice and discipline. Thus the early Minoan and Cyprian metal tools are much more clumsy than the Sumerian originals.

Hoever, a true Metal Age arises only when there are permanent settlements of smiths in a certain region. Itinerant smiths or prospectors in quest of ore may produce a "chalcolithic Age" by importing a few metal objects which are used side by side with the aboriginal stone and bone tools, or they may give instructions as to the shaping of metal objects. But a true Metal Age can only arise with the advent of the smith. The diffusion of metallurgy need not differ from that of the potter's lore, where new types often herald the settling of new inhabitants. Archaeology affords us definite proof of the continuity of diffusion of metallurgy from a certain centre. Gordon Childe pointed out that the same hammer made of a grooved stone lashed to a forked stick heralds early mining in Sinai, Caucasia, the Alps, Spain and Cornwall and that the oldest metal tools and weapons are very similar both in Mesopotamia and Egypt and tend to differentiate from protodynastic times only. Still certain common tools remain identical for a very long time over vast areas.

It would appear from archaeological data that the oldest smiths moved about quite freely in prehistoric Europe. But this is not strange as we have many historical examples to prove the same. Thus we remind the reader of the stimulating influence of Bohemian and Bavarian coppersmiths on the bronze-craft of Benin. Manipuri workers were carried off to Burma in 1760 where they became responsible for many crafts (36). For Chingiz Khan's successors worked Chinese, Persian and even German miners and a French jeweller!

Of course the itinerant specialist occurs less frequently among primitive people and tends to be restricted by the deposits of ore and fuel to the country of his tribe. But their wanderings may be prompted by pressing needs or social conditions and warfare. There seems no reason to doubt the diffusion of metallurgy at least in its primitive stage. Later and especially in developing the metallurgy of iron there are indications that we must be careful in applying the diffusion principle. We must not fall into the mistakes of de Mortillet who contended that iron metallurgy was discovered in Africa, or Bataillard who thought that the gipsies were the initiators of the Bronze Age.

3. *Technical background of the primitive smith*

Before discussing the characteristics of the primitive smith another problem must needs occupy us for some time. We mean the *technical background of the primitive smith*.

We have already discussed the difficulty of applying the well-known series of Copper-, Bronze and Iron-Ages to certain tertiary and fourthly centres of metallurgy, but the sequence propagated of old holds true for the Near East. However, these Ages can hardly be said to characterize true stages of metallurgy, these stages are far better characterised by modifications of metal technique.

The study of material things has helped to illustrate man's efforts to utilize his environment, but not only this, his tools and implements are the outward signs of peculiar ideas in his mind. Materially speaking there is a close interrelation between tools, processes, raw materials and finished products, but above these there is the presence of motive and insight of the creator. In his gradual conquest of the metals man has not proceeded by small variations to a gradual change of metal technique, but there are certain periods in which inventions have created new paths and technique advances in leaps along lines drawn by experiment and practical science. Each of these stages creates its own means and processes. Thus the Bronze Age smiths elaborate casting methods, the Iron Age smiths of La Tène develop rivetting. We have already sketched these three stages of metallurgy.

The earliest stage, the "native metal stage" is the transition from Stone Age to the Metal Age. Man had already learnt to use the native metals gold and copper (and also silver and meteoric iron), but he had only treated them as he worked bone, stone and wood. But now he learnt to appreciate their true metal character by heat-treatment and discovered that the "mysterious stone" could be shaped by tempering, hammering, cutting and grinding. Soon, and this phase of the use of native metals already falls within the second stage of metallurgy, casting and shaping the metal when hot joins these treatments to complete the cycle of operations. The new possibilities of casting and heat-treatment have impressed themselves so deeply in the mind of early mankind, that some of the stone objects of the Late Stone Age take the form of metal objects in regions that border upon others where metallurgy has already become a regular craft (37).

But true metallurgy begins with the "ore stage", with the discovery that certain stones, which we call ores, could be reduced to metals (first copper, then lead and silver, etc.) and that metals could be heated until they could be cast when molten. Here again we have another, but completely different cycle of operations and processes, of discoveries

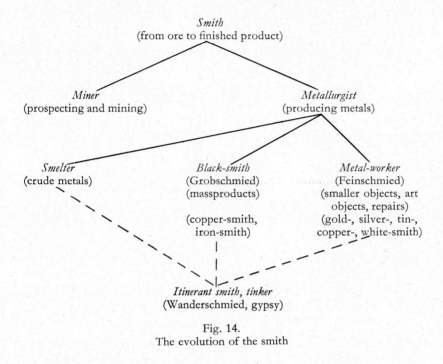

Fig. 14.
The evolution of the smith

and inventions. Here the smiths have struck an entirely new line and several generations of experimenting and trials must have preceeded a long line of masters in the "new art" and their pupils. It is practically certain that this new stage of metallurgy brought along specialisation. Especially when the surface deposits of certain ores grew rare and the smith had to work deeper strata and start vein mining, he could no longer dig the ore and produce the metal and the finished metal object from it. There arose the craft of the *miner* who did the prospecting and mining side of the job and the *metallurgist* who reduced the ore and worked the metal. The new element in this stage of metallurgy is not so much the metal as the processes, the many phases of working and reducing the ores, the preparation of new metals and of alloys (bronze) and the gradual insight into the proper field of application to which each of these metals and alloys were destined by their nature.

The preparation of alloys was no mean task. They could be prepared by the smelting of two different ores, by smelting a metal with another ore or by melting certain metals in the appropriate proportions. The first two methods were the oldest, the last was not used until the end of the Bronze Age. Therefore alloys vary greatly in composition in the Early Bronze Age and only late could their composition be kept within a close range. But this meant no disadvantage for the alloys in their early stage for their applications were far less differentiated than they are nowadays and their composition could vary within wide limits without decreasing their usefulness to the early metallurgist. Neither was the purity of the metals of great importance at this stage, though the practical and unscientific (and therefore uneconomical) preparation with primitive apparatus and methods often yielded remarkably pure products. The formidable growth of the mysteries connected with the extraction of metals led to further specialisation. Gradually three different types of metallurgists are evolved. The first of these is the *smelter*, whose task it was to produce the crude metal or the alloy from the ores. Then there arose the *blacksmith*, who manufactured mass products from crude metals, first copper objects (coppersmith) then mostly those of iron, a task which we have come to identify with the name "blacksmith" though the metal-workers of the early Assyrian and Babylonian texts were certainly copper- and bronzesmiths of mass products. Finally there were the *metal-workers*, who produced the smaller objects, art objects and who repaired or decorated metal objects. As such we find gold-, silver-, tin-, white- and copper-smiths. It is quite probable that the earliest specialists of this type were the gold- and silver-smiths, who very early in the history of metallurgy reached a skill that is hardly less than that of his modern colleague. Thus for instance the gold objects from Dashur in Egypt show us that the Egyptian goldsmith was a master of many a technique which is still practised in the same form (at least in principle) as so many centuries ago. The value of his experiments for the development of copper metallurgy remains to be studied.

A third and most important step was the discovery of iron metallurgy and the preparation of iron from its ores. The "iron-stage" meant a new series of discoveries and inventions again. For here the composition of the metal or alloy is of secondary importance. The ancients could prepare wrought iron and steel, though cast iron was probably beyond their pale and produced incidentally now and then. The different forms of iron which we know are essentially alloys of iron and carbon. By introducing a small percentage of carbon in the practically pure wrought iron we obtain an alloy which by appropriate heat-treatment can be transformed into steel. This introduction of a small percentage of carbon was achieved in Antiquity by frequent re-heating of the wrought iron in a charcoal fire between the hammerings. But the essential factors for the properties of the resultant iron or steel lay in the quenching, tempering, forging and re-heating, in short in the working of the material. The iron stage therefore means a completely new cycle of processes and operations, mainly centered on the working of the metal. The new smith of this iron stage is the smith whom the word always evokes in our mind. His stock of trade is different from that of the older smith of the "ore stage" though he has of course built up his world of knowledge on the foundations of practice and experience of the earlier type. In the Iron Age the specialisation at which we have already hinted was completed. In classical times there is a fairly complete differentiation between the miner and prospector, the smelter, who prepared the crude metal and the alloys, the work of the blacksmith (Grobschmied), which consisted in the making of large pieces and mass-products and the metalworker (Feinschmied) who shapes the crude metal to small objects, art objects and who effects small repairs.

In Homeric and classical Greece the *metalleus, chalkeus* or *sidèreus* was still one who worked his own ores and produced finished metal objects. But in Roman times the differentation had already proceeded very far. Mining is conducted on truly industrial scale, metallurgy is a real industry, that produces metal in bars and blocks; the blacksmith and the different types of metalworkers are common figures in Roman public life.

Apart from the different types of smiths already mentioned we meet the itinerant smith or tinker (Wanderschmied). He is sometimes a blacksmith, but more often shows the characteristics of the metalworker and is either a copper-smith or a white-smith or both. The few examples of tinkers or smith-tribes, that are nomads and who still work their own ore, may go to show that this type of smith existed before the Iron Age. That the type became general with the coming of the Iron Age is clear from many data. The typical tinker is the gypsy,

whose history is full of curious sidelights on the history of metals.
The Hungarians say "there are as many smiths as there are gypsies".
They seem to have come from India and indeed their language is intimately related with Sanskrit. Their word for metal or iron is *saster*
(compare the Sanskrit *sastra*!), copper is called *lolo* (red) *saster*, brass
dscheldo saster (yellow iron), a typical nomenclature of a people that
was originally a tribe of iron-smiths, now the traditional tinker and
copper-smith! We remind the reader of a similar feature in Negro
nomenclature, which also shows the precedence of iron to copper in
Africa! The gypsy is the typical tinker who carries his smithy, anvil,
firehearth and tools along and who works sitting, a position quite
impossible for a black-smith. At the same time he is the fortuneteller
and the musician, a combination that is a regular feature of itinerant
smiths in other regions. The Roumanians call him *calderari* or tinker,
and *spoîtori* or white-smith and this again illustrates the evolution of
a people that left India as a tribe of iron-smiths. Still this original
occupation is extremely useful for the explanation of many of the
features of gypsy technique and this again shows the extreme importance of the technical background of the smith.

Schrader had pointed out, that there is no general Indo-European
term for smith (38), but that terms were formed in the languages
belonging to this family after their separation and that the introduction of metallurgy among several of these peoples occurred at a stage
when specialisation of the smith's craft had already proceeded quite
far. Some of the terms for smith are connected with certain metals
(chalkeus, sidereus, smith (from smîda: metal?)), others point to
certain operations (kovaçi, compare the Latin cudere: cutting, a word
that was taken over by the Magyars, the Letts and the Esthonians) and
finally some which simply mean a worker, one who fashions (Lat.
faber). The same holds true for the names of the smith's tools. The
identity formerly claimed for the Negro terms for smith and shaman
seems incorrect (39). Thus for instance the Bantu word "ngangu"
means skill, cunning, art and applies to the smith as the shaman as
well! The material given above will have convinced the reader that
even the most primitive smith must have been a very skilled person and
therefore Childe is quite correct in calling him the first expert (40) whose
work was a "full time job". Though he works for the community of
his tribesmen, he is unable to help them in producing food, but they
have to feed him in return for the goods produced by him. The
coming of the smith is therefore a social revolution, the effect of which

is still visible in the regard which both parties have for each other among primitive people. It is true that the technical background on which his trade was built up has changed considerably in the course of many centuries, but it remained a factor which can not be disregarded if we want to discus the social and religious status of the primitive smith. There may be something in the saying that "the smith has always a spark in his throat" but his thirst was not always materialistic and he acquired a wealth of knowledge and applied science which were of the greatest importance to the evolution of mankind.

4. *Social and religious status of the smith*

Apart from the materialistic factors and the technical background of the smith, which emerge clearly from the archaeological data, there is little to help us in describing the *social and religious status of the primitive smith*. Still the ethnographical material of which we gave a summary will help us to determine the main characteristics.

1—First of all the place of the smith in primitive society wavers between extremes. He is either *honoured or despised*, but always held in awe. We cited Cline's opinion which is essentially true. The smith is bound to the place where he finds his ore and fuel (wood or charcoal), often for long, though he may wander away after a short time, when the surface ores are exhausted as in the case of the Asûr.

Among nomads or pastoralists he is a social outcast, there he is despised most because of his manual labour and the nomad treats him with contempt and fear, because he does not understand his trade and never will. There he belongs to the lowest castes or is simply a pariah, his name is a term of abuse. Still they suffer him, for he is useful, he forges the weapons which they use in warfare, which he is not allowed to join. If his wives and daughters practice a little agriculture or collect fruits, berries and the like, they despise them the more.

But his share is a honourable one with the agriculturalists, who as a matter of course leads a sedentary life. He forges their implements and he is the wise friend of his villagers, who come to his smithy to study him at work, he is their councillor, because he is clever, an expert who often is an important trader and go-between, often chief, village-head or councillor of kings, often priest or even a prince of the blood. Here wehre social life is differentiated in the extreme he is at home and he can display his influence to its limits.

This of course holds good for the sedentary smith only, for the tinker is truly despised everywhere though feared, just as the modern peasant still identifies every gipsy with a thief.

Before proceeding let us survey the interesting details on the Javanese smith given in two publications by Rassers (41).

Nowadays the smith in Java is a poor, humble man, but all the same he is still a special and honoured person. From the way in which he is treated and also from his own behaviour it is clear that the belief that his profession brings him into contact with supernatural powers has not yet entirely disappeared. The word for smith is pande (expert), a word used especially for the black-smith and empu or kyai (Lord, master) as used for the armourer.

Gold-, silver- or copper-smiths were called empu, but this term was formerly used in Java to denote the iron-smith in general though it came to mean armourer later. In Bali not every armourer is called empu but only those who forge superior weapons of magical power or those destined to be used by princes.

In ancient Java forging was veiled in mystery and since the introduction of the Javanese kris, the dirk of ancient Java, in the Iron Age (between the fourth and seventh century A.D.) a whole literature arose around the mysterious figure of the kris-smith, who often was honoured like a prince of the blood. Under the government of the princes they are said to occupy honoured positions at the court. The smith could under certain circumstances represent the entire community.

In ancient Java the rôles of smith and prince more or less overlap, sometimes their relationship is compared to that of brothers. Their genealogy like that of the princes goes back to the gods. In Bali the *bangsa pande* or guild of the smiths was originally a clan or genealogical group.

Even nowadays when a kris will be manufactured the shabby smithy is decorated to become a *kayon*, the stage for the performance of a masked play or sacred ground. The smith is obliged to hang the small model of a tent (*taroeb*) under the eaves outside, thereby making his smithy a *taroeb* or sacral ground and a meeting place of the community. Originally the *taroeb* was the primitive tribal temple dedicated to Banispati, the canibalistic Lord-of-the-Forest who is also Panji, the tribal hero.

The *pandjaq* is not only the smith's assistent, but the assistent of the gamelan or sacred band is also called *pandjaq*!

The sacred offerings before starting the work on a kris are exactly the same as those of other "rites de passage", such as circumcision and wedding ceremonies. Not only are the regulations of the decoration of the smithy very strict, but the details of the fashioning of the kris and the ornamentation of the weapon are carefully fixed in tradition. The smithy is more or less the space in which the adventures of the tribal hero Panji are enacted and the decoration of the kris inevitably recalls the picture of the kayon, the triangular screen used in wayang, which represents Panji or Banispati. Shape and motifs used for damascening the weapon have acquired special significance and so every wearer of a kris has chosen his weapon a shape and pamor most suitable and auspicious!

2—It is clear that the early smiths were organized either in *castes or guilds*. Among nomads and pastoralists we mostly find smith-castes which are always endogamous. The smith-caste lives apart in semi-nomad tribes in a special quarter. They are often members of aboriginal subjects or strangers without rights but often members of the same tribes without any anthropological or ethnological distinction. Among the agriculturalists the stress lies on the guild-form of organisation, but the smiths often retain traits of their original clan organisation. Even here they often form a proud endogamous line of families with long genealogies who ply their trade from father to son. The pupils are initiated, a rite sometimes even applied to strangers and strong links bind masters and pupils. Their pride often culminates in their claim of royal blood. The trade secrets are jealously guarded, ethics are very strict among the guild-brethern and their number is often limited. Gradually the guilds of gold- and silver-smiths, copper- and bronze-smiths separate from the iron-smiths, who are generally held in higher esteem as they forge the weapons and implements. Even here the iron-smith is seldom at the same time a warrior, he remains at home to look after the supply and repair of arms. Sometimes the smith-clan also embraces members who are leather-workers, wood-carvers or who ply any other trade.

3—The smith is always a mysterious figure, whose work apart from being a continuous source of wonderment to the primitive tribesman, is generally bound by traditional rites and ceremonies. The *ritual of the smith's craft* is generally determined by the religious systems of their fellow-tribesmen. The primitive societies hold that many processes can not be carried out by anyone, at any time or in any circumstance. The operatives should be in a state of ritual purity and as it is essential to ensure this various ceremonies and abstinences may be necessary. The Bambala iron workers consider it impossible to smelt iron without the medicine which they say transforms iron ore into iron. The principal person therefore is the "iron doctor", who has jealously guarded knowledge of the different medicines. The work is carried out in spring only! During the work the smelters live in temporary shelters in a state of strict taboos. They may not enter their own home, nor shall their wives wash, anoint themselves or put on ornaments that would attract the attention of men, e.g. they are to remain in the same state as bereaved widows. The men moulding the kiln for smelting the ores are not allowed to drink any water (42)! This example is typical for many other taboos and rites. Practically every operation such as the lighting of a kiln, the starting of a new piece of smithing, etc. are carefully regulated and they should be accompanied by certain offerings or ceremonies. This even covers the digging of the ores. Especially sexual taboos are prescribed all over the world. The smith has to avoid the company of women: no woman, more particularly pregnant woman shall enter the smithy; the workers often work naked. The fire shall be kept pure, for does not the god who gives the smith power reside in it? The earth-fire is his assistent and the invisible power that helps him to smelt the stones and transform them into metals. The fire shall always be kept burning and shall by purified by regular offerings. Religious hymns are sung during the work, and the connection between the smith and music is one of the most interesting themes of the many legends and myths.

The smith is often identified with the magician or priest as is evident from the examples which we have cited; even the nomad who despises and fears the smith always considers *the power of the smith* awe-inspiring. Does he not possess the power of the medicine-man as he transforms the ores into metals? He must possess "strong medicines", often he is considered to be the only one, who should be allowed to touch and work the "dangerous stones". The power of the expert is soon expanded in different directions in the mind of the primitive tribesman. He is often depicted as a great warrior, a magician, a robber, a merchant and he acquires important social functions such as magician, master of the ceremonies in secret societies, etc. His power is derived from the spirit-world with which he is in constant contact. In European legends he learns his craft from higher beings, dwarfs help him, the gods visit him or his power comes from the "swarze Meister", the devil, and he takes part in the "wild hunt" of the spirits of the dead!

His power is also evident outside his craft. According to Philon of Byblos the ancient Phoenician author Sanchuniaton says that his countrymen called the iron-smith "chorosh" which also meant "magician", probably because of the intricacies of iron metallurgy and his knowledge of the secret manipulations and necessary rites to purify the "new, unclean metal" (43). In ancient Java (44) the smith bears the same title as a priest. One of the most renowned magicians of ancient Java, who floated on a leaf from India to Java and who understood the art of making gold, was called Loh-Gawé, that is the Sanskrit "loha-kara" (metal-worker) rendered in Javanese. And nowadays the Protestant minister is often honoured with a title closely related etymologically to the Javanese word for smith. Javanese literature abounds with wonder-tales of the smith, whose sakti (mana) is considered to be enormous.

Fig. 15.
Smithy in ancient Egypt

His curse is very effective and "biting". It is expensive to buy off the curse of a smith" as the Negro saying goes. He has special powers to detect thieves and to ban the devil. Because of his relations with the spirit world he can see into the future and he often prophesies from the slags of his furnace or the charcoal, etc. He has healing powers, especially if his line has practised the craft for generations, he can prevent illness by hardening men like his iron. A special trait is the power of the blood of the smith. This plays a large part in several rites, for instance in the special ablutions necessary when one marries the daughter of a smith.

Spilling the blood of a smith is a dangerous thing, it is followed by a curse which only blood can wipe out, and killing a smith can only be attempted by one who possesses considerable "mana".

But often his personal power is not considered sufficient for the work. The Ba-Ila say that the efficiency of smelting operations depends on the ritual purity of the smith, the power of the foreman of the smith or iron doctor and his medicines; the Pangwe ascribe the succes of these operation to the power of the ancestors, the spirits of the fire, the magic of the plants and herbs, that are often added to the furnace for reasons of the "sympathetic magic" type and the strictness with which the sexual taboos have been observed. The smith is also considered to be dependent on the power of the metal and his tools.

5—*The power ascribed to the smith's tools* is considerable. An old Dutch

Fig. 16.
Metalworkers at work in the grave of Ipu-im-re

rhyme says that "to touch something in the smithy, to taste something in the chemist's shop, and to read in a book of legends and ghost stories can be dangerous". As we saw, it is often said that the tools do the work, not the smith. This applies especially to the smith's hammer, which is often "loosened" by special rites (45). When making the hammer, it should not be touched before it is finished. In Angola the hammer is worshipped because it is connected with the earth-spirit, as it forges the adze and other agricultural implements. It is treated as a prince and fondled as a baby. The hammer is worshipped all over the world, it is the symbol or implement "par excellence" of the

Fig. 17.
Smiths in the grave of Ipu-im-re

thunder- or fire-god, viz. Thor's hammer, etc. The Evhe smith of Togo talks of his tools as "the hammer and his family". The bellows are often worshipped, even by tribes who have no smiths, and hung in the fetish-houses. The anvil plays a large part to, for are not powerful medicines and curative mixtures "forged" on the anvil? An oath on the anvil is considered to be particularly binding and many a magical rite of the smith is connected with the anvil. The furnace also plays a part. The building is often accompanied by imitative rites. Two children are placed in the new furnace and crack beans to imitate the crackling fire, so that the furnace shall burn well later on. When building it special taboos are observed.

Below it are buried medicine or some sacrifice (often an embryo!) to make it more efficient. The smith shall never give his tools away, lest he die!

Fig. 18.
Goldsmiths in the grave of Ti

6—Still more *powerful is the metal* itself. This belief dates back to the period before the smith when mankind learnt to know the native metals gold, copper and meteoric iron. The awe for these "special stones" only grew when the smith learnt to smelt, melt and cast them. In this respect we consider the awe for the power of the metal primary and the belief, that metals were endowed with a particular power because of the miraculous transformations that attended their manufacture, as a secondary factor in the wealth of beliefs.

The Negroes thought that the metals possess inherent mysterious qualities either by virtue of their hardness and brightness when found native or by the effects of the smelting operations. This latter belief in the power of the metal as a "condensate" of the power of the smith is later. A very general belief is that fashioning a new metal may bring along an epidemic to man and beast or a failure of crops.

The power of the metal is ascribed to its connection with the earth, it is produced from a stone by fire. The metal is no less than a piece of earth purified by fire, a piece of earth charged with *mana*, earth of

great potency. They who produce or handle these stones charged
with mana should possess mana themselves lest they incur all kinds
of dangers. The spirits of the earth and protectors of the metals should
be propitiated when digging the ores, a belief that is still strong in
fifteenth century mining and later. These charged stones from heaven
(meteorites) and earth carry along part of the power of the element
from which they sprang. This is why both mining and metallurgy have
always had strong religious traits until very recently. The fire plays
a large part in these beliefs, especially the earth-fire, that brings forth
the metal in the womb of the earth. These charged stones have the
regenerating powers of the earth, they are less transitory than other
stones. They are born from the earth and are still born everyday! The
legend of the growing metal is a very persistent one, which lived until
recently and played a large part in the world of the alchemists. Just
like everything that came forth from the earth the metals possess the
qualities of regeneration, growth and propagation. The sexuality of
the metals is a very early belief that is not yet dead. By "marrying"
male and female ores metals are born, these too have a gender and the
"marriage of the metals" is a special feature of medieval alchemy. This
belief in the gender of ore and metal reaches back to Babylonian times
and possibly earlier, it created an organic cosmos, which was generally
reshaped by the reasoning of modern science into a world of laws and
mechanical processes.

Metals like the earth from which they sprang were subject to the
cosmic laws of birth, growth and death. We read in a Chinese book,
that when the people were ordered to dig for gold in the T'ung-t'ing
mountains, the metal assumed the shape of a cow which fled over the
crest of the range (46). Death and resurrection was their fate and the
smith, who worked these "charged stones", performed a rite full of
secret dangers. As he conjured the metal out of its ore with the help
of the fire-god, his patron, he interfered with the harmonious growth
of the metals in the earth. Perhaps the sacrifice of an embryo when
building a furnace has the meaning of an expiatory offering, giving
one life for the other, or should we read in it the "charging" of the
metal with the budding life of the embryo? Purification and sacrifice
were necessary when interfering with the processes of Mother Earth,
abstinences and purity of the officiant necessary. The smithy was a
temple of the spirits of the earth and the fire; the smith a priest who
by certain rites could accelerate or cause the birth of the metals, the
furnace an altar on which the rite was enacted. The belief in the growth

of the metals led to the idea of their transmutation, inherent in our mind to the doctrines of alchemy. Every metal was gradually transfered to the highest state of perfection, gold, by the care of its mother, the earth. Men could accelerate this process under certain circumstances. But the idea of transmutation is a late one and even the doctrines of the gender and growth of ores and metals may not be as old as they are sometimes believed to be. But it is certain that the belief that metals were bearers of power, earth charged with mana, was very old. The rarer the metals were, the greater was their power (47). Later these doctrines were extended by connecting certain metals with planets and gods, and colour symbolism was introduced into the theories. The astrological theory of metals is probably not older than Neo-Babylonian times, though the connection of certain metals with gods may be older. The theories about colours connected with certain metals are older too, at least in part. This may be due to the fact that ancient nomenclature was often based on the colour of the metal or alloy as we shall have occasion to point out. Gold for instance is of old the metal of the sun, it has the power and life-giving properties of the sun. Masks for the dead are made of gold and the Egyptian king rewards his faithful subjects with the "gold of victory".

But the field of study of this subject still lies fallow, at least for the objective student. A mass of literature exists on the subject that is written in a spirit of enthousiasm, bias and ignorance rather than in a cool and critical state of mind. These questions of symbolism especially the interpretation of pre-Hellenistic texts belong to the most intricate problems of the history of religion and only a thorough knowledge of the texts and the world in which they were written, in which these beliefs grew and flourished, will really help us. It will be seen, that many of these magical beliefs and rites go back to the times when primeval man believed that by following the example of the cosmos he could attain more power and become perfect. But there are also traits that go back to the technical facts behind the craft of the primitive smith. In different beliefs in the power of smith and metal we find again the struggle between the world of the Stone Age and the new world of the Metal Age. We think of the part played by the different metals in magic, especially in the taboo on several metals in certain rites and ceremonies (for instance the unhewn altar of Jos. 8.31 or the circumcision rite). We also see the struggle between the worlds of bronze and iron, especially in the strange rôle of iron in certain rites. It should not be used for certain magical ceremonies, or it is expressily mentioned to give protection over other metals. It bans devil and witch, horse-shoes are used against evil spirits, a knife thrown into a whirlwind will strike the demon who inhabits it; iron may give protection or even invulnerability against rain, illness or even abortion. In short iron protects against the demons and spirits of the Bronze Age, but it should never be used when evoking these powers.

Thus the use of certain metals in magical rites is a sure proof of their antiquity, the frequency with which a metal occurs in these rites an indication of their relative age. "Late" metals like tin and zinc are practically absent from magical precepts. But this leads us from our subject and lest the reader becomes like "the smith's dog that sleeps at the noise of the hammer and wakes at the crunching of teeth" we must revert to our original theme.

5. *Gods and heroes of the smith*

This survey of the powers of the smith should be completed by a summary of the *gods and heroes of the smith* though it belongs rather to the domain of the history of religion. Many decades ago Rossignol (48) collected much evidence in a nearly forgotten but excellent book which gives much information on semi-mythical smiths-tribes, demi-gods and gods of the smith and though much of his interpretation will no longer stand in the light of modern evidence, we are at least indebted to him for having pointed out and studied this very important material which is not yet exhausted by far. Among the historical smith-tribes the *Chalybes*, the classical smiths of Pontus are prominent. The discovery of iron is ascribed to them (49). They are said to descend from Ares (50) and live in the region south of Trebizond, Sinope and Amisus, in the country of the iron-ores. Probably they are the tribes that make iron for their Hittite masters and later for their new masters, the Mossynoeci and Chaldaioi (51).

The *Tibareni* (Tabareni) are probably identical with the Tubal of the Bible (52). This people comes together with the Mossynoeci as a Thacian-Phrygian tribe from the Balkans, but whether there is any historical evidence to prove that they were smiths is still an open question. Probably their fame was partly due to the Chalybes who were their subjects. This is certainly the case with the *Mossynoeci* (Muski), the later masters of the Chalybes (53). There is nothing of the smith about the Tibareni as the classical authors describe them, on the contrary they are said to be a care-free and gay people (54), that lived partly in the Pontic plain, partly remained like the Muški, their kinsmen, in Cilicia after the Cimmerian migrations, which broke their power as the heriditary enemy of the Assyrian kings.

Semi-mythical and partly historical are the legends about the *Telchines* (55). They consist of seemingly historical traditions of smiths that peopled Crete, Rhodos and Cyprus (from the continent of Asia Minor?), but these traditions have been greatly overgrown by traits of demon-smiths, powerful magicians with the "evil eye", who could change their shape at will and who were not always the friends of mankind. They were often connected with the sea in later time. Four namen are often given, Aktaios, Megalesios, Hormenos and Lykos, who are said to have been born from the blood of Uranos. They belong to the sphere of Rhea, the mother of the Cretan Zeus. Crete is often called Telchinia! But it is very doubtful whether these pre-Greek figures belonging to the sphere of Rhea and Zeus, really hail from Crete; it is more probable that their original home was Phrygia or at least the continent of Asia Minor. For the historical part played by Crete in the evolution of metallurgy is far less important than the legends of Greece would have us believe, they may be founded on the fact that many metallurgical achievements may have come to that country from Crete. According to Wissowa the words "chalkos" and "telchein" go back to the same root, that is probably of Asiatic origin (56) and connected with the Old Norse dfelch, dwarf. It may be that the Telchines represent old gods or spirits of the Bronze Age pushed back from prominence by the Olympians.

Prominent among the mythical figures are the *Dactyloi* who were the first to discover and forge the iron of the mountain-valleys. They too seem to belong to the sphere of the Cretan Rhea (57), though there are other traditions that bring them from Phrygia (58). Mostly five male and five female figuers are mentioned. They come from Crete to Samothrace and Olympia, in which latter place they are worshipped together with Heracles. They are not only skilful smiths but also musicians (59). They have many traits of the European dwarfs and elves, who protect and watch their treasures in the mountaincaves, work gold and silver and forge iron into steel.They serve mankind by forging implements for house and field. But the European dwarfs seem more than the Dactyloi, for are they not imbued of the characteristics of the old nature-, earth- and death-demons and at the same time half-buried memories of older cave-dwellers who forged iron and raised cattle, of aborigines, nomads, Finns, Celts and Gypsies?

The *Curetes* are their kinsmen, whom Homer described as a tribe of Aetolia. Later they are said to be the children of the Dactyloi. They belong to the followers of the young Zeus and are also said to have accompanied the child Dionysos in Phrygia. The myth of their shield-dance which saved the life of the child Zeus is wellknown. Later they are said to have discovered the manufacture of arms, especially in Euboeia. They were also worshipped in Ephesos and Priene, but they are soon absorbed by the Corybantes, who came from Eastern Asia Minor as their orgiastic traits show.

In close connection with the smith stand the *Cyclopes*, thunderstorm- and fire-demons, often connected with volcanoes, smiths and metal-workers of great skill. They were worshipped in the Peleponese, Corinth, Argos, Thrace, Rhodos and Asia Minor, some legends tell that they were killed by Apollo who is also said to have killed the Telchines. They are the smithing assistants of Hephaistos, who later are afterwards located with him in the Etna. They are often pictured with traits of satyrs (pointed ears, etc.) (60).

As in primitive times all crafts is sacred, the evolution of smithcraft had great influence on creation myths and we find smith-gods or fire-gods among all peoples of Antiquity. Everyone will recall Agni, Vulcan and Hephaistos and perhaps also the Babylonian Girru. Brahma as a blacksmith creates man and the Michoacans of Mexico believed that they were created from metal by a smith-god. The Toradja's of Celebes have a subterranean smith-god, called Langkoda ("the Lame"), who tests the souls of the Toradjas as to their "quality" and the Smith of the Upper World (*Proeë m Palaburu*, the Lord Creator and at the same time the Great Physician) reforges the souls that have failed (61)! In the Rgveda Indra is the smith of the gods and the Avesta recognizes the Ameneshpent Kshatra Vairya as the genius of the metals. But the god of the smith, often the god of the earth-fire is a typical example of an ambivalent god, both a saviour and a demon. Loki guides the hand of the blind Hodur when he kills Baldur, just as the smith Kedalion guides the blind Orion and a Jewish legend says that Tubal-Cain guided the hand of the blind Lamech when he murdered Cain, Adam's son.

Vulcan is the most debated of the two classical smith-gods (62). The French school of Carcopino and Toutain make him the god of the Tiber who later on inherits traits of Hephaistos, others see him as an old Roman god of the fire as the destroying and purifying element, who later on becomes the god of the smith-fire. But he is also the god of the earth-fire (63) and he is worshipped with the vegetation- and earth-godess Maia, perhaps because of the fertility of the volcanic ashes. The arms of the conquered enemy are burnt in his honour. Then he appears as the divine smith of the tubae for the Tubilistrum and he adopts the attributes of Hephaistos, felt cap, hammer, tongs and apron. His cult in Ostia is very old, but he has been coupled in vain with the Etruscan Séthlans who is far more like Hephaistos and works at Populonia as Hephaistos did at Lemnos. His son Cacus is nursed at Praeneste by the Digidii (Dactyloi) and the Etruscans say that he forged the lightning.

One does not find these traits in the oldest texts on Vulcan and Rose therefore is inclined to believe him to be a god who came from the eastern part of the Mediterranean, a god of the earth-fire, who has similar traits to Hephaistos, who also hails from these regions. But Vulcan must have come to Ostia at a very early date.

The figure of *Hephaistos* is better understood. His home country seems to have been the Phrygian-Carian region, more specifically the region of Phaselis and the Lycian Olympos (64) where he manifests himself as a god of the earth-fire in the many burning gases and where he was worshipped of old. He was also at home in Lemnos, Naxos and Samos and came to Athens with the Carians or the Pelasges where he was "married" to Athene. He is often pictured on the coins of Asia Minor, but he is hardly ever shown as a crippled man, which he is according to every legend. His assistents are the Dactyloi and other dwarf-like figures who forge steel in the fires of the mountains. Hephaistos is not the smith who forges the sun at dawn as Mannhardt claimed, but a fertility god of volcanic nature, the god of the earth-fire. The Hephaistos of Lemnos was originally the lover of Kabiro, the earth-goddess, who had accompanied him from the East. Kinai-thon calls him a cousin of Daedalos and Hesiod marries him off to Charis or Aglaia (both earth-goddesses) but it was Homer who claimed his marriage with Aphrodite. The wild, elemental side of his nature remains much longer with him than with other gods. Still in the Iliad (65) he is entirely the divine smith. Sometimes, for instance when the fire is carried out into the world during the Hephaistia he shows some traits in common with Prometheus.

He has also much in common with some of the *supersmiths* of the legends like Wieland or Völundr, Mimir, Ilmarinen and many others. Wieland is lamed to keep him, Hephaistos limps like Vulcan. But the Amazones used cripples as leather workers and copper-smiths and many craftsmen are said to be cripples in Antiquity. Just as Jacob is lamed in his struggle with God, Hephaistos is lamed by Zeus. But he is generally represented (if so) as having only one lame foot, though the legends say that he is lame on both. The most beautiful of all the legends of supersmiths is that of Ilmarinen who forges the metal vault of the high sky and the magic weapon "sampo" in the Kalewala (runes 8 & 9). Much remains to be done in further studies of this chapter of the history of metalworking. This must, however, be left to the ethnologist and the historian of religions.

6. *The smith in Antiquity*

The discussion of Vulcan and Hephaistos has led us back to our original plan of describing, at least in outline, the gradual social evolution of the smith from clan to caste and guild. Having surveyed his early status in primitive societies and the characteristics of the early smith we must now discuss the meagre data on the story of *the smith in the civilisations of Antiquity*.

We shall start with *Egypt* because Greek writers always stress their identification of Hephaistos and Ptaḥ, the creator-god of Memphis. The first to do so was Herodotus (66) and many followed. He was said to be the son of Nilus, to have reigned over Egypt and some authors like Joannes Malalas and Joannes Antiochenus even contend that he taught the Egyptians to forge iron weapons. But Egypt did not come to use iron generally before 1200 B.C.! Diodor (67) even calls him a fire-god. Sometimes the name Hephaistia is used for Egypt (68).

This identification is made on very loose grounds. Ptaḥ is first of all the divine creator and earthgod, later on he becomes the patron-god of all craftsmen, more specially of the carpenters and smiths. But all the important texts such as the famous Shabaka-text represent him in his creative function only.

Now and then Ptaḥ is called the "creator of all handcraft (69)" and he is said to have formed "the mountains, the beautiful precious stones and great mighty monuments". There is also the expression "electrum from the mountains and native gold from... the workshop of Ptaḥ", but in these text the Egyptian god is not mentioned as a pigmy. Hephaistos is always lame and Rosner (70) takes it that this was due to the fact that the Anatolian metallurgists of the third millennium B.C. often suffered of chronic arsenic-intoxication (due to the smelting of arsenical copper-ores or arsenic-copper alloys), which led to arse-

neuritis and lameness of the extremities, which picture remained in the mind of people long after other "healthier" ores were worked.

Now the passage from Herodotus mentioned above tells us how Cambyses was struck by the image of Ptaḥ in his temple of Memphis "for the image of Hephaistus is very like the Pataeci of the Phoenicians, wherewith they ornament the prows of their ships of war... it is a figure resembling that of a pigmy". Now Ptaḥ is usually depicted as a mummy, but on the other hand we have a cippus in the British Museum (72) showing Ptaḥ as a dwarf on the top of a staircase! Later figurines of the god Ptaḥ often take the form of the later and foreign god Bes, the sockles usually mention his name as Ptaḥ-Sokaris. It is of course claimed by the Greeks that there was a tradition which made the Egyptian god lame because of the fall from a horse and they also identify him with the element of fire. Though there was much in his nature and his later images to support the Greek identification of Ptaḥ and Hephaistos (71) this identification is an "interpretatio Graeca" and not supported by Egyptian texts, describing the nature of their god.

In the same passage Herodotus mentions that Cambyses entered also the temple of the Cabeiri where he "not only made sport of the images but even burnt them. They are made like the statue of Hephaistos, who is said to have been their father". Ptaḥ is assisted in his creative activities by the ḥmww (HWB III.83), the artisans and craftsmen, who are often called his childern. Now in Old Kingdom mural paintings we find (73) that the goldsmiths in particular are represented as dwarfs. Now dwarfs from Inner Africa were quite popular in Egypt, where they were employed as servants, dancers and shepherds, but these were normal dwarfs called iwḥw (HWB I.57.15) or more commonly dng(HWB V.470.6)(compare the Amaharic "denk"). However, Egyptian pathology also knew a type of dwarf with bow-shaped legs, called dnb (HWB V.576.3), a term derived from a verb "to be curved". In certain crafts and more particularly in the workshops of goldsmiths and jewellers we find a peculiar type of pigmy, called nmw (nmj) (HWB II.267.5), a pathological chondrodysplast, who is especially employed in the last stages of making jewelry. The earlier stages like melting and refining gold are carried out by normal workmen and somehow these pigmys seem to have been a closed group of skilled workmen cherishing and cultivating the secrets of older generations. There is no reason to think that the Egyptians used dwarfs as smiths to prevent them from running away or because they had especially strong arms! The combination smith-dwarf is known in many countries and may be a reminiscense of the earliest smith who may have had a short stature as a mountain people working in the mines.

Metallurgy was an early art in Egypt and the silver- and goldsmiths were exceptionally clever. Perhaps when we read in Weill's study on the word "bi3" which originally meant "copper" but also came to mean "something rare, curious or wonderful" we may infer that we find here something of the astonishment of the primitive man at the products of the first smiths.(74)

It was formerly often stated that one of the invasions in prehistoric Egypt was that of "the smiths of Horus" but this thesis of Maspéro rested on the wrong translation of the word "mśntyw" which has nothing to do with smiths but means "harpooners". But unfortunately this story is still found in many a handbook where it serves to prove the originality of Egyptian metallurgy!

It is strange that we know practically nothing of the metal-workers of ancient Egypt themselves. Whereas the ordinary metal-worker does not seem to have been respected any more than his fellow craftsman (75), the goldsmith seems to have formed an exception. Though he is a little his own master as any other craftsman and though even the goldsmith of the viceroy (in the New Kingdom period) has to ask his master for leave to attend a feast for Amon, they seem to have enjoyed more respect from the higher classes. Generally speaking, the goldsmiths and chiefs of the goldsmiths have fathers and brothers excercising the same trade, in the same way as the craft of the painter or sculptor seems to have been handed down from generation to generation in the same line. Under the Old Kingdom the smiths (or perhaps only the gold- and silver-smiths) formed a guild that worked under the supervision of the temple. It was thought until recently that this guild was presided over by a priest with the title "high inspector of the artists" (wr ḫrp.w ḥmw. t) but this is now doubted as Junker has argued very plausibly (76) that we should read this title "ḫrp ḥmw.t Wr(Atum!)" and that therefore the high-priest of Ptaḥ in Memphis bore the title of "inspector of the artists of Atum" and was not the chief of all the smiths in Egypt. Though there is no early sign of centralisation of the smiths, many priestly titles show their importance.

Only during the eighteenth and nineteenth dynasties documents tell us about a factory and arsenal of weapons at Memphis. They speak of a foreman of the workshop, a scribe and an inspector of the "arsenal of Pharaoh" (77). There was also a leader of the maker of war chariots, a surveyor of the workshop of the Master of the Two Lands, a manager of the workshop in the arsenal. Here were concentrated the manufacture of leather cuirasses, arrows chariots, bows and other war material. It is quite possible that there was a similar arsenal in other towns, notably in Upper Egypt, such as Memphis, the town of the jewellers devoted to Ptaḥ-Sokaris. At this date and certainly right into the twentieth dynasty such craftsmen lived close together in the same quarter of the town or on the temple grounds.

We also read of metal-workers but apart from a few texts without much information this word is not used. It seems to form part of a surname sometimes, thus in the papyrus Abbott someone bears this name with the suffix "p3 ḫ3rw" (the Syrian). But Eerdmans is not right in saying (20) that we see only pictures of gold- and silver-smiths on Egyptian reliefs, for though they are rarer we know of pictures of copper-smiths, the casting of copper and furnaces.

We do not know either what the esteem was in which the smith was held in ancient Egypt. One should not believe the words of the papyrus Sallier (2.4.6): "Never did I see a smith as an envoy or a gold smith with a mission, but I saw the smith at work in front of the hole of his furnace. His fingers were like the hide of a crocodile and he stank of the spawn of fishes", for we read here a song of praise of the trade of the scribe. It reminds us of Eccl. 38.28: "The smith sitting by the anvil and considering the ironwork, the vapour of the fire wasteth his flesh and he fighteth with the heat of the furnace: the noise of the hammer and the anvil is ever upon his ears, and his eyes look stil upon the pattern of the thing he maketh" or of Is. 44.12: "The smith with his tongs both worketh in the coals and fashioneth it with hammers and worketh it with the strength of his arms; yea, he is hungry, and his strength faileth, he drinketh and is faint". But here too the prophet is apt to exaggerate the fatigues of the smith's work.

Nor is very much known about the smith in ancient Mesopotamia. A Sumerian term for smith, simug, is written with a complex sign that is made up of two others, viz. that for "smith's fire" (Falkenstein No. 325, which author calls it a smelting furnace, though the pictograms very clearly show the picture of a basin with burning charcoal as used by the smith) and that for "foreman". It seems certain that the word smith meant "foreman of the smith's fire", which we can compare with the later Accadian *nappâḫu*, which literally means "one who blows the (smith's) fire".

The smith in ancient Sumer was not a free craftsman; he was linked closely to the temple-state economy that characterizes this ancient civilisation. He belonged to the GIŠ-KIN-TI (craftsmen), who were controlled by a priest-smith called SANGU. During Urukaginna's reign he was even elevated to the higher rank of SANGU-GAR. So he was a bondman and remained so for many a century. Even the Codex Hammurabi (par. 274) ordains that the smith shall receive a lower pay than the peasant, because he is only a *muškênu*, a bondman, controlled and fed by the temple. This does not mean, however, that he was a slave. He was only controlled by the temple authorities and received his raw materials from them to obtain his wages in return for the finished goods. We hear that the temple-state had central storehouses called AZAG-AN distinguished by a suffix running "place where... is kept" where the imported metal and other goods were stored (78).

However, the Sumerian TIBIRA covered both the Accadian tamkaru (merchant) and qurqurru (metallurgist), like the mercatores of the Middle Ages who were often both artisans and merchants at the same time. Hence the trade was only partly a State-affair and the dam-gàr (tamkaru) was allowed a certain latitude to do some business of his own. Hence the lots of 6—12 talents of metal sometimes go to the é-DUB-ba, the State storehouse, also called "house of the silver and the lapis lazuli, the great storehouse". Several tons of copper were consumed yearly in each Sumerian town and the gold-smith's shops seem to have worked some 6 K of red gold, 8 k of refined gold and nearly 6 k of silver in one year at Ur (79).

The large part of the metal still arrived at the storehouse at Ur around 2000 B.C., where a large staff looked after the eight groups of workers for the administration: sculptors, goldsmiths, lapidaries, carpenters, founders, fullers, tailors and shipbuilders. Each of these "guilds" had a supervisor and the chief of each section also assisted in surveying certain activities of the other sections. The supervisor was the assistent of a gašam: enqu, imqu, the master of a workshop. The controlling office (tùn-lal-me) might employ him upto thrice a month. The directors of the storehouse act through inspectors or controllers, who mostly check the weight of metal and objects fashioned from it.

The storehouse bought its copper or other metal from the merchants and laid it up. Here the smith came to receive his assignments and the necessary raw materials to work them at home in his smithy. In return of the finished goods he received his pay. Several contracts between the storehouse keepers and the individual smiths have been found. As we shall see this system persisted even after the smith had become a free man. During the Ur III period he was already a settled citizen with a plot of land, whose fashioned articles were carefully weighed, checked and registered as he brought them back to be paid a salary expressed in units of barley. We read of contracts for making hoes from 600 K of copper, or a number of tools to be made from 500 K. In the fifth year of Šu-Sin 20 talents of copper were thus issued to the smiths of Ur, and other contracts speak of several hundreds of hacks being made from one lot of copper (80). A similar organisation existed at Tello-Lagash, at Umma the controllers were mainly scribes.

The kings of Ur had a great entrepôt of metals and other base materials at Drehem (Puzuriš-Dagan), where there was no industry, but the craftmen lived in towns like Sippar ("town of bronze") and Eridu ("town of smiths").

We hear about a town called Dûr-gurgurri (BAD-TIBIRAᴷᴵ) that was founded by Sin-iddinnam of Larsa and which seems to have been an old Sumerian metallurgical centre as the name means "fortress of the copper-smiths". Its location is unknown but it flourished for many centuries at it still figures in the correspondence of king Ḫammurabi, when transports of wood-blocks for the metal-workers are mentioned and when it is the scene of an inquiry of bribes taken by officials (81) from the tribute of silver. Unfortunately its exact location is unknown, but its excavation might yield interesting results.

We know little of the religious status of the smith in Mesopotamia. His patron-god was Ea, who is the patron-god of all craftsmen, later on special patrons of every craft were created and the fire-god Girru became patron of the smiths, and the goldsmiths. Some time ago Hrozny pointed out that the oldest Fara texts (27th century B.C.) gave the following version of the name of the hero Gilgameš: "(DINGIR)GIŠ GIBIL. GÍM. MES" which means "the man of the fire and the axe". This might stamp the national Sumerian hero as the patron of all those who work metals and wood, e.g. smiths, gold-smiths, carpenters, etc. (82). This interesting suggestion, however, remains to be proved.

The recovery of the archives from the ancient Alalakh (Tal 'Atsha-nah) and from Mari on the Euphrates (82) have shed much light on the state of metallurgy during the eighteenth century B.C.

The metallurgical knowledge revealed by these tablets reflects the apex of the Bronze Age. Weapons and tools are made of bronze, large quantities of gold and silver are collected and reported. Iron, if mentioned, is a rarity used to indicate wealth, its uses are limited and it plays no part in common life. In fact we find here the same type of technical skill that is reflected in the stock epithets and phrases dating back to the Bronze Age but used by Homer when writing his Iron Age epic.

The more common metals of these days are mentioned together in a letter stating that Thamarchi, by decision of the priest, is to obtain certain garments and portions of silver, gold, tin, copper and lead or objects shaped therefrom. At Alalakh two goldsmiths, Abban and Abiadu, are mentioned by name. Mostly the total weight of gold objects is specified, for instance "objects each weighing $22\frac{1}{2}$ shekels of gold", but in certain cases a more elaborate description is transmitted such as "a dagger with a gold sheath", which served as a betrothal gift of king Ammitaku.

Large amounts of silver, probably from the mines in Asia Minor (the most important source of Near Eastern silver) are mentioned. We have mentioned the large amount distributed by the king, but private persones like Echli-Ishtar could expend 250 shekels of silver. However, this silver was in the form of different vases and cult objects used in the temple. Another tablet tell us that 685 shekels of silver were disbursed for the overlay and fashioning of a statue, shoes and horse trappings, larger cult vessels, etc. to be endowed to the temple of Ishtar. The Mari tablets inform us how such silverware was ordered. Here the Assyrian king Shamshi-Addu writes to his son Iasmach-Addu, governor of Mari: "I have sent you 20 mana of silver for the incrustation of your statue. The statues which have been made here (at Assur) and at Shubat-Enlil, their accounts have been made in the temple of Assur... their accounts were correct... Now, on the matter of this work consult Mâšum and Mašiya. The tablets of the accounts of the silver of this statue, the silver of the incrustations, the work lavished on this statue... on the casting, which have been used, let them be written down accurately on a tablet and send this to me. Those responsible and the entire amount of silver which has been used to complete it on the statue shall be inscribed. In the temple of Assur it will be installed...".

Another tablet from Alalakh mentioned a total of $33\frac{1}{3}$ shekels of silver to be collected for a "GAL-vessel" when the daughter of the priest of Ishtar was married to Kuzzi, the barû-priest. The silver of these tablets is sometimes specified as "pure" (gabbu) or as "extra fine" (atru). The latter quality is mentioned in a memorandum on the excess of the assignment of the town of Kunuwa, which is declared to be silver acquired by illegal dealers (83).

Three centuries later we find that the town of Alalakh still has a predominantly Hurrian population (and hence ties with the north) though the percentage of Amorites has increased. Regular contacts have now been established with the Hittites and Mitanni to the north but also with the small city-states of Canaan. At Alalakh smiths (SIMUG, nappachu, "those of the bellows") appear in several census-lists and even as landowners. In the earlier period they figured already together with barbers, goldsmiths, leatherworkers, cooks, dyers, tailors, weavers, carpenters and cartwrights in the ancient counterpart of the modern Syrian bazaar. A fifteenth century tablet bearing the seal of Idrimi lists the products of 64 business houses (bîtatu) in this bazaar: "(x) smiths made (x) namcharu (part of a waggon) and 9 copper tišnu-vessels, 5 pair of garuwe, 20 copper daggers and 1500 copper arrowheads, 22 leatherworkers, 5 houses of the martatu-trade, 3 houses of jewellers, 1 house of the seal-cutter, 16 houses of the joiners who make the offering-tables manufactured 16 tables, 80 seats, 80 stools, 5 couches without sides, 4 couches, 2 footstools for a couch and 2..., 11 cartwrights manufactured 9 chariots and 2 aššis-carts. Total 64 houses doing the work of the district".

During this period copper has taken the place of silver as a medium of exchange. It is usually weighed in local "talents" (in kakuru of 1800 shekels or half a Babylonian talent of 30 kgr), its value is about 1/450th of that of silver. The copper is received in bars and handed over to the smiths to be worked into vessels, rings, baskets, braziers, door-panels and parts of furniture, tools and weapons. In certain cases we are sure that copper metal is actually meant. Thus we have a note on "3 talents of copper, and 1200 shekels for the smiths of Berâšena, 7,000 shekels of copper for Bentamušuni", 400 shekels of the sum here being for arrow-heads to be made by one person. Then there is a note on "7 talents of copper for the smiths to make 2000 copper baskets for the town of Nichi", and another reading "4 talents of copper for the men of Berašena. 4000 shekels of copper for arrow-heads and 600 shekels for copper doors". A receipt for weapons includes "copper made into bars (ZAG. ipiša) and 30 copper eriga delivered to Šuwa". Then there are the texts on copper objects such as the note on 4 bronze drinking vessels weighing in all 4200 shekels and a list of bronze utensils, e.g. 2 picks of 400 shekels each, or the note on two loads of bronze chains weighing 2750 shekels of bronze, which have been sent to the town of Zalche. Bronze (ZABAR) is employed in the manufacture of most weapons, bows and chariot fittings (84).

In the reign of king Ḥammurabi and his successors the old temple-economy of the Sumerians broke up. The temple-guilds seem to have declined and though they still have a certain religious prestige they have a difficult time which grows worse in the Cassite period when the guilds break up into guilds of free craftsmen. A great change is wrought by the dissolution of the Hittite Empire about 1200 B.C. under the pressure of migrations of peoples from the Balkans. The monopoly of iron manufacture which this empire had for several centuries was broken and many a craftsman and iron-smith was driven from his home in Asia Minor. Already in the days of Ḥammurabi we read of "$\frac{1}{3}$ mina of copper-ore (?) (erêm) which they have added for the Subartan" (85), which probably means that there was a smith or metal-worker from Subartu, the mountain region to the north working in Mesopotamia at that time. In Assyria Tiglath Pileser already possesses large quantities of iron which becomes quite common in the eigth century for the manufacture of weapons and clamps for architectural purposes. Then of course Mesopotamia must have possessed its own iron-smiths, though we can not expect any smelting on a large scale in these river-valleys without sufficient fuel and ores, but there seem to have been blacksmiths and metal-workers (86). They remained valuable craftsmen and Sennacherib mentions expressily that he carried off the smiths of Babylon and Nebuchadnezzar did the same with those of Jerusalem (87).

There was already much specialisation by those times. We hear of the nappâḫu or blacksmith and the gurgurru or metal-worker, the latter executing more delicate work like casting, chasing and embossing; while the jeweller or gold-smith is called nappâḫ ḥurâṣi (KUG DIM).

The later dynasties have kept the old system of central stores of raw materials which were given out to the smiths for refining and working. If we take for instance Assyrian letters of the Sargonid era (722—626 B.C.) we read (88): "We have seen, we have examined what was placed in the house of the scribe. We have smelted 23 minas of aššapi gold together with the alloys, it has been worked up into foil, according to the measure which the king commanded. Then it was locked up." Another letter runs: "During the month of Tishri the gold that the abarakku official, the court secretary and I examined, -viz.: 3 talents of refined gold, 4 talents of unrefined gold, was placed in the store house of the chief of the danibe-workers (metal-workers); he has sealed it. May the king issue orders to the abarakku chief and the court secretary to open up the gold, the beginning of the month being favourable, let them give it to the artisans, so that they may proceed with the work". But there is always some danger in this system, for "The iron which the king my lord gave to the smith for the work was sold by him to certain merchants of Caleh... they are not willing... five minas they are giving. Having taken courage they will bring it down below", so after all there seemed some chance of recovering the stolen iron. But even at that time there was a lot of red-tape for: "In regard to the wooden building wherein the iron is stored which is in the palace of Aššur and about which the king my lord wrote. I have interviewed prefects, city magistrates and elders. (They say) "the district-chief tears down and rebuilds. Inasmuch as he manages the affairs of the palace he is bound to repair the cracks and should roof the building. But if a rafter decays the city magistrate of Aššur should repair the damage. Now (I am telling) the district chief to gather my helpers, he is willing. I shall replace those rafters which are weak. This year is far advanced, but by the month Shebat the king my lord can come and give orders."

We have already seen that the dissolution of the Hittite Empire accounted for the wandering of many Pontic smiths over the Near East. Otherwise the quick spread of the working and use of iron at that time would be much less intellegible. It is logical that these groups or clans of iron-smiths were not allowed to immigrate everywhere. As far as we can judge from the meagre data the frontiers of the bigger states like Egypt, Assyria and Babylonia were officially closed against these immigrants, whom the inhabitants of these civilised countries would hardly have distinguished from the wandering bands of ma-rauders in these troubled times. Therefore the earliest signs of these iron-smiths are found with the nomads of the Syrian and Arabian desert, where they were the ancestors of the typical tinkers which we find at the present time in Arabia. These iron-smiths possessed a mass of lore and knowledge quite different from that of the copper- and bronze-smiths who had already been at home in the towns of Syria and Mesopotamia for many a century.

The *Kenites* of the Bible must have formed a group of these iron-smiths driven from their homesteads, though we would not contend

that there were no Kenites before 1200 B.C. or perhaps other bands of
tinkers outside the Hittite Empire, but the majority will have spread
over this region after the fall of the empire. Eerdmans has published
two studies on the Kenites (89), these despised and feared smiths and
tinkers of the desert.

The nomads of the desert were those who despised them most, for
the Hebrews treated them with much more sympathy. Eerdmans
proved beyond doubt that they were tinkers, who did not belong to
the nomads but who were originally at home in towns, who lived in
the oases at that period and only took to nomad life much later. In
the Old Testament they live in the North (90) and in Amalek (91), the
Rechabites were their kinsmen (92). Their name is derived from Qain,
which means "smith" (93). In this passage the original Hebrew text
reads "a hammerer, an artificer in copper and iron". Then we saw that
Tubal has some connection with the Tibareni of Pontus but not with
the Persian tûbâl (slag) (Gesenius) or with the name of the god Gibil
(now read Girru) (Partington). They were mainly iron-smiths, who
worshipped a thunder- and fire-god in Sinai and Eerdmans suggests
that the sympathy between Hebrews and Kenites was caused not in
the last place by their god, who showed some traits of the God who
gave the Israelites the stone tablets. Moses takes the daughter of Hobab
the Kenite as his wife in the land of Midian that was rich in ore, so
that here again the Kenites live in a country where they could get the
ores which they required as good smiths. They seem to have worn a
tribal "sign of Qain" by which their god protected them against evil
spirits, in the same way as modern Arabs use such signs. The despise
in which these "townsmen" were held by the true nomads is well
expressed in the story of the shepherds and the daughter of Ruel the
Kenite (94). But the Hebrews were not their enemies, the tribes seem
to have intermarried freely. Even the later Rechabites who lived in
tents were looked upon with friendship as a tribe who lived in a way
that was not quite according to the Law, as a type of Nazirites, who
prohibited strong drink and wine and who did not practise agriculture. By then the Kenites have already become the wandering
desert-smiths which Doughty described so lively (95). If they are said
to raise cattle even in the older periods, this can of course not be taken
as a proof that they were nomads.

Some like Rowley and Meek hold that Qenite views had a profound
influence on the origins of Yahwism and Budde and Weber hold that
the Kenite totemistic prohibition of making fire on the weekly rest-

day gave rise to the Hebrew Sabbath (96). These are, however, problems which the historian of religion should study, as we are looking at the smith merely from the point of view of discovering whether there was anything in the nature of his work and status in ancient times which is to be considered of importance for the technico-historical development of his craft.

These smiths were of the greatest importance to the nomads, for they alone forged the iron weapons, which helped the nomads to attain that superiority over the bronze-using troops of the civilised states into which they carried their raids. The superiority of the Hittites, which seems to have been due largely to the possession of iron and other superior weapons, and also the domination of Palestine by a handfull of Philistines seem to have been due to their excellent smiths. For "there was no smith found in all the land of Israel, for the Philistines said, lest the Hebrews make them swords and spears!" (97)

The gradual evolution of the tinker to the state of a true nomad, did not heighten the respect of the desert tribes for him, he remained despised as the smith of the Somali or Masai or the Jewish smiths of the Faladshas of Abyssinia. But he had become a necessary part of the tribe, may be despised but suffered and even held in awe. His status is a strange one. In every camp (98) there are one or more families of smiths, who stand outside the Bedâwîn community. They are generally "strangers from the Euphrates country or Iran". They marry among themselves or very occasionally with slaves, but they are never permitted to take a bedu woman. These smiths work for the camp as a whole, shoeing horses, making swords and reparing rifles. In summer they receive their fee based on the number of horses to buy clothing, grain and other supplies for the ensuing year. They take no part in raiding and are not attacked by raiders. Their losses during raids are recovered by their fellow-smiths in the enemy tribe and usually they get some of the profits of raiding.

Nothing is known of the smith of the Indus civilisation, but in Hellenistic India we find that the craftsmen and tradesmen are mostly associated in guilds. Some crafts like mining, gold- and silver-working and the manufacture of arms were government undertakings (99).

The manufacture of arms and agricultural implements were probably wholly in the hands of the state, and the craftsmen employed by these government factories received food and wages for their labour.

The factories for the working of base metals were supervised by

the "inspector of the base metals" (*Lohâdhyaksa*), a central authority
for urban workshops and those in the country. But on the royal
domains the *sitâdyaksa* supervised the smiths who worked there and
saw to it that their work was properly done. Therefore, there does not
seem to have existed a strict centralisation, but the situation that most
of the country smiths obeyed another authority than the urban smiths
is wholly in the line of the Arthacâstra, the leading manual of state-
craft of the times.

Still from Buddhist texts we learn that not all the smiths were
employed by the state, as they seem to have lived in villages too and
to have fashioned agricultural implements freely for their brethern.
These smiths seem to have been placed under the supervision of the
local authorities.

In the Aegean world (100) the documents have informed us that
there were different types of smiths, bronze-smiths (ka-ke-u), goldsmiths (ku-ruso-wo-ko) and cutlers (pi-ri-je-te). The Pylos tablets
record the issue of weights of bronze (like in Mesopotamia) to smiths
living in a number of localities. As some of the headings look more
like clan-names than place-names Ventris suggested that the smiths
might have formed small closed communities of tinkers, may be working local ores. May be their work was on a part-time basis like the
seasonal iron smelting by Hittite peasants which Gurney (101) believes they practised. Of course peasant communities have sometimes
practised such smelting which took place during the winter and which
supplied them with the necessary metal for their own community.
This happened in Scandinavia not very long ago in the same way as
in the Iliad, where Achilles says that the winner of the ingot of pig-
iron (102): "Even if the winner's fertile farm is at a remote spot, he
will be able to go on using it for five revolving years; his shepherd or
ploughman will not have to go to town through lack of iron, but will
have it at hand."

On the other hand the variety of objects which the smiths are
ordered to make precludes such part-time occupation of peasants, it
rather seems a full-time job. The allotment at Pylos deal with $1\frac{1}{2}$ kg
of bronze (sufficient for some 100 arrow-heads) or 5 Kg (for a number
of spear-heads of sword-blades). The Pylos smiths are also distinguished by the possession of "doeloi" (slaves) and they work bronze, gold,
silver and lead. The contents of various tablets are the equivalent of
saying "the village of X is excused payment of so much in recognition
of the fact that it has so many smiths (khalkêwes) working on govern-

ment contracts". More than 25 of these tablets mention smiths "with (or without) a talasia", the word talasia (like the Latin pensum) being used in the general sense of "an amount of metal allocated by weight for processing", which reminds us of the situation in ancient Mesopotamia and its palace- or city-storehouses.

The smiths seem to have a higher proportion of unmistakable Greek names than appear on most lists of Pylos, one of them being "a-pa-i-ti-jo", probably Hâphaistion. The tablets mention smiths being "slave of the god", "belonging to a god" and "taught by a god", which may represent various stages of teaching and skill, the "smiths of Potnia" probably being apprentices as they are listed separately from other smiths. They are certainly honoured skilled craftsmen, though the tablets do not call them specifically "demiourgoi" (those who work for the demos) they seem to have been sent for (like the seer and the doctor or the shipwright) from outside the community. In the Homeric poems they are certainly creative craftsmen excercising their trade for the service of the community. Their patron god was probably Hephaistos, whose ambiguous character in the Homeric epics Wace condensed into these words: "Hephaestus is at once the somewhat comical figure of A and theta, the glorified craftsman of sigma and holocaust of Psi and the flame over which man broil their meat in B."

Homer is of course not a historian of metallurgy and his ideas about this craft were rather vague, the more so as he is an Iron Age poet, writing an epic about a Late Bronze Age situation. In his story of Hephaestus making the arms for Achilles he describes a divine smith who works gold and silver, bronze and tin with the same tools and crucibles! On the other hand the poems show us how important the smith had become and how important a place metals had already conquered in the Mycenaean world. Homer may not be too clear on the functions of the smith, but in classical Greece we already find specialisation of different branches of metallurgy even going as far as specialisation in different types of arms. Between the sixth and fourth century B.C. hours and markets were fixed for metal products in the different Greek towns and in the course of our discussions we will be able to mention many important metallurgical centres of Hellenism.

In Republican Rome different types of independent smiths are to exist, for instance they buy the crude metal of the Elban mines and work them up to products which they sell again to merchants. They seem to have been organised in guilds, for Pliny says (*Nat. Hist.*) (104): "In the distant past, a guild of copper-smiths was third among those established by Numa" and Plutarch mentions this guild as the seventh of ancient Rome. Every large city in the Roman Empire had its smiths who worked the blooms of iron into tools and implements for some of the local needs. Rome, for instance had a local guild of smiths (fabri ferrarii) (105), but also several individual ferrarii and the guild contained a lot of specialists apart from the ordinary iron-smiths. At Milan there was a very large Collegium Aerariorum of twelve centuries of members and that of Brixia (Brescia) had an unusually large number of members too. Aquilea counted many smiths among its inhabitants for it was deeply interested in the mines of Noricum, where Roman state contractors lived but only few fabri. On the other hand it seems that something approaching a factory system prevailed in Imperial times at the iron mines of Virunum in Noricum, which were nearly 100 KM north of Aquilea.

Republican Rome had needed its smiths for the manufacture of arms and weapons, they seem to have worked mainly in Rome itself or in the region between Capua and Rome. An army of eight legions would need some 1600 skilled fabri (carpenters and smiths) (106). The smiths of Populonia working the iron from Elba concentrated on the manufacture of implements and tools (107), and the specialists living in the Vicus... ionum Ferrariarum (108) in Imperial Rome had concentrated on the manufacture of helmets, shields, swords, knives, locks or nails. May be the difficulty of working iron led to a greater specialisation than in copper and bronze metallurgy, but still the principal-cities had enough smiths to forge the arms for Vespasian (109), and a chalkeus or two were found in nearly every town of the Empire. Pontic iron was still most favoured but other qualities were used for specific purposes too.

In the Imperial period Italian metal industry shows a generous investment of capital and far-reaching division of labour.

At Puteoli it would be incorrect to speak of iron factories. Undoubtedly there were establishments of slave-worked forges under one roof which specialised in certain articles for a wide market, but the products carried no trade-marks. A dealer and wholesale merchant is mentioned in an inscription. At the iron mines of Noricum it is more likely that there was something approaching a factory system prevailing. Noric iron had a good name all over the Roman world, but always as a blade or tool not as the ore or unworked wrought iron.

But again plain kitchen utensils and farm implements require the service of many individual shops. These copper- and iron- smiths combine the functions of craftsmen and salesmen, often melting down articles of stock to supply material for immediate need. Even at Capua where silverplate manufacture was more or less a factory system, the production of iron implements was often conducted in small shops and in Rome we found many individual iron workers. Terra-cotta tablets of the oldest tombs at Ostia mention ironmongers, cutlers, etc. At Pompeii there were many retailshops of iron-ware probably supplied from the factories of Puteoli and Capua.

Thus in our survey we found that the characteristics of the primitive smiths have disappeared in the civilisations of the Ancient East and that later on, we find guilds of smiths with little to distinguish them from other craftsmen and little of the original peculiar social and religious status. Only the tinkers of Arabia and their ancestors, the Kenites and other itinerant smiths of Antiquity descended from the Pontic smiths still have some of these characteristics. The other smiths have evolved from clan and caste to guild and the individual smith would have disappeared in the factory system of the Later Empire had not the Dark Ages and the Middle Ages put a stop to this proces and returned to the smith some of his original individuality and craftsmanship!

What the smith gained in individuality and craftsmanship in the Middle Ages and after was largely lost again in the Industrial Revolution and the great social revolution that accompanied it. We all know what happened after that and how the old rhyme:

> "I heard that Smug the smith for ale and spyce
> Sold all his tools and yet kept his vice"

has come to be only too true! If to pursue the study of the ancient smith further would mean understanding the factors which determined this great change better, this alone would already make it worth while to amplify and to go more deeply into the outlines of his craft and his social and religious status sketched above. But even without such an important return "a good peice steil is worth a pennie".

BIBLIOGRAPHY

1. G. Cozzo, *Le origini della metallurgia, i metalli e gli dei* (Roma, 1945)
   Eliade, M., *Metallurgy, magic and alchemy* (Paris, 1936)
   Eliade, M., *The Forge and the Crucible* (London, 1962)
   Forbes, R. J., *Metaal en Metaalbewerking in mythe en maatschappij* (Mensch en Maatschappij XVIII, 1942, 3—32)
   Napier, J., *Ancient workers and artificers in metal* (London, 1856)
   Robins, F. W., *The smith, traditions and lore of an ancient craft* (London, 1953)
   Sébillot, P., *Les travaux publics et les mines dans les traditions et les superstitions de tous les pays* (Paris, 1894)
   Zippelius, G., *Die Urgeschichte des Schmiedes* (Würzburg, 1901)
2. Andrée, R., *Ethnographische Parallelen. Der Schmied* (Berlin, 1878, 153—159)
   Andrée, R., *Die Metalle bei den Naturvölkern* (Leipzig, 1884)
3. Huntingsford, G. W. B., *Free hunters, serf-tribes and submerged classes in East Africa* (Man, 31, 1931, no. 262)
   Bent, J., *The sacred city of the Aethiopians* (London, 1893, 212)
   Hollis, A. C., *The Masai* (Oxford, 1905, 330)
   Merker, A. C., *Die Masai* (Berlin, 1904, 110, 207, 246, 265, 306)
   Paulitschke, P., *Ethnographie Nordostafrikas* (Berlin, 1893, 202, 236)
   Perkyns, M., *Life in Abyssinia* (London, 1886, 300)
4. Hollis, A. C., *The Nandi* (Oxford, 1909, 36)
5. Nachtigal, G., *Die Tibbu* (Z.f. Erdkunde 5, 1870, 312)
6. Lippmann, E. O., von, *Entstehung und Ausbreitung der Alchemie* (Berlin, vol. I, 1919, 267, 273, 521, 525, 608, 626, 682; vol. II, 1932, 81, 190)
7. Gutmann, B., *Der Schmied und seine Kunst im animistischen Denken* (Z.f. Ethn. 44, 1912, 81—93)
8. Spieth, J., *Die Ewe Stämme* (Berlin, 1906, 776)
9. Frazer, J., *the Golden Bough* (London, 1920, vol. I, 349; vol. III, 237)
10. Waitz, Th., *Anthropologie der Naturvölker* (Leipzig, 1859, vol. 2, 97)
11. Lenz, O., *Skizzen aus West-Afrika* (Berlin, 1878, 184)
12. Forde, C., *Daryll, Habitat, economy and society* (London, 1934, 165, 169, 298, 344, 350—358)
13. Becker, C. H., *Vorbericht Innerafrikaexpedition* (Der Islam III, 1912, 261)
14. Cline, W., *Mining and metallurgy in Negro Africa* (Paris, 1937)
15. Lowie, H., *Introduction to cultural anthropology* (London, 1934)
16. Partington, J. R., *Origins and development of applied chemistry* (London 1935)
17. Colani, M., *Ethnographie comparée* (BEFEO 36, 1936, 197)

DOUTTÉ, E., *Ethnographie, magie et religion de l'Afrique du Nord* (Paris, 1912, 40)

ROHLF, G., *Reise durch Nord Afrika* (Peterm. Mitt. Erg. Heft 25, 1868, 30, 54)

SCHURTZ, H., *Das afrikanische Gewerbe* (Leipzig, 1900)

POTTIER, R., *Les artisans sahariens du métal chez les Touaregs* (Métaux et Civilisations I, 1945, 31—40)

MASON, O. T., *Origins of invention* (Cent. Sci. Series, London, 1895)

18. GORIS, R., *De positie der Pande Wesi* (Med. Kirtya Liefrinck-van der Tuuk, afl. 1, Singaradja, 1929)

KAT ANGELINO, P. DE, *Over de smeden en eenige andere ambachtslieden op Bali* (Tijdschr. Bat. Gen. 60, 1921, 207; 61, 1922, 370)

OSSENBRUGGE, F. D. E. V., *Het primitieve denken op Java* (Bijdr. Taal-, Land-, Volkenk. in Ned. Indië, 71, 1916, 241)

19. OSSENBRUGGEN, F. D. E. VAN, *Over het primitief begrip van grondeigendom* (Indische Gids, XXVII, 1915, i, 368)

KRUYT, A., *Het ijzer op Midden-Celebes* (Bijdr. Taal-, Land-, Volkenk. 6. ser. vol. 9)

20. NIEUWENHUIS, A. W., *Quer durch Borneo* (Leiden, 1907, II, 198)

21. ANDRÉ, R., *Die Metalle bei den Naturvölkern* (Leipzig, 1884)

GILLE, B., *L'ancienne métallurgie du fer à Madagascar* (Techniques et Civilisations IV, 1954, 144—147)

22. ANDRÉ, R., *Ethnographische Parallelen. Der Schmied* (Berlin, 1878, 153)

23. DUNBAR, G., *Other Men's lives* (London, 1939, 38, 259)

24. FORDE, C. DARYL, *Habitat, Economy and Society* (London, 1934)

ALFÖLDI, A., *Schmiedehandwerk und Königtum in Nordasien* (Magyar Nyelv XXVIII, 1932, 205—221

25. GOWLAND, W., *Metals and metal working in Old Japan* (Trans. Proc. Japan Soc. (London) XIII, 1914/15, 20)

26. MATTHEWS, *Sc. Ann. Report Bur. Ethn.*, Washington 1883, 171—178

NORDENSKJÖLD, E., *Modifications in Indian culture* (Comp. ethn. Studies VIII, 1930)

27. PHILLIPS, J. A., *Thoughts on ancient mining and metallurgy* (Arch. J. XVI, 1859, 12)

28. SCHRADER, O., *Sprachvergleichung und Urgeschichte II.i, Die Metalle* (Jena, 1906)

29. SCHUBERT, H. R., *The Anglo-Saxon smith in about* 1000 *A.D.* (J. Iron Steel Inst. 163, 1949, sept., 8)

30. CHILDE, V. GORDON, *Dawn of European civilisation* (London, 1939)

31. ANDRÉ, R., *Die Metalle bei den Naturvölkern* (Leipzig, 1884)

32. WAITZ, TH., *Anthropologie der Naturvölker* (Leipzig, 1859, II, 97)

33. RUBEN, W., *Eisenschmiede und Dämonen in Indien* (Leiden 1939, 4, 11, 130, 302)

34. SAYCE, R., *Primitive arts and crafts* (London, 1933)

35. CLINE, W., *Mining and Metallurgy in Negro Africa* (Paris, 1937)

36. SAYCE, R., *Primitive arts and crafts* (London, 1933)
37. DUNBAR, G., *Other men's lives* (London, 1939, 38, 259)
38. SCHRADER, O., *Sprachvergleichung und Urgeschichte, II,i, Die Metalle* (Jena, 1906)
39. CLINE, W., *Mining and Metallurgy in Negro Africa* (Paris, 1937)
40. CHILDE, V. GORDON, *The Bronze Age* (Cambridge, 1930, 4, 10)
    CHILDE, V. GORDON, *The Most Ancient East* (London, 1934, 224)
    CHILDE, V. GORDON, *Man makes himself* (London, 1935, 130, 200)
41. RASSERS, W. H., *Inleiding tot een bestudeering van de Javaansche kris* (Med. Kon. Ned. Akad. Wet. N.R. 1, 1938, no. 8)
    RASSERS, W. H., *On the Javanese kris* (Bijdr. Taal-, Land-, Volkenk. Ned. Indië, 79, 1939, 501—582)
42. SAYCE, R., *Primitive arts and crafts* (London, 1933)
    BRAUN, P., *Les tabous des Feriae* (Année Sociologique 1959, 49—125)
43. DAUBRÉE, A., *La génération des minéraux métalliques* (J. des Savants 1890, 379, 441)
44. BERG, C. C., *Tooverij in de Hindoe-Javaansche Maatschappij* (In: La sorcelerie dans les pays de mission, Brussels, 1936, 361)
45. OHLHAVER, H., *Der germanische Schmied und seine Werkzeuge* (Leipzig, 1939)
46. GROOT, J. J. M. DE, *The religious systems of China* (Leiden, IV, 1901, 52)
47. LEEUW, G. VAN DER, *Phänomenologie der Religion* (Tübingen, 1933, 35)
    KRETSCHMER, P., *Zu den ältesten Metallnamen* (Glotta XXXII, 1952/53, 1—16)
    GOLDZIHER, I., *Eisen als Schutz gegen Dämonen* (Arch. f. Religionswiss. X, 1907, 41—46)
48. ROSSIGNOL, J. P., *Les métaux dans l'antiquité* (Paris, 1863)
49. AISCHYLOS, *Prometheus* 714; STRABO 12. cap. 549; ARISTOTLE, *De mirab. ausc.* 481
50. HERODOTUS I. 28
51. EISLER, R., (Ch) *Alybes, Chaldaioi* (Caucasia V, 1928, 97)
    ZAKHAROV, A. A., *Etudes sur l'archéologie de l'Asie Mineure et du Caucase* (Rev. Hitt. Asian. I, 1931, 111)
    XENOPHON, *Anabasis* IV.3.4; V.5.17; *Cyrop.* III.2.7
52. SCHARFMEYER, F., *Eisen* (In: Reallex. d. Assyr. II, 318)
53. WAINWRIGHT, G. A., *Tabal, Tibareni, Tabareni* (OLZ 39, 1936, 481)
54. HERODOTUS III. 94; XENOPHON, *Anabasis* V.5.2.; DIODOR 14. 30.7
55. LAUNAY, L., DE, *Les Telchines et les origines légendaires de la métallurgie* (Rev. Gén. des Sci. 19, 1908, 449)
56. MOTZ, F., *Ueber die Metallarbeiter der heroischen Zeit* (Meiningen, 1868)
57. DIODOR V. 64—65
58. PLINY, *Nat. Hist.* 7. 57
59· PLUTARCH, *de musica* c. 5,8.3

ろo9o९

60. KLINKENBERG, C., *Rhodische Urvölker* (Hermes 50, 1915, 271—303)
61. BAUMANN, E. D., *De mythe van de manke god* (Varia Antiqua, IIe reeks, Arnhem, no date, 3—28)
62. ALTHEIM, FR., *Griechische Götter in Rom* (Berlin, 1930, 172)
    DUVAL, P. M., *Notes sur la civilisation gallo-romaine I, Vulcan et les métiers de métal* (Gallia X, 1952, 43—57)
    DUVAL, P. M., *Le dieu Vulcan en Gaule* (BSAF 1952/53, 55)
    ROSE, H. J., *The cult of Vulcanus at Rome* (JRS 23, 1933, 46)
    TOUTAIN, J., *Sur un rite curieux et significant du culte de Vulcain à Rome* (Rev. Hist. Rel. 103, 1931, 136)
63. PLINY, *Nat. Hist.* 2. 240
64. PLINY, *Nat. Hist.* 2, 106
65. ILIAD 18. 369
66. HERODOTUS III. 37
67. DIODOR I. 12—13
68. HOPFNER, *Fontes...* 301, 673
69. Ancient Records III. 28
70. ROSNER, E., *Die Lahmheit des Hephaistos* (Forsch. u. Fortschr. XXIX, 1953, 362—363)
71. MORENZ, S., *Ptah-Hephaistos, der Zwerg* (Festschr. ZUCKER, 1954, 277—290)
72. B.M. 36250
73. MONTET, P., *Ptah patèque et les orfèvres* (Rev. Archéol. 40, 1952, 1—11)
74. WEILL, R., *Les mots "bi3", cuivre, métaux, mine, carrière, blocs, transport, merveille et leurs déterminatifs* (Rev. d'Egypt. III, 1938, 69)
75. ERMAN, A. & RANKE, H., *Aegypten* (Tübingen, 1923, 550)
76. APAW 1939, no. 23, 29
77. SAUNERON, S., *La manufacture d'armes de Memphis* (BIFAO LIV, 1954, 7—12)
78. SCHEIL, V., *A propos des métaux d'Umma* (RAss. XII, 1915, 60)
    LIMET, H., *Le travail du métal au pays de Sumer au temps de la IIIe Dynastie d'Ur* (Paris, 1960)
    NORTH, R., *Sociology of the Biblical Jubilee* (Rome, 1954, 58)
79. CT X, nos. 14333, 21394; IX, no. 19031
80. UET III. 346, 296, 721; REISNER, *Tempelurkunden no.* 124
81. VAB VI. no. 17 & 54
82. HROZNY, B., *Le nom et le caractère de Gilgames* (C.R. Acad. Inscr. Bell. Lett. 1938, 114—118)
82. WISEMAN, D. J., *The Alalakh Tablets* (London, 1953)
    Archives Royales de Mari (Paris, 1952 —, 5 vols.)
    FORBES, R. J., *New evidence on Late Bronze Age Metallurgy* (Sibrium III, 1956/57, 113—121)
83. AL 414, 348 & 376; 371, 409, 369, 366, 378, 368, 33; ARM I. 74
84. AL 69, 143, 153, 161, 213, 227, 401, 397, 402, 431, 406, 407, 396
85. CT VI, 25

86. UGNAD, A., SUBARTU (Berlin, 1936, 179)
87. 2. Ki. 24. 14; Isa. 24. 1; 29. 2
88. HARPER 1194, 114, 1317 (K. 5397), 91 (K. 620)
89. EERDMANS, B. D., *De Kenieten en het Jahwisme* (Theol. Tijdschr. XLI, 1907, 492)
    EERDMANS, B. D., *Alttestamentische Studiën* (Giessen, 1908, II, 44, 85)
90. JUDGES 4. 11
91. *i. Sam.* 15. 6
92. *i. Chron.* 2. 55
93. *Gen.* 4. 22
94. *Exod.* 2. 17
95. DOUGHTY, *Travels in Arabia Deserta* I, 137, 278
96. BUDDE, K., *The Sabbath and the Week* (J. Theol. Stud. 30, 1928, 14)
    MEEK, J., *Hebrew Origins* (New York, 1936, 86)
    ROWLEY, H. H., *The Re-Discovery of the Old Testament* (London, 1945, 82)
    WEBER, MAX, *Das antike Judentum* (In: Aufsätze z. Religionssoziologie, Tübingen, 1921, 64)
97. 1. Sam. 13. 19
98. FETTICH, N., *Bronzeguss und Nomadenkunst* (Skythia II, 99)
    ANDREAS, M., *Gypsy coppersmiths in Liverpool and Birmingham* (London, 1913)
99. TIMMER, B. C. J., *Megasthenes en de Indische Maatschappij* (Amsterdam, 1930, 149, 154)
100. VENTRIS, M. and CHADWICK. J., *Documents in Mycenaean Greek* (London, 1956)
    WACE, A. J. B. and STUBBINGS, F. H., *A Companion to Homer* (London, 1962)
    LEJEUNE, M., *Les forgerons de Pylos* (Historia X, 1961, 409—434)
101. GURNEY, O. R., *The Hittites* (London, 1952, 83)
102. ILIAD XXIII. 832—835
103. GRAY, D. H. F., *Metal-working in Homer* (JHS LXXIV, 1954, 1—15)
104. PLINY, *Nat. Hist.* 34. 1
105. C.I.L. VI. 892
106. LIVY I. 43; DIONYSIUS 7. 59; CICERO, *de Repub.* II. 39
107. DIODORUS V. 13
108. C.I.L. VI. 9185
109. TACITUS, *Hist.* II. 82

Chapter Four

TOOLS AND METHODS OF EARLY METALLURGY

> Behold, I have created the smith that bloweth the coals
> in the fire and that bringeth forth an instrument for
> his work. (Isa. 54 : 16)

1. *The essentials*

Four things were essential to the early metallurgist, viz. ores, fuel, blast air and tools, furnaces and crucibles.

In an earlier volume of this series (1) we have set out that the ancients were conversant with most of the *ores* they needed for the production of metals. Through the centuries they had come to recognize their outer characteristics, they had systematized this knowledge and had discussed them in various ways. They knew how to find and mine them, and above all they knew how to select and prepare them for smelting. Basing itself on the experience of many generations each Greek or Roman "metallon" (mine) not only extracted and produced the ore needed, but near it was usually one or more "ergasterion" (workshop) like those of Laureion (2), where the selection, pounding and washing of the ores was carried out. The "kegchrion" (kegchros: millet) was the pounding shop, the broken ore was concentrated by sieving and washing on tables with running water. There is no doubt of the efficiency of these establishments and the fact that the ancient smelter could disposed of properly cleaned and selected ore to start with.

But the *fuel* was often rather a problem. For the quantity and above all the quality of the fuel determine to a large extent the temperature attained in the furnace and this again is largely responsible for the possibility of working certain ores and of using certain processes. In other words the fuel determines to a certain degree the melting and smelting activities of the early smith.

In this respect ancient metallurgy was seriously handicapped for the production of coke from coal which gave an excellent hard and well-burning fuel for the reduction of ores in large quantities is a recent invention. Coke was not used for metallurgical purposes before the end of the eighteenth century, at least on a large scale. However, charcoal was an excellent though relatively expensive fuel which burned well and was capable of reducing ores, though it was not hard enough to bear heavy loads of ore and therefore charcoal-burning furnaces could never attain the size of modern smelting appliances.

We have argued earlier (3) that hampered with fuel as it was ancient technology was largely a charcoal-technology and hence metallurgy too was charcoal-dominated until the eighteenth century A.D. The ancient smith and metal-worker was dependent on a charcoal-fire to achieve high temperatures and hence his techniques were limited to a certain extent by the lack of means of producing higher temperatures (such as we use in oxygen-welding) and the means of controlling such a charcoal fire very closely (4).

Fig. 19.
Gathering brushwood for charcoal manufacture in Palestine
(after Dalman, Arbeit und Sitte)

In ancient Egypt charcoal was available to the smith. It was extensively burned in the eastern desert and the Sinai peninsula which accounts for much deforestation in these parts. Samples of charcoal have been found in Early Dynastic tombs at Naga el-Deir, in a First Dynasty tomb at Saqqara and in the storerooms of the pyramid temple of Menkaure. Though charcoal was found in Sinai too, this may be charred wood, the latter being the original fuel. Apart from this charcoal (d'b.t; HWB V.206) they used fire-wood (ht.n.sdt; HWB III.340), mostly and tamarisk wood, though wood was very expensive in Egypt. Theophrast tells us that they often used the roots of the papyrus plants and sari-grass (5) along with straw, chaff, animal dung, rushes and sedges.

Grass and camel dung are used by the modern fellahin, they are collected by children and dried in the sun to flat cakes, which form an inferior fuel, that was certainly known in Antiquity too.

Portable charcoal fires are depicted on ancient Egyptian reliefs. The use of olive wood and charcoal made from it is mentioned in late Hellenistic Gnostic papyri. These charcoal fires easily attain a temperature of 900° C., and the temperature can be raised by the application of blast air, it was therefore eminently suitable for the production of small quantities of metal and it served the skilled Egyptian goldsmiths well.

In ancient Mesopotamia charcoal was known from times immemorial, as powdered charcoal was even used as a pigment in prehistoric pottery. The charcoal called *pêntu*, though used early always remained expensive in a treeless country like Mesopotamia. The most common wood used for the manufacture of charcoal was ṣarbatu-wood, which is almost certainly either styrax wood or a similar gummy wood. It was cut up into logs (*kurû*) in the hot month of Api and the logs were not bound up in bundles but stored under hides, if they were not used for the manufacture of charcoal immediately.

Also date-kernels, thorny shrubs, chopped straw and reeds and camel-dung were used as they were in ancient Palestine which was not blessed with good fuel for the smith. In the Old Testament fire-wood ('êsîm) is often mentioned, though it seems to have been scarce on occasions (II. Sam. 24.22; I.Ki. 19.21), and the glowing embers (gahelet) are often mentioned as equal to charcoal. This live ember (Prov. 25.22; 26.21; II. Sam. 22.9,13) is different from the charcoal called pehâm (Prov. 26.21) which is prepared in heaps and is used by the smith. Only the fire transforms it into live ember. Then dung and hay or chopped straw (ḳaš) (Ez. 4.15; Matth. 6.30) were used, the remnants of olivepressing (géphet), kernels (gal'inîn), thistles and shrubs (sîrîm, hamâsîm) also served for burning.

In the classical period charcoal remained the principal metallurgical fuel. We have several reports on its manufacture from classical authors, such as Pliny (6) but none is so well-informed as Theophrastus whose description is not only correct even for present conditions but his arguments on the properties which a good metallurgical charcoal should have are quite sound and could hardly be improved. We will therefore quote the relevant passage from his *Enquiry into plants* (7) in full:

"The best charcoal is made from the closest wood such as the holm oak, for these are the most solid, so that they last longest and are the strongest; wherefore these are used in the silver-mines for the first smelting of the ore. Worst of the woods mentioned is oak, since it contains most mineral matter (ash!) and the wood of older trees is inferior to that of younger, and for the same reason that of really old trees is especially bad. For it is very dry, wherefore it sputters as it

Fig. 20.
Burning charcoal-heap in Palestine
(after Dalman, Arbeit und Sitte)

burns; whereas wood for charcoal should contain sap. The best charcoal comes from trees in their prime and especially from trees which have been topped, for these contain in the right proportions the qualities of closeness, admixture of mineral matter and moisture. Again better charcoal comes from trees in a sunny dry position with a northern aspect from those grown in a shady damp position facing south. Or if the wood used contains a good deal of moisture, it should be of close texture; for such wood contains more sap. And, for the same reason, that which is of close texture either from its own natural character or because it was grown on a dry spot is, whatever the kind of tree, better. But the different kinds of charcoal are used for different purposes; for some uses men require it to be soft; thus in the iron-mines they use that which is made of sweet chestnut when the iron has already been smelted, and in silver-mines they use charcoal of pine-wood; and these kinds are also used by the crafts. Smiths require charcoal of fir rather than of oak; it is indeed not so strong, but it blows better into a flame as it is apt to smoulder less; and the flame from these woods is fiercer. In general the flame is fiercer not only from these but from any wood which is of open texture and light, or which is dry; while that from wood which is of close texture or green is more sluggish and dull. The fiercest flame of all is given by brush-wood; but charcoal can not be made from it at all, since it has not the necessary substance."

"They cut and require for the charcoal-heap straight smooth billets for they must be laid as close as possible for the smouldering process. When they have covered the kiln, they kindle the heap by degrees stirring it with poles. Such is the wood required for the charcoal-heap."

"For the crafts requiring a furnace and for other crafts various woods are servicable according to circumstances. For kindling fig and olive are best, fig, because it is tough and of open texture, so that it easily catches fire and does not let it through, olive, because it is of close texture and oily."

In another passage he adds: "The scrub oak gives poor wood for burning charcoal as does the sea-bark oak... The wood of the Turkey oak is even more wretched for burning and for making charcoal for the charcoal is entirely useless except to the smith, because it springs about and emits sparks."

Furthermore he discusses the manufacture of tar as a by-product of the production of charcoal.

Pliny recommends the use of wood from coniferous trees, cypresses or terebinths for the manufacture of charcoal in the passages mention-ed above, but he is mainly concerned with the manufacture of tar and similar products, which we discussed elsewhere.

In Populonia Simonin found the remnants of oak and chestnut char-coal; Straker found birch, oak, hazel and maple charcoal on Roman smelting sites in the Weald, and he gives further information of the fuel of post-Roman metallurgy.

The charcoal-heap or pile (pit) is called Meiler in Germand and myt in Dutch, words both derived from the Latin "meta", (a cone-shaped heap) and thus here is another proof that little has changed in the method of charcoal-burning. Charcoal and wood were the two popular types of fuel in the classical world and charcoal had the advantage of being "more concentrated heat". As Pliny expresses it (8): "It is only when ignited and quenched that charcoal itself acquires its characteristic powers, and only when it seems to have perished that it becomes endowed with greater virtue". It was exported from production centres like Magna Graecia and Macedonia, Mt. Ida and Gaul to many other quarters of the Roman world, where the price was usually carefully regulated as was the sale of fuel. We have a good example of the regulations from Delos (Inscr. Délos, 509).

It is often said that many regions of the Ancient Near East were deforestated by the cutting of the trees for the burning of charcoal, but this is largely exaggerated. Of course the fuel supply for the metallurgical centres was an important factor in this process, and as Strabo says: (9) "In ancient times the plains of Cyprus were thickly overgrown with forests, and therefore covered with woods and not cultivated. The mines helped a little against this since the people would cut down the trees to burn the copper and the silver and the building of the fleets has further helped...". But there are certainly other and more important factors that stimulated deforestation and one of these was formed by the numerous goat-herds kept in the Mediterranean region since Antiquity. It can be said without exaggeration that the goats have denuded many a fertile region in Greece, Malta and other parts of the Ancient World. Still in the neighbourhood of mines charcoal burning must have done much damage. On the island of Elba the best iron ore of the Roman world was found but the local wood and charcoal had apparently already given out before the Empire and the ore had to be transported after roasting to Populonia to be smelted there, where wood and charcoal could be easily obtained from the Ligurian mountains. Pliny complains that "the effect of the shortage of fuel on the roasting operation is particularly noticeable in Gaul, where the second roasting is carried out with charcoal instead of wood" and he also comments on the shortage of fuel in Campanian metallurgy (10) and therefore there is some truth in the statement of the effect of metallurgy on deforestation. But the supplies of wood and charcoal remained plentiful in Antiquity even if cheap local resources may have given out and smelting continued to use these fuels for many centuries without difficulties except perhaps somewhat higher charges on the fuel bill.

According to Theophrastus (11) briquettes were also made in Antiquity by pressing together charcoal, pitch and tar, the latter serving as the cementing medium. It is not known whether these briquettes were ever used in metallurgy, but this is improbable.

A similar exceptional case is the furnace mentioned in the apocryphal "Prayer of Azaniah" (written after 170 B.C.) which is said to be heated with naphtha, a fuel which was also used in certain baths of Byzantium, but which is not known to have been used in metallurgy until very recently, for special metallurgical furnaces.

There are, however, different members of the coal family which are mentioned as fuels by the Ancients. Bailey in his note on the gagates mentioned by Pliny (12) says that "Theophrastus gives an account of quite a variety of minerals from Thrace, the Lipari islands, Sicily and Liguria, all of which burn, an account which leaves the writer in no doubt that, in addition to asphaltic materials, some varieties of coal were known to the ancients" though their inflammability when moistened with water and the subsequent quenching with olive oil is a fable of course.

There are some references to lignite such as the passage in Theophrastus (13): "Those products of mining which are called carbo (anthrax) are found as earthy stones, they can be kindled and burn up wholly like charcoal. They occur in Liguria and in Elis on the road over the mountains to Olympia. These coals are used by the smith" and Dionysios Aphrus refers to "an earthy and sulphurous mass, like coals, which the smiths and inhabitants of Britain use to a large extent as fuel". They do not seem to be true coal as Davies supposed. At Velem St. Vid there is certain proof that lignite was used in the metallurgical processes.

There is, however, no proof that peat was ever used, though it is mentioned by Tacitus and Pliny: (14) "the Chaucians collected mud with their hands dried more by means of the wind than by means of the sun and therewith warm their limbs which are stiff because of the northern colds". It would have been of little use. But in the case of true coals we have certain proof that they were used by the metallurgists of the classical world. Its value was not appreciated quite fully by the Romans and they neglected such coalfields as Esterel and Clermont-Ferrand in Gaul. Owing to its impurities (especially sulphur!) it was always a bad substitute for charcoal until coking was discovered in the eighteenth century and the noxious substances could be removed to obtain a fine, hard fuel. But coal was used for domestic purposes in provinces where it occured in surface outcrops especially in Britain. Cunnington (15) gave quite a list of references on finds of coal in the remains of Romano-British villas which go to show that in Roman times coal was certainly used and even transported over rather large distances probably by means of packhorses. This coal was often found in association with iron slags and it was apparently used for smelting lead at Pentre. After surveying all the archaeological evidence obtained in Roman Britain we can say that in most places where coal crops out within the Roman area it was worked more or less systematically in Roman times. This exploitation was most systematic in the civilised south-west, where Somerset coal came into extensive use even among the poor and secondly in the military north where Tyne-valley, Cumberland and Scottish coal were regularly used

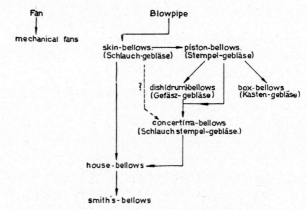

Fig. 21.
Evolution of the means of producing blast-air

in the frontier-forts. The collieries of the Wall districts were no doubt under military control, but we have no evidence as to the control and management of the others. From the association of coal and iron slags it would seem that coal was used in smelting iron though not frequently. Summing up our evidence we must conclude that charcoal was and remained the principal metallurgical fuel in Antiquity and that wood was also used extensively. In the Near East certain local fuels were certainly used as they are nowadays and in some Roman provinces coal seems to have been used to some extent. Once the different types of furnaces are known in detail it will be interesting to measure the temperatures obtained with these fuels in the ancient kilns, as such figures would go far to help us to understand the metallurgical processes, usually described so loosely by the ancient authors.

The third important factor in ancient metallurgy, the *production of blast air*, still is more or less a mystery. Blast air was not necessary for all metallurgical processes, but only for those that required high temperatures or when larger quantities of ores were smelted. There is no doubt that the simple means of raising the temperature of glowing charcoal such as the fan and the blowpipe belong to the oldest tools of the smith. Both are still widely used with charcoal fires all over the world (16).

The fan is known in different forms and it has gradually been mechanised. But however elaborate mechanical types of fans or fan-like apparatus were developed, none of them would have more effect than a good natural draught and for many metallurgical purpose it would be of no use. The fan was, therefore, more and more used for air-conditioning and similar applications for which work it was better suited. We find it in use in primitive mines, etc. but less and less in metallurgy.

The blowpipe was far better suited for the work of the smith. It gave a stronger air-blast which could be directed on the exact point of the fire where it was wanted. It raised the temperature of the glowing charcoal far better and it was eminently suited for the work of the goldsmith and the jeweller, for which purpose (granulation-work, etc.) it must have been used very early, for the oldest Egyptian pictures of blowpipes often occur in scenes depicting the work of goldsmiths. Bergsøe's studies have shown what primitive South-American Indians were able to do with this simple instrument. In Egypt the blowpipe is depicted on Old Kingdom reliefs, one of the best known pictures of this instrument is found in the Fifth Dynasty tomb of Ti at Sakkarah (17). The Egyptians probably used metal pipes with clay tips, possibly also reeds like the Sumerians and Babylonians. The New World seems to have known the blowpipe only, Mexican and Inca smiths never seem to have developed any form of bellows. For the evolution of the blow-pipe, which is too small and too difficult to handle for larger fires, led to the invention of bellows (18). The clay-nozzle or tuyère at the end of the older types of bellows conducting the concentrated air-blast into the fire, can be more or less regarded as the condensed survival of the old blow-pipe, the rest of the bellows merely representing an evolved better and larger form of producing the necessary volume of air. These tuyères have often been found in ancient smelting furnaces or on smelting sites, and though they have often been disregarded they form certain evidence that blast air has been used. The ethnological evidence and theories on the evolution of the bellows have been neglected by the archaeologists, but we must necessarily draw on them to supplement the very meagre archaeological data.

Several authors, especially Foy and Klosemann have traced the evolution of the bellows. By general consensus the earliest form of bellows was the *skin-bellows* (Schlauchgebläse) formed by sewing together the skin of an animal (often a goatskin), attaching the pipe and tuyère to one of the leg and using a slit with two wooden rims as the opening for introducing fresh air into the bag. This is, according to all authorities, a very old form evolved in the Near East, but more probably in Western or Central Asia. It is the form described by the ancient authors (19). For though Cline says that the skin- or bag-bellows admits little variations it is certainly the parent of all modern forms of bellows. Frobenius was of the opinion that two categories of bellows were evolved from these primitive form, viz. the wooden forms of Asia (pump-bellows, box-bellows, and drum-bellows) and the typical African drum-bellows, in the latter case because the climate of Africa does not allow a long span of life to leather or skin forms. He regards the pump-bellows as the typical Malayan form, the box-bellows as the Far-Eastern form and the wooden dish- or drum-bellows as the East-African form possibly introduced under Malayan influence. But his theory is sketched rather rapidly and without due attention to the facts and we think that Foy, who studied the problem in detail, gave a more consistent story.

The skin- or bag-bellows was according to Foy the oldest form, evolved in Central Asia and the Near East. As practice demanded a constant supply of air, two or more pairs of bellows were used, each smith working one pair. Are we not told about Hephaistos' forge that "through twenty pipes at once forwith they poured their diverse-tempered blasts"? And does not the Pythian priestess describe the smithy at Tegea with the lines (20):

> "There is a place, Tegeë, in the level plain of Arcadia,
> Where by stark stress driven twain winds are ever a-blowing,
> Shock makes answer to shock and anguish is laid upon anguish."

These old skin-bellows came to Africa and Europe from the Near East, not as Luschan contended from Africa to the rest of the world. They are depicted on ancient Greek vases and they are still used by primitive tribes in Africa and India. They are the typical bellows of the gypsies.

A second group of formes was evolved from the *pump-bellows* (Stempelgebläse), a type akin to the bag-bellows and probably evolved in Southern or Eastern Asia. The blast air is forced into the tuyère from a wooden or bamboo cylinder in which a piston is moved up and down. Here again, two cylinders are worked alternately to maintain a constant stream of air. It is found in the Far East, Farther India, Malaya and Indonesia and in East-Africa as far as the Islam penetrated from the coast, for instance up the Zambesi river. One form with

Fig. 22.
Primitive skin-bellows of the Gypsy-smiths according to Kopernicki

horizontal pistons belongs to the Far East and was elaborated and mechanised to form the *box-bellows* or "tatara" of the Japanese and Chinese. The second type with *vertical pistons* is still characteristic of Farther India and Indonesia, but it occurs in Burma, India and Madagascar too.

The *dish- or drum-bellows* are an intermediate form between the bag- and the piston-bellows. This form, probably developed in Central Asia or India on the border of the region covered by the two primary types, spread over the Near East to Africa, where it is still the dominant type in the region of South and Middle Africa between Liberia and the Upper Nile. It consists of a loose diaphragm fitted over a solid chamber. The air is inhaled either through a slit in the diaphragm which is closed when depressing the diaphragm or else through a flue leading into the chamber. In the latter case the spout of the bellows is inserted far enough into the broad end of the tuyère to direct the blast straight into the fire, but not far enough to prevent the intake of fresh air when the diaphragm is raised. The dish-bellows (Gefäsz-blasebalg) is moved by a set of sticks (Africa) or with a pair of strings (Near East, India and Malaya), but in other forms the diaphragms are moved with the hands, are at the same time used to shut the slits through which the air is sucked in, which are found especially in these sub-forms.

A hybrid form that came originally from Eastern Asia (as parallels are found in Siberia!) are the *concertina bellows*, a cross between the piston- and dish-bellows. They resemble the double-bodied dish-

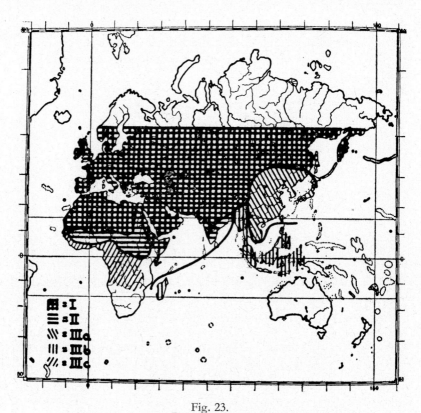

Fig. 23.
Types of bellows and their distribution after Klosemann
I.   Original leather skin-bellows
II. Dish-bellows, intermediary form, partly clay
IIIa. Far Eastern box-bellows (late wooden form)
IIIb. Malayan piston bellows (late wooden form)
IIIc. African dish-bellows (late wooden form)

bellows except for the larger size of the body and the voluminous skin, which encloses a large stack of rings which are drawn apart by short pistons and allowed to fall as the bellows is raised and lowered. They are found in Africa, being probably introduced from the Mediterranean lands. For they were introduced into Europe from Asia and there crossed with the skin bellows to form our leather *house-bellows* with an accordion-like bag expanded and collapsed between two wooden boards. Others have suggested, that the house-bellows were evolved in Europe from forms of dish- or drum-bellows. The earliest reference to these forms of bellows can be found in Ausonius' *Mosella* (V. 267), a poem of the fourth century A.D. Theophilus (21) gives an adequate description of their construction and manufacture. The dish-bellows with their wooden or earthenware chambers are now more or less African forms, showing the great ingenuity of the native smith; but they have disappeared from Europe.

The house-bellows grew larger as the volume of air necessary for smelting was increased by the evolution of iron metallurgy. In general we can say that the evolution of the bellows is intimately linked with the development of iron metallurgy. As in the Middle Ages and perhaps even in Roman times water-power was used to produce blast air, the typical long-levered *smiths' bellows* were evolved. The dish bellows survived especially in those countries were leather was less common or where the climate was not suited to this material (Africa), for the same reasons the piston bellows maintained themselves in Indonesia, etc.

It might seem from these lines that the evolution of the bellows is quite clear, but only the outline can be barely traced as we possess very few details on the bellows of Antiquity. Probably much material is still buried in texts and in the pictures of reliefs, vases, etc. but no adequate study of the subject has yet been made. Most authors mention that bellows were known in Egypt in the XVIIIth dynasty but they take that period for the date of the invention of these apparatus without ever looking at the details of its construction which undoubtedly point to a much earlier date for its conception. For it may be true that the earliest pictures of bellows are found on the walls of XVIIIth dynasty tombs, such as those of Rechmire and Menkhepherrasonb (22) but these are dish-bellows, probably with earthenware chambers and a skin moved by strings. The assistants of the smith stand upon the top of the chambers and seem to have closed the slits in the diaphragms with their feet when pushing it down. However, the details are not clearly visible and we might also suppose that the blast air is blown into the tuyère from some short distance leaving a space through which the fresh air can be sucked into the body of the bellows by lifting the diaphragm by the string, a method which we have already described as still used in Africa. Anyhow, the forms of bellows shown here are far from primitive forms and they must have had quite a long history behind them. How long, we do not know, for there are no other pictures to guide us at present, either from Egypt or from Mesopotamia. The blow-pipe is certainly used in the earliest historic times in Egypt and the Old Kingdom texts have the expression "rkḥ śḏt" (fanning, blowing the fire) (HWB II.458) (compare the Coptic rokh, rakhe and the Greek anthrakia, a coal-fire). Another very old Egyptian word "hwt" (fire-glow, blaze) (HWB II.485) is related to the Coptic "hôt" (blow-pipe, bellows, but also vent, see the Greek physetér in Job 32.19 and Herodotus IV.2) or the Coptic "hoi n.nifi" (bellows) (The Coptic "nife, nifi" being the Egyptian "nfj, nf", wind, air). But no Egyptian term for blow-pipe or bellows is known notwithstanding the pictures we possess of these apparatus.

Bellows are mentioned in the Bible, once directly in connection with lead-smelting (23) (Jer. VI.29) and five times indirectly (24) but the smith is traditionally called nappaḥ, that is the "user of bellows". But these passages do not allow us to draw conclusions on the date of their introduction into Palestine.

But in Mesopotamia where the blowpipe is certainly very old and perhaps depicted on a seal of the Uruk-period from Susa (25), both blow-pipe and bellows are represented by terms which occur in fairly old texts. Both Accadian words are derived from the same root "nph" which means "to blow, fan (a fire), set ablaze". The blow-pipe is called *nappaḥu* and we know a Sumerian ideogram for this apparatus written GI plus KA.IM (26) which occurs in a text going back to the Kassite period (seventeenth century B.C.) at least, if not earlier. This shows us that at the earliest time a reed, tipped with clay was probably used (27).

The bellows were called *nappaḥtu* and the metallurgist and more particularly the smith was called *nappaḥu*, the "user of bellows" as in Hebrew. As no Assyrian or Sumerian picture of a complete bellows is known nor one found in the excavations probably as no attention was given to the remains of dish-bellows or other forms (consisting for a large part of easily corrodable materials) we must rely at the present on the philological evidence which shows that these words belong to the earliest Accadian stratum that is at least to the beginning of the second millennium B.C.

A diligent search for properly dated tuyères might help to solve the history of the bellows both in the Ancient Near East and in the classical world. This is of the greatest importance to the historian of metallurgy as several techniques and especially iron metallurgy are closely related to the evolution of the bellows, without which we can not picture the smith. Of course many other techniques such as the smelting of certain copper and lead-ores were wholly or partly possibly without blast air, but the most economical processes wanted it badly and on the evidence of their development we must guess that the evolution of the bellows from the blow-pipe dates from the third millennium B.C. The evidence of tuyères found in early smelting sites had often been disregarded, but they were found near a furnace at Telloh (Ur III period, 2000 B.C.) and other early sites in the ancient Near East and Bronze Age Europe. As they either represent the clay nozzle of the bellows themselves or the clay pipes let into the wall of the furnace into which the nozzles of the bellows were introduced, they may prove that bellows were used at those periods, for at least in the latter case the use of blow-pipes is impossible.

In the classical world bellows are regularly used in metallurgy (28) and Strabo (29) ascribes their invention to Anarchasis, a Thracian prince, who was said to live about 600 B.C. Homer (30) knows the skin-bellows (askos) which are depicted on many Greek vases. The other word used for bellows is "physa" (31), which is said to have been applied in an early form of flame-thrower. Still the common Greek word for bellows was "physeter", e.g. "blow-pipe". In Latin we usually read of the "follis" or "fabrilis" which hardly changed until well in the Middle Ages.

Bellows are quite indispensable to certain metallurgical processes, thus the discovery of the production of cast-iron was the result of better and larger bellows, whereby the temperature in the furnace could be raised above the melting point of iron.

The fourth essential is a good *metallurgical hearth or furnace*. We have discussed these industrial furnaces in a previous volume when we dealt with the methods of heating in the ancient world (32).

It is difficult to write the story of the *metallurgical furnace* for not only are data in certain regions as the Near East practically absent, but on the other hand the abundant data from other regions such as prehistoric Europe show such a welter of types and are so lacking in correct observation and detail, that one can not but wish, that many of these excavated furnaces should be studied and described again by specialists and that in such important regions as the Near East more attention should be given to furnaces and other details of smelting sites. Excavators should call in experts to review these finds, for is it not strange that we know next to nothing about these things from the actual centre of ancient metallurgy and should depend on descriptions by laymen who more than often use wrong or misleading terms for what they believe to have found. Thus for instance Flinders Petrie's description of the important Gerar furnaces is not only lacking in detail, but as far as one can judge from the scant data and photographs entirely wrong. No piece of ore was ever smelted in these "smelting furnaces" and they seem to represent a "military forge" in which blooms of iron (or perhaps bars) were reheated for further forging. Now in this case Wyndham Hulme gave the correct interpretation, but many other descriptions of other furnaces remain uncriticised by experts and their "evidence" is used in building up theories on the story of metallurgy. What we want at present is a re-examination of the existing data by experts and more expert attention to new finds.

In view of this situation we need not wonder that few have ever tried to find the threads of the story of the furnace as most writers have shunned this labyrinth and skipped this subject with a few paragraphs of generalities. The only one who to the knowledge of the writer has tried to systematize the data on primitive furnaces is Klosemann but this author was misled by his theory of the African origin of iron metallurgy. Recently Weiershausen and Deichmüller have summed up the data on furnaces in prehistoric Europe, but more essays of this type are needed before an adequate picture can be formed (33).

What we will give in the following lines is a very tentative picture, more or less a discussion, of some of the principles underlying the different types of furnaces with a few details on ancient types.

A furnace is a contrivance in which the metallurgical operations are carried out under the influence of heat derived from either the combustion of some kind of fuel or in modern types from the heating effect of electrical current. The temperature of such a furnace varies according to its size and purpose. A furnace consists of two essential parts: a) the fire-box in which the fuel is burnt, and b) the hearth in which the actual operation is carried out. In many primitive furnaces these two parts are actually one. Many furnaces are now built with chimneys and they are also provided with some contrivance for the production of blast air if they work under "forged draught".

We can distinguish three types of metallurgical furnaces, viz. 1) those in which the fuel and the substance to be heated are in contact, 2) those in which the ore is heated by the products of combustion, and

3) those in which neither fuel nor products of combustion come into contact with the substance to be heated.

If fuel and ore or metal come into contact we speak of shaft-furnaces or hearth-furnaces. In the case of *shaft-furnaces* the height is consider-

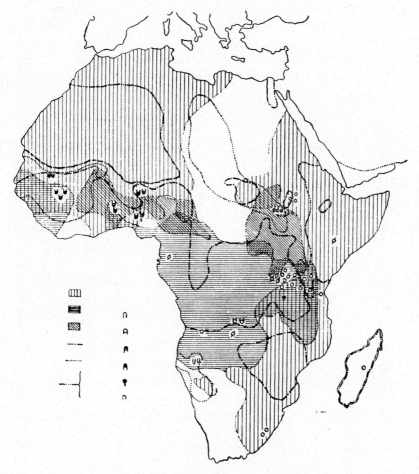

Fig. 24.
Distribution of types of bellows and furnaces in Africa
according to Frobenius (Das Unbekannte Afrika)

ably more than the diameter and two types can be distinguished. The shaft-furnaces worked with natural draught do not generally yield a very high temperature, but they are used for calcining ores, burning lime, etc. They can be used for continuous work, being fed at the top while the end-product is withdrawn from the bottom. They are also called *kilns*. Similar furnaces but used with blast air or forced draught are called *blast-furnaces*. These blast-furnaces are used for the smelting of iron, copper and lead. The ancient type had a square section, but now these furnaces, especially those used for producing iron are round. The bottom is generally conical to form a well in which the metal collects. Both kilns and blast-furnaces show a great variety of types, each appropriate to some specific purpose, each of these has some special name like "rapid cupola, fire-hearth furnace" etc.

In the case of *hearth furnaces* the height is the same or less than the diameter. They can also be worked with forced draught. Here too there is direct contact between fuel and ore and the process can be guided towards an oxidising or reducing reaction. These furnaces comprise liquation hearths, finery fires, etc. They are used for the production of lead from galena, for the production of wrought iron directly from iron ore (Catalan forge, etc.) and as a smith's hearth.

The second category of furnaces, in which the products of combustion heat the ore or metal are called *reverbatory furnaces*. They are quite modern apparatus and entirely unknown in Antiquity. They are now used for many roasting, calcining and melting processes.

The third family of furnaces protects the ore or metal from contact either with the fuel or with the products of its combustion. They are all derived from the crucible. In the case of the *crucible furnace*, the heating chamber (which may be a simple crucible!) is movable. Such a process is used in Antiquity for refining gold, for producing "wootz" steel, etc. In other, so-called *muffle furnaces*, the heating chamber is a fixed part of the structure, which may for instance be used to store crucibles during the heating period. Small models are used for testing ores and metals in the laboratory since the sixteenth century A.D. Some kinds of furnaces are built to volatilize and condense certain compounds or metals recovered from the ore. These retort furnaces are especially used in modern zinc manufacture.

In most furnaces there is certain zone in which the essential reactions take place or where the temperature is such that corrosive compounds are formed (which may again be destroyed or bound in other parts of the furnace). Such conditions determine the life of the furnace and many of the most primitive furnaces served only once. That is why we often find the remains of thousands of ancient furnaces on these smelting sites. Once, however, the furnace is built up of stone (on the inside at least) its life is considerably longer and the way is paved for the evolution of furnaces which can produce continuously.

The type of stone used in building these furnaces should be carefully selected and adjusted to the peculiarities of the ore treated. We distinguish *acid* materials such as flint, ganister, sand and fireclays, *neutral* materials such as graphite and chromite and *basic* materials such as limestone, dolomite, magnesite and bauxite.

The choice of these materials depends on the gangue of the ore and it will aid the flux in destroying the effect of the gangue on the process. In the case of acid, siliceous gangue a basic lining of the furnace will be chosen and renewed after the furnace has worked for some time.

When we turn to ancient furnaces we find that this truth has been realised quite early and that their construction ranges from the very simple open-hearth-furnaces to the precursor of the blast-furnace, the Stückofen. Simple types often had a very long life if they were suited to the particular use and the rather mild demands of the early metallurgist, but it was realised that furnace lining lengthens their life. Thus certain types of furnaces were developed by Illyrians and Celts and taken over by the Romans, whose simple "lip-fires" survived until the puddling process was invented in the XVIIIth century. The Romans merely increased number and size of the furnaces but they were singularly uninventive as to new types. The original bloomery fire of the Celtic iron-smiths was long in use side by side with the larger and better Stückofen or shaft-furnace, which latter type survived until the thirteenth and fourteenth century A.D. in Central Europe and even later in the North.

It is yet impossible to trace many of the older types, as we possess so few data on furnaces in the Ancient Near East. Gowland held that two centres were responsible for the evolution of different furnace types, viz. the Sudan and Nubia and the Near East (Asia Minor). He was wrong about the former centre, the date of which is no longer believed to be much earlier than 700 B.C., but he is probably quite right about Asia Minor, which played so important a part in the technique of many metals and the mountain-region between Mediterranean and Caspian Sea was probably responsible for the development of many furnace types. If we see among the scanty data such specialised furnaces at Gerar in the fourteenth century B.C. far earlier than the development of iron metallurgy in Europe, we may regard these as a proof for Gowland's theory.

The early development of copper, gold, silver and lead metallurgy in the Near East undoubtedly led to a vast amount of experience in smelting and furnace building, so that it was comparatively easy to adapt certain types to the new smelting technique of iron. Further analysis of metal remains and slags will no doubt cast further light on the temperature and efficiency of these early furnaces, as well as on the connection between the furnaces of the Near East and those of prehistoric Europe. There are certain signs that the gradual evolution of iron smelting furnaces from prototypes destined for the treatment of copper ores took place in different regions locally. Thus there

Fig. 25.
Clay crucibles found in El Argar, Spain
(after Gowland, JRAI XLII, 1912)

seems to be a link between the older Schmaltalgraben copper furnace and the later Tarxdorff iron furnace. But the existence of pre-Roman specialised furnaces in the Near East gives support to Gowland's theory of a development of the furnace in these regions and spread of its construction with the metal techniques.

A type of furnaces quite common in Antiquity is the *roasting fur-nace*, which was used in the case of iron ores to drive off the water and make the ore more porous and in the case of galena and pyrites to expell the larger part of the sulphur and arsenic from the ore. The most primitive roasting furnaces were just heaps of ore on fuel (wood), but in prehistoric Mitterberg long narrow buildings were used for the roasting of the copper ore, in which a bed of slag carried the

charcoal on which the ore was heaped. The Romans used either large
bowl-shaped hearths (sometimes even equipped with tapping chan-
nels!) and also round open-hearths. In Hüttenberg roasting furnaces
and smelting furnaces were built in pairs, both being of the bowl-
furnace type. Generally speaking we can say that the most suitable
types of smelting furnaces were selected and used for roasting.

The most primitive and probably the original "smelting furnace"
is the *bon-fire* or open hearth fire, as this was only suitable for some
very readily reducible ores, we do not often find their remains, though
they were long used for the reheating of blooms, etc. in the smithy.
The most primitive type generally found, because it had such a long
life, is the *bowl-furnace*, a clay-lined hole in the ground which, when
blast air was used was provided with a tuyère blowing over the rim
on the contents. The furnaces of Hüttenberg consisting of pairs of
bowl-furnaces seem to have combined roasting and smelting in one
pair of furnaces, the latter operation being conducted in the larger
one. This type of furnace was very common in the Ancient Near East
as it still is with many primitive smiths. It is mentioned by Hesiod (34)
and it was used by the Romans side by side with more sophisticated
types. The German bog-ore smelting continued to use it for many
centuries.

The bowl-furnace was the ancestor of many new types, one of
which was the figure-of-eight furnace, consisting of two bowl-furnaces
sunk in the ground, of which the front one seemed to have received
the slag from the other. This furnace was fitted with a hood-chimney
and probably the blast was not introduced at the base but continued
to be applied over the rim. This type of furnace, possibly a Roman
invention, was not much used afterwards.

The bowl-furnace was not very efficient, the chief waste arises from
the total loss of the heat escaping from the zone of combustion and
from the great loss of metal in the slag. Therefore, the *pot-furnace* is
an improvement. The neck of the bowl-furnace was contracted so as
to form a dug-in pot, blast and tapping hole were built in at the base,
but the walls remained of clay, the furnace did not yet rise above the
ground. This development can be traced in its different stages in
Central Europe quite clearly, for instance in the earlier furnaces at
Lausitz and in Silesia. In Tarxdorff a special hour-glass type is found,
consisting of two chambers above each other, of which the top chamber serves to hold the bloom, the lower chamber collects the slag.
Other varieties of this Tarxdorff furnace were found at other sites.

The pot-furnace seems to have been in general use in England, and possibly in Bavaria too, in Roman times.

A further development of the pot-furnace is the Jura-type, built in the hill-side, which is also found in Carinthia. They are mostly vertical holes in the hill close to the face of a steep bank, with lateral apertures near the base, to which wind is admitted through a horizontal channel lined with stones. They seem to have been worked with natural draught, though free-standing furnaces of this type would be more suitable for natural blast.

Fig. 26.
Bronze Age anvil found in Augsdorf near the Wörthersee, Austria
(Museum of Klagenfurt)

Another development of the bowl-furnace is the *ditch-furnace*, of which the sloping types seem to be the earlier, the horizontal form the later one. They were mostly used for roasting and they are the ancestors the *roasting-hearth*.

Further types of the bowl-furnace were lined with stones and the walls were raised above the ground. Some of these stone-walled bowl-furnaces were covered up after filling them with ore and fuel, such covered types are still in use in Madagascar and may be the ancestors of the cupola-furnaces of much later date, which at the same time remind us of the old type of baking furnace in use in the Near East.

If the bowl was simply lined with stone, we get the *bloomery fire* from which the later *Catalan forge* and *Corsican forge* descend and the *hearth-furnace* to which class the liquation hearth and the finery fire belong. Furnaces with a fore-hearth also seem to descend from the bloomery-fire, possibly combined with the figure-of-eight furnace.

Most of these types have separate chimneys built over or next to them. But by raising the walls over the bowl a structure containing both furnace and chimney was obtained which could be worked with natural or artificial blast like the bloomery fire and its descendants. This is the *shaft-furnace*, which in its primitive forms is called *Osmund*

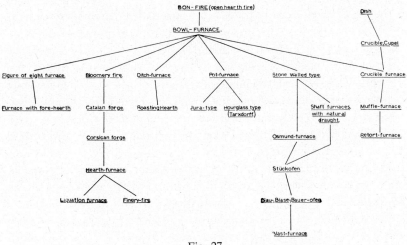

Fig. 27.
The evolution of the metallurgical furnace

furnace, or if double the latter's size *Stückofen*, from which type through such varieties as the Bauer-, Blau- and Blase-ofen the *blast furnace* was evolved. The blast furnace is now the most typical iron smelting apparatus, but many types such as cupola-furnaces, the rapid cupola or the fire-hearth furnace are used for preparing other metals as well and more primitive forms were applied to the same use in Antiquity, though generally with natural draught if such easily smelted metals as copper or lead were prepared. It is, however, very difficult to generalise, as ancient metallurgy was still trying out types of furnaces and many combinations are known which disappeared again in the centuries to come. Gilles traced the gradual development of the prehistoric bee-hive furnace through the shaft-furnaces to the early blast-furnace of the twelfth century A.D., but there are still many gaps which research will fill up.

Transitional types from bowl-furnaces to shaft-furnaces can be observed in prehistoric Europe in Carinthia, Epernay and the Jura. Types partly built into the hill-side and not yet free-standing, more or less constructed round the charge, were found at Eisenberg. These shaft-furnaces usually built of stones and lined with refractory clay seem to come to central Europe from the Eastern Mediterranean at the end of the Bronze Age. They are found in very early remains at Mitterberg and Velem St. Vid, though the old bowl-furnaces remain supreme in the Eastern Alps. Shaft-furnaces at Hüttenberg and Lölling were used with artificial blast quite early, but as often old furnaces were torn down to build new ones, the dating of these remains is often very difficult. At Laurion the lead furnaces are shaft-furnaces, and the type is common in Siphnos in the sixth century. Gradually they are improved especially the Stückofen used for the production of iron. This is clear when the Hallstatt furnaces of Neuwied are compared with the La Tène types from Siegerland. The Celts developed a type with a chimney and tapping hole. Other types have been found at Bibracte, Cartagena and in Etruria and they grow very common in Roman times.

Mingazzini reported on two bronze-models of what seems to be an early type of shaft-furnace found in Sardinia, which earlier generations had believed to be models of sanctuaries of some kind.

These Roman types are usually small cylindrical shafts of 3'—4' high and working with artificial blast through tuyères. In Populonia both natural and artificial blast is used and some types with 6 blast-holes have been found. In Moravia the type is used continuously from Hallstatt times upto the tenth century A.D.

As water-driven bellows increase the quantity of blast-air, the height of the furnace can be increased and the medieval blast-furnace is evolved which is able to produce cast-iron, a substance unknown to Antiquity.

In Roman times such special furnaces as welding furnaces, examples of which were found so much earlier at Gerar, Palestine, now spread over the Empire (Corstipitum, etc.).

The future student of this problem will do well to remember that we have pointed out the profound influence of the potter's furnace on early metallurgy. Early Susan pottery was burnt at temperatures ranging from 900 to 1200° C. though temperatures as high as 1400° C. do not seem to have been reached in these early times. We must also remember that baking furnaces (for bread, etc.) and glazing-furnaces were well known in these early times and that there is almost certainly a bond between these types and their evolution.

From reliefs of the Old Kingdom period we know that a small portable (charcoal) fire with checks was in use in Egypt, especially by goldsmiths. This is probably the brazier called '*ḫ* (H.W.B. I, 223) which corresponds with the Coptic *âsh*, which is often translated with *kaminos* (furnace). Apart from thist he Egyptians had different kinds of furnaces, the potter's kiln *t3* (HWB 228) mentioned in very old texts the baking furnace *trr* (HWB V, 318) (Coptic *trir*) and the furnace

Fig. 28.
Smithy of the primitive metalworkers of Bḥapath, India
Note the dish-bellows and the combination of modern and primitive tools

of the metallurgists *ḥrj.t* (HWB III, 148) (Coptic *ḥro*) are both late terms which occur only at the end of the New Kingdom, though the appliances were certainly known earlier. A general Coptic term for furnace, *intok*, seems to have been derived from an Egyptian *pr(nt)k3*, literally "house of the burning".

The ancient Sumerian sign for "smith" is nothing but a brazier (SIMUG) which is exactly the same as the modern "manqal" still used in Iraq. The smelting furnace was called GIR₄ in Sumerian, "keru, kûru" in Accadian though the term UDUN or Accadian "utunu" is also used. The latter term which is related to the Hebrew attûn seems to denote more especially a kiln such as is used for burning lime or bricks (35). The Bible uses the word "kûr" in several passages (36) or "kibšân" which seems to denote the smelting furnace (37), while "kûr" is the refining furnace. Apart from these the Bible also mentions the baker's oven ("tannûr") (38), the potter's furnace (39) and the blacksmith's furnace (40). The Mesopotamian texts mention furnaces for smelting gold, etc. but they give no details of their construction, at least in the case of metallurgical furnaces and therefore we depend entirely on the finds of such furnaces at Ur, etc. None of these have been described in sufficient detail to enable us to express a further opinion of their efficiency. But apart from these different smelting furnaces we find *crucibles* in general use in Antiquity. The Egyptian sign for copper ("bi3") is accompanied by a determinative which pictures a crucible and crucibles are shown in mural paintings and reliefs. Examples were found in Sinai and elsewhere, clay crucibles used in iron manufacture were found by Sayce at Kerma (Sudan). Eighteenth dynasty reliefs depict the casting of bronze doors from crucibles, which are about 5" high and 5" in diameter. Clay crucibles were also found in Mesopotamia (Ur, etc.). Crucibles were found among the remains of Troy II and a lump of stamped silver from Zendjirli (700 B.C.) retains the form of the bottom of a crucible. Herodotus mentions the melting down of gold and silver in crucibles ("pithos") (41) as practised by the Persian treasury. Crucibles have been found at Gezer, they are called "alîl" and the "fining pot" mentioned in different passages of the Bible (42) is either a crucible or a cupel.

It is quite probable that the earliest *crucible* was a smelting pan of refractory clay or sand mixed with clay used for the melting of metals in a pottery kiln. Both crucible and cupel were developed as the smelting melting and refining of metals came to be more known and the proper refractory ingredients were soon found in a world which had a thorough knowledge of the potter's art. Of course each of these crucibles could be heated separately in a bowl-furnace or even an open hearth fire if the required temperature was not too high, but as more difficult operations such as the preparation of steel were carried out in crucibles, the experience gained in glass-making, in pottery and in the construction of bowl-furnaces was combined to construct *crucible-furnaces*, in which the crucible protected its contents against the fire and other possible sources of impurities. A further development was the *muffle-furnace*, in which the heating chamber is fixed but admits the introduction of one or more crucibles. This furnaces was known to Agricola and his generation and was already used for assaying in those days. As far as we know the Romans have not used the muffle-furnace, it was invented later.

But the Romans were well informed on the proper materials for making cupels and crucibles and the selection of the proper refractory clay. Pliny (43) mentions "tasconium (from the Spanish *tasco*: crucible or cupel), a white earth-like potter's clay, which is the only substance which can endure the combined efforts of the blast, the heat of the fire and the glowing charge of the crucible". The term *kálathos* (44) seems to denote the melting crucible, another term, *periodos*, said by some authors to denote the smelting crucible for the preparation of crucible steel, can not be traced.

2. *The Tools*

Even the primitive smith could not work without tools, but they need not be very sophisticated, for the ancient smiths produced their best work with very simple tools. When discussing the story of gold we will have occasion to point to the interesting studies by Bergsøe on pre-Columbian Indian metallurgy and a quotation from the native author Garcillasso de la Vega will show how in the New World too the smiths often worked with very primitive tools. In his chapter on the arts and crafts of the Incas he says: "The gold- and silversmiths had no anvils made of iron or any other metal. This was because they could not produce iron, though they had iron-mines (sic!). In their language iron is called "quillay". They use hard stones of a yellow-green colour as anvils, they polish them on each other and regard them as one of their most treasured possessions.

Neither did they possess handled hammers. They use tools of copper or bronze in the form of dice with rounded corners and of different sizes. Files or engraving needles were unknown, neither had they bellows, but they blew the fire with copper tubes of half an ell or less in length, which had a small opening at the end, through which the air was forced out with great speed. Sometimes eight, ten or twelve men were blowing the fire as required. Neither were they able to make tongs to pick the metal out of the fire. This they did with two pieces of wood and then they placed the hot metal on wet sand, which lay before them; there they turned it round and round before they dared to touch it. Notwithstanding these difficulties they produced beautiful metalwork and even objects, that were hollow inside (hollow castings!). They also knew that the vapours of metals were unhealthy and therefore they never had their smithies or smelting sites indoors but always on an open space in the courtyard."

Unfortunately the history of tools is still a gravely neglected subject. A few picture books of early tools were published like Sir W. Flinders Petrie's Tools and Weapons, but these contribute little to an understanding of the development and handling of such tools. The only attempt at a history of tools in the Ancient Near East (45) is unfortunately based on untrustworthy or out of date information culled from books by Feldhaus and Neuburger.

Much can be learned from the ethnologist's study of primitive tools. The strange fact emerges, that in principle most of our tools go back to the Palaeolithic or early Neolithic age, the cutting edge, its position in relation to the handle (and hand) and many other details being the same in the early stone, flint or obsidian tool as in the modern steel tool (46). Hence the story of tools will have to be built up from the study of properly dated pieces from excavations and museums, and their handling can still be studied in primitive smithies, which prove to be well arranged and properly planned for the execution of the various operations of the primitive smith. This can be seen from illustrating the plan of a Bikom smithy. A number of such detailed studies is already available (47), but a synthesis is not yet possible. Gordon Childe attempted such a synthesis (48) and the following extract of his lecture on the archaeological significance of metalworking techniques held in 1956 may show what important conclusions can be drawn already from the few data in our possession:

"The early development of the saw directly affected carpentry, stone-working, architecture and, by making wheels possible, revolutionized transport and thereby other industries. Though wheels and ploughs could have been made with stone tools, neither is known before the beginnings of metalworking. Ashlar masonry was probably impossible without a saw, and seals were normally engraved using metal drills and gravers. Nearly as old is the cauldron, which made possible cooking by suspension.

Later, though still in the Bronze Age, came nails, wire, springs, hinges and adjustable compasses. With the Iron Age came tongs, shears, scythes, horseshoes, tyres and ploughshares. Metal further encouraged the specialization of tools, but the general spread of its influence was limited by cost. Thus flint sickles were usual until the Late Bronze Age and log-cabins do not appear in Europe until after the cheap socketed celt. No intensification of forest clearance is noticed until the Iron Age when, in Norway for example, the first smeltidg of bog iron ore is followed by a great expansion in this

respect. Food production was then also greatly affected by the introduction of iron scythes and other agricultural implements".

In some cases it was possible to find the set of tools a smith worked
with. Gordon Childe drew our attention to part of the furniture of a
Bronze Age smithy found in Inshoch Wood near Inverness which
consisted of a small socketed hammer, an anvil made of a rich 30%
tin-bronze and a broken spear-head, part of the smith's stock of scrap
metal (49).

Maryon, to whom we owe many careful studies of the tools and

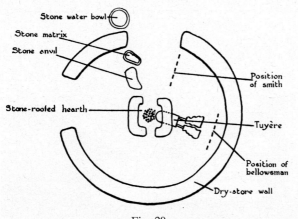

Fig. 29.
Plan of a smithy in Tula (Nigeria)

methods the early smiths used has ventured a reconstruction of the
inventory of Bronze Age workshops from the finds and the methods
used in metalwork of that period (50). He holds that this was "a simple
workshop with a paved hearth, casting pit, pounding stone with
stone mullers, anvil, a light bronze hammer, a mallet of stag's horn,
a perforated stone hammer, a cake of lead and a small L-shaped anvil
of bronze, square-shanked flint chisels and chasing and repoussé tools.
Here the smith could practise smelting and casting, produce sheet
metal and wire, solder and make repoussé work."

Leaving aside such well known instruments as the saw, the chisel
and the adze or axe we will give a few details on some other implements such as hammer, tongs and files.

Though the mallet was used very early in the carpenter's trade, no
longhandled hammer was used in metallurgy in early Egypt. Practically all the copper and bronze objects were shaped with stone

hammers without a handle. These polished stone hammers held in the first were also used to beat gold-leaf and similar thin sheets of metal. The hammer-stone developed into the long-handled hammer, the ancestor of our sledgehammer, in the Iron Age only, when the head was also made of iron and no longer of stone. Coghlan (51) has traced the history of this perforated stone hammer down in Ireland where it was early associated with metal work among the tools of the copper-smith and the gold-smith, indeed with any worker in sheet metal and hence it seems to go back to the Early Bronze Age at least. Stone

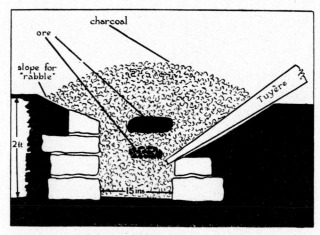

Fig. 30.
Forge of a Bikom smith (After Jeffreys)

hammers of this type were found at Troy I, followed by a series of copper, bronze and finally iron, sub-rectangular sledges which continue down to the present steel age.

In Mesopotamia stone hammers were used originally, some beautiful small haematite hammers have been found. Later, however, copper and bronze hammer-heads were used, and as soon as commercial iron appeared iron hammers. Several objects resembling the heads of sledge hammers were found in Assur-nasir-pal's palace at Nimrud.

The same sequence of stone and iron hammers is found in Palestine, Malta and Crete, but in Cyprus bronze hammers were found in a bronze factory at Enkomi. Bronze tools (axe, adze, drill and dowels) are used in Mycenaean shipbuilding. Anvils are usually made of stone and later on of iron. Some anvils are hardly distinguishable from hammers and the nail-like anvils of Africa probably find their proto-types in the

Near East. The Greeks had small hammers and larger sledge-hammers, while the Romans possessed different types each specially adapted to the farriers, coopers, carpenters, and other trades, and knew several forms of adze-hammers. Many tools were adapted from the Celtic smiths.

Other important metallurgical implements are tongs and forceps. Tongs work on the hinge-principle, forceps are made by bending a piece of flexible metal until the ends can be forced to touch. Different types of tongs, forceps and tweezers were found in Egypt and they still retain their spring perfectly. Some New Kingdom examples are in the British Museum. The forceps are undoubtedly the older type, they are depicted on Old Kingdom reliefs. Round-tipped copper tongs have been found in a glass-factory at El-Amarna. In the Iron Age both types are made of iron and they become fairly common, examples from the clasical world and from prehistoric Europe are well-known. Still the early metallurgist was able to work without them using green twigs or pieces of wood as the African smiths still do. Both the jointed tongs with two jaws and the one-piece pincers or forceps seem to be foreign imports in Negro Africa, even of late date, simple wooden forms are used very frequently as they are in primitive Indian metallurgy.

Bronze files were known in Old Kingdom Egypt, but the first iron file is that belonging to the Assyrian set of tools found at Thebes and dated 666 B.C. Bronze files were common in Antiquity but later they were quickly replaced by iron and steel files.

Maryon (52) has pointed out that the decoration of gold and bronze ornaments and weapons with patterns of incised lines or dots show that the smiths used different types of "tracers" (chisel-shaped punches such as chisel, punches and awls) and "trunnion-anvils" to obtain such effects. The charcoal fire was used for welding, soldering and other operations.

These few lines may serve to show that rich material is still awaiting a future student though the evidence is of more importance to the history of metal-work than to the evolution of metallurgy itself.

3. *Metallurgical techniques*

A few words remain to be said on the *working of metals*. We can not enter into details on this subject, partly for the lack of proper analytical data and other evidence, partly because many of these processes do no longer belong to the production of metals, our proper subject, but to the history of metallurgical art, a chapter of the history of art in general. Still it may prove useful for our further discussions to present a general outline of the different processes and to classify them according to their technical principles.

A number of older publications are still of value for survey of the techniques used by the ancient smith (53), but of late Maryon has contributed (54) to a more systematic treatment of our subject, which provides an excellent start for the future student of these techniques.

Sometimes metals were used in their *native state*, but this practically limits their application to ornamental uses. In the overwhelming majority of cases the metal is worked by some process, the earliest group of processes being those of mechanical working and heat treatment. *Heat treatment processes* include simple heating (for instance before hammering), glowing, case-hardening (cementation or carburisation, so important in iron technology, where we shall discuss its merits and effects), hardening, tempering or annealing (used especially in the case of copper and iron) and quenching (so important for the preparation of steel). Subjecting a metal to such an amount of heat, that it melts, is the first step in the important process of *casting* (55).

Bronze Age casting methods were far from primitive, such processes as "casting on" being neatly handled. The smith watched his crucibles with molten copper or bronze carefully and avoided oxydation and the formation of a porous bronze with a high cuprous-oxide content.

The earliest form of casting was *open mould casting* using stone, loam or clay moulds and even wooden moulds in the case of making tin coins (56). Hodges reported on the casting methods of Bronze Age Ireland:

"The finishing of sandstone or steatite moulds harked back to Neolithic stone working, and the form of cast implements was dictated by the limitations of carving in stone. Clay moulds usually consist of an inner (fine) and outer (coarse) sheath. Particle size and mineral analysis of moulds (for swords) found in Lough Eskragh has shown that the clay in both sheaths came from the same deposit, but that the inner sheath had been made of levigated material, as used in making slips and thus showing the potter's hand. The patterns for such moulds were often made of wood (as found at Tobermore, Co. Derry). Wood grain is evident in some bronze implements, and casting is here dependent on wood-carving technique. Casting in two-piece moulds made of bronze, and running-on, appear to owe nothing to other technologies, although bronze shields and early cauldrons, for which there are no bronze prototypes on the Continent, may be copies of leatherwork."

Sand casting was not practised in Antiquity, this is an invention of the eighteenth century. The moulds were either temporary or permanent. The use of moulds of several parts, valved and closed moulds comes later. Permanent open and closed moulds of stone (steatite, etc.) were generally used for small mass products such as votive and ornamental objects, and coins. Temporary moulds were often formed over stone models.

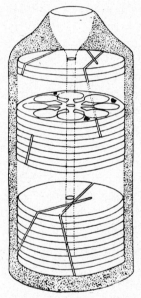

Fig. 31.
An Indian coin mould

Piaskowski described an Iron Age bronze foundry in Poland, where the metal was cast in clay moulds from clay laddles with a capacity of 40—60 gr of bronze heated at 600—900° C. Three to five foundries in the settlement produced bronze ornaments at a rate of a total annual weight of 30 Kg mostly by the cire-perdue method of casting. In some cases as in ancient Indian coin-casting most intricate moulds were used.

Open mould casting was soon replaced by a far better process, the *cire-perdue process* or wax casting process (57) which has become of great importance in industry shortly ago. At the same time we see a gradual tendency to replace solid casting by hollow casting, the core used often being made of oiled sand or a bituminous mixture (especially in Mesopotamia). Temporary moulds were made of loam or clay here again sand casting came only very late. *Valve moulds*, moulds with permanent parts seem to have been used in classical Antiquity, their use was part of the everyday routine of the metallurgist of the tenth century A.D. (Theophilus III. 84) and its proficiency shows that it was already known and used for many centuries. It is, however, doubtful whether metal moulds were already used in Antiquity and it is of course quite certain that *chill casting* and *steel casting* were still unknown. Among the metals cast in Antiquity we find, gold, silver, lead, copper and its alloys such as bronze, brass, lead- and antimony-bronzes. Cast-iron was probably unknown in Antiquity as the furnace temperature for the proper carburizing and melting of crude iron were unattainable. Apart from the heat treatment and casting processes both machining and mechanical working processes are known in Antiquity.

The *mechanical working processes* deform the metal, the *machining processes* take away parts of the metal with tools. The most important mechanical operations are hammering and forging, the latter operation embracing not only plain forging, but also forging with a mandrel, swaging, stamping and punching, the latter two operations being often used in coining. Like all mechanical operations these treatments can be executed with cold or heated metals. Other mechanical operations are bending, including the making of rims, cutting and spinning (as often used with precious metals). Akin to spinning is the modern operation of rolling. Press operations include raising (stamping out or bending in), jumping, drawing down, flattening, shearing, blanking and ironing. Drawing tubes from metal was of course unknown in Antiquity, but it may be that the drawing of wire was known at that period. However, ancient wire is very often cut from metal sheet or foil and hammered (sometimes in V-shaped stone moulds) (58) we very often still recognize the peculiar square section of such cut wire. Gold, silver and copper wire were used very frequently in Antiquity, often the wire is plated before use. True drawn wire is said to have been found in Troy II, but confirmation is still lacking. Multiple wire or wire coiled into spirals is very frequent in ancient jewelry and copper wire was used in Saqqarah (27th century B.C.) for attaching glazed tiles in king Zoser's pyramid. Cutting metal was of course a very common operation. Many of the *machining processes* were known too such as reaming, boring, planing, grinding and smoothing, scraping, drilling and filing. Even turning seems to have been practised but milling seems to have been unknown.

Different *joining methods* were practised. *Riveting and caulking* were known quite early in ancient metallurgy. The plates of the statue of king Pepi of Egypt were riveted with copper bolts, tang and rivet were used in that country for axes upto the twelfth dynasty, when casting was introduced for this kind of work. Even the earlier iron objects are often rivetted with bronze nails. The pieces of larger bronze and copper objects were rivetted all over the Ancient Near East since the third millenium and often already earlier. Both *soldering and welding* are further ancient methods of joining. Though these terms are often used very losely, soldering should be used only in the case of the use of any metal or alloy whose melting point is lower than that of the metal or alloy to be soldered, which may be run between the parts to be joined to fasten them together. Two types of solder are known, viz. soft solder and hard solder, a classification based upon the melting point of the solder. Ancient soft solder are very often lead alloys, among which alloys of lead and tin are very popular up to the present time. Hard solders may be alloys of the type of brass or alloys containing silver, etc. Solders of the latter type were often used by ancient jewellers, natural alloys such as electron being often used in Ancient Egypt. Mötefindt claims that soldering was an Egyptian invention, but since very early examples have been found in Mesopotamia. Gold beads from the Royal Graves at Ur were found to be soldered, the Entemena vase is an example of the soldering of silver with copper, other objects (from AlUbaid) were soldered with lead. Soldering copper or bronze does not become general until the classical period, though a few Old Kingdom examples are known soft solder does not seem to have been used very early. Maryon, who studied this technique very carefully, came to the following conclusions (59):

"Joining pieces of metal can be achieved by

a. Soldering. This may be divided into: (1) hard soldering on gold, electrum, silver, copper, bronze, and iron, and (2) soft soldering.

b. Welding. This may be divided into: (1) pressure welding, cold or hot, without fusion; (2) sweating together, or surface welding, without pressure; and (3) fusion welding, a term which includes autogenous welding, burning together, fusing together, electric welding, acetylene welding, etc."

Observation of the earlier mobility of some (that is, the more impure) metals during a melting run may have suggested the process of soldering. Hard soldering (above 550°) dates back to 3400 B.C. and was common practice in Ur; soft soldering was known before 2500 B.C. Extremely fine granulation work was produced by the Greeks and Etruscans in the sixth century B.C. Often wrongly described as 'welded', non-ferrous metal joints were invariably soldered, with the exception of a set of small gold boxes (Early Iron Age) showing cold lap welds. Repairs were often made by 'burning' (or running) together: the fracture was, in effect, enveloped in a clay mould and fresh metal was cast on.

The oldest metal statues were made of copper sheets either riveted or nailed to wooden cores, and riveting was also common in domestic ware and for decoration. Bowls were made from early times by sinking (hammering on the inside) or raising (from thin sheet by hammering on the outside), and there are thousands of early examples of repoussé, chasing and engraving, as well as of work done with tracer or punch, or in high relief. All these processes require much annealing and the products show that this was well understood. Other methods of decoration were 'inlay', that is, the tracing of a recess into which a piece of another metal was inserted and fixed, and 'overlay', which involves attachment by cold flow to a surface that is merely roughened and not recessed.

Ferrous (true) welding is in evidence from the beginning, as in a tiny model head-rest of Tutankhamen (1360 B.C.). Warriors of Asshur-nazir-pal had iron swords (ninth century B.C.), and the Luristan finds (1200—900 B.C.) show some steel containing 0.5 per cent of carbon, demonstrating that forging and carburization developed quickly. Ultimately welding also came to be used successfully in massive structures such as the Colossus of Rhodes (280 B.C.; $7\frac{1}{2}$ tons of iron frame) and the Delhi pillar (A.D. 310; 6 tons), as well as in delicate work, involving the 'piling' of many sheets into a composite laminate, and developing into pattern-welding.

Hence the ancients did not use cold *pressure-welding* and hot pressure-welding only in some cases with iron, because copper, bronze or brass never join properly this way. They applied *fusion welding* only in the form of "casting on", e.g. either by preheating the edges of the pieces to be joined and pouring molten metal in the welding zone, or by laying a piece of weld metal on the edges to be joined and heating them together with a blowpipe until they became fused. Such methods were already in use during the Bronze Age though not for fine metal-work or jewelry, this was the common method of manufacturing lead water-pipes in Roman times. There are also such methods as *brazing* (hard-soldering iron, copper, brass or bronze by means of a low-fusing brass solder, mostly of copper and zinc) and *sweating* (joining two surfaces already coated with a film of solder), but it is not clear whether such methods were already in use during these early days. Special joining methods were used in *granulation* work. The Columbian Indians "sintered" gold and platinum grains together with a blow-pipe. The ancients of the Old World used colloid soldering for their granulation work, e.g. a copper salt plus a flux like borax, which permitted soldering at low temperatures. For soldering jewelry and the like their charcoal fire and also oil lamps (for quite small work) were the source of heat. The real autogenous welding with the gas blow-pipe belongs to the nineteenth century. Apart from the classes of operations mentioned there are many *decorative and ornamental processes* which figure largely in art objects and the story of which forms part of the history of ancient art. There is the old process of beating, beaten copper and gold leaf being very old both in Egypt and Mesopotamia. Other beaten work includes the beating of copper leaf or sheet over a moulded bituminous core such as the famous Sumerian lion heads and others. The beating of gold leaf in Egypt differed from that in Mesopotamia for in the latter country no gold-beater's skin was used but the gold was beaten between two stones, haematite hammers such as found at Ur may have served for this purpose too. Beaten bronze and copper strips figure largely in Assyrian and Egyptian decorative art. Other decorative operations are chasing (engraving), cutting (incising), drilling (punctuating), embossing (raising in relief), moulding (shaping), punching or stamping, raising, repoussé (chased relief) and many others. Some of the most important surface treatments of metals are encrusting, cloisonné or inlay-work, ornamentation, brazing, plating and enamelling (60). Many of these techniques were known in Antiquity. Assyrian bronze objects were embossed over clay cores and the famous treasure of the Oxus contains many embossed gold and silver objects. Repoussé work was known in ancient Egypt and Mesopotamia, the technique was used in Crete and Phoenicia and it was well known in Neolithic Europe. Punching belongs to the stock in trade of the Mesopotamian artists, actual punches have been found at Tell Halaf and are said to date from the early third millennium. It is used in Egypt, though not frequently until later periods but this technique is quite common in the Aegean. *Cloisonné* work was found at Ur but remains rare in these regions. It is, however, quite common in Egyptian jewelry of the XIIth dynasty onwards, and the art was practised in Sidon and Tyre from 2000 B.C. onwards. Plating, if we mean applying sheet metal to wood and other materials, is a very early technique but true plating, the covering of a metal surface by another metal is not so common. Still in the Gudea period copper was plated with gold and the plating of silver and copper with gold was quite well known in Egypt and Mesopotamia at an early date.

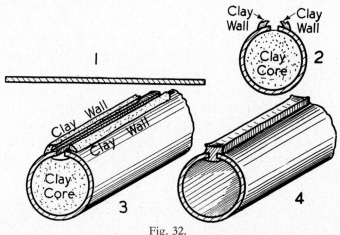

Fig. 32.
How a Roman lead pipe was soldered

The earliest cloisonné work was made by soldering wires to a metal base thus forming little cells to be filled with enamel. The later champlevé technique, said to have started in India or China around 800—850 A.D.) formed these cells by gouging out part of the metal and thus leaving ridges to contain the enamel.

Inlay work was popular as early as the Bronze Age but it spread very quickly in the Iron Age especially among the tribes living on the fringe of the Roman world in the fourth century A.D., when iron knives and the like are decorated with stars and circles of inlaid bronze. The inlay was hammered into previously prepared grooves or a sheet of inlay metal was beaten into the body, which was previously scored with the pattern, and then cut away so that the body surface underneath showed up the design. After the transition period this art reappears again in seventh and eighth-century Frankish art and in Viking objects.

The older *niello*-technique used silver sulphide for inlay work, it could be properly moulded below its high melting point (835° C), subsequently to be gently heated and burnished. After the eleventh century A.D. more easily fusible mixtures of the sulphides of silver, copper and lead were used for this type of inlay-work.

There were several methods of obtaining colour effects on the surface of metal objects, one being the "mise en couleur" process by which the baser metals are dissolved out of the surface of cast gold by a corrosive paste, fusing the surface with a blow-pipe followed by polishing. Such techniques were known to Negro goldsmiths as well.

The later iron swords have attractive "damascene" patterns which were due to the technique of manufacturing and which were later obtained on purpose. The early iron of North Germany and Scandinavia was made from bog-iron ores, having a high phosphorus content, so that they can be reduced at low temperatures. The result, however, was a very soft iron product, too soft for practical use. Only when steely iron, or steel, which could be hardened, was employed as it was by the Romans, could efficient weapons be made. So the smith tested iron from every available source, forging and welding it; heating, quenching and tempering it, until he found a steely iron which would stand up to its work. He would then also decorate not only the handle and scabbard but the very blade itself with inlays of silver, copper or gold, sometimes building up the actual fabric of the sword with strips of steel, twisted or plain, all welded together. Maryon examined a sword of the Nydam type composed of (a) two cutting edges, (b) a separate core, and (c) on either side of the blade four rods or bundles of strips, each rod first twisted, the left straight, alternately, for a repeat of about $1\frac{1}{6}''$. Each rod or bundle appearing on both side of the blade. Hence the sword was made up of strips of metal, cutting edge, core and twisted strips, all being welded together into one sword blade with a typical surface pattern.

Maryon examined another sword with letters forming an inscription. The letters were built up from a number of short lengths of iron rod, each about $\frac{3}{4}''$ long. The smith made a deep chisel-cut to mark the exact position of each part of a letter and then heated the blade white hot. With his tongs he lead the little iron rod over the chisel-cut, and struck it with a blow with his hammer so that the cold iron was driven into the surface of the blade, which was now reheated to welding heat (say 1300° C) and the safety of the inlay was assured by careful hammering. Anstee reported on a test to produce such pattern-welded iron swords with simple means: "All the work was carried out single-handed under primitive conditions, using a small forge with Chinese-type box bellows, hammer, tongs, vice and a crude anvil. Supplies of home-made charcoal were insufficient (about two hundred-weight would be required for one sword) and coke was used in all cases except three.

The first six experiments served to eliminate various points of technique as being impossible or unnecessary. No. 7 produced a specimen sword in which the various stages were left unfinished to show the details of the method. No. 9, a similar but fully finished sword, was produced as follows. Three rods of good, Victorian wrought iron, each 0.22 in. in diameter, were forged out into strips in which the ratio of width to thickness was 9 : 1. The strips were laid flat one on the other and forge-twisted into a two-start screw, two 'filler rods' of square section being at the same time incorporated into the valleys. The resulting composite bar was flanked on either side by a straight packing rod, and by another composite bar of opposite twist the units of which had undergone a home-made case-hardening treatment. This assembly was forge-welded together, using a sliding wire-clip and proceeding in inch-heats, to give a triple band of characteristic herring-bone pattern, tapering to a point at one end where it had been gripped by the tongs.

Cutting edges were welded on to this core by doubling a forged half-inch rod around the point. Fullering, final forging, and grinding completed the sword blade for which a hilt, scabbard and belt fittings were also made. The total working time was seventy-five hours, of which forty-three had been spent on the blade, involving 128 separate forging and welding heats. The finished blade weighed 1 lb. 10 oz.; 1 lb. 3 oz. had been removed from the rough forging by grinding, and the total cross-sectional area of the original core-assembly had been reduced by 70 per cent. The work showed that any of the patterns observed on ancient swords could be produced in this manner by twist-welding and grinding".

Apart from these techniques there are the *finishing operations*. Apart from such techniques as etching, varnishing, brushing, pickling and cleaning with a sand-blast (the last two are quite modern) metal surfaces may be finished by *abrasion*, that is cleaned and polished using abrasive materials like sand and emery with leather-covered or wooden wheels (cutting down or buffing as the jeweller calls these techniques) and with covered or solid wheels (grinding).

A second class of finishing operations, *polishing*, is effected by very fine abrasives with cushioned wheels of felt, chamois, etc. These include the techniques called glazing, dollying, colouring, finishing and lapping. Finally the surface may be finished with steel or agate burnishers, an operation called *burnishing*.

The ancients also worked out methods for reproducing metal objects. Miss Richter drew attention to the fact that enormous quantities of embossed silver, gold and bronze were brought to Italy after the conquest of Greece (62) and soon after an era of collecting started which demanded a supply of copied ware. All that was needed was the taking of an impression in plaster or terracotta of the original and casting it in metal or clay. The originals of such copies often clearly show that they were not cast but hammered over a die. Finds from Begram (Afghanistan), Egypt and the Chersonnesus on the Black Sea have proved the effect of the Pax Romana and the possibility of obtaining copies of works made in the Golden Age of Greece throughout the Empire.

It is to be hoped that soon a larger amount of objects will be examined by experts, for at present it would be extremely difficult to trace the evolution of these techniques from the scant data, partly buried in literature on the history of art and partly in excavation and museum reports. A thorough study of this subjects is sorely wanted, for it will throw much light on several outstanding questions of the history of metallurgy too. Again this re-examination of published analyses seems important as many reports are incomplete and some results seem very doubtful, terms being used very losely indeed.

But we should not tarry long in the wilderness of these untrodden paths for as the Walrus said:

"The time has come to talk of many things".

BIBLIOGRAPHY

(For further details we refer the reader to our Bibliographia Antiqua, Philosophia Naturalis, section II, B and C. & Suppl. I & II)

1. FORBES, R. J., *Studies in Ancient Technology vol. VII* (Leiden, 1963) (Mining and Geology)
2. HOPPER, R. J., *The Attic silver mines in the fourth century B.C.* (ABSA XLVIII, 1953, 200—254)
3. FORBES, R. J., *Studies in Ancient Technology vol. VI* (Leiden, 1958) 13—28
4. MARYON, H., *Metal-working in the ancient world* (AJA LIII, 1949, 93—125)
5. THEOPHRASTUS, *Hist. Plant.* IV. 8. 4—5; STRABO 3. 2. 8. cap. 146
6. PLINY, *Nat. Hist.* XIV, 122, 127; XVI. 38, 52
7. THEOPHRASTUS, *Enq. into Plants* V. 9; III. 8. 5—7; IX. 2. 1
8. PLINY, *Nat. Hist.* 36. 201
9. STRABO 14. 6. 5
10. PLINY, *Nat. Hist.* XXXIV. 67 & 96
11. THEOPHRASTUS, *De igne* 37
12. PLINY, *Nat. Hist.* XXXVI. 141
13. THEOPHRASTUS, *On Stones* 23—28
14. TACITUS, *Annals* 13. 57; PLINY, *Nat. Hist.* XVI. 1
15. CUNNINGTON, M., *Mineral coal in Roman Britain* (Antiquity VII, 1933, 89)
16. FORBES, R. J., *Studies in Ancient Technology* (Vol. VI, 81 ff, Leiden, 1958)
17. STEINDORFF, G., *Das Grab des Ti*, pl. 134
18. FOY, W., *Zur Geschichte des Eisentechniks insbesondere der Gebläse* (Ethnologica I, 1909, 185)
    FRÉMONT, CH., *Origine et dévélopement de la souflerie* (Paris, 1917)
    FRÉMONT, CH., *Evolution de la fonderie de cuivre* (Paris, 1903)
    HAMZA, H., *The cylindrical tubes or nozzles of the ancient Egyptian bellows* (ASAE 30, 1930, 62)
    KLOSEMANN, K., *Die Entwicklung der Eisengewinnung in Afrika und Europa* (MAGW 54, 1924, 120—140)
    LOHSE, U., *Die Entwicklung der Gebläse bis zur Mitte des XIX. Jahrhunderts* (Stahl und Eisen XXXI, 1911, 173)
19. ILIAD XVIII. 468; VIRGIL, *Georgics* IV. 171; LIVY 38. 7; HORACE, *Saturn.* I. 4. 19; THEOPHILUS III. 82—84
20. ILIAD XVIII. 468; HERODOTUS I. 67
21. THEOBALD, W., *Des Theophilus Presbyter Diversarium Artium Schedula* (Berlin, 1933, III. 82—84)
22. NEWBERRY, P. E., *The Life of Rekhmara*, plate XVIII; DAVIES. N. and N. G., *The Tomb of Menkhepherrasonb*, Plate XII

23. *Jer.* VI.29
23. *Isa.* 54. 16; *Ezech.* 22. 21; *Job.* 20. 26; 41. 21; *Sirach* 43. 4
25. LEGRAIN, DP XVI, 31
26. ŠL no. 85 plus ŠL no. 30; MEISSNER, BR., *Seltene Assyrische Ideo-gramme* no. 1470
27. CT XI. 47, 111. 26
28. DAVIES, O., *Roman Mines in Europe* (Oxford, 1935)
29. STRABO 7. 3. 9. cap. 303
30. ODYSSEY X. 19—20
31. ILIAD XVIII. 372; HERODOTUS I. 68; THUCYDIDES IV. 100. 1
32. FORBES, R. J., *Studies in Ancient Technology* Vol. VI, 73 (Leiden, 1958)
33. CZÖRNIG, C. VON, *Das Land Görz und Gradisca* (Wien, 1873, 141)
    DEICHMÜLLER, J., *Tonofen und Ofenmodelle der Lausitzer Kultur* (Leipzig 1941)
    DICKINSON, H. W., *Elinghearths* (Trans. Newcomen Soc. XVIII, 1937/38, 274—277)
    GILLES, J. W., *Der Stammbaum des Hochofens* (Archiv Eisenhütten-wesen, 23, 1952, 11/12, 407—415)
    GOLDSMITH, J. M., and HULME, E. W. *Sketch of the history of natural draught furnaces* (Trans. Newcomen Soc. XXIII, 1942/43, 1—13)
    HURST, J. E., *The history of the cupola foundry* (Engineering 124, 1927, 830—831)
    KLOSEMANN, K., *Die Entwicklung der Eisengewinnung in Afrika und Europa* (Mitt. Anthrop. Ges. Wien, 54, 1924, 120—140)
    NICHOLS, H. W., *Models of blast furnaces for smelting iron* (Field Museum Chicago, 1922)
    MINGAZZINI, *Santuari o Alti-forni* (Studi Sardi X—XI, 1950/51, 3—17)
    PENNIMAN, T. K., ALLEN, I. M., and WOOTTON, A., *Ancient metallurgical furnaces in Great Britain to the end of the Roman occupation* (Sibrium IV, 1958/59, 97—128)
    SOUTHERN, H., *The historical development of furnaces* (Edgar Allen News, XII, 1933/34, 313—315; 330—333, 345—347, 357—359, 374—376)
    WEIERSHAUSEN, P., *Vorgeschichtliche Eisenhütten Deutschlands* (Leip-zig, 1939)
    VOGEL, O., *Zur Geschichte des Schmelztiegels* (Glashütte 65, 1935, 722)
    WRIGHT, H. E., *History of the development of blast-furnaces in Great Britain* (Iron Coal Trade Rev. 150, 1945, 733—736, 777—780)
    COGHLAN, H. H., *Some experiments on the origin of copper* (Man, 1939, July)
    —, *Prehistoric copper and some experiments in smelting* (Trans. Newco-men Soc. XX, 1939/40, 49—65)
    —, *Some fresh aspects of prehistoric metallurgy of copper* (Ant. J. XXII, 1942, 22—38)

34. Hesiod, *Theogony* 864
35. *Dan.* 3. 6
36. *Deut.* 4. 20; *Isa.* 48. 10; *Prov.* 27. 21
37. *Gen.* 19. 28
38. *Gen.* 15. 17; *Isa.* 31. 9
39. *Eccles.* 27. 5; 28. 30
40. *Deut.* 4. 20; *Jer.* 11. 4
41. Herodotus III. 96
42. *Prov.* 17. 3; 27. 21, etc.
43. Pliny, *Nat. Hist.* 33. 69
44. Pollux VII. 99
45. Gompertz, *The Master Craftsmen* (London, 1933)
46. Fairchild, M. and Hart, H., *A million years of evolution in Tools* (Doylestown (Pa.) Bucks County Hist. Soc., 1929, 338)
    Herig, Fr. and Kraft, G., *Die Form der Palaeolitischen Geräte* (Archiv f. Anthrop. N.F. 22, 1932, 177—255)
    Leroi-Gourhan, A., *L'Homme et la Matière* (Paris, 1943)
    —, *Milieu et techniques* (Paris, 1945)
    Little, J. D., *The antiquity of tools* (Metal Finishing 41, 1943, 495—497, 562—563)
    Wilkie Foundation, Civilisation through Tools (Des Plaines (Ill.) 1954)
47. Cline, W., *Mining and Metallurgy in Negro Africa* (Paris, 1937)
    Coghlan, H. H., *Metal Implements and Weapons* (In: Singerc. s., History of Technology I, 1954, 600—622)
    Coghlan, H. H., *The perforated Stone Hammer in Ireland* (J. Cork Hist. Arch. Soc. LX, 1955, 97—116)
    Coghlan, H. H., *Evolution of the axe from prehistoric to Roman times* (JRAI 73, 1943, 27—56)
    Coghlan, H. H., *Some problems concerning the manufacture of Copper shaft-hole Axes* (Archeol. Austrica 29, 1961, 57—75)
    Coghlan, H. H., *Notes on the Prehistoric Metallurgy of Copper and Bronze in the Old World* (Oxford, 1951)
    Curwen, E. C., *Implements and their wooden handles* (Antiquity 21, 1947, 155—158)
    Duval, P. M., *Ascia and asciculus à la lumière des documents figurés* (REL XXXI, 1953, 45—46)
    Dick, O., *Die Feile und ihre Entwicklungsgeschichte* (Berlin, 1925)
    Bernt, W., *Altes Werkzeug* (Mьnchen, 1939)
    Evrard, R., *Forges anciennes* (Liège, 1956)
    Frobenius, L., *Kulturgeschichte Afrikas* (Berlin, 1938, 197)
    Klosemann, K., *Die Entwicklung der Eisengewinnung in Afrika und Europa* (MAGW 54, 1924, 120—140)
    Maryon, H., *The technical methods of the Irish smiths in the Bronze and Early Iron Ages* (Proc. R. Irish Acad. XLIV, 1937/8, 181—224)
    Lansing, A., *A pair of Graeco-Roman shears* (BMMA 34, 1939, 244)
    Ohlhaver, H., *Der germanische Schmied und sein Werkzeug* (Leipzig, 1939)

48. CHILDE, V. GORDON, *The story of tools* (London, 1944)
—, *Man* 1956, no. 4548, page 1432
49. CHILDE, V. GORDON, *A Bronze-worker's anvil and other tools recently acquired by the Inverness Museum* (Proc. Soc. Ant. Scotland 80, 1945, 8—11)
50. MARYON, H., *The technical methods of the Irish smiths in the Bronze and Early Iron Ages* (Proc. R. Irish Acad. XLIV, 1937/38, 181—224)
51. COGHLAN, H. H., *The perforated Stone Hammer in Ireland* (J. CORK Hist. Archaeol. Soc. LX, 1955, 97—116)
52. MARYON, H., *Some prehistoric metalworker's tools* (Ant. J. XVIII, 1938, 243—250)
53. BAUME, W. LA, *Zur Kenntnis der Metalltechnik in der Bronzezeit und der ältesten Eisenzeit* (Schr. Naturf. Ges. Danzig N. F. XIX. 3. 1930, 141)
BLÜMNER, H., *Technologie und Terminologie der Künste und Gewerbe bei Griechen und Römern* (Leipzig, 1887, vol. IV)
COGHLAN, H. H., *Metalli Lavorati* (Enciclopedia Univ. Dell'Arte, 1962, vol. IX, 225—232)
JAHN, O., *Darstellungen des Handwerks und des Handelsverkehrs auf Vasenbildern* (Ber. Verh. K. Sächs. Akad. XIX, Leipzig, 1867)
JUNKER, H., *Die Hieroglyphen für Erz und Erzarbeiter* (MDAIK 14, 1956, 89)
HOSTMANN, CHR., *Zur Technik der antieken Bronzeindustrie* (Arch. f. Anthr. 10, 1878, 41—62)
MISKE, K. VON, *Bergbau, Verhütting und Metallbearbeitungswerkzeuge aus Velem St. Veit* (Wiener Präh. Z. 16, 1929, 81)
MÖLLER, G., *Die Metallkunst der alten Aegypter* (Berlin, 1925)
PIWOWARSKY, E., *Form- und Giesstechniek in vorchristlicher Zeit* (Beitr. Gesch. Techn. Ind. 22, 1933, 25)
RAINBIRD, CL., *The Iron Age treasure of Snettingham* (Proc. Preh. Soc. XX, 1954, 27—86)
ROEDER, G., *Aegyptische Bronzewerke* (Glückstadt, 1937)
ROEDER, G., *Komposition und Technik der altägyptischen Metallplastik* (Arch. Jahrb. 57, 1933, 226)
SQUARZINA, *Le piu antiche lavorazione minerarie e metalluriche in Italia* (L'Industr. Minerarie sett. 1951)
THEOBALD, W., *Des Theophilus Presbyter Diversarium Artium Schedula* (Berlin, 1933)
WILLERS, H., *Neue Untersuchungen über die römische Bronzeindustrie von Capua und Niedergermanien* (Leipzig, 1907)
54. MARYON, H. and PLENDERLEITH, H. J., *Fine Metalwork* (Singer c.s., History of Technology vol. I, 1954, 623—662; vol. II, 1956, 449—484)
55. BECKER, E., *Von der Bronzegusztechnik unserer germanischen Vorfahren* (Gieszereipraxis 57, 1936, 409—413, 440—442)
EMBDEN, H. J. MEERKAMP VAN, *Modern vormgietwerk* (Philips Technisch Tijdschr. 15, 1953, 137—150)

Homma, M., *Materials used in the ancient casting art of Japan* (Kokka, no. 759, 1955, 159)

Drescher, H., *Der Ueberfanggusz* (Mainz, 1958)

Coghlan, H. H., and Raftery, J., *Irish prehistoric castingmoulds* (Sibrium VI, 1961, 223—244)

McIntyre, J. B., *Metal casting methods* (Metallurgia 48, 1953, 123—129)

Kluge, K. and Lehmann-Hartleben, K., *Die antiken Groszbronzen*, vol. I. *Die antike Erzgestalltung* (Berlin, 1927)

Lamarre, H., *La cachette de fondeur de Longueville* (Revue Archéol. XXIII, 1945, 98—115)

Maréchal, J. R., *Evolution de la fonte en Europe et ses relations avec la méthode wallone d'affinage* (Techniques et Civilisations IV, 1954, 129—143)

Maryon, H., *The Bawsey Torc* (Antiq. J. XXII, 1944, 149—151)

Piwowarski, E., *Form- und Giesstechnik in vorchristlicher Zeit* (Giesserei 38, 1951, 548—556)

Richter, G. M. A., *Ancient Plaster Casts of Greek Metalware* (AJA 62, 1958, 369—377)

Somigli, G., *Breve storia della fonderia* (Milano, 1953)

Yetts, W. P., *The technique of bronze casting in ancient China* (Ostas. Z., N.F., V, 1930, 84)

Zannoni, G., *La fonderia de Bologna* (Bologna, 1888)

56. Hodges, H. W. M., *Studies in the Late Bronze Age in Ireland. I. Stone and clay moulds and wooden models of bronze implements* (Ulster J. Arch. 17, 1954, 62—80)

Hodges, H. W. M., *The Bronze Age moulds of the British Isles I. Scotland and Northern England* (Sibrium IV, 1958/59, 129—140)

Hodges, H. W. M., *The Bronze Age moulds of the British Isles II. England and Wales* (Sibrium V, 1960, 153—162)

Homma, M., *Materials used in casting art of Japan* (Kokka no. 759, 1955, 159)

Paret, O., *The remains of moulds from a bronze foundry of 3000 years ago* (Giesserei 43, 1956, 159—163)

Piaskowski, J., *Foundry technique in a fortified town in Biskupin, District Znin, in the period of the Lusation culture* (550—400 B.C.) (Polsk. Akad. Nauk, Warzawa, 1957, Engl. summary)

Rosenqvist, A. M., *Studies in the bronze-technique in the Vestbye find* (Viking, 1954, 125ff)

Thompson, F. C., *The technique of casting coins in ancient India* (Nature 162, 1948, 266—267)

57. Embden, H. J. Meerkamp van, *Modern vormgietwerk* (Philips Techn. Review 15, 1953, 133—146)

Hart, R. Raven-, *The casting technique of certain Greek bronzes* (JHS 78, 1958, 87—91)

Neil, H. O', *Metal founding through the Ages* (Foundry Trade J. 1949, 575—581)

ROEDER, G., *Herstellung von Wachsmodellen zu ägyptischen Bronze-figuren* (Z. Aegypt. Spr. 69, 1933, 1, 45—67)

58. ANASTASIADES, E., *Bronze welding, riveting and wiremaking by the ancient Greeks* (Metal Progress 58, 1950, 322—324)

DÖHNER, O., *Geschichte der Eisendrahtindustrie* (Berlin, 1925)

LINDBLOM, K. G.,*Wire-drawing especially in Africa* (Stockholm, 1939)

THEOBALD, W., *Das Drahtziehen in der lateinischen Literatur vom Altertum bis zur Renaissance* (Glasers Annalen 115, 1934, 57)

59. ANASTASIADES, E., *Bronze welding, riveting and soldering by the ancient Greeks* (Metal Progress 58, 1950, 322—324)

MARYON, H., *Soldering and welding in the Bronze and Early Iron Ages* (Techn. Studies Field Fine Arts V, 1936, 75—108)

MARYON, H., *Archaeology and Metallurgy. I. Welding and Soldering* (Man, 1941, no. 85, 118—124)

MARYON, H., *Welding in ancient times* (Welding and Metal Fabrication, London, Oct. 1955, 383—389)

MARYON, H., *The Fashioning of Metal Artefacts* (Man 1956, page 1432)

MÖTEFINDT, H., *Zur Geschichte der Löttechnik in vor- und frühge-schichtlicher Zeit* (Bonner Jahrb. 123, 1916, 132)

MARTIN BURGESS, E., *Technical Note on the fragment of Iron mail* (Roman) *from Carlingwark Loch* (Proc. Soc. Antiq. Scotland 57, 1952, 50)

60. BERTOLONE, M., *Ceramiche villanoviane decorate con lamelle metalliche* (Riv. Scienze Preist. IX, 1954, 3/4, 180—185)

CALEY, E. R., *Examination of two gold objects of aboriginal manufacture* (Ohio J. Sci. LIV, 1954, 149—150)

CHAIT, R. M., *Some comments on the dating of early Chinese cloisonné* (Oriental Art III, 1951, 67—78)

GORDON, D. V. VAN, *Japanese Shippo-art enameling* (cloisonné) (Amer. Ceram. Soc. Bull. 33, 1954, 37—40)

HOLMQVIST, *Tauschierte Metallarbeiten des Nordens aus der Römerzeit und Völkerwandrung* (Stockholm, 1951)

JOPE, E. M., *An inlaid knife from Winchester* (Antiq. J. XXVI, 1946, 70—72)

MOSS, A. A., *Niello* (Studies in Conservation I, 1953, 49 ff; Ant. J. XXXIII, 1953, 75—77)

RIETH, A., *Anfänge und Entwicklung der Tauschiertechnik* (Eurasia Sept. Ant. X, 1936, 186)

THEOBALD, W., *Herstellung des Blattmetalls im Alterum und Neuzeit* (Diss. Hannover, Berlin, 1912)

A. WOOTTON, *Some notes on the Antoninianus, a Roman "silver" coin* (SEABY's coin and medal Bulletin, March 1958, 103—105)

A. WOOTTON, *A further note on the Roman blanching technique* (SEABY's coin and medal Bulletin, September 1958, 363—364)

A. WOOTTON, *The Roman "silver washed" coinages, on the probable evolution of an early blanching technique* (SEABY's coin and medal Bulletin, June 1958, 229—232)

61. ANSTEE, J. W., *Pattern-welded Iron Swords* (Man 1956, no. 4548, pag. 1432)

BELAIEW, N. T., *Sur le "damas" oriental et les lames damassées* (Métaux et Civilisations I, 1945, 10—16)

JANSSENS, M., *Essai de reconstitution d'un procédé de fabrication d'épées damassées* (Conservation 3, 1958, 93—106)

LANORD, A. FRANCE-, *Les techniques métallurgiques appliquées à l'archéologie* (Revue de Métallurgie XLIX, 1952, 6, 411—422)

MARYON, H., *A sword of the Viking period from the river Witham* (Antiq. J. XXX, 1950, 175—179)

MARYON, H., *A sword of the Nydam type from Ely Fields Farm* (near Ely) (Proc. Cambridge Antiq. Soc. XLI, 1943/47, 73—76)

REGGIORI, A. & GARINO, C., *Esame tecnologio di un gruppo di spade galliche della Lombardia nord-occidentale* (Sibrium II, 1955, 43—55)

SALIN, E., *Trois damasquinures romains* (BSAF 1952/53, 122—125)

SMITH, C. S., *Decorative etching and the science of metals* (Endeavour XVI, 1957, no. 64, 199—208)

SMITH, C. S., *A metallographic examination of some Japanese sword blades* (Symposium La tecnica di fabbricazione delle lame di acciaio presso gli antichi, Milano, 1957, 43—68)

SMITH, C. S., *A History of Metallography* (Chicago, 1960)

VOGEL, O., *Entwicklung der Metallbeizerei* (In: Handbuch der Metallbeizerei, Berlin, 1938)

62. PLINY XXXIII. 148, 157; XXXIV. 47, LIVY 27. 16. 7; CICERO, *in Verrem* 24

CHAPTER FIVE

GOLD

> Cest or auquel chacun tend, chacun vise, pour lequel
> nuyt et jour ce misérable monde vit en continuelle
> peine et tourment de corps et d'âme.
>
> Jacques Gohory (1)

1. *Introduction*

Probably ever since gold came into use in the Ancient Near East men have both cursed and blessed this glittering metal. Many a philosopher before Pliny will have expressed in his own tongue the words: "Gold is accursed by reason of the hunger with which it is sought, censured and reviled by all really good men, and discovered only to be a scourge to life" (2) and many a document will have weighed the merits and disadvantages of gold for mankind with the same fairness as Agricola did in *de Re metallica* Book I (3).

But the speculations of moralists and philosophers have not been able to stem the stream and since the discovery of gold its production and value have been determined by the greed so well expressed by the words of Ferdinand, king of Spain in his letter to the colonists of Hispanola (July 25th 1511): "Get gold, humanely if you can, but at all hazards get gold" (4). It would be futile to speculate on the name of the discoverer of gold, Pliny half-hearted contributed a few names of mythical persons such as Cadmus, etc. (5). A metal like gold is not suddenly discovered by one person, but its characteristics are slowly recognized by a long series of observations. It is more profitable to enquire whether the common opinion is true that gold was the first metal discovered by man. There is probably no general answer to this question. We must remember that the first metal must have been a native metal; it is extremely improbable that man had any knowledge of metallurgy and the smelting of metals from ores before he had appreciated the specific "metallic" properties of these "shining stones" found on the earth's surface. There are only four metals (gold, copper, meteoric iron and more rarely silver) which are found in sufficient quantity in their native state to rank amongst the earliest metals discovered. Therefore, neglecting the extreme "diffusionist" attitude it depends on the mineral wealth of a country, on the contact of its inhabitants with other metal-using people and on their own degree of civilisation which is the first metal discovered or known in that region. Generally speaking the common opinion that gold was this metal is right, but there are some striking exceptions to this rule. We should remember, that in few places in the ancient world was gold worked on the spot where it was found, Colombia being one of the few exceptions to the rule. What the Neolithic goldminers collected with their horn picks, wooden shovels and stone hammers was passed on to those tribes or peoples who were interested in the "yellow stone" (6). Many primitive people have no use for it. The Portuguese invaders of Brazil found the natives using golden fishhooks! Hence many primitive tribes in Agrica, Polynesia, Melanesia, etc. had no special term for this stone and have adopted foreign words for gold in the course of the ages.

In Egypt copper was known much earlier than gold, if we judge from the excavations at prehistoric sites. Though copper was known in earlier periods, gold appears more generally only in the Badari period but it is worked like copper e.g. as if it were a kind of stone (7). Again in Africa in general gold seems to have come after copper or other metals. Thus the Katanga negroes say that "yellow copper (gold) is easier to make into bullets than ordinary red copper", calling it thus because they knew copper before gold (8) and some Kaffir tribes call gold "yellow iron" (9). The North American Indians probably knew copper before gold. On the other hand in South America and Mexico gold seems to have been the earliest metal and in Chinese chin[1] (金) meant gold before it acquired the more general present meaning "metal" (10). As for Iran and Mesopotamia we have expressed the opinion that the science of metallurgy originated in the Armenian mountains or the highlands of Iran, where native gold occurs fairly frequently and we think it highly probable that in these regions gold was the first metal too. Archaeological discoveries lead us to place this discovery of gold in the early Fourth Mill., but we can not ascribe the priority of such a discovery to any region because the evidence is still very slight. But after all the priority question is not very important.

We will not dwell on the rôle which gold played in religion, myth and magic (11), though we should like to point out that many authors show a tendency to overstress the available evidence (12). This glittering yellow metal was very early connected with the sun and even in the sixteenth century A.D. Agricola had to protest against the idea that the native gold found in river gravels is drawn out of the earth by the sun (Book III).

Its supposed mystical and philosophical (but later often its more material) qualities were the driving force of early chemistry and alchemy (13) from which after nineteen centuries of strenuous research our modern chemistry arose.

2. *Early gold technology*

The metallurgy of gold clearly passes through three phases (14):
1. The cold deformation of nuggets and placer-gold
2. melting and casting of gold
3. working of gold with harder metals from the Iron Age onwards and tooling.

There is a long period between the first discovery of gold and the Egyptian texts extolling the King's virtues in such words as "the hills and the mountains pay thee impost of gold" (15) or "gold comes forth from the mountain at his name". Though it is very probable that in most regions gold was the first metal to be used, it must be remembered that the early use of gold falls in the Neolithic Age and that this gold was not recognized as a metal in its early days. In this early phase gold was simply a tough material, worthless for practical purposes of life (16) but collected for its aesthetical or supposed magical properties. It could in no way compete with wood and stone as base material for the making of tools and weapons. Still in those early days when the possibility of melting gold had not yet been discovered and only its *malleability* was known, it was collected in small quantities from surface deposits and fashioned as stone or wood objects would be manufactured. In the case of wood or stone the final object was formed by cutting away from a crude piece of wood or stone (64) all the unnecessary parts. The final object was therefore contained in the spatial limits of the original stone or piece of wood. It seems that some of the earliest gold objects found in Egypt were actually fashioned on this principle but soon the malleability of gold was discovered and objects were made by hammering out gold nuggets and bending or cutting the small sheets or wires obtained. Hence all the techniques of the goldsmith employing gold sheet or foil gold go back to this oldest phase as do the techniques of pasting such foil gold on wood, stone, etc. and so do the techniques of chasing and embossing for which stone and wooden forms were used.

The *melting and casting* of native metals are discovered in the transitional period between the true Neolithic and the Metal Age.

We will have occasion to discuss the fact that gold occurs always as a native metal in all of its commercial ores and deposits (18). Gold technology therefore never contributed in the same way as copper technology to the development of metallurgy; the characteristic smelting process was only developed in the case of a metal like copper, which though it occurs in fairly large quantities as a native metal, can be obtained easily by the smelting of widely distributed copper compounds or copper ores. In this sense we agree with Garland that there was no connection between the technology of copper and gold (19) but of course many metallurgical processes such as bending, beating, embossing, boring, welding, turning, raising, etc. which were developed in the Metal Age are not characteristic of one metal only but are used for all other metals after their discovery. The goldsmiths of all ages must have adapted these metallurgical processes to their craft quite freely. The early metallurgy in the Ancient Near East and indeed for many centuries after was greatly impeded by the lack of good smelting processes and apparatus, and we can safely state that the production and refining of metals up to the eighteenth century A.D. was completely limited by such apparatus as ovens, crucibles, etc. Metallic silver, for instance, occurs rarely in nature, it is mostly produced from lead ores and therefore the production of silver was limited by the development of smelting lead ores and refining lead. Gold never suffered from such a hindrance, the metal was easy to work even without the application of heat and, since only small quantities were worked at a time there was no need for large and intricate apparatus.

3. *Gold Mining*

Before enumerating the different gold deposits known in the Near East in ancient and modern times we will give a survey of the *nature and characteristics of these deposits* (20).

Gold is rather widely distributed in nature, it occurs in minute quantities in almost all rocks. Even such common rocks as limestones or sandstones contain gold and so does seawater. The amount of gold in a ton of ore is usually so small that even if the ore is concentrated by washing away the gangue, it is generally impracticable to smelt the ore so as to collect the precious metal in lead or copper and to remove the base metal afterwards by some process. The present economic limit for the extraction of gold from auriferous rocks is about 2—3 grains per Ton (0.0001%), a considerable advance on the limit given by Agricola for sixteenth century gold technology (0.188%). At present a considerable percentage of the world's gold production is produced from copper or silver ores as the by-product from lead or copper mines. This production of gold as a by-product from other ores was probably started by the Romans who in the first century B.C. began to work pyrites and other sulphides for gold. Still as late as 1875 this process was not in common use and 90% of the gold was collected from placers. We will therefore direct our attention to the production of gold from auriferous rocks only and we can, for the development in the Ancient Near East, safely disregard the extraction of gold from other ores or metals.

We can distinguish two types of gold, v.i.z. *reef gold*, irregular masses of gold occuring in quartz veins or lodes and *alluvial or placer gold*, deposits representing the detritus, gravels and sands derived from the desintergration of auriferous rocks and veins. Often this debris is washed far away from the original rocks and the gold is deposited amongst the river gravels and sands. The gold is often crystallized (filiform gold, wire gold and other dendritic forms) which fact gave rise to the legends about "growing gold", which even Agricola did not succeed in weeding out .

A century ago an author (21) deplored that "the ancient leaders sought the precious metals not by exploring the bowels of the earth but by the more summary process of conquest, tribute and plunder", but the ancient miners must have had some more scientific method of prospecting. We can not say whether the search for gold deposits (*prospecting*) (22) was conducted along certain empirical lines in early times, but we do hear that the Roman geologists looked for certain white gravels near which they expected to find gold placers and that the prospector has a good chance of finding gold in certain oxidized top-layers of veins of copper ores in Spain.

The ancient *mining or extraction processes* (which are still used) were very simple because *gold always occurs as a metal in all its ores* and though a few compounds of gold exist, they play no rôle in the production of gold. Even in the quartz or quartzite the gold occurs in the metallic state. Therefore after mining the gold is simply extracted and though it is never quite pure but practically always alloyed with silver, copper or traces of iron, it is practically ready for use and no special treatment of the rock containing the gold is necessary. The mining processes though differing according to the nature of the deposit and the ore, consist mainly in the freeing of the gold particles by crushing or sifting the ore and separating the gold from the rest by making use of the high density of the precious metal.

Most of the gold produced in Antiquity was placer gold (or alluvial gold). In these placers the gold is often derived from auriferous rocks whose exploitation would not have been profitable but erosion of the matrix and subsequent concentration by water have left accumulations of economic value. The gold occurs scattered as dust, grains or pellets (*nuggets*) and hand picking, dry-blowing, winnowing or sifting may suffice to collect it. We may say that nature has opened the lodes and veins. These nuggets may be of considerable size, the largest ever found (at Ballarat) weighed 190 lbs. The sand can also be washed over smooth sloping rocks by running water, when the gold particles have a tendency to sink to the bottom of the stream owing to their high density.

The following methods are used in the case of *alluvial gold*, their principles probably date back to the earliest historical periods.

- a. *Panning or pan-washing.* The sand or gravel is agitated with water in pans, troughs, or "cradles" of various forms (usually shallow basins), the rocky matter is floated off and the gold particles collect on the bottom as gold dust or nuggets.

- b. *Placer mining.* The sand or gravel is shoveled into a "sluice", a long flume or trough with transverse cleets, riffles or obstructions along the bottom. Water streams through and sweeps along the sand, the gold collects in the crevices. The sluices may be covered with fat to retain the nuggets or the riffles may be covered with skins of certain animals. The legend of the Golden Fleece is often connected with the production of gold by washing sands containing gold over sheep skins.

- c. A later process better suited for organized gold production and probably not used before the Romans, is called *hydraulic mining* (*hushing*). Softer beds were broken down by strong currents of water in Antiquity, these were the "arugiae" of the Romans in Spain (23). At the present time water is directed under high pressure from a reservoir through a special nozzle against the gold-bearing earth. In both cases the washings are conveyed in sluices and treated as described under *b*.

These methods were applied very efficiently in Antiquity. English engineers exploring the Egyptian gold mines in the Nubian desert found that the ancient Egyptians were "very thorough prospectors and no workable deposits were found which they had overlooked". We must remember a very important factor in these processes, the fairly large amount of water essential to the washing of the sands or gravels. This water was the determining factor for ancient gold mining and no mines could be opened up if water could not be procured. The more difficult extraction of gold from quartz rocks is called *vein or reef mining*. Agatharchides has given us a very exact description of the use of this method in Egypt and if we translate this passage preserved for us by Diodor (III, 12—14) into modern technical language, it would run like this: "In Egypt dark rocks traversed by veins of white quartz containing the native gold are exploited by means of adit-levels. The rock is broken up by the fire-setting method (because the ancients lacked proper explosives) and the pieces broken up further into small pieces by hammers. These small pieces are reduced in mortars to pea-size and these pellets are transferred to handquerns fed through the upper stone. The pulverized product is then spread over sloping boards or stones and the gold separated from the gangue by the aid of water. Clotted lumps are rubbed by hand to expedite the concentration. The gold is then collected and weighed".

Reef mining was conducted to depths of nearly 300' in Egypt and tunnels of upto 1500' followed the veins into the rocky slopes of the valleys of the desert region.

4. *The goldfields of Antiquity*

If we want to draw a map of the gold deposits (28) known in Antiquity, adding as we have done in the appended map the deposits discovered by modern geologists and not mentioned in ancient literature, we must not forget that we must distinguish carefully between the ancient deposits mentioned as mines (which are very rare) or those regions and places from which gold is said to come as tribute, booty or object of trade. The latter may be countries like Libya, where modern prospecting has failed to find any trace of gold placers, ancient or modern, or like the Western Oases, where no gold deposits of any kind are mentioned in modern handbooks. All doubtful evidence has therefore been omitted in this map and the arrows indicate regions from which gold may have been imported or possible trade routes along which gold traveled. As far as possible ancient, but exhausted deposits have been indicated as well as deposits not mentioned in ancient texts.

A short survey of the deposits indicated on the map leads us first to *Egypt* (29) where the principal gold mines were situated on the coast of the Red Sea, in the desert along it and in the Nubian desert. More than 100 old mines were found in these districts and in the valleys the schists are full of alluvial workings. The following groups of mines can be distinguished: 1) Wadi Dara, Wadi Dib and Wadi Um Mongul (all about 27′50″ N. 33′ E.), 2) Wadi Foakhir between 26′48″ N. and the route to Qoseïr, 3) Djebel Zebâra (Wadi Hamesch, Bir Sighdit, Umm Rus, 25′40″—25′15″ N.), mentioned in AR III. 289 because of the energetic exploitation by Seti I, 4) the region between 25′ and 24′ N., 5) the coastal region near Râs Benâs and Berenice (23′ 27″ N) and finally 6) Wadi Allâqi, especially near the Nile and to the east of its middle course (AR I. 520). The importance of Nubia as a gold producing province of Egypt can hardly be exagerated, the yearly production of these mines has been estimated as high as 600—800 lbs. As early as the Old Kingdom we hear of military expeditions to Nubia for negroes and gold (30), but the gold must have been mainly Nubian gold. For though the possibility remains that real "Negro gold" from the interior of Africa came to Egypt as early as the VIth dynasty, authorities on African metallurgy state (31) that not until the Middle Ages did the gold trade from real negro areas assume any great value. The important work of Merenre had opened the First Cataract for the Egyptian ships under Pepi Ist's reign and made the approach to the gold mines possible. When Senusret I conquered the Third Cataract and Senusret III fortified the Second, the approach to these gold mines was finally safeguarded and we can state safely that the Egyptian administration of Nubia since the Middle Kingdom guarded one of the most important sources of income of the XIth and XIIth dynasties. Though Coptos does not produce gold it is often mentioned as a "gold country" or the texts mention "gold from Coptos". This is probably due to the fact that Coptos ows its importance to the gold trade passing through this town at the Nile head of the road to the coast of the Red Sea and its goldmines. Close by the Wadi Hammamat, in the Wadi Ballat a location of gold-bearing quartz was mined, and a number of huts were found (32) which housed the 100—200 miners who worked in this locality. It is probably of Roman date, but on the other hand the Turin papyrus shows a settlement on the very spot on the geological map of the region which it contains.

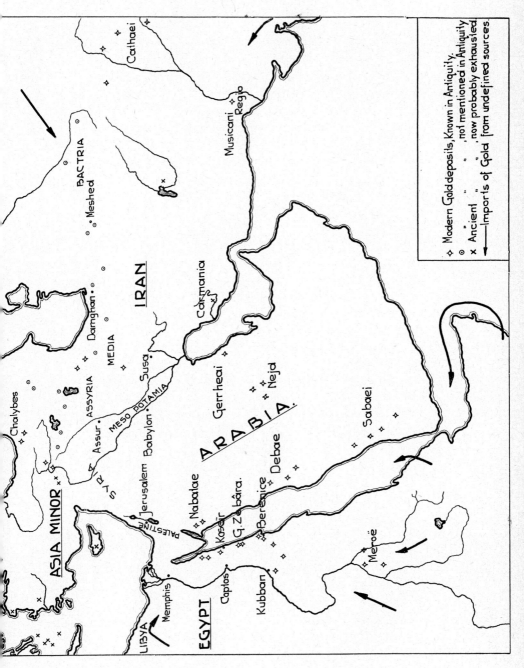

Fig. 33.
Map of the gold ores of Antiquity

Much of the "Nubian gold" may have come down from more southerly regions like Aethiopia, Napata or Kush, where the classical writers found it at Meroë (33) but it may have come from the region of the Blue Nile (Sennar district) or even farther down in Abyssinia, Somaliland or Madagascar. The ancient Egyptian records often refer to gold and antimony being obtained from "Punt" which is a rather vague designation of Somaliland or Inner Africa beyond Ethiopia. Quiring has tried to prove (34) that South Africa was meant because this is the only country besides Algeria, Morocco and West-Africa where both gold and antimony are found, but this hypothesis is very doubtful, the more so as the author goes as far as make the Egyptians reach India and China in their efforts to round the Cape of Good Hope!

Contrary to the fairly common reports that Egypt imported gold from the Sinaï (35), we must state that this can not be true, though imports from Midian were possible. The West coast of *Arabia* is rather rich in gold and several regions are mentioned by ancient authors. Midian is represented by the "region of the Nabatae" (36). There are several deposits near the coast of Asir (region of the Debae) (37) and Jemen (38), the country of the Sabaeans. We are told that the inhabitants of these regions do not know how to work gold "which was obtained by digging and found not as gold dust but as nuggets". They make collars with these nuggets, perforating them and stringing them alternately with transparent stones by means of thread". which means that they still treated gold (in Strabo's time!) as they would treat stone and had not recognized it as a metal. It is probably in South Arabia too that we must locate that evasive country of Ophir, though many other locations have been suggested, such as Somaliland, South Africa, Malaya, Sumatra, etc. The suggestion made by Dahse (39) who thought that Ophir was the Gold Coast is obviously wrong, because the ships for Ophir sail from the recently excavated Red Sea harbour of Ezion Geber. This Ophir occurs in many passages of the Bible (40) but other sources mentioned are Sheba (41) which certainly is South Arabia, Uphaz (42) and Parvaim (43). The last two are not identified, but we think that they are to be located in the same region, the West coast of Arabia.

Apart from these locations gold occurs in the highlands of Nejd which is probably identical with the Havilah of the Bible (Gen. 2 : 11— 12, *hawilah*). The genealogies of Havilah given in two passages (44) are contradictory and vague on the point of the location of this country. It has been suggested that Nejd or at least the highlands of Arabia were meant by the "Meluchha" of the Mesopotamian texts (45), but the identification can not yet be accepted as final as long as the "Meluchha-Magan" problem remains unsolved. On the coast of East Arabia gold is already mentioned by Strabo (Country of the Gerrheans) (46) and even in the tenth century A.D. Arabia was still an important centre for silver and gold (47).

India may have been an important source of gold, though the texts which mention Indian gold are mostly from classical authors. We do

Fig. 34.
Querns for grinding gold ore in an ancient
Nubian mine (After Gowland, *Metals*)

not find any mention of the most important modern gold deposits (Deccan, Jashpur, Nilgiri, Malabar), though the "desert east of India" of Herodotus (III. 98) may be the Central Indian Desert. The gold deposits of Haiderabad are mentioned by Strabo as in the "country of the Musicanes" (48) and the "country of Sopeithes" (49) is probably identical with the "Indian rivers" the Sutelj and other rivers of Kashmir which are still reported to carry down gold from the mountains, as is the Ganges which Pliny mentions (50). In India also the famous "gold-digging ants" lived (51) though they are sometimes said to be gryphons or to live in Aethiopia or among the Scythians instead of in India (52). It is often suggested that this legend refers to the gold from parts of Afghanistan or Chinese Turkestan imported into the Hellenistic world. Laufer (53) has published a valuable study of the gold deposits in these parts, which should be consulted by those who wish to disentangle the weird legends of the gold-digging ants or griffins of the Arimaspi. The same question was recently discussed very fully by A. Herrmann (54). Of course there is always the possibility that gold was imported from Inner Asia (Bochara, Amur Daria, Turkestan, and Siberia) (55) or even from the Far East (Malaya, Sumatra) (56) though exact records on this subject do not exist and we would not dare to suggest any of these sources for periods earlier than the Hellenistic Age.

In *Persia* several gold deposits are known from modern surveys of the country but very few ancient texts mention them. There is of course the river Hyktanis in Carmania mentioned by Strabo (57) and it is probable that the "Media" mentioned in Assyrian inscriptions ("*Sikraki* in Media", ii R. 67. 32) refers to the gold in Kawend (Zendjan). The other important deposits near Damghan, between Nishapur and Meshed, two miles east of Meshed, in the Tiran Mts. (W. of Ispahan near Hamadan), the region S.E. of Teheran and that N.W. of the Takht-i-Suleiman do not occur in any of the texts published up to now. There are of course the various legends on the rich gold bearing regions of Northern Europe (58) on the Massagetae or the "Hyperborean rivers" (59) and the famous stories of the Golden Fleece, but more definite locations of gold deposits are given in Colchis and surrounding regions, the country of the Suanes or Soanes (60), mentioning the use of "fleeces".

South of the Caucasus (61) in *Armenia* the famous metal workers, the Chalybes, are credited with rich mines (62); this probably refers to the deposits near the Taldjun river near Artwin. The region of Alindjeriv near Batoem and the gold mines in "Syspiritis near Caballa" visited by Menon, general of Alexander (63) are probably identical. Other deposits known are south of Lake Van and in the Kedabekbegh and W. Karabegh Mts. In general Assyrian texts often vaguely mention "the highlands" as the source of imports of gold (64). Gold is said to come from Aralu (the Assyrian Underworld) "the dust of its mountains" (65).

In the rest of *Asia Minor* gold is conspiciously absent. Only two gold deposits were known there in Antiquity, the more famous one embracing the banks of the Pactolus and the slopes of Mt. Tmolus (68). Literary and archaeological evidence (69) go to show that the actual gold metal found in the mountains and the river was not exploited before the Iron Age and that this gold formed the basis of the wealth of Croesus and his family. Unfortunately both literary and historical evidence show that this gold was exhausted not long after Croesus and that mining and washing stopped in this region. The persistence of the legend is probably due to the fact that the clay of the Pactolus used for the pottery and terracotta of Sardes is sprinkled with innumerable minute particles of goldencoloured mica.

The second deposit was near Astyra in the Troad, and it is reported to be the source of the riches of Priam of Troy (70) but it is exhausted too, now. In Cyprus gold and electrum seem to have been rare before the Classical Age (71).

There were of course many gold mines and placers in *Thrace, Macedonia and Greece*, but they were exhausted soon after their tapping begin in the Bronze Age (72), though a few remained to be exploited in historical times up to the Roman conquest. We cite just the most important of these: 1) the Hebrus in Thrace (73), 2) also the Strymon-Maritza district, 3) the slopes of the Rhodope Mts., 4) Skapte Hyle (74) and several of the islands, Andros, Thasos, Thera, Melos, Kimolos, Seriphos and Siphnos (75). When the gold fields, from which the Hellenistic kings drew their wealth, were confiscated by the Romans (167 B.C.) they were closed for a time and then reopened (158 B.C.), but their production seems to have dropped fairly rapidly (76)

In preclassical days this gold did not play an important part in the world, though Petrie (77) believed that the Egyptians imported gold from the Caucasus and the Pactolus region. Egypt remained the main producer of the Ancient Near East and in this country silver being rare, was valued even higher than gold. Though its value in relation to gold dropped in the course of time and the rate became practically the same as in other countries of the East, this had no effect on the part which the large output of the Egyptian gold mines played in the Ancient Near East (78). This position of Egypt could be maintained thanks to the fact that the civilised river-valley lowlands of Egypt, Syria, Mesopotamia and the Indus were devoid of important gold mines. The metal had to be imported and except in the case of Egypt none of these civilisation was permanently in control of the source of their gold. The early appearance of gold in Assyria (Tepe Gawra VIII) and in the early dynastic Royal Tombs of Ur show that there was an early contact with the gold-producing highlands or desert regions and that the goldsmith's craft in these regions could point to a long history.

On the other hand the Aegean gold was the source of the wealth of the Minoan and Myceneaen civilisations. The finds at various sites in this region (79) have confirmed the reports of the Homeric poems, which do not only mention gold objects by the score (80) but which also mention gold used as a means of exchange (81), as a precursor of minted coins. A tablet from Knossos (82) gives a list of the tribute in gold demanded from various villages of the region, which might be native gold collected from local placers but which might also be meant to indicate the value of the tribute to be paid. There is no doubt that "polychrysos" Mykene, Pylos or Troy could obtain its gold from the region and would not need imports from Egypt.

Prehistoric Europe did not lack gold either, though the production was mostly small until the Roman conquest. There were only few deposits of gold in Italy in the Alpine region, the most important of which were at Victumulae, near Vercellae, where the Salassi had collected placer gold as early as 143 B.C. and after Roman conquest of this region they were worked somewhile with a maximum of 5000 labourers imposed by the government (83).

Far richer were the placers of Transsylvania, Hungary and Dacia and also those in Noricum, the present Carinthia, which placers were discovered by the local Celtic tribes, the Taurisci. This discovery attracted the attention of the Italians, who flocked to this ancient "Klondike" in such masses that the price of gold in Rome dropped to one third. The Taurisci then drove out the Italians to re-establish their monopoly, until the days of Augustus when this region came under Roman control and continued to yield gold in small quantities (84).

Smaller amounts of gold came from the mountains of Saxony and Bohemia and there were local placers on certain large rivers like the Rhine, but they never achieved more than local importance. In the British Isles (85) gold was found and collected in Cornwall, Scotland, Wales (Dolaucothy and Dolgelly) and Ireland. Here the gold-gravel of the Wicklow mountains yielded gold from the Early Bronze Age till well in the La Tène period and it is claimed that much of it was exported and that objects made of this gold were found in Central Europe (86). Though Tacitus gives an exaggerated picture of the mineral wealth of Britain there is no doubt that the Romans undertook the exploitation of the goldmines of Wales (87) and even built a bath-house near these mines.

Gold mining was rather frequent during the early history of Gaul, but it seems to have suffered a set-back until it was taken up again in Roman times. There were gold placers in the Cevennes and the

Pyrenees, in the valleys of the Garonne, Ariège and Tarn, the Haute Vienne, Creuse and Cantal regions and in several Alpine valleys (88) where Caesar is reported to have taken vast quantities of gold as booty. The main stream of gold in Roman times came from the "arrugiae" of North-Western Spain and the terms used by the Iberians point to an old tradition of collecting nuggets on these gold placers (89). The stream of gold increased when the kinghts' companies started their work in Spain in 178 B.C.

5. *The application of native gold*

The gold collected in the mines and places was either refined on the spot, as the description of the Hellenistic gold mines by Agatharchides in Egypt would suggest, or it was exported in the form of gold dust, nuggets, bars, etc. to be refined by the buyer. The original form of the Chinese sign *chin*[1] (gold) represents, according to the explanation given by Li-šsu in the *Shou-wên*, four nuggets in two layers of earth under the earth's surface. In the same way we would like to see the natural form of gold represented in the early pictographic signs for Kù (90), these early pictograms look very much like nuggets. The Egyptian *nub* shows a much later stage of gold technology. Though Lepsius, Champollion and Wilkinson have held this sign to represent a bowl with a folded cloth over it used for washing gold from auriferous sand (91) and Crivelli thought that it was a portable furnace used for casting gold (92), the consensus of opinion regards it now (as Birch and Petrie (93) suggested) as the picture of a collar or necklace of gold beads, the "gold of honour" so frequently mentioned in Egyptian texts. We may mention here that *nub* appears early in the King's "Gold-name" as a symbol of the victory of Horus over Seth, the god of the gold town Coptos (94).

It has been wrongly supposed that the native gold was very pure and that all alloys with silver were compounded from the pure metals. Petrie, for instance, supposes that the Egyptian gold containing 16% of silver or more was a technical alloy. The reverse is true. Nearly all the native gold from the mines and placers is a natural alloy of gold with sometimes considerable quantities of silver, usually some copper and traces of iron. Other impurities such as tellurium, bismuth, antimony, mercury, platinum, etc. occur alongside these more common elements. Nor are any of these impurities sufficiently characteristic of certain localities to warrant theories like the Transsylvanian origin of the sceptre of Khasekhemeui as propounded by Petrie and Peake. Modern gold deposits very rarely produce pure gold. Though 99.9% gold was found in California, the average from that country was 88.4%; in Australia it was 95%; in Japan 62—90% for placer gold and 57—93% for vein gold. The same holds good for ancient deposits. Davies reports 75—92% gold for the Aegean islands and W. Anatolia (95), Lucas found 77—90% gold in the product of the six most important Egyptian gold mines (96) and nuggets from the Caucasus region are reported to contain 57—70% of gold (97). Garland considers any alloy containing less than 60% of gold an artificial one, for he states that no lower fineness of natural gold has been found anywhere in the world (98).

It is very interesting to compare these figures with the analyses of gold objects from excavations. For Egyptian objects Lucas found 72.1—99.8%, Williams 71—92% (99) and Thomas 84—90% (100) of gold. In Mesopotamia the composition of gold jewelry, etc. is according to Partington 30—48% of gold, 8—59% of silver and 0.3—10% of copper (101). This means that the *gold used in the Ancient Near East was mainly the native alloy* and that *refining of this native gold was not practised until the later phase of the period under discussion.*

This conclusion was confirmed when new non-destructive X-ray analysis was introduced in the examination of metal objects (102) which permitted the inspection of many museum treasures made of native gold. Not only were Iron Age gold objects from prehistoric Britain made of unrefined native gold (103), but this also held true for the majority of ancient Egyptian objects tested. A hoard of Greek jewelry found near Patras consisted of many gold fragments of late Hellenistic and Roman date, made of native gold containing over 12.5% of silver (104), and even in Roman times unrefined native gold was frequently used.

Native gold was, however, not only used because of the lack of refining possibilities during the earlier stages of gold metallurgy. The ancients used such native gold with more or less impurities of varying character on purpose because they considered them related types of metals of the gold family.

The alloys of gold and silver present a *range of colours* varying according to the increasing silver content from reddish yellow through pale yellow to white. For instance the modern alloy of silver and gold called "electrum" (spec. grav. 12.5—15.5; 22—55% of gold) varies from pale yellow to white. By adding copper to a silver-gold alloy containing 10% of silver we get the modern alloy known as "green gold". A gold-silver-copper alloy was known in Antiquity as "Corinthian bronze" (105). The modern "white gold" is a gold-platinum or a gold-nickel alloy and has nothing to do with the ancient "electrum" or "white gold" (106). This wide range of colours which of course occurs just as well in the native gold containing varying amounts of silver was appreciated by the ancient Egyptians and applied to art objects to attain certain aesthetical effects. It played a large role in the philosophy of the early Coptic alchemists and even their predecessors the jewellers and artisans of Egypt (107) and in Mesopotamia the different colours of the types of native gold were appreciated by the artists too (108). In Egypt these colour effects were produced artificially not only by selecting (and later by compounding) the silver-gold alloys but also by colouring gold itself or by colouring the surface of base metals to give them the appearance of the appropriate gold alloy. Thus the "purple or red" gold was produced by dipping the gold object in a solution of an iron salt and heating it afterwards, as Wood proved by his experiment (109). A bronze with a blue tinted platina was produced by alloying the bronze with small quantities of gold, and the *"Leiden-Stockholm" papyri* give many recipes for the colouring of metal surfaces to give them the appearance of precious metals. In Lydian objects the silver is sometimes dissolved from the surface to fake a more valuable appearance (110), and electrum long remains a favourite metal for making mirrors.

The complicated *nomenclature of gold* in the Ancient Near East proves our view, that the different types of native gold were held to be members of a family. In Fig. 36 it will be seen that there are a number of Accadian terms denoting gold (111) and this is in accordance with the fact that the oldest golden artifacts have a gold content ranging from 29 to 91% (112). The Sumerians have fewer terms, Limet believes that the GUŠKIN.SÁR.DA is a gold-alloy halfway between the gold-copper alloy, called "red gold" (GUŠKIN.ḪUŠ.A) and the pure gold (GUŠKIN.SI.SÁ) but this presupposes intentional alloys, whereas native gold would be a more pronounced red, when containing more gold. On the other hand we know that the Sumerians worked native alluvial gold, only in exceptional cases we hear of reef gold being imported. This is the case with the "gold in its powder" (GUŠKIN SAHAR.BA ḪURSAG) which Gudea obtains from the Ḥaḫ-ḫum-mountains (113), and a later text from Ur mentions reef-gold too (114).

The red gold is definitely considered superior in later texts, it is also called "dark gold" (115). It is noteworthy that during the second millennium terms like "fine gold" (ellu), "washed" (misû), "refined" (sirpu) and "superfine" (damqu, SIG₅) begin to crop up, whereas the older "white (pisû) gold" was simply the natural electrum containing much silver. The Accadian ḫurâṣu for gold is related to the Hebrew hârûṣ and by way of the Hurrian ḫiaruḫḫe to the Greek chrysos. In Hurrian there are also the terms zalḫu and aiarḫi (116) and in Hebrew a number of terms denote the native gold, ḥašmal being reserved for electrum (117). In Syria too the documents of the middle of the second millennium (118) begin to speak not only of yellow and red gold, but also of "simple, double, triple and quadruple gold (titturu, tumusse, sirwanase)!

Erman-Grapow's Egyptian dictionary mention the following terms for gold in the ancient Egyptian language:

nb	(II.237.6)	gold
nb n st		reef gold
nb n mw		alluvial (river) gold
nb ḥr ḫ3ś.t.f	(II.237.8)	gold-bearing rock
nkr	(II.344.12)	(sieved) gold-dust
nb n śṯnj	(IV.358.17)	excellent gold
nb nfr	(II.237.11)	beautiful gold
nb sp 2	(II.237.12)	second-quality gold (twice refined?)
nb sp 3	(II.237.13)	third-quality gold (thrice refined?)
nb ḥḏ	(II.237.9)	white gold, electrum
nb n' '	(II.208.7)	multicoloured gold
nb n ḳnj	(V.52.15)	yellow gold
ś3wj	(IV.13.10)	"two-thirds" (66%) gold from Nubia
ḳtm.t	(V.145.6)	(Nubian) gold: Hebr. kethem, Greek
ḏ'm	(V.537.13)	light-coloured gold, electrum

The last term was formerly read "uasm" by the generations of Lepsius and Sir. W. Flinders Petrie, but now the reading "d'm" has been accepted universally (119). The word is rarely used after the XXVth dynasty, like many other terms denoting a particular quality of native gold, probably as by then such impure gold was generally refined. There is considerable confusion in the Bible between amber and electron (120) but Pliny rightly points out that it is a gold-silver alloy with some 20% of silver (121).

The conclusion we can draw from this riot of Accadian and Egyptian terms is that they fall in several classes. Some actually mean the metal gold or electrum or indicate its provenance, form and shape; others mention the colour or give information on the purity, degree of refining, etc. Another class embraces the terms with poetical or symbolical meaning, and then there are some terms which are typically "slang" words (122). Most of these terms disappear as the gold collected from rivers and mountains is being purified in one way or other.

6. *The refining of native gold*

We have no direct evidence where and when the refining of native gold started, but from some of the "quality" terms for gold mentioned above and other circumstantial evidence its seems that refining did not start in Egypt but somewhere in Syria or Mesopotamia. One of the fourteenth-century Amarna letter, written by Burraburiaš to Amenhotep IV of Egypt, reads: "The 20 minae (of gold) which he (the messenger) brought were not "full", when they were put in the furnace only 5 minae came out" (123). There is also the expression NE.KÚ, "what was eaten by the fire", which was originally held to be the name of a metal but various Ur III texts were found in which the figures given show that it meant "loss on smelting or melting", (NE.KÚ.LUH.HA.BI) or refining loss. When gold was delivered to the goldsmiths the weight of the original gold and that of the manufactures objects was carefully noted and apart from this refining loss, there was also a NE.KÚ.AG.SU.BI, a "loss on hammering or flattening" and a NE.KÚ.AG.BI, a "loss on working" in the reports, all of which are sometimes measured carefully (124). Its Accadian equivalent is the "ḫurâṣu sagiru" pointed out by Meissner in a Sargonid text. These indications seem to point out that the separation of silver and other impurities from the gold from mines or placers was invented long before the Amarna Age and possibly during or shortly after the Ur III period (2200—2000 B.C.). But as usual centuries were to elapse before this technical process became common in other countries such as Egypt. From analyses of gold objects in Palestine Macalister concluded that the gold imported in Palestine in the twelfth century B.C. was so pure that it must have been refined in some way. Unfortunately this is a dangerous argument for the gold of Troy II (2600 B.C.) is very pure too (96) and we have shown that this is the case with native gold from various sites. Hence the purity of the gold itself is too dangerous an argument to be used, we should base ourselves on textual evidence that the possibility of recognised to separate the "pure" gold from the native form, and its use as a test, a feature which is very different from a large scale application of this knowledge to produce pure (100%) gold or something very closely approaching this. The evidence from Egypt is much fuller. Since the XVIII dynasty we find the practice of debasing gold by alloying with copper, a procedure probably found so lucrative that in the later periods of Egyptian history compounds containing up to 75% of copper are found. In the XX and XXI dynasty the texts begin to mention more and more qualities of gold like "gold of two times", "gold of three times", etc. which must mean gold refined twice, thrice, etc. (AR. vol. IV). Since the XXVI dynasty the word for electrum disappears from the texts and in the Persian period (525—332) the first objects of pure gold appear. Then Diodorus informs us of Agatharchides personal observations of the refining process ("parting") used in his days in Egypt.

The refining processes being expensive their use, except on a small scale for assaying, it seems that their commercial use does not go back much beyond the sixth century B.C. The various types of native gold were available in various parts of the Near East and hence it is extremely improbable that gold-silver alloys were compounded on a large scale from the pure metals but native gold must have been used. The spread of the refining processes may have been retarded by the natural advantages arising from the use of native gold instead of pure gold. When gold is alloyed with silver (and the same conclusion holds good for alloys containing (smaller) percentages of other metals like copper) the alloy is harder than the pure gold, it will stand tear and wear better and it can be applied in the same way as pure gold. This native alloy was found in practically every gold mine in Egypt, electrum is mentioned even to have come from Punt, Emu, the Highlands, mines east of Redesiâ, the South Countries, the mountains. Therefore there would have been no need to compound it from the pure metals prepared at much cost. Only when obtaining varying qualities from a few localities or from the only source available to him the goldsmith must have been forced to refine and compound his gold in order to obtain the quality he needed. However, by applying his skill to refine gold on a smaller scale he possessed a proper means of evaluating the native gold than by its colour or other external characteristics. This means that together with the refining methods the *art of assaying* was born. We mentioned the letter from the Amarna files which refered to the "testing" of gold. The Old Testament has various passages mentioning the "fining pot" (125), "the refiner" (126) and gold that is "tried" in the fire (127). The cuneiform texts use the word "su'udu" for refining (128), later "ṭubbu" (to improve by heat) or "zanu" (an equivalent for "bašalu, cooking).

However, a simpler way of testing gold was found, the *touchstone*, called the Lydian stone or basanos by the ancients (129), which according to Dana (130) is "a velvet black siliceous stone or flinty jasper used on account of its hardness and black colour for trying the purity

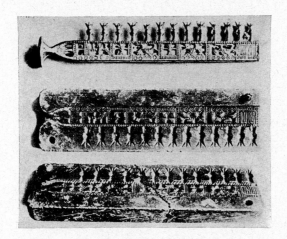

Fig. 35.
An Ugarit goldsmith's double mould and a wax copy
of the cast object (After Scheaffer)

of precious metals. The color left on the stone after rubbing the metal across it indicates to the experienced eye the amount of the alloy". The practice of the modern jeweller is somewhat different from that of the ancient goldsmith. He takes the object to be tested and rubs it on the stone till a small yellow mark appears. Then he drops nitric acid (which the ancients did not know) on the mark. If the gold is of poor quality — or is not gold at all — the yellow streak at once disappears. Pure gold will, of course show no discolouration, and gold of 20 or 18 carats shows very little. Some jewellers have several bottles of nitric acid of different degrees of strength. If dilute acid fails to dissolve the streak on the touchstone, more concentrated acid is used. The quality of the gold is thus more accurately determined.

Pliny refers to it (calling it *coticula* instead of *basanos*) (131) in the following passage:

"The discussion of gold and silver suggests the stone called *coticula*. This used to be found only in the River Tmolus, as Theophrastus says, but now it is found in many localities. Some call them Heraclean stones, others Lydian. They are of moderate size, not more than four inches long and two wide. The side that has been exposed to the sun is better than the lower side. Those who understand the use of these touchstones, when they have taken a specimen from a piece of ore as they would with a file (i.e. by rubbing) tell you at once how much gold there is in the ore, how much silver or how much copper. They are so skilful that the maximum error is less than a scruple".

The term Heraclean stone is usually reserved for the magnet (132). The ancients not disposing of nitric acid used needles of standard quality to test their gold, as is clear from the passage by Theognis "when I am put to the test I am tried even as gold is tried by rubbing besides lead". But apart from the touchstone another way of expressing the purity of gold was developed, the carat-weight (134). This unit of 200 mgrs has by tradition been derived from the seeds in the pod of the Ceratonia aliqua L., the carob (Arab. harrub or hurnûb). The word "carat" comes from the Greek "keration", which is both the seed of the carob, and the equivalent of the Latin siliqua, carat. Keration is in its turn derived from keras, a horn, from the crescent-shaped pods of the tree, usually called St. John's Bread. The Assyrian unit of weight "kisal" (KI-SA-AL) is the seed of the carob-pod. The carat as a standard of purity indicates "a twenty-fourth part".

Touchstone and refining methods opened up an important application of gold, coining gold pieces in the mint. The development of minting in Lydia and the rest of the Greek world dates from the centuries when refining methods had come into common use. We will return to some aspects of the minting of gold later but must now needs turn to a discussion of the refining methods and their history:

7. *Cupellation and other refining methods*

The refining methods fall in two distinct classes:
  a. methods for the separation of precious metals (gold and silver) from base metals such as copper, and
  b. methods for the separation of gold from silver or native gold.

a. The *cupellation* process is probably the oldest and most efficient way of separating the precious metals from the baser ones (135). Its principle is alloying the gold with lead in a special pot or crucible ("cupel") and oxidizing the product by means of a strong current of air blown into the surface of the molten metal. The base metals are "consumed" or "drossed" (the oxides formed are absorbed by the wall of the porous cupel) while the gold and silver pass "unscathed through the ordeal" (136). For this trial by fire a special crucible was made porous enough to absorb the oxidation products of the base metals, which seemed to disappear in the "fining pot". The modern cupellation hearth is lined with bone ash, calcareous clay (marl) or magnesia; the ancient cupels which Agatarchides called "kerameon" (137), Pliny "catini" (138) and Cassiodorus "fictilia" (139) were all made from a special type of clay, which Pliny calls "tasconium". This cupel is distinct from the usual "melting pot", the "choanos" of Homer (140). We have very detailed descriptions of the ancient process in Theophilus' manual (141), which agree completely with the fragmentary information given by ancient authors. There is no reason for supposing with Davies (142) that this cupellation process was invented in the Iron Age only for the method described by Agatarchides, on which he bases this assumption is already a complication of the older simpler method in use in much earlier times. Beneviste (143) has made it clear that the Greek "obryza", Latin "obrussa" means cupellation and he derives these terms from a Hurrian "ḫubrušḫi", meaning the "earthen"-vessel, the cupel. This is quite plausible for the process came to Greece from Anatolia-Syria in the way the very word for gold entered the Greek language.

This process could also be operated on a commercial scale by treating washed gold ores (to which fluxes were added to form a slag with the gangue remaining in the gold ores) with lead in the way indicated above, oxidizing the molten alloy in cupels or melting pots and recovering the "regulus" of pure gold (and silver) after the slag has been removed. This process is called *liquation* and it was used from the time when the Romans started to work more complex ores (sometimes sulphidic ores) for gold (144). We have no evidence that this large-scale "cupellation" was used in earlier periods.

The *amalgamation* process (extraction with mercury) was known to the Romans "in laboratory and factory" (145) and Pliny describes the way in which mercury is used to recover gold from gold cloth (146). The richer gold ores are crushed and mixed with mercury, the gangue is separated by forcing the mercury through leather, and then the amalgam (solution of the gold and silver in the mercury) is heated to recover the precious metals (147). We have a fairly good description

of the process by Vitruvius, who confounds vermillion with red lead
(a lead compound) (148): "The workshops which were in the Ephesian
mines are now removed to Rome, because this kind of vein has been
discovered in parts of Spain. The ore from the Spanish mines is conveyed to Rome and dealt with by the farmers-general (publicanes).
The workshops are between the temples of Flora and Quirinus.

I will now go on to describe the treatment of minium or vermillion.
It is said to have been discovered in the Cilbian Fields of Ephesus. The
material and its treatment is sufficiently wonderful. For what is called
the ore is first extracted. Then using certain processes, they find
minium. In the veins the ore is like iron, of a more carroty colour,
with a red dust around it. When it is mined, and is worked with iron
tools, it exudes many drops of quicksilver, and these are at once collected by the miners. When the ore has been collected in the workshop, because of the large amount of moisture, it is put in the furnace
to dry. The vapour which is produced by the heat of the fire, when it
condenses on the floor of the oven, is found to be quicksilver. When
the ore is taken away, the drops which settle because of their minute-
ness cannot be gathered up, but are swept into a vessel of water:
there they gather together and unite. Four sextarii (4 pints) of quicksilver when they are weighed come to 100 pounds (70 lbs.).

When quicksilver is poured into a vessel and a stone weight of 100
pounds is placed upon it the stone floats to the surface. For it is unable
by its weight to press the liquid down and so squeeze it out and separate it. If the stone is take away and a scruple of gold is placed upon
the quicksilver, it will not swim, but is pressed down to the bottom
of itself. We cannot deny that the gravity of bodies depends on their
species and not on their volume."

"Quicksilver is adapted for many uses. Without it neither silver nor
brass can be properly guilt. When gold is embroidered in cloth, and
the garment, being worn out by age, is no longer fit for use, the cloth
is put in earthenware vessels and burnt over the fire. The ashes are
thrown into water, and quicksilver is added. This collects all the
particles of gold and combines with them. The water is then poured
away and the remainder is placed on a cloth, and is pressed by hand.
Under this pressure the quicksilver being liquid passes through the
pores of the cloth and the pure gold is retained within."

The finds at Suplja Stena, some 12 Km. from Vinča proved beyond
doubt that the Romans produced mercury on a large scale here (and
in Spain too!). The kiln used in the process was a closed type of the

ordinary baker's furn, slanting towards a fore-hearth in which the mercury collected. The ore worked was cinnaber, crushed in sandstone mortars with stone pestles and heated in the furnaces, where the mercury distilled off to collect in the fore-hearth. Perhaps mercury was identical with the "water of separation" of the Bible (149). The

Accadian	Sumerian	English	Notes
ḫurâṣu	GUŠKIN (KÙ.GI)	"the yellow", gold	Hebr. ḫârûṣ; Hurr. ḫia-ruḫḫe; Greek chrysos; Arab ḫrḍ
ḫurâṣu ḫuššu	GUŠKIN-ḪUŠ.A	red gold	
ḫurâṣu arḳu	GUŠKIN-SIG₇	yellow gold	arḳu is the yellow-green of young shoots (Gr. chloros)
ḫurâṣu šadi		mountain gold	
	GUŠKIN.SÁR.DA	alloyed gold	
ṣarirû	AN.TA.ŠUR.RA	"the ruddy", red gold	from root ṣ r r
pašallu		gold leaf	compare Syr. p'šâlâ = texture
šaššu		"the sun-metal"	compare Syr. šamša = sun
zûzu		mint-gold	compare Syr. zûz = coin
ṣaidu	GUŠKIN.SI.SÁ	refined red gold	from root ṣwd = shine red
misû		washed gold	from root msh
anaku		(lit."tin") gold coin	compare Engl. „tin" = gold coin
dalbu, daiâlu		"the circulator"	from root djl = walk to and fro
zalḫu		(Subaraean) „the ruddy"	compare Syr. z'liḫê = patina
sâmu		"the red"	often combined with 2
sakîru		reef gold	compare Syr. 's'Kar = rubrum facit

Fig. 36.
The Accadian nomenclature of gold

process was in common use during the Middle Ages (150) and introduced in the silver industry of Mexico in 1552 by Bartol. Medina.

b. There are several methods to separate gold from silver, but we usually find them combined with the cupellation process. The parting methods in use in ancient times were probably:

1. *Salt process.* The principle consists in the addition of salt to the silver-gold alloy, some reducing agent like straw, charcoal or other

organic material being added. The salt attacks the silver and forms silver chloride which is absorbed by the walls of the crucible. It is still used in Japan where the gold is mixed with clay and salt, and the crucible containing the mixture heated in a charcoal furnace for 12 hours at red heat. Then the dish is removed and the gold is washed with hot brine to dissolve the silver chloride formed (151). A slightly different version is given by Theophilus (III. 33—34) and Agricola (Books VII and X). Another version using powdered bricks or tiles instead of clay and adding sulphates is given by Biringuccio. Though Gowland thinks that gold was refined by this salt process in the Persian period, we have only indirect evidence that these cementation processes were known because we find its principles applied in the more complicated processes which are discussed by the classical authors.

There we usually find a combination between the salt process and the cupellation method. Thus the important information given by Agatharchides on gold refining in Egypt states that the gold was purified by mixing it with tin (lead?), salt and some barley husks, enclosing the mixture in a crucible with a luted lid and heating it for five days in a fire of straw. On cooling the pure gold remains, the base metals would be oxidized and absorbed by the pot, the silver chlorinated by the salt and absorbed, and the bran would prevent the base metals from being oxidized too rapidly. The low temperature obtained by a straw fire which is said to be specially adapted for gold refining (152) would prevent the evaporation of too much metal; for gold evaporates appreciably if heated above its melting point. Here gold remains solid but is gradually penetrated by the refining agents.

This combination of cupellation and cementation by the salt process is not only mentioned by Agatharchides, Strabo takes "styptic earth" instead of salt; Pliny refines with lead, *misy* or *alumen nigrum*. The *misy* is translated by copper or iron pyrites (Bailey) (153) and the *alumen nigrum* by a salt of aluminium or iron, borax or salpeter, or a nitrate, chloride or bromide.

Agricola (Book VII) mentions a similar process with salt and lead, using urine as the reducing agent and in Japan Gowland found a process for refining gold using clay and lead oxides (154).

2. *Sulphur process*. This parting method consists of heating the gold-silver alloy with sulphur-compounds (sulphides) and charcoal. This treatment transforms the silver into black silver sulphide and leaves the gold as a residual *regulus*. The silver can be recovered from the sulphide by cupellation with lead. It is very probable that the processes

with *misy* mentioned by Pliny are of this type. Davies considers de-silvering with stibnite (antimony sulphide) very probable in the Ancient Near East and he ascribes the antimony content of some gold objects in Egypt to the use of this refining method. The method is described in detail by Theophilus (III. 69), Biringuccio and Agricola (X. 254—280).

3. Parting methods involving the use of *nitric acid* are not used before Agricola's time.

8. *The goldsmith*

We do not propose to discuss in detail the development of the goldsmith's craft, a subject which should be left to experts, but a few words on the place of these highly skilled craftsmen in ancient society seem justified. The KÙ-DÍM (kutimmu or nappâḫ ḫurâši), the "fashioner of gold", the goldsmith was an important person in ancient Mesopo-tamia. According to the cuneiform texts he obtained his gold from the "gold-mountains", the KUR A-ra-li and KUR HUḫu-uḇLUL (155) or the KUR A-ra-lu and KUR Ḫub-u₅ (156). Gudea imported it from the mountain Ḫa-ḫu-um, or Meluhha, which in later texts seems to denote Ethiopia (whence ivory and ebony came too) but which in the Larsa period may have indicated the Indus valley (157). This gold arrived in the form of gold dust, bars or rings. Texts of the Early Larsa Period (1900 B.C.) mention small quantities arriving from abroad (158) and in the Code of Hammurabi (§ 112) there is a special clause on the risk of transported goods handed to third parties for delivery in Mesopotamia by merchants residing abroad.

Gold is often mentioned in Ur III tablets, but more in the south than in the north of lower Mesopotamia, the gold may have been imported mainly from overseas in those days. It appears that different qualities of gold were in circulation and this implies that from these texts no general conclusions should be drawn from the gold/silver ratios mentioned in various texts, the more so as gold was not a means of exchange in this early period (2000 B.C.) but simply a precious metal upto the Old Babylonian Period. Only in the Cassite period (1500 B.C.) the situation changes (159) and gold is being used as a means of fixing prices. In the north, in Assur, gold seems to have been available in large quantities, for as much as 30 minaes of gold are sometimes supplied as trading capitals (160). The normal rate gold/silver seems to have been 1 : 8, if certain texts allude to a rate 1 : 4

(161) this seems to have been fixed for an alloy less fine than the monetary gold which a goldsmith needed. A text from Larsa (162) mentions a rate 1 : 6½.

No doubt the goldsmith received native gold of varying purity, for a text of the days of Rim-Sîn (163) speaks of:

"8 shekels of gold, its rate 1 shekel equals 4 shekels of silver,

5 shekels of gold, its rate 1 shekel equals 3 shekels of silver."

Then the goldsmith prepared certain alloys for specific purposes. Gold

Fig. 37.
Egyptian goldwork as depicted in the tomb of Zenone

in the form of leaf of sheet gold for overlay work, was usually an alloy of copper and gold, such alloys as two parts of gold on one part of copper (164) or five parts of gold on two parts of copper (165) are mentioned. For objects subjected to wear an alloy (zahalu), may be richer in gold was used. Texts of the first millennium mention alloys of gold and "haematite" (166), may be a gold/iron alloy.

The goldsmiths, like other craftsmen were organized in guilds, Late Assyrian texts mention the "rab nappâḫ ḫurâṣi," the chief of the goldsmiths. His skill is obvious from the various technical terms for the operations and tools he uses (167). The gold-bar (ni-pištu) is melted (ba-zi-ir) in a crucible and refined (BAR.GIR, ṣurrupu), cast and

shaped or worked in various ways (šub-ba, labânu), sometimes used
for inlay-work (gar-ra, šakânu). If the goldsmith is later admitted to
the membership of the Academy, the "bît mummi" (168), it is because
of the great skill he showed in the many works which have survived
to our days.

There is no doubt about the skill and the specialisation of the goldsmiths of ancient Egypt. The gold-miners (ķwr, V. 21. 9) washed the
native gold (i'j nb, I. 39. 19), after having estimated the probable output of the sands (bj3w, II. 237. 7) and deliver the gold dust (nķr nb,
II. 344, 12) in special pouches ('rf n nb, I. 210. 21 or krś n nb, V. 135.
13) to the merchant who finally brings it to the "place where the gold
is worked" (ḥ.t nb, II. 238. 16), the jeweller's shop. The goldsmith,
the "worker in gold" (ḥmw nb, III. 82. 12) is organised, we read about
the chief of the guild of the goldsmiths (mr w'nt n nbj.w, I. 287. 16).
There is a considerable number of terms for the methods he uses to
transform the crude gold into the beautiful objects we admire in our
museums. In several cases we do not know precisely what is meant by
a range of what seem to be synonyms at first sight, a study of these
terms in their proper context might reveal more than the dictionary
gives:

b3k m nb	II. 238. 2	sheathe or cover with gold
nbd	II. 247. 1	sheathe or cover with metal
dg3	V. 499. 2	sheathe or cover with metal
mk	II. 162. 1	cover with gold
gnh	V. 176. 9	gold-sheathed (wooden objects)
śśr m nb	IV. 294. 12/13	to gild
tjś m nb	V. 243. 3	to gild
mḥ	II. 119. 18	inlay
ḥt	III. 204, 1—5	inlay with copper-gold alloy
ś'b m nb	IV. 44. 4	to decorate with gold
im3 m nb	I. 80. 15	to beautify with gold
t3j	V. 347. 14	to engrave metals
3h'	I. 19. 10	to engrave or incise signs
skr	V. 306. 11	to beat gold
dķ'	V. 495. 7	to polish
śn''	IV. 156. 10	to polish

No wonder that the Egyptian texts prove that there was a certain
amount of specialisation in the goldsmith's craft, for apart from the
general term "goldsmith" (nbj, II. 241. 1) we find the "gold worker"

(ḥmw nb, III. 82. 12), the "gold beater" (šsp nb, III. 485. 8), the "engraver" (t3j bsnt, I. 477. 5), the "maker of necklaces" (str, IV. 344. 5) and the "maker of beads" (irw wšbt, I. 373. 8).

Gold foil and sheet gold were applied widely in ancient Egyptian art, it was applied to columns, doors, obelisks and bas-reliefs (169), Vernier doubts whether the stories of the large gold reserves of Egypt (170) were true and suggests that gilding a silver core may have been far more common than supposed upto now. This can only be proved by a thorough examination of our museum objects. On the other hand it has recently been stated that two solid gold obelisks, some 7 M high were erected in the temple of Ammon at Karnak (171), but this would mean that the pair of them represented 2500 talents of solid gold, e.g. some 38 Tons of gold! It is not explained to us how such large castings were executed by the ancient goldsmiths, even if they disposed of such enormous quantities of gold. It is certain that gold was simply a precious material and did not play its part as a medium of exchange before the conquest of the country by the Persians and Alexander the Great (172). Specimens have survived of gold and silver pieces issued during the reign of Tachos (361—359 B.C.) minted after the pattern of the coins of Athens, the silver pices being inscribed with the words "good gold" (nfr nb) in Demotic characters. Coins with hieroglyphic inscriptions date from the reign of Nectanebo II (359—343). When the papyri mention tributes of gold exacted from the villages of Egypt (173), this is native gold, and in some cases silver is allowed as a substitute.

There is no doubt of the prominent place of the goldsmith in the Mycenaean civilisation. In the Pylos tablets (174) the ku-ru-so is frequently mentioned though we hear no details about his work. The kurosowoko, the chrysochóos, also appears among the tradesmen and he may have imported his own gold to work it into the gold ornaments, discs, masks, diadems, sheet gold ornaments on swords and daggers, earrings, necklaces and pins which are so abundantly found in Late Helladic graves. The "sacred gold" mentioned in a Pylos tablet may be a golden ritual or votive object. In classical Greece the goldsmith is often called chalkeus, but his proper name is χρυσοχόος or χρυσουργός. A certain specialisation is indicated by such terms as "gilder" (χρυσωτής), "bracelet-smith" (ψελλιοποιός, Latin armillarius), assayer (χρυσογνώμον) and "gold-worker" (χρυσοτέκτων). It would be interesting to examine the Talmud and other Jewish texts to find out what part the gold-smith played in Jewish society. In Roman society the aurifex is a honoured craftsmen, who is sometimes also called maragritarius (jeweller or dealer in pearls), and mentioned in many inscriptions (175). Some towns besides Rome have a guild of goldsmiths like Smyrna (176), in other towns no such organisation is mentioned specifically though individual goldsmiths are (at Aquilea, 177) (at Capua, 178). Strong guilds existed at Palmyra (179) and at Alexandria (180) in which town a freedman was magister of the guild. The goldsmith's shops of Roman Egypt were private property, not only in Alexandria but also in other towns like Tebtynis and the Fayum. It seems that the government controlled the industry by granting rights to individuals to operate in certain districts after payment of a fee for this privilege (181).

We have mentioned the fact that proper method for assaying and refining gold formed the basis for the development of coinage. From Lydia gold coinage spread to Greece, but smaller silver coins were not struck before 560 B.C. (182). Gold coins played a secondary role only, the value of gold and silver falling slowly until Alexander the Great released the huge stores of precious metals of the Persian kings. Only then a regular circulation of golden coins can be said to start. Rome originally had bronze coins, later silver ones too. Then Augustus establishes a fixed value between gold and silver and makes gold coins an essential part of the monetary system. It gradually began to replace silver as the most important monetary metal. Byzantium struck but few silver coins, but circulated mostly gold and bronze coins. The gold value fluctuated and there was a gradual depreciation upto 30%, the causes of which were political rather than economical. This is for instance the cause of the debasement of the coins of Orodes I. The prolonged warfare between the Parthians and Romans led to the need of a greatly expanded coinage (183), probably achieved by melting down silver coins of Orodos' predecessor with early Parthian bronze coins.

The oldest form of gold is sheet or foil gold and so are the techniques derived from it, pasting and glueing it on wood and stone and chasing and embossing it when forms of wood and stone were available. The ancient Egyptians beat nuggets into gold foil upto 0.001 mm thick which was pasted on the support or objects were dipped in a mixture of gold dust with powdered lead and paste and then heated. The Old Kingdom foil gold is seldom thinner than 0.01 mm, but later sheets are ten times thinner. The Romans improved the technique of making gold leaf (184) but did not get much beyond 0.0002 mm, the limit which stood until the 18th century (185) when it fell to 0.00008 mm. Rolled gold is a late development (186). The *granulation* techniques were practised in Egypt and Mesopotamia but particularly by the Etruscans (187) who were masters in the field. The story of the development and spread of this technique has not yet been written, it became known in China in late Chou-early Han times (188), but it is particularly interesting to note a completely independent development of the art in South America (189). Bergsøe first drew the attention to the fact that pre-Columbian Indians of Ecuador were able to melt and granulate the high melting native gold-platinum alloy of their country, using very simple methods though from time to time they alloyed it with copper. Gold/copper alloys were very popular in South-American metallurgy and determined the development of the metallurgy of gold in these regions, this alloy had a melting point some 200° C lower than its components and the early Spanish explorers found "tumbaga" everywhere. It made casting easier and yielded a harder metal, a small amount of gold went further and it was a way of colouring copper!

Further historical studies on the goldsmith's craft by experts are urgently wanted if we want to trace its spread over the Old and the New World. Excellent books have been written on ancient jewelry (190), but more work is needed to link this up with Chinese and Far Eastern techniques (191) and with those of the New World mentioned above.

A thorough study of the history of the goldsmith's craft and the recognition of its services to the development of metallurgy in general will more than compensate the impressions evoked by the pessimistic words of Timon of Athens:

"Gold, yellow, glittering, precious gold... Much of this will make black, white; foul, fair; wrong, right; base, noble; old, young; coward, valiant."

BIBLIOGRAPHY

1. GOHORY, JAQUES, *L'histoire de la Terre Neuve du Pérou* (Paris, 1545)
2. PLINY, *Nat. Hist.* XXXIII, 4—52
3. HOOVER, H. C. and L. H., *Agricola's de Re Metallica* (London, 1912, 279—281)
   AGRICOLA, GEORG, *Zwölf Bücher vom Borg- und Hüttenwesen* (V.D.I. Verlag, Berlin, 1929)
4. HELPS, A., *The Spanish Conquest of America* (London, 1857)
5. PLINY, *Nat. Hist.* VII, 197
6. J. F. GLÜCK, *Der Gelbe Stein* (Z. Metallkunde 44, 1953, 277—281)
7. FRANKFORT, H., *Studies in the Early Pottery of the Near East*, 1927, vol. II, 21
   LUCAS, A., *Ancient Egyptian Materials and Industries*, London, 1962
8. CAMERON, V. D., *Across Africa* (London, 1885, vol. II, chapter 17)
9. PARTINGTON, J. R., *Origins and Development of Applied Chemistry*, London, 1935
10. COLLINS, W. E., *Mineral Enterprise in China*, London, 1912, 244
11. GRAPOW, H., *Die bildlichen Ausdrücke des Aegyptischen* (Leipzig, 1924)
    LORIMER, H. L., *Gold and Ivory in Mythology* (Essays pres. to Murray, 1936)
    THORNDIKE, L., *History of Magic and Experimental Science* (London, 1929, vol. I)
12. SMITH, G. ELLIOT SMITH, *The Ancient Egyptians* (London, 1923, 205—206)
13. E. HOLMYARD, *Makers of Chemistry* (London, 1931, 6)
    FORBES, R. J., *Studies in Ancient Technology*, Vol. I (1955), 121
    LIPPMANN, E. O. VON, *Entstehung und Ausbreitung der Alchemie* (Berlin, 1919/1954, 3 vols.)
    THORNDIKE, L., *History of Magic and Experimental Science* (London, 1929/1958, 8 vols.)
14. J. F. GLÜCK, *Der "gelbe Stein"* (Z. Metallkunde 44, 1953, 277—281)
15. BREASTED, *Ancient Records*, III, 285 & IV. 33
16. PLINY, *Nat. Hist.* XXXIII. 59
17. KÖSTER, W., *Der metallische Werkstoff* (Ber. D. Museum VII, 1935, iii, 77—104)
18. PLINY, *Nat. Hist.* XXXIII, 62. 77
19. GARLAND, H. and BANNISTER, C., *Ancient Egyptian Metallurgy* (London, 1927)
20. LOCK, C. G. W., *Gold, its occurrence and extraction* (London, 1901)
    LONGRIDGE, C. C., *Hydraulic Mining* (London, 1903)
    —, *Gold Dredging* (London, 1905)

ZERRENNER, C. *Gold, Platin und Diamant wasschen* (Leipzig, 1851)

21. JACOB, W., *An historical Inquiry into the Production and Consumption of the Precious Metals* (Philadelphia, 1832)
22. FORBES, R. J., *Studies in Ancient Technology*, Vol. VII (1963), 109ff
23. QUIRING, H., *El laboreo de las minas de oro por los Romanos en le Peninsula Ibérica y las arrugias de Plinio* (Investigacíon y Progresso IX, 1935, 6—8)
    —, *Der Römische Goldbergbau in Hispanien und die Arrugien des Plinius* (Z. f. Berg-, Hütten- und Salinenwesen 81, 1933, 270—279)
    —, *Der Römische Goldbergbau und die Arrugien des Plinius* (FuF 10, 1934, 34—35)
    TÉGLAS, J., *Studiën über den Dacischen Goldbergbau der Römer* (Ungarische Revue IX, 1889, 331)
24. *For further details see my Studies vol. VII* (1963), 201 ff
25. LUCAS, A., *Ancient Egyptian Materials and Industries*, London, 1962
26. BREASTED, *Ancient Records* III, 166, 198, 259
27. DIODOR III, 12—14
28. EMMONS, G., *Gold Deposits of the World* (New York, 1937)
    FREISE, E., *Berg und Hüttenmannische Unternehmungen in Asien und Afrika während des Altertums* (Z. f. Berg-, Hütten- u. Salinenwesen, 56, 1908, 347 ff)
29. FITZLER, K., *Steinbrüche und Bergwerke im Ptolemäischen und Römischen Ägypten* (Leipzig, 1910)
    FUTTERER, W., *Afrika in seiner Bedeutung für die Goldproduktion in Vergangenheit, Gegenwart und Zukunft* (Berlin, 1895)
    GARDINER, A. H., *The map of the gold mines in a Ramesside papyrus at Turin* (Cairo Scientific Journal VIII, 1914, 42)
    HUME, F., *Geology of Egypt* (3 vols. Cairo 1931—1937)
    H. M. E. SCHÜRMANN, *Alter Goldbergbau im Wadi Ballat* (Geologie en Mijnbouw N.S. XIV, 1952, 113—114)
30. BREASTED, *Ancient Records* vol. II
31. CLINE, W., *Mining and Metallurgy in Negro Africa* (Paris, 1937)
32. H. M. E. SCHÜRMANN, *Alter Goldbergbau im Wadi Ballat* (Geologie en Mijnbouw, 14, 1952, 113—114)
33. STRABO XVII. 2.2. cap. 821; HERODOTUS III, 23, 114
34. H. QUIRING, *Die Lage des Gold- und Antimonlandes Punt und die erste Umfahrung Afrikas* (Forsch. & Fortschr. 21/23, 1947, 16—18, pags. 161—163)
35. BREASTED, *Ancient Records* IV, 408—409
36. STRABO XVI. 4. 26. cap. 784
37. STRABO XVI. 4. 18. cap. 777
38. STRABO XVI. 4. 19. cap. 778—780
39. DAHSE, G., *Ein zweites Goldland Salomos, Vorstudien zur Geschichte Westafrikas* (Z. f. Ethn. XLIII, 1911, 1—79)
40. 1 *Ki.* 9. 28; 10. 11; 22. 48; 1 *Chron.* 29. 4; *Job* 22. 24; 23. 16; *Ps.* 45. 9; *Is.* 13. 12
41. 2. *Chron.* 9. 1; *Ps.* 72. 15
42. *Jer.* 10. 9; *Dan.* 10. 5

43. 2. *Chron.* 3. 6
44. *Gen.* 10. 7; 10. 28—29
45. VAB I, 70b; VI, 33 & 39; *Thureau Dangin, Rituels Accadiens* (1921, 132)
46. STRABO XVI. 4. 22. cap. 780
47. D. M. DUNLOP, *Sources of gold and silver in Islam according to Al-Hamdânî* (Studia Islamica vol. VIII, 1957, 29—49)
    ALLCHIN, F. R., *Upon the antiquity and methods of gold mining in ancient India* (J. Econ. Hist. Orient V, 1962, 1/2)
48. STRABO XV. 1. 34. cap. 701
49. STRABO XV. 1. 30. cap. 700; XV. 1. 68. cap. 718
50. PLINY, *Nat Hist.* XXXIII. 36
51. STRABO XV. 1. 37. cap. 703; XV. 1. 44. cap. 706; PLINY, *Nat. Hist.* XXXIII. 66; VII. 10; XI. 111; ARRIAN, *Indika* XV. 6; HERODOTUS III. 102—106; APOLL. VIT. VI. 1—2
52. HERODOTUS III. 116
53. T'OUNG PAO IX, 1908, 429
54. *Das Land der Seide*, Leipzig, 1938, 10
55. LEVAT, *Richesses minérales des possessions russes en Asie centrale* (Ann. des Mines 1903)
56. SCHOFF, G., *Periplus of the Erythrean Sea* (Philadelphia, 1912, 160)
57. STRABO XV. 2. 14. cap. 726
58. HERODOTUS III. 116; I. 215
59. STRABO XV. 1. 58. cap. 711
60. PLINY, *Nat. Hist.* VI. 14; VI. 30, XXXIII. 52; STRABO XI. 2. 19. cap. 499
61. JESSEN, A. A. and PASSEK, T. E., *Zoloto Kavkaza* (Das Gold des Kaukasus) (Izvestija Gosurdarstenoj Akademii Istorii Materialmoj Kultury, Fasc. 110, 162—178)
62. ARISTOTLE, *de Mir. Ausc.* 26
63. STRABO XI. 14. 9. cap. 529
64. *Tigl. Tt.* 27; VAB VII. 164. 1
65. II R. 51. I—II. 11; LUCKENBILL, A. R., II. 261; K. 2801. r. 36; MEISSNER-ROST, B. A., III. 295; KAH 75. r. 14
66. BA III. 234. 21
67. VAB I, 70b; VI. 33; W. CAMPBELL, THOMPSON, *Dictionary of Assyrian Geology and Chemistry*, Oxford, 1936
68. DAVIES, O., *Bronze Age Mining round the Aegean* (Nature 130, 1932, 985/7)
    SHEAR, TH. L., *The gold sands of the Pactolus* (Class. J. XVII, 1924, 186/8)
69. HERODOTUS I. 93; V. 49 & 101; PLINY, *Nat. Hist.* XXXIII. 66; STRABO XIII. 1. 23. cap. 591; XIII. 4. 5. cap. 626; SCHEIL, MMAP, XXI. 8
70. STRABO XIII. 1. 23. cap. 591; XIV. 5. 28. cap. 680
71. REGLING, PW VII. 978
72. DAVIES, O., *Bronze Age Mining round the Aegean* (Nature 130, 1932, 985—987)

DAVIES, O., *Roman Mines in Europe* (Oxford, 1935)

GAUL, J. H., *Possibilities of prehistoric Metallurgy in the East Balkan Peninsula* (AJA 46, 1942, 400—409)

A. S. ARVANITOUPOULOS, *Peri tou chrysou tes Makedonias* (Polemon V, 1952, 83—119)

73. PLINY, *Nat. Hist.* XXXIII. 66

74. HERODOTUS VI. 46

75. HERODOTUS III. 57, PAUSANIAS X. 11. 2; BENT, A., *Researches among the Cyclades*, JHS VI, 195

76. LIVY, 45. 29. 4—14

77. PETRIE, W., *Flinders, Arts and Crafts of Ancient Egypt* (London, 1909, 83—94)

78. ROLFE, R. T., *Gold and Silver in Ancient Egypt* (Metal Ind. (London) 31, 1927, 433 & 481)

THUREAU DANGIN, F., *Le rapport entre le valeur de l'or, l'argent et le cuivre à l'époque d'Agadé* (RA VIII, 1911, 92)

—, *Le rapport entre valeur de l'or et l'argent en Babylonie* (OLZ XII, 1909, 382)

UNGNAD, *Das Wertverhältnis der Metalle* (OLZ XIV, 1911, 106)

79. WACE, A. J. B. and STUBBINGS, F. H., *Companion to Homer*, London, 1962

80. ILIAD VI, 48; X. 379; XI. 133; XX. 268; XXI. 165; XXIII. 549; X. 315; VII. 180; XI. 46; XVIII. 289

ODYSSEY 10. 45; 21. 10; 2. 338; 13. 11; 3. 304

81. ILIAD IX. 122, 264; II. 229; XIX. 247

82. Kn Ol (Ventris and Chadwick no. 258)

83. STRABO 4. 6. 7; 5. 1. 12; PLINY 33. 78

84. STRABO 4. 6. 12; 5. 1. 8; WOGRINZ, A., *Zur Geschichte des Tauerngoldes* (Metall und Erz 36, 1939, Heft 8)

85. R. F. TYLECOTE, *Metallurgy in Archaeology*, London, 1962

86. OTTO, H., *Die chemische Untersuchung des Goldringes von Gahlstorf und seine Beziehungen zu anderen Funden* (Jhresschr. Focke Museum, Bremen, 1939, 48—62)

87. TACITUS, *Agricola* 12. 6; C.I.L. VII. 151

88. DIODOR V. 27; STRABO 3. 2. 8. cap. 146; 4. 2. 1. cap. 190; 4. 1. 13. cap. 187; 4. 1. 13. cap. 188; 4. 3. 3. cap. 193; SUETONIUS, *Ceasar* 54

89. FORBES, R. J., *Studies in Ancient Technology* VII, 1963, 158

90. FALKENSTEIN, no. 703; LANGDON, Pict. Inscr. no. 264

91. WILCKINSON, J. G., *Manners and Customs of the Ancient Egyptians*, vol. III London, 1837, 224

92. HOLMYARD, E., *Makers of Chemistry* (London, 1931, 6)

93. PETRIE, W. FLINDERS, *Medûm*, London, 1892, 33

PETRIE, W. FLINDERS, *Arts and Crafts of Ancient Egypt*, London, 1909, 83

94. SETHE, K., *Urgeschichte und älteste Religion der Aegypter* (Leipzig, 1920)

95. Davies, O., *Bronze Age Mining round the Aegean* (Nature, 130, 1932, 985)

96. Lucas, A., *Ancient Egyptian Materials and Industries*, London, 1962

97. Danilevskij, V. V., *Historisch-technologische Untersuchungen der alten Bronze- und Gold-Erzeugnisse des Kaukasus* (Russ.) (Izvestija Gosudarstevannoj Akademii Materialnoj Kultury Fasc. 110, 215—252)
    Zhemchuzni, J., *Russ. Chem. Soc.* 1923, 545

98. Garland H. and Bannister, C., *Ancient Egyptian Metallurgy* (London, 1927)

99. Williams, C. R., *Catalogue of the Egyptian Antiquities, gold, silver, jewelry and related objects* (New York. Hist. Soc. 1924)

100. Thomas, E. S., *Notes on the Mining Industry of Egypt* (Cairo Scientific Journal, III, 1909, 112)

101. Partington, J. R., *Origins and Development of Applied Chemistry* (London, 1935)

102. Weill, A. R., *Un probléme de métallurgie archéologique* (Rev. d. métall. 48, 1951, 2, 97—104)
    Weill, A. R., *Etude aux rayons X d'objects égyptiens et romains à base d'or* (Revue de métall. XLIX, 1952, 4, 293—298)
    Weill, A. R., *Analyses aux rayons X de deux plaques d'or provenant de fouilles archéologiques* (La metall. Ital. 1951, 12, 3—7)

103. Rainbird Clark, R., *The Early Iron Age treasure from Snettishham, Norfolk* (Proc. Preh. Society 1954, 20 (1955), 27—86)

104. Comfort, H., *A hoard of Greek jewelry* (A.J.A. 54, 1950, 121—126)

105. Pliny, *Nat. Hist.* IX. 139; XXXIV. 5—8; XXXVII. 49

106. Herodotus I. 50

107. Hopkins, *Alchemy*, New York, 1934

108. Plenderleith, J., *Ur Excavations* (London, 1934, vol. II, 394)
    Smith, E. A., *Rolled gold, its origin and development* (J. Inst. Metals, 44, 1930, 175—205)

109. Wood, R. W., *The purple gold of Tutankhamûn* (JEA XX, 1934, 62—65)

110. Davies, O., *Bronze Age mining round the Aegean* (Nature 130, 1932, 985)

111. Bottéro, J., *Archives R. de Mari* VII, 184
    Chicago Assyrian Dictionary VI, 245
    Limet, H., *Le travail du métal au pays de Sumer au temps de la dynastie d'Ur* III, Paris, 1960, 41
    Levey, M., *Chemistry and Chemical Technology in ancient Mesopotamia* (Amsterdam, 1959, 187—195)
    Levey, M., *The refining of gold in ancient Mesopotamia* (Chymia V, 1959, 31—36)

112. Bottero, J., RA 43, 1949, 17

113. Thureau-Dangin, F., *Inscriptions de Sumer...*, Paris, 1905, 110—111

114. Legrain, UET III, no. 414 & 418

115. Strassmaier, J. N., *Inschriften des Nabonidus*, Leipzig, 1889, 489

116. UNGNAD, A., *Gold, Orientalia* n.s. IV, 3/4, 1933, 296—299
117. KENNETT, R. H., *Ancient Hebrew Social Life and Customs*, London, 1933, 83
    HAUPT, J., *Hebrew terms for gold and silver* (JAOS 43, 1923, 116—127)
118. VIROLLEAUD, CH., *Les tablettes de Mishrifé-Qatna* (Syria IX, 1928, 90—96; XI, 1930, 311—342)
119. BISSING, W. VON, *Zur Geschichte des Silbers und des Elektrons* (Acta Orientalia IV, 1925, 138—141)
    GARDINER, SIR A. H., *cited in: The early chronology of Sumer and Egypt by St. Langdon*, JEA VII, 1921, 150
    LEPSIUS, C. R., *Les métaux dans les inscriptions égyptiennes*, BEHE, fasc. XX, Paris, 1877
    PEET, T. E., *Review of Petrie's History of Egypt* vol. I, JEA IX, 1923, 124
    WILCKEN, Z. f. Ä. LX, 1925, 86
120. *Ezech.* 1. 7; 7. 2; *Dan.* 10. 5—6; *Apoc.* 1. 15; JOSEPHUS, *Antiq.* VIII. 8
121. PLINY, *Nat. Hist.* XXXIII. 80
122. THOMPSON, W. CAMPBELL, *A Dictionary of Assyrian Geology and Chemistry* (Oxford, 1936)
123. KNUDTZON, J. A., *Die Amarna Tafeln*, VAB II. 1, 92
124. LEGRAIN, L., *Temps des rois d'Ur*, p. 84, no. 1
    FOSSEY, C., *Rev. Étud. Sém.* 1935, II, pags. II—VI
125. *Prov.* 17. 3; 27. 21;
126. *Mal.* 3. 3
127. *Zech.* 13. 9
128. KNUDTSON, *Amarna Tafeln*, VAB II, 70
129. BACCHYLIDES, *Fragm.* 10 (edit. Jebb); PLATO, *Georgias* 486 D; SOPHOCLES, *Frag.* 800; THEOGNIS 449, HERODOTUS VII. 10, PLINY, *Nat. Hist.* XXXVI. 58, 147, 157; THEOPHR., *peri lith.* 4. 45; ARISTOTLE, *Hist. Anim.* VIII. 12.
130. DANA, *Systematic Mineralogy*, 242
131. PLINY, *Nat. Hist.* XXXIII. 126
132. PLINY XXXVI. 127; PLATO, *Ion* 533 D
133. STOCKDALE, *Historical notes on the assay of gold* (Science Progress XVIII, 1924, 476)
    SETHE, K., *Die Bau- und Denkmalsteine der alten Aegypter und ihre Namen* (Sitzber. Berl. Akad. Wiss. Phil. Hist. Kl. 1933)
    LORD, L. E., *The Touchstone* (Class. J. XXXII, 1936/37, 428—431)
    HRADECKY, K., *Geschichte und Schrifttum der Edelmetallstrichprobe* (V.D.I. Verlag, Berlin, 1942)
    H. QUIRING, *Forsch. und Fortschritte* 19/20, 1949, 238
    CALEY, E. R. and RICHARDS, J. C., *Theophrastus on Stones* (Columbus, 1956)
134. THOMPSON, R. CAMPBELL, *The Assyrian Kisal as the origin of the caratweight* (Iraq V, 1938, 23—30)

135. PLINY, *Nat. Hist.* XXXIII. 59—60; Bab. Talmud, Erubim (B) 53b
136. *Ezech.* 22. 18—22; *Num.* 31. 22; *Zech.* 13. 9; *Mal.* 3. 3
    GUILLAUME, A., *Metallurgy in the Old Testament* (P. Exp. Q. 1962, 129—132)
137. DIODOR III. 14
138. PLINY, *Nat. Hist.* XXXIII. 69
139. CASSIODORUS, *Varia* IX. 3. 3
140. HOMER, *Iliad* 18. 470
141. THEOBALD, W., *Technik des Kunsthandwerks im zehnten Jahrhundert* (Des Theophilus Presbyter Diversarium Artium Schedula) (Berlin, 1933, III. 22, III. 68)
142. DAVIES, O., *Bronze Age Mining in the Aegean* (Nature 130, 1932, 985)
143. E. BENEVISTE, *Le terme obryza et la métallurgie de l'or* (Revue Philol. XXVIII, 1953, 122—126)
144. PLINY, *Nat. Hist.* XXXIII. 79; XXXIV. 177
145. DAVIES, O., *Roman Mines in Europe* (Oxford, 1935)
146. PLINY, *Nat. Hst.* XXX. 32; *wrong facts in* XXXIII. 99
147. VASSITS, M. M., *Vitruve et la métallurgie de Vinča* (Revue Archéol. 43, 1954, 60—66)
    WEHRLY, CH. S., *Mercury down the Ages* (Chem. Industries 44, 1939, 139—142; 257—260)
148. VITRUVIUS, *De Archit.* VII. ix. 4; VII. viii. 1—3; VII. viii. 4
149. *Num.* 31. 22
150. THEOPHILUS III. 35—36; AGRICOLA, *de Re Met.* VII
151. GOWLAND, W., *The Metals in Antiquity* (R. Anthr. Inst., London, 1912)
    GOWLAND, W., *The art of working metals in Japan* (J. Inst. Metals IV, 1910, 2)
    SCHIFFNER, C., *Die Entwicklung der Gold-Silberscheidung* (Frankfurt, 1923)
152. PLINY, *Nat. Hist.* XXXIII. 60; XXXIV, 121; XXXV. 183; STRABO 3. 2. 8. cap. 146
153. BAILEY, K. C., *The Elder Pliny's Chapters on chemical subjects* (London, 1932, 2 vols.)
    TÄCKHOLM, *Studien über Bergbau der Römischen Kaiserzeit* (Uppsala, 1937)
154. GOWLAND, W., *Archaeologia* 69, 137
155. LANDSBERGER, B., JNES XV, 1956, 146—147
156. REISENER, E., JNES XV, 129
157. LEEMANS, W. F., *Foreign trade in the Old Babylonian Period* (Leiden, 1960)
158. UET V. 292 & 526
159. EDZARD, D. O., JESHO III, 1960, 38 ff
160. LANDSBERGER, B., *Dergi* IV, 1940, 25
161. LEWY, H., JAOS 67, 1947, 309, note 21
162. YBT V 207

163. TCL X 72 (AO 8464)
164. DOUGHERTY, *Records from Erech, time of Nabonidus* (New Haven, 1920, 54)
165. DOUGHERTY, *Archives from Erech* II, 1933, 367
166. DOUGHERTY, *Archives from Erech* I, 1923, 372
167. LIMET, H., *Le travail du Métal au Pays de Sumer* (Paris, 1960, 140—164)
    GURNEY, O., *Sumer* 9, 1953, 21—35; *Iraq* XI, 1949, 131—142
168. *Beitr. Assyr.* III, 234, 21 ff
169. LACAU, P., *L'or dans l'architecture égyptienne* (ASAE LIII, 1955, 221—250)
170. VERNIER, E., *L'or chez les anciens Egyptiens* (BIFAO XXV, 1924, 167—173)
171. NOBLECOURT, CHR. DESROCHES DE, *Deux grandes obélisques précieux d'un sanctuaire de Karnak* (Revue d'Egypt. VIII, 1951, 47—61)
172. CURTIS, J. W., *Media of exchange in Ancient Egypt* (Numismatist 64, 1951, 5, 482—491)
    JENKINS, G. K., *An Egyptian gold coin* (Brit. Mus. Quart. XX, 1955/56, 10—11)
173. KALBFLEISCH, K., *Edelmetallbeschaffung* (Arch. f. Pap. forschung, 15, 1953, 104—105)
174. VENTRIS, M. and CHADWICK, J., *Documents in Mycenaean Greek* (London, 1956)
175. GUMMERUS, *Die römische Industrie* (Klio XIV, 1915, 129—189; XV, 1918, 256—302)
176. S.I.G. III. 1263
177. C.I.L. V. 785
178. C.I.L. X, 3976, 3978
179. C.I.S. II. 3. I, nr. 3945
180. C.I.L. I. 1307
181. BGU 1127
182. MICKWITZ, G., *Le problème de l'or dans le monde antique* (Ann. Hist. écon. et soc. VI, 1934, 235—247)
183. CALEY, E. R., *Notes on the chemical composition of Parthian coins with special references to the drachms of Orodes* I (Ohio J. Sci. 1950, 107—120)
184. PLINY, *Nat. Hist.* XXXIII. 19. 61
185. THEOBALD, W., *Technik des Kunsthandwerks im zehnten Jahrhundert* (Des Theophilus Presbyter Diversarium Artium Schedula) (Berlin, 1933)
    THEOBALD, W., *Eine Goldschmiedewerkstatt im Zehnten Jahrhundert* (Forsch. und Forsch. XI, 1935, 77)
    THEOBALD, W., *Die Herstellung des Blattmetalls im Altertum* (Hannover, 1912)
186. SMITH, E. A., *Rolled gold, its origin and development* (J. Inst. Metals 44, 1930, 175—205)
187. CHLEBECK, FR., *Beitrag zur Technik der Granulation* (Stud. Etr. XXII, 1952/53, 203—205)

PICCARDI, G. and BORDI, S., *Sull'oreficera granulata etrusca* (Stud. Etr. XXIV, 1955/56, 354—363)

188. VISSER, H. F. E., *Some remarks on gold granulation work in China* (Artib. Asiae XV, 1952, 125—128)

189. BERGSØE, P., *The metallurgy and technology of gold and platinum among the Precolumbian Indians* (Copenhagen, 1937) (see also Nature 137, 1936, 29)

PAUL BERGSØE, *Metallurgiske og tekniske Undersøgelser af Saakaldt "Incaguld"* (Ingeniøren 1936, no. 68, VI, 217—223)

PAUL BERGSØE, *Kemien og Fortiden* (Kemoteknik, Ingeniøren, 1939, no. 59, 65—72)

EARLE R. CALEY, *Examination of two gold objects of aboriginal manufacture* (Ohio J. Sci. 54, 1954, 149—150)

CRUELLAS, J. and RETAMAR, J. A., *Metallurgical knowledge in northwestern Argentina before the Spanish conquest* (Rev. facul. ing. quím.) (Argentine, 24, 1955, 24, 57—63)

EASBY, D. T., *Ancient American goldsmiths* (Nat. Hist. 65, 1956, 8, 401—410)

ROOT, W. C., *Gold-copper alloys in ancient America* (J. chem. educ. 28, 1951, 76—78)

190. BECATTI, G., *Oreficerie antiche dall minoiche alle barbariche* (Roma, 1955)

BAXTER, W. T., *Jewelry, Gem Cutting and Metal Craft* (New York, 1948)

CONTENAU, G., *Manuel d'Archéologie Orientale* (Paris, 1927, vol. I)

FORBES, R. J., *Bibliographia Antiqua, Philosophia Naturalis, parts I—X* (Leiden, 1940—1950), Supplement I (1952), Supplement II (1963)

HOURS, MAGD. *Les chemins de l'or dans l'antiquité* (Plaisirs de France, Dec. 1953, 16—25)

KELLY, M. J. O', *Excavation of a ring-fort at Garryduff* (Antiquity XX, 1946, 122—126)

NEEDLER, W. and GRAHAM, J. W., *Jewelry of the ancient world* (Bull. R. Ontario Mus. Arts 20, 1953, 1—36)

PLENDERLEITH, J., *Ur Excavations* (London, 1934, Vol. II, 394 ff.)

ROSENBERG, M., *Geschichte der Goldschmiedekunst auf technischer Grundlage* (Frankfurt, 1924/25, 2 vols.)

ROQUE, F. BISSON DE LA, *Trésor de Tod* (BIFAO, Caire, 1950)

SCHÄFER, H., *Aegyptische Goldschmiedearbeiten* (Berlin, 1910)

VERNIER, E., *La byouterie et la joallerie égyptienne* (Caire, 1907)

VERNIER, E., *Byoux et orfèvreries* (Caire, 1927, 2 vols.)

WOOLLEY, C. L., *The Development of Sumerian Art* (London, 1935, 75)

191. ANDERSSON, J. G., *The goldsmith in ancient China* (Mus. Far East. Antiq. Bull. no. 7, 1935)

JASPER, J. E. and MAS PIRGANDIE, *De inlandsche kunstnijverheid in Nederlandsch Indië*, vol. IV. *Goud- en zilversmeedkunst* (The Hague, 1927)

GYLLENSVÄRD, S., *T'ang gold and silver* (Bull. Far. East. Ant.) (Stockholm, no. 29, 1957, 1—230)

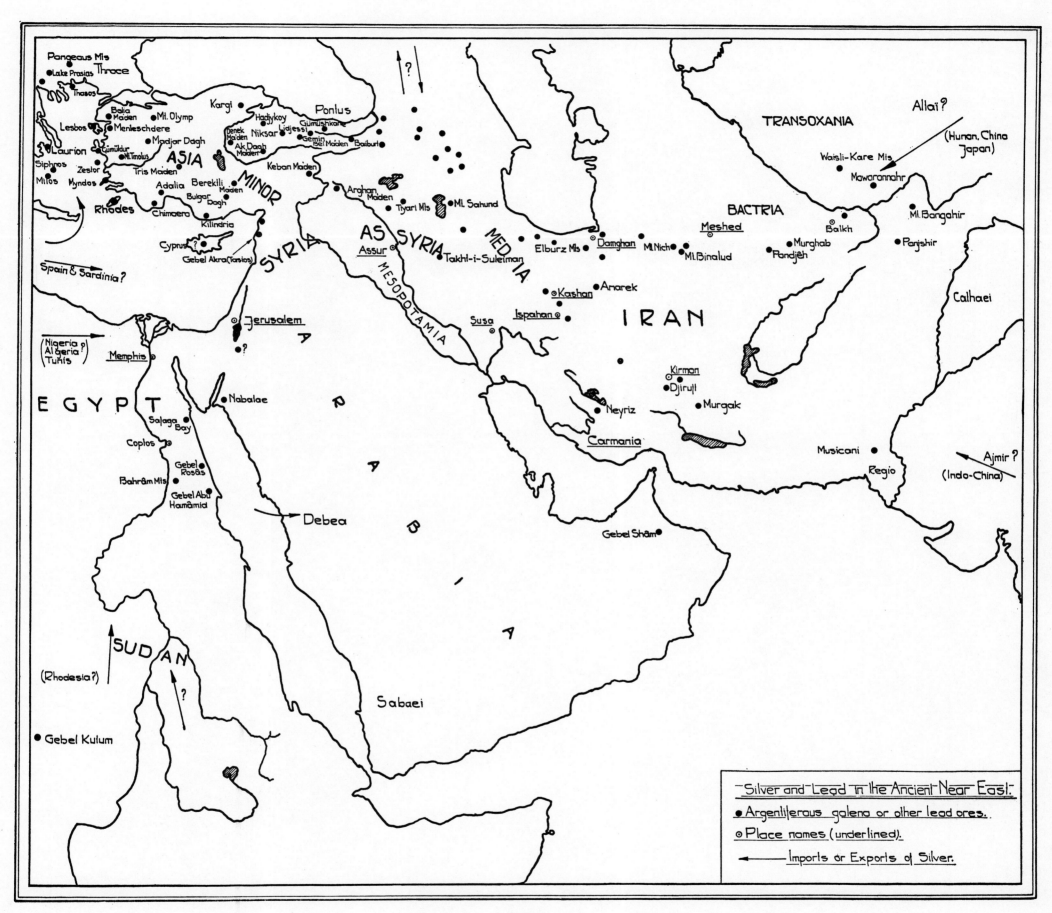

Fig. 38.
Silver and Lead in the Ancient Near East

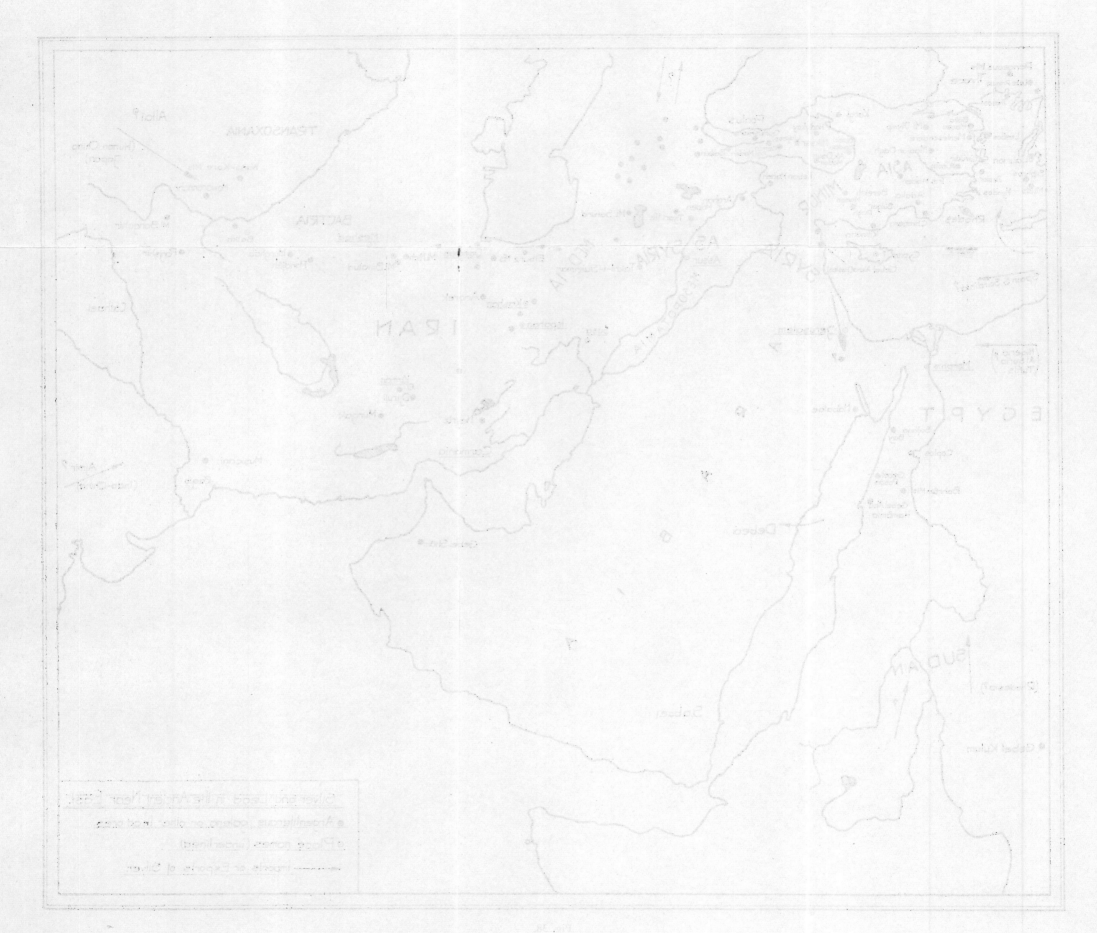

CHAPTER SIX

SILVER AND LEAD

> "Our next subject is the mining of silver, a
> second manifestation of madness."
> (Pliny, *Nat. Hist.* XXXIII, 95)

Pliny's stinging remarks on the greed evoked by the discovery of the noble metals are less bitter in the case of silver, for he justly remarks that the search for silver led to valuable discoveries of other ores: "A small thing it was to have discovered one plague for humanity, but we must needs set a value even to the corruption of gold. Greed sought silver but did not fail to rejoice at having found minium" (1). But here again moralists and philosophers have combined gold and silver in their denunciations. Many of the classical authors are quoted by Agricola (2), but to such unfair words as "Silver is the life and blood of human beings; whosoever has not collected a large amount of it, wanders about like a ghost amongst the living" he adds the very just remark that greed is not caused by the metals but by the sinful mortals who handle them. His first Book is a very fair exposition of the usefulness of metallurgy and the misconduct of humanity after the discovery of the properties of metals.

After a discussion of time and region where silver was discovered we will survey the nature and characteristics of lead and silver deposits, the different mines in the Ancient Near East will be discussed, followed by a review of the refining methods used for these metals in Antiquity.

Our present essay will confine itself to the early history of silver and lead, their production and refining in the Ancient Near East.

1. *The origin of silver*

It is futile to speculate on the name of the discoverer of silver, for the recognition of a metal is the result of a long series of observations of its properties. Even classical authors have hesitated to mention any name. In fact, silver, being one of the metals found in their native state, occurs very seldom in workable deposits and there is strong technical and archaeological evidence that the real discovery of silver, that is its production and refining, is intimately linked with the production of lead. Natural silver was collected from the earliest times in different regions but its role in metallurgy remained insignificant until men learned to produce silver from lead and lead-ores.

Further details will be discussed in next section, but we can anticipate these discussions and state that the production of larger quantities of silver by treating lead-ores was a very complicated series of metallurgical processes, the development of which entailed so many trials and observations that, in the case of silver, the priority of a certain region in the development of this technique may be safely assumed. If we propound a diffusion of silver technology from Asia Minor (probably Pontus) this does not mean that the production of silver could not have been invented or improved in any region independently. For though our knowledge of early metallurgy on the American continent is still very incomplete, modern research has proved that silver was very scarce in Aztec and even in Inca culture. The natives of Peru had indeed collected and melted natural silver, possibly even produced it from the rich argentiferous lead-ores at Potosi and spread its use for ornaments over the South American continent. The early Chimu silver objects are probably made of the native metal. This is certainly the case with Colombian silver objects, which are either silver-greenish because of admixture of gold or reddish because of admixture of copper, two types of natural alloys which occur in these regions, but which could have been produced by the peculiar 'blowpipe and charcoal' technique so ably described by Bergsøe (3). Lead does not seem to have been used to any extent. In Central America the knowledge of silver may have been derived from the South, for the Mayas do not seem to have shared it, but it appears in the XI—XIIth centuries together with other metallurgical knowledge amongst the Toltecs. When the Spaniards conquered Mexico, the Aztecs did use silver occasionally, as silver objects were found on their markets, but they must have depended on natural deposits for their supply, because lead seems to have been unknown to them.

In the Ancient Near East things were different. Silver occurs in *Egypt* from the Middle Predynastic Period (Sequence Date 42) onwards; small pieces of lead of the same period were found and Petrie discovered a wooden hawk coated with sheet lead in Naqada (4).

Egypt, however, can never have been the centre of silver production, because lead and silver do not become common until fairly late. Nor did this knowledge come to Egypt from Africa, for, according to a leading authority on Negro metallurgy, Cline (5), silver was probably never smelted and rarely worked by the indigenous Negro cultures. Early references to this metal in Africa seem to indicate no more than its discovery and working by foreign pioneers. Even Egyptian influences on Negro metallurgy seem excluded as this art reached the height of its development in those parts of the continent where no early Egyptian contacts can be demonstrated. Indeed in the long history of Negro metallurgy Egypt plays no role, neither having been a leader in the craft. Lead or zinc are seldom mined by Negroes. The Stone Age of Africa is immediately followed by the Iron Age, metallurgical techniques having been brought from the West by the Berbers around 400 A.D. and from the East Coast by Arab traders around 600 A.D.

In Palestine both silver and lead come late, apart from a few early finds at Gezer, they can not be said to have been in common use before the second half of the second millenium B.C., the Hyksos period.

In Mohenjo Daro and other Indus civilisation cities silversmiths' work was found, but few details on the technique have been published. Silver and lead were not found in Anau I or Anau II. Though silver objects from Persia and Elam do not date back to a very early period, both silver and lead are known in Mesopotamia since Uruk III and were already fairly common in the Al 'Ubaid period, the Ur graves and early Lagaš. In Central and Transcaucasia they are used from the earliest periods onwards. There is no evidence that silver or lead was used earlier in the Far East (6).

In Cyprus silver and lead are rare before the Middle Bronze Age, but in Crete they are found in the Early Minoan Strata, and on the Aegean archipelago they occur since the Early Helladic period; silver objects are also imitated in early pottery (7). On the Greek mainland, for instance in Mykene, silver is still less common than gold in the Mycenean period. In Europe silver does not occur in any Palaeolithic or Neolithic finds, in the Bronze Age some simple objects occur and even in the early Iron Age its occurence is rare.

Only in the La Tène period. in regions like Hungary, Bosnia, Transsylvania and in the Alps wherever argentiferous ores are found, silver becomes more common. Lead is somewhat earlier. In the Lake dwellings of Middle Europe lead balls (weights) have been found which represent exact multiples of the Sumerian minae. Lead percentages from 4—15% have been found in Southern European bronzes of the Late Bronze Age. In Middle and Northern Europe lead bronzes occur in the Imperial period only.

However, in view of the occurrence of workable deposits of native silver and exceptionally rich argentiferous lead-ore in Spain, silver and lead may have been produced at an early date. Indeed, Siret (8) demonstrated that silver was in use in Spain when implements of metal had only partially replaced stone and this again may be proof that no absolute diffusionist theory can be accepted for the history of silver. There is, however, no evidence that this early development in Spain had any links with Asia Minor, nor is there any proof that this development in Spain was earlier than that in the Near East.

The early history of silver and lead in Asia Minor is still sketchy. Both occur in Troy I; in Troy II they are fairly common and six skillets of silver of exceptional purity have been found which may have been made from silver smelted from a small deposit of silver-chloride ore close by. On the other hand much of the early silver is the natural gold/silver alloy called electrum.

Again the Cappadocian tablets prove the existence of a fully developed silver and lead production in the second half of the third millenium B.C. In view of this and the many rich argentiferous galena deposits of Asia Minor, the skill of early metallurgists like the Chalybes and other tribes located mainly in Pontus and the inventions attributed to them, it would seem that the refining of silver and lead was worked out in Pontus in about the early Third Millenium B.C. and that this knowledge spread gradually over the Ancient Near East until both metals were in common use in the fifteenth century B.C. By that time producing centres in Armenia, Carmania and possibly Elam supplied the rapidly growing demand for silver, which metal went south in exchange for Egyptian gold.

We have discussed the simple production methods of gold and made it clear that this native metal was not refined until fairly late, say the first half of the second millenium. In the case of silver we may expect a late development from the triviality of its natural deposits and the relative complexity of its production from lead ores. Metallurgy developed its technique from the smelting of copper ores; bronze and iron production completed its experience and gold technology, especially the craft of the goldsmith has contributed many interesting processes to metallurgical methods. Copper, bronze and iron had their use in daily life; these metals formed a class of superior stones, which were plastic when hot. Indeed the transmutation of these 'stones' by heat constitutes the main attraction of metallurgy But metals and ores could only be handled by smiths having at their disposal a formidable body of experimental experience and industrial lore. Though these were not secrets, in a way, Childe, (9) is right in saying that metallurgy means loss of economic independence.

Silver and lead are useless metals from a technical point of view. Silver had its value as a medium of currency or for the manufacture of ornaments and trinkets. Native silver occurs in deposits too small to produce quantities worth melting (at least in the Near East); silver is therefore, produced from lead-ores by smelting these ores, especially galena, and separating silver from lead. Thus the history of silver is inseparably bound up with that of lead. Silver, therefore, played no part in the culture of early man and has never been found before he became acquainted with copper, gold and bronze, or only occasionally. The first and essential process for the extraction of silver was the smelting of lead ores, a fairly intricate process, which must necessarily belong to the later stages of metallurgical history.

Lead and silver must have become common at the same time in ancient history. The smelting of ores was not a chance operation, but the logical outgrowth of melting experiments. Many centuries must have elapsed between the first melting of metals and the smelting of ores. Metallurgy was blind, not literally, for the early metallurgists were very shrewd observers of the external characteristics of ores and metals, but because no knowledge existed of the composition of materials nor were processes or reactions of working ores and metals understood in our present-day sense. A complex process like the smelting of galena to produce silver must have come fairly late. Childe argues that lead ores were probably at first valued for the silver they contain, but this could only have been a fact if the lead had already been found to contain silver.

Lead again was a metal entirely wanting in physical properties needed in weapons and implements; it was a worthless constituent of bronze when used as a substitute for tin. In the words of Biringuccio (10): "Das Blei ist ein unvolkommenes, aussätziges und wenig festes Metall." Lead appears late in the history of metals, and apart from some applications in architecture and magic, was not widely used before Roman times. Garland and Bannister (11) found that in Egypt lead bronzes were only used for casting bronzes for ornamental and devotional purposes, but never for implements where a metal of great strength was essential.

The actual discovery of the production of silver from lead ores may have been made in a very early period for galena was used as an eyepaint in prehistoric periods in Egypt and elsewhere. Its brilliant metallic appearance, high specific gravity and very common occurence could not have failed to excite the curiosity of early man. Any piece of galena dropped in a fire would be reduced to lead and if left long enough in the fire, the lead burns away leaving a small drop of silver. Indeed there is every reason to believe that the first lead-silver smelting furnace was the domestic fire. These facts were the foundation for lead and silver production, which reached an industrial stage in Pontus many centuries later. In fact, classical tradition states that King Midas was the discoverer of lead and tin (12), which leads us back to Asia Minor again.

The discovery of silver is often attributed to chance, a very common classical theory being the "forest-fire" story (13). This story claims, that forest fires reduced surface-deposits of lead- or silver-ores and a small stream of silver flowed from the burning forest or a lump of metal was discovered after the fire. According to Napier (14) such phenomena have indeed been observed in the Alps and the Pyrenees, but this was surely not a production method for silver. It is more likely that the Pontic metallurgists developed their methods by a long series of trials and heating experiments and that the classical story is due to a desire for a "plausible" explanation rather than to actual metallurgical knowledge.

There are indeed several classical speculations on early silver metallurgy in Pontus. Homer (15) calls Alybe the "birthplace of silver" and Strabo states that the country of the Chalybes "also had silver mines in earlier times" (16) and in a further passage affirms his opinion that the country of the Chalybes should be identified with "Alybe". Bury (17) identifies the Hittite *Khalywa* (Land of the Hittites) with Alybe, and Hehn, Leaf, Blümner and Giles (18) have accepted the identity of Alybe, the land of the Chalybes and the "silver country".

The problem has been approached from another side by Dhorme (19) who remarks that the town of Hatti, capital of the Hittites, is often indicated in Cappadocian texts by the ideogram kù-babbar (silver) followed by the phonetic determinative *ti*. Therefore not only are the mountains giving access to this country called "silver mountains" but the very name of the capital written KU-BABBAR-ti should be read phonetically Ḥat-ti expressing the bond between silver production and the whole country of the Hittites. Though silver was scarce in the earliest periods of Egypt and the metal was imported from Syria and Asia Minor, it must be considered doubtful whether the Egyptian ḥḏ is derived from the Hittite ḥat (silver), for unless the latter is a word taken over by the Hittites from the autochonous population, the Egyptian word antedates it by many centuries. Thus tradition, archaeology, geology, and technical arguments combine with philology to indicate Asia Minor (and probably the Pontic Coast) as the birthplace of that complex of metallurgical processes which we call silver and lead technology.

The most prominent characteristic of silver is its brilliant lustre, which plays a large role in *ancient nomenclature*. "I think that pride of place is given to this substance (gold), not by reason of its colour, for silver is brighter and more sun-light; that is why it is commonly used for military standards, since its gleaming is visible at greater distance" explains Pliny (20). We need not wonder that this colour is prominent in ancient names for silver. If ancient nomenclature of metals is found to be vague, we must remember that many names must have arisen out of observations confined to external characteristics of fundamentally one (rather impure) substance. When raw materials are used as they are found or acquired by trade, an enormous variety of composition of metals and alloys will be the outcome and an equally bewildering variety of names.

The common Egyptian word for silver is ḥḏ, literally "white". As we explained in discussing the history of gold the natural gold-silver alloy, electrum—often silver coloured—must have been called "silver" as long as no methods for the separation of silver and gold were known. "Silver" was everything that had the external characteristics of silver. Therefore the words "white gold" could hardly have been used for electrum as long as it was not known that electrum was an alloy of silver and gold; indeed both the silver-white electrum and natural silver (rare in early Egyptian history) must have been called "silver". Though ḥḏ is often accompanied by the determinative *nub* (gold), this combination of signs should not be read "white gold". According to de Buck *nub* is purely a determinative and therefore silver was called simply "white, white metal". If Strabo applies the term "white gold" to electrum (21), he knows that he is dealing with a mixture of silver and gold.

In the Graeco-Roman period another term for silver occurs in Egyptian texts. This word *rkwr* (Erman-Grapow, *HWB* I. 213) seems to have been derived from the Greek *argyros*, it may denote the pure metal. Lepsius (22) gives another late term *ru* or *ruā* which has not been identified.

The Hebrew *keseph* (silver and later a silver coin) denotes the same white, brilliant metal as the Accadian *kaspu* (*ṣarpu*). The Sumerian kù-babbar is said to mean 'White brilliant'. It is not known whether the Hittite word *ḫat* means 'white' too, Schrader points out that many Indo-European terms like silver, *Silber*, etc. are derived from the Accadian *ṣarpu* travelling along trade routes from the Euxine to the Baltic coasts and that the variety of terms in Indo-European languages proves that silver was not known until late in these regions (23). He derives the terms *argentum*, *argyros*, etc. from a root *radj* or *arg* meaning 'white, bright shining'. Thus in most languages the term for silver means 'white and shining metal', showing a singular uniformity as compared with the complex nomenclature of gold and electrum. This again may point to the comparatively late appearance of silver in history.

In the case of lead the ancient nomenclature presents many difficulties which are the outcome of defining materials by their external characteristics. There is considerable confusion in ancient texts when dealing with lead, tin, zinc (?), antimony and arsenic, terms for each of these metals being used fairly freely for the others. Only from the context and careful study of the technical possibility of the translation can one sort them out. Thus Campbell Thompson (24) very aptly pointed out that Sumerian a-bár or agar$_5$ (A. GÚG) and the Accadian synonym *abâru* generally mean lead, they are occasionally used for plumbago or antimony; and the Sumerian nagga (AN. NA) (Accadian *anâku*) though generally denoting tin is sometimes used in texts where it can only mean lead. *Abâru* seems connected with the Syriac *Abbârâ* the Hebrew *ôphĕrêth* and the Arabic *abbâr*; *Anaku* is related to the Hebrew *anak* (plummet) and the Syriac *ankâ* (black and white lead) or the Arabic *ankum* (lead). In Cappadocian tablets *anâku* is used very frequently and can denote nothing but lead. The Egyptian word for lead is *dhty* (Erman-Grapow, *HWB*, 1921, 221), and as lead was generally regarded as a kind of inferior silver, we find the word used to express 'a worthless thing' in later periods. Schrader derives words like *Blei* and *molybdos* from a root *'mliwom* meaning 'blue', which Meillet considers to have been taken from an Aegaean language. Our word lead is derived from an old Celtic term *luaide* and the Latin *plumbum* originally meant "tile, bar".

The confusion of lead, tin and antimony (which will be discussed more fully in our chapter on these metals in Vol. IX) is very obvious to anyone consulting classical authors. Pliny calls lead *plumbum nigrum* and tin *plumbum candidum* or *album* (25), his *stagnum* meaning "Werkblei, crude lead, work-lead", and not *stannum* (tin). Medieval alchemists call lead and tin masculine and feminine lead. But then even Agricola talks of *plumbum nigrum* (lead), *plumbum candidum* (tin) and *plumbum cinereum* (antimony) and modern Arabs distinguish tin and lead as white and black lead (26); which terms will remain confusing if one does not take into account the external characteristics of lead, tin and antimony in studying the ancient texts. It must be left to expert philologists to decide whether these ancient terms for lead are based either on its dark-grey-blueish colour or its easy fusibility.

Both metals play an important part in religion, mythology and magic (27). Silver is the metal of the moongod Sin, both being described as "green". In a Sumerian hymn Gibil, the god of fire, is said to purify gold and silver. The connection between silver and moon is common all over the Ancient Near East. In Egypt Hathor, the moongoddess, is goddess of silver (28), while in the magical papyrus Harris (IV. 9) and other papyri the bones of the god Rê and other gods are fashioned of silver. Silver was often called Luna or Diana by the later alchemists, its symbol is a crescent moon because it has the silvery colour of moonlight. Silver weapons or bullets never fail to kill and there is no charm against them. This is a very presistent tradition in the East. Silver is one of the most frequent metals used for charms and amulets, it has special affinity for some precious and semi-precious stones, which should on no account be set in gold. The fact that crude lead can be reduced to plumbago and silver is the basis of ancient technological processes. This may have led to the early Syriac tradition of the transmutation of lead into silver, which was repeated in the Middle Ages, in the heyday of alchemy, by Vincent of Beauvais and others, who considered lead to be debased silver.

Lead plays a very peculiar part in magic. Its dark colour and high specific gravity must have led to the superstition that it had chtonic connections. It is also said to be a "very cold" metal. In Egyptian magic it is the metal of Osiris, in Babylonian magic that of Ea; later alchemists call it the metal of Saturn whose symbol is used to denote lead. Both Theophrastus and Galen are the first to call it "cold". It is considered eminently suitable for magical tablets containing inscribed curses or prayers for the sick; lead being used for "defixiones" from Assyrian times onwards. The lead tablet mentioned in Zech. 5. 7 was probably inscribed with the figures of demons. In Graeco-Roman times lead tablets are in common use for devotiones and carmina and continue to be used for these magical purposes and practises up to the present day. Again the future can be read from figures formed by congealing lead poured into water, and many other magical rites are performed with leaden objects (29).

2.   The ores of silver and lead

When Demas tempted Hopeful on Lucre Hill saying: "Here is a silver mine, and some digging in it. If you will come with little pains you may richly provide for yourselves", Christian is right in deterring his friend from following this advice. There is more truth in the old Spanish proverb, which states that it takes a gold mine to run a silver mine.

Silver is fairly widely distributed in minerals in quantities less than $\frac{1}{2}\%$. Very few gold ores are free from silver and it is almost invariably found in sulphides, that is in ores consisting of sulphur compounds of lead, copper and zinc. Granitic rocks contain on the average 6 parts of silver per million, sandstones 0.44 parts, marbles about 0.2 parts and silver is invariably found in minute quantities in ashes of land-plants, blood of herbivora, corals, volcanic ash, etc.

The largest part of the present world's production is derived from lead and copper ores because smelting lead and copper includes the production of silver (and gold) as by-products, whose market-price does not have such a strong influence on the amount of the silver production. The discovery of America opened up new sources for the production of silver and 1.511.050 Troy ounces were produced between 1493 and 1520, a figure which increased enormously after copper and lead began to be extensively worked and reached a total of 171.200.000 ounces in 1920. More than two-thirds of this silver were produced in Mexico and the United States.

Silver in comparison with gold is of rare occurence in nature in the native state. *Native silver* is not found in alluvial deposits or sands and gravels of rivers, but has to be sought in mountainous regions where it is embedded in mineral veins. Except for the extraordinary deposit in Kongsberg, Norway, silver is not found in lumps or nuggets but in delicate filaments and foils formed by the oxidation and decomposition of lead and silver ores. Native silver rarely occurs at the surface or in outcrops of veins because it is liable to have been converted into chloride by traces of chlorine invariably present in rain water, and washed away. When tracing the history of silver it is important to remember that silver objects which remain in the earth for a long period come to be covered with a white greyish crust by the action of chlorine or converted entirely into soluble chlorides by the action of rain and salt sprays from the sea. Even Roman objects have by now often been converted into unrecognisable masses. No wonder that such masses may have been missed in excavating! The absence of silver in early periods does not prove with absolute certainty that the metal was then unknown.

Native silver is usually found in quantities not worth melting to larger lumps which can be worked. It crystallizes in cubic crystals which may be very pure (30) but are usually alloyed with gold, copper (in France up to 10%), mercury, arsenic, antimony, iron, etc. Native silver rarely occurs in lumps or leaves which without melting can be fashioned even into the simplest objects and therefore we may safely conclude that it can hardly have played a part in the life of early man.

Several *silver ores* are known such as Argentite (silver glance, black silver, ore, glance ore), a sulphur-silver compound, Proustite (light red silver ore, arsenical silver blende), Pyrargyrite (dark red or ruby silver ore, antimonal silver blende) and Cerargyrite (silver chloride, horn silver) which all occur in the strata overlying lead ores as decomposition products of such ores. Deposits of these ores are rare; apart from rich deposits of this type in the New World, they are found in the deposits of lead ores in Spain and in parts of Cornwall and Hungary, but they are of no importance in the Near East. Though Hiller (31) concludes from a passage in Pliny (32) that these ores were worked in Spain by the Romans, we can safely assume, that they were included in the silver production from lead ores, if they were ever worked to any extent in the Ancient World. Simple heating (or roasting) and reduction of these ores with charcoal will produce silver.

Native gold alloyed with silver, the ancient *electrum*, formed an ancient source for silver production as we have pointed out in chapter V. Even nowadays 1.500.000 ounces of silver are extracted from bullion gold though more than two-thirds of the worlds' silver supply is produced from lead, zinc ores and copper ores containing less than 0.5% silver.

The ores from which the metal was first produced in larger quantities were no doubt ordinary *lead ores* and not the rather rare silver ores associated with these lead ores. Prominent amongst the lead ores in *galena* (lead sulphide a compound of sulphur and lead), which is of very common occurence. In many localities, e.g. in Asia Minor, vast almost inexhaustible deposits occur on or close to the surface. Its brilliant metallic appearance and high specific gravity can not fail to excite the curiosity of the primitive miner. After using it as an eye-paint he invented methods of smelting it and producing lead and silver. The indirect method of producing silver from galena must have impeded silver technology. For though practically every deposit of galena is argentiferous, the quantities of silver (usually not expressed in percentages but in ounces of silver per Ton of lead) are minute. The average silver content of various galena samples lies between 20 to 200 ounces per Ton of lead; 0.5% of silver (150 ounces per Ton of lead) being regarded as very rich. In some cases special lodes or veins may contain higher amounts, one of the richest being the veins at Karahissar (Asia Minor) containing 600 ounces or 1.84% of silver. The majority of the lodes have some 0.15% (50 ounces) or less. By selecting special lodes for production in periods when refining methods were still wasteful material containing a high average of some 3% of silver could be obtained. This is the category which Agricola calls a rich ore, but we call it quite exceptional now as improved methods enable us to work much poorer ores. It is possible that Agricola meant true silver ores when he speaks of such rich lodes. In the production of lead from these ores all the silver, which readily dissolves in the lead, is concentrated in the baser metal and not in the other by-products from the lead-ore. This fact may have led many an alchemist astray and led him to believe that he had transmuted lead into silver when he started refining crude lead.

Apart from galena, two other lead ores have a certain importance as raw materials for the production of lead only. The more plentiful of the two is *Cerussite* (lead carbonate), clear or slightly coloured crystals like calcite, but rather soft and brittle. Campbell Thompson has identified the *ḫulâlu* stone (or ᵃZa-Ṭu-Kur), which occurs so often in the Amarna letters, with cerussite, and though these brilliant crystals could have been used in the ornamental objects in which they are stated to have been applied, there is no doubt that their brittleness must have been a serious hindrance for a wider application as a semi-precious stone. The second lead ore of some minor importance is

Anglesite (lead sulphate) forming crystals like gypsum but with a more brilliant lustre. Both cerussite and anglesite occur with native silver and silver ores in the oxidized portions of lead ore outcrops on the surface of the earth for instance in Asia Minor and Armenia. There is no doubt that the ancient miners knew this connection between the ores of the oxidized top portions and the lowerlying lodes of unchanged galena. This is what Pliny says about silver-mines in Spain (33): "Silver is only found in shaft-mines and there is no previous indication of its presence for there is no glinting spark as in the case of gold. The earth is red in places (by the presence of minium, a natural lead-oxyde) and ash-coloured in others (unoxidized galena). Silver is found in almost all the provinces but the best comes from Spain. Like gold it occurs in barren soil and even among mountains and wherever one vein is found another is not far to seek. This is the case also with most ores, and seems to be the source of the greek name metalla. It is wonderful that the mines opened by Hannibal in Spain are still productive. The vein of silver that is found nearest to the surface is called *crudaria*. The early miners use to cease operations when they came to alumen, seek no further, but the recent discovery of veins of copper below that alumen has removed this limit of their hopes. The exhalation from silver-mines is poisonous to all animals but especially to dogs (evolution of sulphur-dioxide gases)". Indeed lead ores are very often associated with copper ores, many examples of this association are to be found in the mines of the Ancient Near East. Theophrastus mentions the same facts and states that such minerals as Arrhenikon, Sandarake, Chrysocolla, Minium, Ochre and Kyanos are very common in gold and silver mines. Also minerals containing gold and silver are much heavier in weight and smell according to Theophrastus, but only the silver is visible (that is, the mineral has a silvery colour because of the high silver content (34). In the days of Agricola and Biringuccio this was common knowledge.

In mapping out the lead and silver deposits in the Ancient Near East we have therefore confined ourselves to the indication of the galena deposits because any one of them will have native silver, silver ores or the less important lead ores associated with galena in its surface outcrops, in more or less important amounts.

The *mining of galena* for silver and lead production was similar to that of gold to a certain extent (35). Of course here the surface lodes were far less important and silver is never produced from alluvial deposits. Therefore, panning, placer mining and hushing as described for ancient gold were rarely used. The only way of approach to the deeper galena deposits was vein-mining by means of shaft-mines. In Laurion alone, more than 2000 shafts have been found on a depth up to 250'. Pliny states (36) that the silver mines of Spain had shafts which extended 1500 paces into the mountains and the Romans were the first to achieve the tapping of the veins below the subsoil water level by complicated systems of drainage using water-wheels, pumps, Archimedan screws, etc. Primitive lead-mining practice as used at the present time at Ajmir (India) (37) may be used to illustrate mining practice in the Ancient Near East. After collection of the galena mixed with gangue and other useless stony material from the lead-bearing stratum, the ore was brought to the surface, crushed, washed with water and sieved to concentrate the ore. These methods are discussed in detail by Agricola (38), whose books show clearly that the methods described are survivals from Roman and pre-Roman times, like so many technical processes, but gradually perfected by many generations of miners and metallurgists. Strabo gives a good description of what happened in Spain (39): "Silver bearing ore is carried along in the streams, is crushed and disengaged in water by means of sieves, then the sediment is again crushed and again strained through (the water being in meantime poured off) and crushed; then the fifth sediment is smelted and after the lead has been poured off, yields pure silver." The sieving of the crushed ore in a stream of water is called *jigging*, during the process the heavy particles of galena fall through the sieve to the bottom, the lighter gangue forms a layer on the top of the sieve and is thrown away. The sediment, as Strabo calls the galena particles, is washed five times to remove all the stony particles and concentrate the ore. Concentration of the ore to a lead content of 70—85% means the possibility to use simple smelting processes for the production of silver and lead. The preparation of the ore for smelting has been discussed in an earlier volume of this series (40).

3.   *The Lead- and Silver-mines of Antiquity*

If we wish to draw a *map of the silver- and lead-ore deposits* known in Antiquity there are more reasons than one why we should confine ourselves to the mapping of the galena-mines. We have mentioned the geological reasons which urge us to simplify matters by selecting galena as the representative of the complex of silver, silver-ores and lead-ores. A second reason is the lack of proper mineralogical information about the deposits in the Ancient Near East. Even such hand-books as the *Handbuch der Regionalen Geologie* rarely state any details about the minerals found in a certain region and, as a matter of course, archaeological handbooks are still more vague and mention silver-mines without even saying whether the silver is found native, in the form of silver ores or in lead-ore. Both history of science and archae-ology would profit by an exact and complete compilation of all geo-logical data on the Ancient Near East. A third point is equally con-fusing to any student: different writers on these subjects use various spellings of geographical names; not only the ancient names but even modern Turkish towns are spelt in so many versions that without detailed maps it is impossible to find them at all. Again a mine is said by one writer to lie in a certain district, the other will locate it near a town or a hamlet, the third will mention the province or river only, so that one mine is mentioned under five or more different guises by the authors. It would be most important if some agreement could be achieved inter-nationally to use a given standard map as a basis for all geographical details, this would avoid much confusion for expert and layman alike.

Too few details are known about the different galena deposits to sort out mines that have been worked in Antiquity, those that have been abandoned and those which are new discoveries. Such details, as far as known to the present writer, will be given in the discussion below. There are hardly more than vague indications about the lo-cations of mines in the pre-Roman texts known up to the present.

Again we must carefully avoid taking too much notice of texts mentioning silver and lead as tribute, because in many cases ther regions paying this tribute could not have produced the metals in question from their own mines. The many tributes of silver paid to Egypt by Syrian towns, for instance, must be interpreted as tribute only; Syria and Palestine had only few feposits and probably got all their silver and lead from other districts such as Asia Minor.

In the map we have also indicated by arrows trade-routes by which these metals may have been imported, though the countries mentioned between brackets can hardly have been engaged in silver and lead trade with the Near East in Antiquity.

In *Egypt* there are four important galena deposits apart from the numerous gold mines, the gold of which always contains silver, but unfortunately the lead ores contain only slight amounts of silver. There is the argentiferous galena containing only about 30 ounces of silver about two miles south of Safaga Bay near the Red Sea near the ancient Mons Claudianus (41), where in Roman times lead and silver were exploited. Galena practically free from silver occurs in large quantities at Gebel Rosâs (25°.17′) about 70 miles south of Qoseïr (42) and cerussite and native silver are found associated with it in small quantities. This deposit was certainly worked for lead during many centuries as even in the third century A.D. the Romans exploited it and a tax was raised on the production which must have been important enough to justify such a measure. These mines were reopened in 1913 by an European company. A third deposit of galena is found in the Bahram Mts., 25 miles east of Syene in the Thebaid, south of Apollinopolis Magna (Edfu) (43). A last deposit of galena is associated with the Um-Samiuki copper ore at Gebel Abu Hamamîd, 50 miles north-west of Râs Benâs near the Red Sea coast (44). Thus, contrary to Gowland's opinion that there were no silver ores at all in Egypt (45), deposits do exist (46), but they are practically valueless for silver production, although rich in lead.

Lead and above all galena has been used from predynastic times to the Coptic period, the mineral is very common as an eye-paint throughout these centuries. The lead used for small ornaments, sinkers of nets, plugs and rings since Old Kingdom times may have been of local origin, but it becomes common only during the XVIIIth dynasty, together with silver imports, which facts tend to show that a local industry did not develop until late when the correct methods were learnt from the North. Thothmes III brought back large quantities of lead from his Syrian campaigns, the total tribute obtained from Retenu, Isy, Tunip and Syria in general amounting to 90 blocks of lead, 1200 pigs of lead and a quantity of over 1760 kg. In the XXth dynasty the Papyrus Harris mentions such large quantities as 3090 kg (twice) and 7100 kg (47)! But a XVIIIth dynasty lead net sinker was not desilvered and indeed pure lead remains rare until Roman times. Lead was used in glazes from the XVIIIth dynasty onwards and Saïtic and later bronzes contain appreciable amounts of lead instead of tin (6—12% average and sometimes up to 20%) (48). These lead bronzes were of course more fusible and fluid and easier to cast, engrave, etc., probably also cheaper, but they were suitable only for casting ornaments and devotional objects where no great strength of the bronze was required. Lead coffins are found in Egypt since the Ptolemaic period. If Hellenistic papyri mention *kollytis* and *molybdourgos*, plumbers, who repair and make water-pipes, this is a clear proof of the penetration of Graeco-Roman technique into Egypt.

Both lead and silver occur in Egypt since the Middle Predynastic Period (49), the sign *ḥḏ* for silver occurs since the Third Dynasty but the metal remains rare for many centuries. In the Pyramid Age it is rarer than gold and preceeds this metal in lists and texts. It may have been imported from Syria and Asia Minor, but because the silver production was hardly developed in those regions, it is more probable that the 'silver' used in Egypt was the silver-coloured electrum. The analyses given by Lucas of silver objects dating before the XVIIIth dynasty prove this as they contain far more gold than would occur in silver derived from galena. Early silver contained 60—92% of silver, 3—38% of gold and traces of copper, certainly a natural product not obtained by smelting. This silver is often patchy from gold particles as a natural product would be, but not a molten one.

The beautiful silverwork of the Middle Kingdom (50) and the picture of rings and necklaces in the tombs of that period (51) show that the Egyptian goldsmiths had turned their experience to this new metal, either imported or held to be pure silver when found as e-lectrum. Silver remains more valuable than gold, even in Hyksos times (*Papyrus Rhind*) it has double the value of gold. In the New Kingdom more plentiful supplies change the ratio gold-silver to 5/3, both lead and silver being imported or taken from Syria and the North mostly in pigs, blocks or rings as the reliefs show us. The *Keftiu* bring silver to Amenhotep III, the silver merchants are Syrians (52), the lead comes from Asia (53). Thothmes III receives silver rings from Ḥatti (54) and the peace-treaty with Hattušil is written on a silver tablet.

But if Egyptian goldsmiths make silver rings (55) and the King of Alašia exchanges silver objects from Egypt for copper, as the Amarna letters prove, this does not mean that a silver industry existed, but only that the clever Egyptian goldsmiths worked imported silver by their own methods, developed by an age-old craft. If, therefore, silverwork in Cyprus shows Egyptian style-elements this is due to the craft of the Egyptian goldsmith and is no proof of a silver production in Egypt. The texts of the New Kingdom mention large quantities of silver (98, 25, 360, 24, 37 lbs, etc.) taken from Naharin, Kheta, Retenu, Zahi, etc. as booty or tribute. The enormous quantities of silver given by Ramses III to the temples (figures like 9 cwt and 20 cwt are given (57) prove that by then silver had become more common in Egypt. Assurbanipal took two silver obelisks weighing 75.000 Kgr. (?) as spoil from Thebes in 661, but still the metal was not as plentiful in

Egypt as in Persia by the Persian period, the gold-silver ratio being still 2/1. Alexander tried to enforce a 10/1 ratio but only in the reign of Ptolemy II did the normal 13/1 ratio exist in Egypt. Before that time Egypt remained a country poor in silver if compared with the rest of the Ancient Near East. Silverwork profited from improved goldsmiths' technique; a XXth dynasty bowl was probably made by spinning and since the Ptolemaic period raising was known to the Egyptian silversmiths (58).

The deposits in *Africa* had no importance in Antiquity. Lead ores occur in the Sudan in the Gebel Kutum and there are deposits at Broken Hill, North Rhodesia. Some authors mention silver imports from Ethiopia into Egypt but it is not clear where these deposits should be sought. The lead-ores of Nigeria, Algeria and Tunis meant nothing to the Ancient Near East and if Herodotus tells us (59) that the Cyreneans gave Cambyses 500 minae of silver this means tribute not production. Indeed silver was so scarce in Africa that Mungo Park finds the gold/silver ratio to be 4/3 in the Sudan in 1796 instead of the Egyptian ratio of 13/1 (60). This and the observations of Cline (61) prove definitely that Africa did not produce silver for Egypt nor was there any diffusion of the knowledge of silver technology from Egypt to the Dark Continent.

Arabia is notoriously poor in lead or silver ores (62). On the east coast of the gulf of Akabah the Midian mountains contain galena rich in silver. This is the source from which the Nabateans produced it (63) and exported it from the harbour of Maknâ. But on the rest of the western coast of Arabia no deposits of lead or silver ores are reported. For Strabo correctly says that the Debae exchanged gold for silver (64), not that they produced it, and the Sabaeans may have had vast stores of gold and silver (Strabo), but no deposits are known to exist in their country. Argentiferous galena is reported from the mountain of Oman.

Both *Palestine and Syria* are very poor in ores, the only two deposits are Gebel Akra (Mt. Tasios), north of Ladikije and the region south-east of the Dead Sea, but silver and lead seem to have been imported in early days. We may be told that Abraham was "rich in silver" (65) or that he paid "Ephron 400 shekels of silver, current money with the merchant" (66) and that Joseph was sold for 20 silver shekels (67), but silver and lead are rare in the remains of ancient cities in these regions. Indeed apart from silver and lead found at Gezer (68), at Ta'anach and the two horned Hathor statuettes from Tell Ajjul these metals are rarely found in early strata in Palestine, but somewhat more abundantly in Syrian cities. The Israelites posses silver in the wilderness and a silver image is cast for Micah from 200 silver shekels (69), but the metals become plentiful in the days of the kings. David stamped silver and it figures largely in the descriptions of Solomon's reign. He is said to have obtained it from Arabian kings of from Tarshish (70). *Tarshish* has been identified with *Tartessos* and this silver was believed to be Spanish silver brought to the East by Phoenician traders. But the Tarshish problem remains unsolved, the "navy" or "ships" of Tarshish may even be just synonyms for sea-going ships and it would be unjustifiable to assume silver production in Spain and trade between Spain and the East at so early a date on such slender evidence. Apart from such finds as the silver vases and objects at Gerar both metals become common only in Hellenistic times. Then it is even reported that the river bed near Jerusalem is lined with lead (71) and Josephus mentions large stocks of lead (72). The Maccabees coined silver money and hence the new meaning "coin" given to the word 'keseph' (silver). Lead is generally considered to be 'reprobate' silver (73), it is mentioned in lists of metals after tin or iron (74) but this means only that it was considered the most worthless metal not the most abundant.

The classical authors tell us many stories about silver deposits in India. According to Strabo it is found in the country of the Musicanes (75) (by which he probably means lead-ores from Baluchistan) and also in the country of the Catheans, in the mountains of the Punjab (76) but he does not indicate any closer location. Nor does Ktesias (77), who remarks that there are many rich mines which were not so deep as the Bactrian mines. There are many galena deposits in India, some of which (Ajmir) have been worked for a very long time, others like those of Upper Burma or those further east in Annam, Tonkin and South China (Fo-kien) can not have been of any importance to the Ancient Near East. The origin of the silver found in Mohenjo Daro is still a mystery (78). Mackay believes that local sources may have been tapped but is more inclined to postulate supplies coming from the argentiferous galena of Afghanistan. On the one hand he rightly remarks that extraction from electrum or galena at so early a date seems doubtful in view of the lack of correct appliances. Still, though less common than copper, bronze and gold, silver is by no means rare in the Indus civilization. The local silversmiths were skilled craftsmen who understood soldering and made beautiful ornaments. He, there-

fore, hesitatingly suggests that extraction from galena may not have
been beyond the local craftsmen. Further detailed study on this silverwork is urgently needed to settle this question; we are inclined to
doubt this early extraction from lead and refining and suggest that
the 'silver' is really electrum, but analysts must have the last word.

There were important sources of silver and lead to the north of
India in Bactria and Transoxania which have been worked from the
Persian period onwards and possibly still earlier. The only excavations going back to very early stages of civilization tell us nothing
about these metals. Pumpelly found lead in Anau I only, but silver
seems to be unknown. Still, Afghanistan and the regions to the north
of the Oxus contain many deposits of lead-ores which like those in
Persia are always argentiferous. Badakshan contains old mines of
silver and lead, which Marco Polo (Book I, XXIV) mentions as very
productive and which occur in the writings of Abulfeda and Ibn
Hauqal. In Ferghana (Transoxania) other deposits are located, especially in the Mawarannahr mountains and the Waisli-kara range.
South of the Oxus, Mt. Bangahir near Anderab on the way to Kabul
was still worked in the days of Abulfeda, and further south halfway
to Kabul the mines of Panjhîr were known to the same writer after
having been seen by the Chinese pilgrim Hiuen Tsang in the seventh
century (79); they are still worked (80). The Chinese valued the silver
from P'o-tzu (Bactria). In Bactria proper there are mines to the north-
east of Balkh, in the neighbourhood of Mughab and in Pendjeh all of
which have been abandoned. The Chaliphs used these mines in
Transoxania, Ferghana, Fars, and Kerman but above all those in
Khorasan, but the mines in Afghanistan and north had to be abandoned in the ninth and tenth centuries because of lack of wood-fuel.
Imports from the Altaï region or further east from China (especially
the central province of Hunan) and Japan are improbable in the period
we are dealing with.

In *Persia* many important deposits are found. First of all in Khu-
rasan there are ancient lead mines near Mt. Nich (81) as well as on Mt.
Binalud and other mountain-sides between Meshed and Nishapur.
In the province of Kerman there are many ancient mines south and
east of Kerman up to Murghab. In the present Fars, the ancient
Carmania, galena is found in the neighbourhood of Niriz. Herodotus
(82) says that Darius got his silver from Cappadocia and Carmania and
Strabo mentions these mines (83) on the authority of Onesicritus.
They may be the silver mines mentioned by Maništusu in the so-called

Cruciform Monument in his story of his wars against a coalition of 32 cities (84). More to the north there are galena deposits in the central mountain range in the district between Kashan and Isfahan, further south near Yezd and north near Anarak. The mountains in Damghan and above all the Elburz range contain many rich veins of galena. Some of the ancient mines near Isfahan were abandoned in the ninth century. There is little lead and silver in Azerbaijan (85) except near Mt. Sahund.

Both silver and lead appear late in Iranian history, but then we must remember that much of the early history of this country is still a blank. In the Elamite period (about 1100 B.C.) fairly pure silver occurs and the lead is practically pure, which would point to a penetration of the processes for desilvering lead to those regions (86). Desch considers the silver used in Luristan to be native metal (87) and King (88) says that supplies of silver came from the hills of S. Elam (89), but no further indication of these deposits can be found, unless those of Carmania are meant. Lead is mentioned in the Vendidad as material for vessels but both metals become common only in the Persian Empire, when the gold Darics and the well-known Persian sigloi were coined. The huge accumulations of gold and silver in the palace of the Persian kings can be judged by the reports that Alexander the Great found 40.000 talents of gold and silver ingots and 9000 talents of coined money.

Mesopotamia did not contain any galena deposits but many rich mines existed in the mountains of *Armenia and Kurdistan*. There is galena on the sloped of the Takht-i-Suleiman near the upper course of the Diyala river. Large amounts of lead-ore containing an average of 20 oz/Ton of silver are found in the mountains near the sources of the Greater Zab and Khabur rivers, especially in the Tiyari mountains, in the neighbourhood of Lisan near Lake Urumiyah, and to the west on the Judi Dagh in the region north-east of Niniveh. From Musasir in this region Sargon II took large quantities of silver and before him Tukulti Ninurta II (90). Further north there are important galena deposits near Erzerum (Carana) on the frontier of Armenia and many other mines round Erivan, north of the Araxes river in the ancient districts of Colchis and Iberia. On the western frontier of Assyria two very important mines are found. The first was Ergenimadeni (Arghan Ma'den) near the ancient Arsinia in the neighbourhood of Diyarbekir (Amida) on the Tigris (91) and the second Keban (Keban Ma'den) on the border of Cappadocia near Harput and Maltya. Keban is regarded by some authorities as the site of the "silver mountains" which Sargon I and Maništusu record (92) but these are more probably the Cilician Taurus (93).

In *Asia Minor* there are no less than 26 important deposits, seven of which are located in Pontus in the district south of Trabzon (Trapezus, Teribizonde). They are located:

1—Near Artvin on the river Chorokh.

2—At Baiburt near Domana and Erzerum on the northern frontier of Armenia, where at the time when Marco Polo visited this district there was still a mine "rich in silver" (94).

3—At Gümüsane (Gümüsh Ma'den) on the Harsut river east of Karahissar, south of Tirebolu (Tripolis, Pharnacia) where the ore contains much silver (like the other galenas in Pontus), about 48-120 oz/Ton. These are probably the mines to which Strabo refers (95) but which were exhausted in his time according to his information, which must be wrong as the mines still contain enormous amounts of galena.

4—At Lidjessi near Karahissar (Colonia), where galena contains over 70% of lead.

5—The Gebel Bel Ma'den.

6—Near Niksar (Neo-Caesarea, Cabira).

We have already referred to the Chalybes-Alybê problem and would only add that these Pontic mines were so rich that Pompey took 6000 talents from them and that they are still by no means exhausted.

7—Gümüshaciköy (Hadjy koï) near Amasya (Amaseia) on the Paphlagonian border (96).

8—Kargi, east of Kastamonu in the Ilgaz Dagh.

9—Ak Dagh Ma'den between Sivas and Kayseri (Mazaca Caesarea), which mines were probably the source of the silver and lead which the Assyrian traders at Kaneš (Kül-tepe) 10 miles north-east of Kayseri buy and send home (97). Tiberius founded a mint at Mazaca, which proves that they were still working in Roman times.

10—Berektlu Ma'den in the AlaDagh (Anti-Taurus), which has been tentatively identified with the "Tunni mountains" where Salmenassar III got his silver. These mines are now exhausted (98).

11—One of the two important mines in the Cilician Taurus is Bulgar Ma'den where the lodes of galena contain up to 600 ounces of silver (1.84%) and which still produces 168.000 Kgr. of lead and 1500 Kgr. of silver per year. Hittite inscriptions were found here (99) and this is more probably the "Tunni" of Assyrian inscriptions (100). The silver was exported to Egypt and shipped from Mallus on the coast.

12—Ala Dagh in the southern Cilician Taurus near Gilindre (Kilindria) where the ore contains the high average of 1% of silver. The Cilician Taurus is probably the silver mountain which Sargon I and Erimuš claim to have reached. It is claimed that the silver was shipped from here to Egypt since the Old Kingdom (46) and Pliny mentions that galena was shipped from the Taurus from Elaeussa, Corcyrus and Zephyrium (101).

Two other deposits are located in the *Lycian Taurus* about which we have no information from ancient texts and so we do not know whether they were exploited in Antiquity.

13—In the Lycian Taurus near *Antalya* (Adalia, Adana).

14—In the *Ak Dagh* south of Kemer (Chimaera).

15—At *Tris Ma'den* in the Sultan Dagh west of Konya remains of old mines have been found (102).

16—In Galatia, *Denek Ma'den* on the Cicek Dagh near Karakecili halfway between Kayseri and Ankara (103). This mine lies to the south of Boğazköy (which name according to Sayce means 'town of silver' (104))and may well have been exploited by its inhabitants.

17—In the *Dumanich Dagh* (Mt. Olymp range) in Bithynia near Karie Seunluk and Bursa (Brussa).

18—*Balya Ma'den* in the Kaz Dagh north east of Mt. Ida in Mysia, which is the Perichraxis worked by the Romans (105) and in 1903 still produced 7.600.000 kg of lead containing 63 ounces of silver.

These two mines were the sources for Trojan silver which was found so abundantly in the Second Town.

19—*Menteshdere*, the ancient Ergasteria, 'between Pergamum and Cyzicus' mentioned by Galen (106).

20—*Mytilene*, the ancient Lesbos (107).

21—At *Gümüldur* near Seferihissar west of Ismir (Smyrna).

22—On the *Gümüsh Dagh* (Silver Mountain) near Bayindir on the Tmolus range in the neighbourhood of the ancient Tralles. Here the galena contains up to 560 ounces of silver but the mines failed in Roman times.

23—The *Murad Dagh* between Usak and Karahissar.

24—*Samos* (Zestor) where old mines were reopened by a Belgian Company.

25—*Gümüshli* (Myndos) near Bodrum (Halicarnassos) where remains of old mines have been found (108).

26—On the isle of *Rhodos* (Rodi) white lead was mined according to Pliny and galena was found (109).

No wonder that with these plentiful sources at hand the Ionians and Lydians were skilled in silverwork (110).

This abundance of silver-bearing rich galena deposits in the surrounding mountains led to an early use of lead and silver in Mesopotamia. Prehistoric silver occurs in the graves of al 'Ubaid and Lagaš. Early lead samples from Kiš seem to have been smelted from simple ores (111). In early dynastic times silver is well known though still rarer than gold, but its use as a medium of currency is very early (112). It was found at Adab, Kiš, Nippur, Tello, al 'Ubaid, and Šurrupak but not at Uruk. But here we must remember that individual silver (and leaden) objects may have been destroyed by corrosion in the wet soil of Mesopotamia. Silver is general in the 'Royal Tombs' at Ur (113) and the silversmith's work is very clever. Some of this silver is of good quality, though much is simply electrum and heavily alloyed with gold or smaller amounts of copper. As there is no proof that this silver was refined at Ur it must have been imported as such either as native alloy or refined near the mines, like that of Lagash. The lead sheat found in the graves of Ur is crude lead smelted from the ore, it was not desilvered.

Presargonic lead is not unknown but still fairly rare, it also occurs in some of the early bronzes, where it must have been alloyed with copper in view of the fairly high percentages found (114). At Kish and Anau I tumblers, beakers and sheet lead have been found and these may represent the first signs of lead produced by smelting galena. The early silver seems to have been mostly native electrum with a high silver content, may be metal obtained from small silver-ore pockets, but by 2500 B.C. silver from galena seems to be flowing in from Pontus. It is obvious from the excavation reports that most of the earlier cities in ancient Mesopotamia had no smelting facilities and that crude or refined lead and silver were imported.

The early texts are not very clear about the sources of this silver. The 22nd. tablet of the ḪAR-ra: ḫubullu series (145) mentions a KUR Ḫáš ha-aš-ba-ár bar as a silvermine of importance, the Lipšur litanies refer to a KUR Zar-su. Sargon I tells us about his expedition to the "silver mountains", and his story is know to us in versions from Assur, el-Amarna and Boğazköy (146). Some like Gadd and Legrain (147) locate these mountains in the extreme west of Cilicia, other in the Taurus in general and even in Elam (148), but the general opinion is now that they should be somewhere in southern Anatolia. The identity of the "Tunni mountains" and the Taurus range (mentioned in Egyptian and Hittite texts) has generally been accepted by Delaporte, Smith and Luckenbill (149). Asia Minor is a far more likely spot for the production of silver, the Cilician ores are far richer in silver than those known from Persia (150).

During Sargon's reign (c. 2300 B.C.) lead weights in animal form became current as money (151), this metal may also have come from the Kurdish mountains nearby. We have already mentioned Maništusu's inscription on the so-called Cruciform Monument referring to an expedition against a coalition of 32 cities in Elam which possess silver mines and diorite quarries. These mines may have been in Carmania, if the cities mentioned were really in Elam. In that case they were the earliest silvermines we hear of in Persia and may be only just opened.

We know, however, that in other cases such an indication of origin may simply be one of quality without any real relation to the source of the silver or lead. The texts often mention "silver of Amurru" and "silver of Akkad" as indications of purity (152), the latter being certainly less pure than the "qalû silver" of high purity (153). The early silver usually contains lead and copper with up to 1% of gold and bismuth.

Maništusu was the first to establish a regular money system of talent, mana and shekel based on silver weighed out by the merchants. Erimuš is said to have been the first to have a statue cast of lead (154), he visited Sargon's silver mountains (155). A lexical list mentions a "silver-weigher" (156) next to a carrier of weights. We also have a fairly clear idea of the trade form of silver, usually rings (157), barsor ingots (kusru) (158), lumps (sibirtu) (159), plates (kappu) (160), wire or just small pieces. The rings and wire often come in units of $1/8, \frac{1}{2}$ and one shekel, such standard pieces of silver, the precursors of money, were found at Khafaje.

Gudea too obtained "silver from the mountains (161). The location of these mountains was sought in the Taurus and more particularly in the Bulghar Dagh or sometimes more vaguely in Asia Minor in general (162), while Woolley thinks that the Zagros region is meant, probably because Meluchcha is mentioned in the next line of the text. We are inclined to accept the first mentioned location as no dates are available on the state of metallurgy in the Kurdish mountain region at this date, where supplies of silver and lead were also plentiful and where Gudea fetches so many other commodities. He is also said to have a store of lead in his palace (163).

In the Agade period the ratio gold/silver is reported to be 8/1 in the reign of Sargon I (164) but in the Ur III period silver seems to have become more common as a ratio of 10/1 under Bur Sin and 7/1 under Gimil Sin would lead us to believe. In Ur III texts (165) sums of silver are lent at various rates of interest. These texts also mention A-bar, abâru (Hebrew 'ôphèrèth) (lead) as a fairly worthless metal (166). It has been Heichelheim who inferred that the production of silver was larger (167) or the contacts between Asia Minor and Meso-potamia may have grown closer as the famous Cappadocian tablets which date from this period tend to show. The Ur texts also mention silver objects such as rings, gems and vessels and silver is taken into the palace as revenue but actual payments in silver are very rare. A tablet from Dungi's reign contains accounts of amounts of silver (168). Imports of silver and lead to early Assyria are mentioned in the Cappa-docian tablets containing the correspondence between Assyrian traders in Asia Minor (Kaneš) and the firms to which they belong in Assur.

The Kültepe tablets (169) prove that during the nineteenth century much lead ore was shipped from northern Assyria into Anatolia where the necessary fuel for smelting and desilvering the lead could be obtained. There was also a large copper trade in Anatolia, but tin and bronze were still scarce in those days.

But silver seems to have remained a money standard only, actual payments being made in copper or lead bars, rings, etc. (170) seldom actually in silver. The lead is said to have come from the "Chachu and Mašgungunnu" mountains which must probably be sought in the Kurdish and Armenian mountain ranges. The silver production of Cappadocia and Elam seem to have become larger, silver in the form of rings or pieces (Hacksilber) is mentioned more frequently than in earlier periods and is now certainly much more common than gold.

Silver still has this function in the Old Babylonian Period (171), not only in Southern Babylonia but at Eshnunna, Assyria and Mari as well. There is no evidence that imports at Ur during the Ur III period were already paid for in silver, but at the time of Rim Sin the metal is indeed used to pay for the copper imported from overseas. This over-seas trade was most important to Ur and silver models of boats were presented to the temple of Ningal (172) and gifts in silver to the god-dess or garments valued in silver abound in the texts (173). As this silver began to serve to pay for the copper from Tilmun its impor-tance began to increase and this accounts for the strict laws and the penalties laid down in the Code of Hammurabi (§ 112) on the transport of silver from Anatolia to Ur.

During the Larsa period silver was imported from Eshnunna into Larsa, being "kaspum ṣarpum", pure silver like that sent from the Assyrian trading colonies in Anatolia to Assur, the local trade at Larsa also acknowledges a third quality "kaspum kankum" (174). In these early periods silver flowed in and out and changed hands within southern Mesopotamian kingdoms being partly employed in the transit trade and for the rest absorbed in the countries' own economy. The value of silver in relation to copper was still high, 1 : 112—140 (175).

Although during Hammurabi's reign the gold/silver ratio is reported to be 6/1 which may point to a temporary shortage of supplies from Asia Minor and Armenia due to the troubled times there and in North Syria, the ratio remains very constant at 10/1 during a long period afterwards. Though some Old Babylonian sites yielded very few silver objects the metal is now commonly used for foundation tablets of temples and even deposits of some value have been found (176) especially in Assyria. Lead seems to have been very common in Assyria from early periods onwards. Weights up to 500 Kgr. are by no means rare in the temples and large sums of lead are mentioned as fines in Assyrian law-texts (177). The metal was probably not obtained in Assyria itself but imported either from Asia Minor or from the mountains in the North. The production of silver from lead becomes more widely known, lead being generally considered as an adulteration of the silver (178). Leaden clamps are used in Assyrian buildings.

Bactria and Carmania have also been suggested as sources for the silver supplies of Mesopotamia but we have no exact data on silver production there, though it would seem from the now more frequent silver finds in Elam and Persia that the metal became more common towards the end of the second millenium and could of course have been produced locally from the deposits mentioned. The location of "Mount Šaršu" has not yet been identified (179).

In the Amarna period silver and lead have taken up their definite places in metallurgy, they are widely spread over the Ancient Near East except Egypt, and huge amounts of tribute and booty are mentioned in the inscriptions of Assyrian kings. Tukulti Ninurta takes enormous quantities of silver and lead from the region of the Tiyari Mountains (180), such quantities as 32 or 11 talents of lead, 18 pigs of lead, 3 talents of silver being mentioned. This would lead us to believe that silver and lead metallurgy was by now well developed in the region between Lake Van and Lake Urumiyah, the ancient Urartu. In the earlier Assyrian tribute lists silver preceeds gold but this is hardly due to this metal being rarer, as the gold/silver ratio proves.

Silver spoils from Syria and Phoenicia are taken by Aššurnasirpal II and by Salmenassar III, Sargon II gets his silver from Musasir near Lake Urumiyah and a tribute of 2100 talents (?) from Carcemiš (181).

The Amarna letters contain several passages that point to the beginning of an export of silver to Egypt in exchange for Egyptian gold. In the Alalakh tablets (182) silver and gold are seldom mentioned but they were not becoming scarce, this is clear from the amounts of precious metals which the Egyptian kings of this period took from Palestine and Syria. However, there is a pronounced tendency already to avoid paying in silver and to use copper as a medium of exchange for day-to-day transactions. In Old-Assyrian times lead crops up now and then as a medium of exchange.

It has been suggested that the Phoenician traders were responsible for the frequency of silver in the Near East in the first millenium and that this silver was obtained by them from the mines in Sardinia and Spain, but the part which Phoenician trade played in early history has been grossly overrated on account of misleading classical information and no value should be attached to such reports for early periods. Closer contacts in the Ancient Near East in this period, the abundance of rich deposits and metallurgical skill in several regions are the reasons for the abundance of silver in this period and fit into the logical development of metallurgy in the Near East. The practice of de-silvering lead was not yet common, Assyrian lead of the VIIIth century still contained 0.11% of silver (183).

Copper and lead money (184) were soon displaced by silver in clippings, bars, rings, spirals or sheets, weighed out on a balance for payment. Refined silver was stamped in each separate town. Refined silver appears in many contracts (for instance at Tell Halaf about 650 B.C.). An early stamped bar from Zindjirli weighs exactly one mina (185) and dates from about 700 B.C. and there are traces of an early pre-Lydian coinage in Assyria. Sennacherib states that he cast shekel and half-shekel pieces in silver in the same period (186). The early Persian and Neo-Babylonian silver pieces had a "GIN"mark, there were heavy penalties for tempering with such coins (187) and we know that the silver was definitely alloyed, probably with copper (188). In the Neo-Babylonian period the gold/silver ratio was 12/1 under Nabonidus, rising to 10/1 during the troubled times at the end of the dynasty but falling to 12/1 to 13/1 during the Persian period, when the kings established silver standard money throughout their Empire. The silver of Carmania and Bactria may have contributed largely to the store of *sigloi* found by Alexander the Great in the King's palace (189). As in the case of gold, when silver refining and testing had become public knowledge this metal could be used for coins and here again we can not ignore the fact that the development of proper testing methods and the development of coinage between the VIIIth and VIth centuries play a large part in the later history of silver.

There are still very few historical data on the silver and lead production from *Asia Minor*, the major producer in Antiquity. Bittel (190) states that in the early third millenium copper, lead and some silver are known, the latter probably produced at the Ak Dagh near Sivas. Analyses have not been published and we can not decide whether this was native or refined metal. It would be interesting to investigate whether this silver was indeed refined for then we would have proof that the refining methods were tried out in those early periods in Asia Minor. In Alishar a few pieces and seals of lead were found (191) and lead occurs in very early bronzes at Thermi and Hissarlik.

Dating early finds from Central and Eastern Anatolia is still very difficult, and we can not fit early silver and lead finds into the scheme we propose here. But the antiquity of refining methods in Asia Minor is definitely proved by both the finds at Troy and the Cappadocian tablets. The latter date from about 2250—1950 B.C. and deal with many transports and sales of lead and silver. The silver is mostly sold in bars in quantities of 4 to 15 minae, a single mention of silver in the form of a chain weighing about $\frac{1}{2}$ mina (a form very common for gold) occurs in the texts. Crude silver called "silver from Kaneš" and "refined silver" are mentioned. Pure lead and "loose lead" in sealed containers (probably pigs of lead) are mentioned. The ratio silver/lead varies from 3.5/1 to 6/1, the average is 4/1; lead is usually measured in talents. These facts prove beyond doubt that both silver and lead were refined at that date and that several grades were manufactured and sold.

In the Hittite Empire both metals were plentiful, supplies being exported by the Keftiu of the south coast to Egypt where it suddenly grows more plentiful in the fifteenth century. Close connections with the Aegean islands and the Minoan civilisation existed without doubt (192). Hittite bronzes, especially those of early periods, sometimes

contain lead, no doubt added intentionally. Six rolls of lead with
Hittite inscriptions were found at Assur (193).

The earliest strata at Troy (Troy I) contained small amounts of
silver and lead but in Troy II refined silver and silverwork appear.
Several techniques like hammering, chiselling, engraving, soldering
and granulation seem to have been mastered by the local silversmiths
(194). The silver objects found include 11 vases (containing up to 5%
of copper), bars with about $2\frac{1}{2}\%$ of copper, crucibles (195) and six
remarkable ingots weighing exactly 40 shekels of the heavy mina,
varying from 6.0 to 6.1 ounces only. These ingots are very pure,
equal to Roman refined silver (196) and their low gold and silver
content point to manufacture from argentiferous lead ore. This is also
the case with the other silver objects from Troy II, the average analysis being 95.61—95.15% of silver, 0.17—0.47% of gold; 3.23—3.44%
of copper, 0.22—0.44% of lead and traces of iron. Though Meyer has
not ventured to locate the galena mines from which this silver was
obtained, we agree with Evans, Cary (197) and many others that there
is no doubt that the galena from Mount Ida and Mt. Olymp was
worked as it was in later times, though of course both the Pontic area
and Bulghar Ma'den may have supplied the ore or the metal at the
beginning of this period. Small leaden idols were also found in Troy
II and some lead was used in the bronzes of this period.

Silver and lead appear in *Cyprus* after copper and bronze in the
Middle Bronze Age about the fifteenth century B.C. Some of the
early silver is reported to be pure (198) but in the Early Iron Age it
was still widely alloyed with lead and only imperfectly refined. Rich
finds date from the fifth century only, silver finds at Amalthus copy
earlier copper and bronze trinkets. Several classical authors mention
silver or lead mines in Cyprus (199) and though some modern writers
repeat this information (200) no confirmation can be found for this
opinion, Strabo mentions silver in connection with copper mines and
possibly the production of silver from copper was meant, though this
is rather early for the intricate methods necessary for this refining.
Oberhummer (201) says definitely that no lead or silver is found on
the island. Lead objects are fairly common in early periods but seem
to have been imported from the mainland together with the early
silver. Only in the Greek period in the fifth century silver is far more
common than gold, this silver is pure and these later silver objects
can, therefore, be distinguished very easily from the earlier manufactures of silver-lead alloy (impure silver either imperfectly refined

or an intentional alloy). In the Amarna letters the kings of Alašia exchange copper for silver objects with Egypt and some of the early silverwork found does indeed show signs of Egyptian manufacture. This proves that local silver production either from galena or from copper ores was certainly unimportant in the fourteenth century B.C.

There is no doubt that *Crete, the Aegean islands and Greece* have learned the use of silver and lead from Asia Minor whatever trade connections they may have had in later periods. There were no deposits worth mentioning in Crete but many on the Aegean islands (202). Milos, Paros, Santorin, Kuphonisia have galena deposits. Kimolos and Thasos had mines which were exploited up to the eighth century like those of Siphnos (203) which were at their height in the sixth century but were flooded by the sea in the fifth (204). These smaller mines were soon eclipsed by the rich galena deposits of Laureion, which though exploited in Mycenaean times began to expand in the sixth century and were the rich strata were revealed after 500 (205). We have many detailed studies of these important mines (206) and also many references from classical authors dealing with these mines and the effect of their great production on the social and economic life of Greece (207).

Lead and silver have been found in the Aegean islands from the Early Cycladic period onwards, lead in the form of small votive boats. In Crete they occur since Early Minoan times, silver daggers have been found at Kumaressa (208) and small lead votive axes occur in E.M. II graves. By trade with Asia Minor they became more common in later periods. Trade connections with the West may have existed in later times and silver may have come from Spain in the L.M. period. The rarity of silver objects at Knossos has been attributed to the fact that the palace was destroyed by plunderers. Egyptian monuments tend to show that the Keftiu or Minoans (?) were engaged in silver trade between Asia Minor and Egypt from the XIIth dynasty onwards. Silver objects are imitated in early pottery in Crete (209). Crete never produced silver and lead but traded them.

Small silver plaques found at Enkomi and Knossos dating from Late Minoan times seem to be coins. They are marked with a sign H or I for the half-bit. Gowland has concluded from parallels from Japan (the manufacture of the so-called Mamma-ita-gin) that they were made by pouring drops of silver on a metal surface thus marked.

In Mycenean Greece silver grew more common though still less so than gold (210). Some of the silver is very pure like that of Troy II,

though some is alloyed with no less than 30% of lead. The analyses
tend to show that refining lead and silver was known, probably from
Asia Minor. In this period the use of silver spread and must have led
to the openings-up of local sources, in the islands and on the mainland. Production at Laurion may well have started by now (211).
Silver was fashioned into jars, rings, wire, and discs at Mykene and
both here and at Tiryns lead was used for clamps and in the form of
sheets, pigs and lumps. In the Iliad and the Odyssey silver is far less
popular than gold, it was used for plates and dishes or for the decoration of swords and other weapons (212). This silver probably came
from local deposits for a Mycenaean site at Thorikos was very close
to the Laureion mines which were worked in those days, though the
real exploitation came in the days of Solon only. Fairly large amounts
of lead were found in the Mycenaean deposits in Athens (213). Lead
is mentioned twice in the Iliad (214) but only as a symbol of a plastic
"weak" metal when a spear-point is "bent like lead", or as weights
attached to nets such as were found at Mycenae, Dendra and Brauron.
Lead was used for vessels for storing water and small lead statuettes
or lead wire were quite common as were leaden rivets. A Knossos
tablet mentions three lots of 3 Kgr. "mo-ri-wo-do" (molybdos) (lead).
The sign for silver in the Pylos tablets (a-ku-ro) is identical with that
of the unit of weight, probably lumps (or rings) of silver of a standard
weight served both a units of currency and weight like the shekel in
the Old Testament (215).

Classical Greece knew silver and lead in large amounts for apart
from the mines in Macedonia and Thrace which we will discuss below
there was the output of the mines at Laurium, which Bromehead (216)
describes in these words:

Coming now to classical Greece we find what are probably the most
famous mines in the world, the silver mines of Laurium or Λαύρειον
at the southern end of the Athenian peninsula. It is far more true that
the battle of Salamis was won in the mines of Laurium than that
Waterloo was won on the playing fields of Eton. The mines were first
worked by Mycenean peoples and then abandoned. Athenian working
began about 600 B.C. Silver was scarce in Solon's time (638—598),
but by 500 B.C. royalties on Laurium appear in the Athenian budget.
The mineral worked was mostly galena, but the silver content was
such that the mines were always spoken of as silver mines; it runs
from 30 to 300 oz. troy per ton, averaging about 60 oz. From the
middle of the last century the area was worked by a French company,

mainly for zinc, and the French School of Archaeology at Athens has been enabled to make a complete study of the mines, which till then had been untouched since about A.D. 100. Classical Greece was flooded with Persian silver and perhaps imports from Spain and Sardinia. The Macedonian conquest of Asia Minor contributed largely to the intensive production from all the deposits mentioned in Thrace, Macedonia and Asia Minor (217).

In Macedonia and Thrace many mines were worked under the Macedonian kings who also vigorously developed production in Asia Minor. There were mines near Kassandra (Salonica) (218), Lake Prasias (219), Pangeaum (220), Thrace (221) and many others (222) but most of those were only tapped in classical times. The royal Macedonian silver mines were taken over by the Romans in 167 B.C. and reopened in 158, but they produced little and seem exhausted by that time, though they had contributed to the wealth of Philip and Alexander. Such resources had been at the disposal of classical Greece, but in Europe there were many more supplies of galena, in Hungary, in Tirol (223) and in the Harz mountains. In Britain there were leadmines in Somerset (Mendips), Shropshire, Derbyshire, Flintshire, Northumberland and Yorkshire (224).

The exploitation of the lead resources by the Romans commenced very soon after their arrival (A.D. 49) and shows every sign of being a well organised trade. Little evidence of deep mining has survived and it is probable that most of the ore was obtained by means of shallow workings, mainly in Somerset, Salop, Flintshire and Derbyshire. Although the silver content does not seem ever to have been as high as that of some well-known mines in the Mediterranean, it is clear that silver has been extracted by the Romans from some of the British lead. The lead was cast in carefully made moulds, producing pigs with inscriptions which indicate their date. These were then used for the pipes, cisterns and pewter tableware which contributed to the high standard living of the period. Pre-Roman lead usually contains 0.04% of silver, but most of the Roman lead pigs marked "Ex. Arg" have only 0.002—0.008% of silver.

In France lead ores were mined near Rodez, Gévandan and other sites in Auvergne, in Britanny and in the Pyrenees even before Roman occupation, in most of these places foreign competition closed the mines soon after the Romans came to stay (225). Here too the lead seems to have been desilvered, for the lead strips and rings recovered from a Roman vessel which foundered about 200 B.C. near the isle of

Riou off Marseilles was very pure and contained only traces of copper, iron and silver (226).

In Italy itself lead ores were mostly mined in Tuscany for some time, here again the refining was most efficient (227), the lead is usually over 99% with only traces of copper, bismuth or silver, two lead objects have some tin alloyed with it, one only antimony.

The mines of Sardinia were worked by the Phoenicians according to Solinus, but modern research would not claim production earlier than the fifth century (228). The rich deposits of Linares, Sierra Morena, Ciudad Real, Murcia and Cartagena in Spain (229) may have been exploited earlier but it is doubtful whether this production reached the Ancient Near East before classical times (230). Though Diodor claims that the Phoenicians found so much silver that they exchanged the stones on their anchors for silver (in ingots) it is doubtful whether this Phoenician trade is earlier than the period of Greek colonisation. The silver mines of New Carthage were for a long time the main source of silver for the Roman State. Sulla took the silver mines from the knight's companies to sell them for ready money, the heighdays of New Carthage were certainly the decade from 145—135 B.C. In later years the yields and profits were smaller but these silver mines remained important (231) and we have recounted their story elsewhere (232).

This is what the data discussed above tend to show:
Silver and lead production started in the early third millenium in Asian Minor gradually spread to the west (Aegean and Crete) and to the east, where first the Armenian mines, then those in Elam, Carmania and finally Bactria were exploited until at the beginning of the first millenium silver and lead were common metals in the Near East except in Egypt where they did not become common until the Persian period.

4. *Refining and smelting methods*

Before discussing refining and smelting methods in Antiquity it will be useful to summarize modern methods of lead and silver production. This will give an opportunity of indicating the principles underlying these methods, introducing the archaeologist to the metallurgical terms and sorting out by a process of elimination those processes which, for various reasons, could not have been known or used in Antiquity.

It is at the same time easier to discuss the reactions underlying the metallurgical processes when discussing modern methods. For in Antiquity, in the early days of metallurgy, processes were found and developed by trial and error, methods and apparatus borrowed by one branch from another, and every student will be struck by the rather haphazard methods used and the lack of uniform technique and implements. Only gradually have countless generations of miners and metallurgists learned to understand the reactions occurring during the treatment of their ores and metals, and gradually several phases of the treatment have been separated. Thus each stage of the production could be better observed and directed, the product profiting from the specialisation. The underlying physical and chemical principles have, of course, only recently been found, studied and developed but the specialisation already existing in the days of Agricola has a very modern appearance; and yet is was developed, by means of shrewd observation and thorough knowledge of every aspect of the trade, by skilled metallurgists, who knew neither physics nor chemistry. Specialisation existed in Roman times and the rudiments date back much earlier. But the undifferentiated early methods will be difficult for the layman to understand as they are even a puzzle to the expert in many cases. Several reactions proceed at the time in the primitive furnace and thus the "primitive method" is much more undifferentiated and far more difficult to guide and to understand than the modern method. For there are very few texts to guide us. Those gleanings which we pick up in Pliny or Strabo have often been written down by elegant writers but bad metallurgists, and it is often difficult to make any sense of their notes.

It should, therefore, always be remembered that the deliberate differentiation and recognition of several reactions is the modern phase and the 'simple' method of primitive metallurgy is really a complicated mess of reactions which could only be duplicated with much practical skill and keen observation of product and process, because the reactions were not understood as they are today.

We will start with the *production of lead from lead ores* because this lead was also used for the larger part of the silver production in Antiquity and even up to modern times. Lead is produced from galena in three stages: I—Smelting of galena, II—Purification of the crude lead, and III—Desilvering of the soft lead.

I—There are three ways of *smelting galena.*

I*a*. In the *Air Reduction* or *Roasting process* the galena is first gently heated in a blast of air. The sulphur-lead compound, galena, is then decomposed, most of the sulphur escapes as sulphur dioxide gas, some is left in the form of lead sulphate, some galena remains intact but most of the lead is oxidised to lead oxide (litharge). When the correct stage of desulphurisation is reached the temperature is raised and litharge, lead sulphate and galena interact to form lead, which collects at the bottom of the furnace, while the remaining sulphur now escapes as sulphur dioxide gas.

I*b*. In the *Reduction process* the galena is first roasted until practically

Fig. 39.
Smelting lead (After Agricola)

all the galena has been transformed into litharge, which is then reduced by means of carbonaceous matter (Charcoal, Coke, Wood) to lead.

I*e*—*Precipitation process* (Matte smelting process) in which galena is heated with metallic iron. This method is a modern refinement unknown in Antiquity and need not be discussed further in detail.

The product obtained by smelting galena is called crude lead (work-lead, base-bullion) (German: *Werkblei*), the 'stagnum' described by Pliny (233), it contains 45—180 ounces of silver, but in case of rich ores these figures can be considerably higher.

At the present time this smelting is carried out in reverberatory furnaces or, in the case of ores containing a low lead percentage or much silica, blast- or shaft-furnaces are used. The primitive furnaces and even those at Laurion were much simpler, the earliest being

2.4% of silver. Then the remaining molten metal will set all at once. By pouring off the molten metal before this happens the silver is concentrated as far as possible and the lead thus enriched can be desilvered by the very old cupellation process and the lead recovered from the litharge formed thereby (see under V*c*). It seems from the muddled account which Pliny gives of the refining of lead (236) that the principle of the Pattinson process was known and probably even applied at least in Roman times. His account becomes intelligible if we take both *stagnum* and *argentum* to mean "crude lead" and the *galena* in this passage to be "purified lead". The passage then clearly illustrates that the first crystals formed after melting argentiferous lead are almost pure and being denser sink to the bottom and can be laddled out or poured off to be treated separately for silver (237).

By cupellation lead was generally desilvered in Antiquity with remarkable efficiency considering the primitive technique. It is true that Friend and Thorneycroft found Spartan votive figures of lead to contain 0.057% of silver but they have no right to conclude on so few figures that desilverisation was not practised before the Romans. We need only point to the analyses of Troy II lead. When considering the development of any metallurgical process it is imperative to draw conclusions on a statistical basis only, every analysis should be taken into account and indeed, owing to the lack of cooperation of archaeologists and museum directors, who do not generally know that modern analytical methods are non-destructive, the analytical data to work upon are still insufficient from a statistical point of view. But we can safely say that the Greeks desilvered lead upto 0.02% of silver. The Etruscans learnt the art from the Greeks and applied it with the same success (238), whereas the Romans could extract down to 0.01% or even 0.002% in some cases. Roman lead pipe was found to be desilvered very completely (239) and contain only slight amounts of oxidic compounds probably due to the recovery methods of the lead. But, in general Roman lead pipe is unusually pure when compared with modern technical material. Agricola mentions that in his days the limit of extraction was 0.008% of silver, not a very appreciable advance on Roman technique, while modern extraction brings the silver content down to 0.0002%. We will see below that this ancient extraction of silver only seemed very efficient but that even the Romans were extremely wasteful in treating lead ores and that part of the silver disappeared in the slag of lead production. If we now turn to the production of *silver from electrum, silver- and lead-ores* we must first mention a method that is now rarely used to produce silver but that certainly played a part in Hellenistic metallurgy.

IV—For *production from electrum* Antiquity possessed two methods which we have mentioned in discussing gold technology. Both are complex methods in which cupellation is combined with conversion of the silver into chloride or sulphide which is taken up by the slag into the cupel. The silver can be recovered from the slag or dross by roasting and reduction with charcoal.

The *Salt process*, IV*a*, (or cementation) is described by Theophilus (III. 69) and after him by Agricola, who calls it "Scheiden im Guss mit gemischtem Pulver", it eliminates the silver in the form of silver-chloride with common salt.

The *Sulphur process*, IV*b*, called "Scheiden im Guss mit Schwefel oder Spiessglaserz" by Agricola, transforms the silver into silver sulphide by the addition of sulphur or antimony sulphide (stibnite). Both methods depend upon a thorough knowledge of the cupellation method which must have been used for centuries before complications like the two methods described above could have become common practice. They were certainly used in the Hellenistic period. We have concluded from evidence given in a former chapter that the cupellation method was known and used about 1500 B.C. but that the desilvering of electrum become common in later periods and was in general use about 600 B.C. We will revert to this method below.

V—For the production of *silver from silver- and lead- ores* (or copper-ores) three types of methods are known:

V*a*—*Wet methods* by which the ore after preparation (by roasting or converting into chloride) is leached with a suitable solvent (cyanide lye, brine or strong salt solutions) from which the silver is precipitated (Augustin process, etc.). Another variant treats the suitably prepared ore with sulphuric acid and converts the silver in solution into an insoluble form (Reduction with copper or Ziervogel process). Both refinements were unknown in Antiquity.

V*b*—*Amalgamation* was known to the Romans (240), it had by then reached the manufacturing stage and it is mentioned by Theophilus and Biringuccio. The latter calls it a secret process. In 1532 it is introduced into Mexico by Bart. Médina and since then it is know as the *Patio* process. Usually the finely divided ore is mixed with salt, copper sulphate and mercury, and exposed to the air in heaps which are constantly worked. The silver amalgam (silver-mercury alloy) is then distilled, the mercury thus recovered, the silver remaining as a residue.

A variant consists of roasting the silver ore with salt, mixing it with metallic iron and then following the procedure described above.

As mercury production started only in Roman times the amalgamation process was not applied in earlier times.

V*c*—Dry methods are far older and have been used from the very beginnings of the silver industry.

The lead ore is first *smelted* (see method Ia) to crude lead, copper ores are treated by liquation (method IIa) and the lead-silver thus obtained is concentrated by the *Pattinson* process (method IIIc). Silver ores are roasted and the oxide formed reduced with coke or charcoal. Both this crude silver and the concentrated silver-lead alloy are now *cupelled*. In the case of lead ores liquation was, of course, unnecessary, but in the case of copper ores it was imperative to extract the silver by alloying the crude copper with lead and liquating it. In Antiquity it was customary to smelt silver ores with lead to ensure complete extraction of all the silver (241). The same method is used by Agricola, but by his time metallurgists have learnt that many ores contain sufficient lead to keep the silver in solution and only in the case of ores containing insufficient lead is this metal added during the smelting process. Though the principle of the Pattinson process seems to have been known to Pliny it is doubtful whether this method of concentrating the silver was applied on a large scale and usually the crude lead was used for cupellation without concentrating. Now *cupellation* was a process that had been known for centuries, this last stage of the process has carried out with extreme efficiency and we have already pointed out the very good results obtained, a thoroughly desilvered lead. But the first stages were not yet differentiated in metallurgical practice and a varying complex involving roasting, smelting, oxidation, liquation and other reactions was the common way of treating the lead or silver ore. This complexity defeated the purpose of the early metallurgist to extract all the silver from the ore, his knowledge was not yet sufficient to control all these reactions happening at different places in his crudely constructed furnace. Though his lead was very completely desilvered afterwards, he was very wasteful of the lead in the original ore and with the lead he wasted a considerable part of the silver, that remained in the lead lost in the slag. The Greeks in Laurion, for instance, treated an ore containing blende (aluminium and zinc compounds) and other impurities and when trying to obtain a fairly pure lead they had to use a high temperature when smelting to ensure a complete slagging of the impurities in the ore. This defeated their purpose as a great deal of lead passed into the slag and some volatilised. Thus the slags at Laurion contain about 10% of lead, those in Sardinia up to 30%, in Cartagena 8—17%, in Arles 10—15%. De Launay (242) calculated that more than $\frac{1}{3}$ of the original silver was lost in the slag, which contained 25—30% of lead with 0.07—0.1% of silver, though the refined lead contained only 0.001% of silver. As Roman silver technology improved and with close attention paid to the furnaces, in several regions less lead (and therefore

Fig. 41.
Oxydation of crude lead (After Agricola)

less silver) was lost in the slag. The circular smelting furnaces of Laurion were constructed of *mica schist* from Laurion and refractory *trachite* from Milo: according to Strabo they had high chimeys to condense the fume. The condensate consisted of καδμια, σποδος and μολιβδος, possibly zinc oxide and antimony oxide respectively and was highly valued for medicinal purposes. The process was probably not unlike the low furnace treatment of Carinthia in Austria, perhaps even like that in the Scots ore-hearth; from existence of partly altered galena modules in the slags it is clear that the temperature attained was not high. The lead content was 10% or more, by Strabo's time it had dropped, probably to 2—3%. Nevertheless retreatment of old cinder was a profitable enterprise, begun in 1864 and still in operation at the turn of this century.

It is evident that cupellation was carried out very efficiently: contemporary Attic coins assay 980 fine white lead pigs have been discovered running 0.025—0.033 oz./ton. It is fairly clear that this was obtained by reduction of by-product litharge. Its price in the free market was about 11/—(gold) per cwt. in 408 B.C., by 395 B.C. it had dropped to 6/—(gold). Metal price fluctuation, that great bugbear of the producer and user, was obviously as rampant 2,400 years ago as in the inter-war period of this century, and rigging the market just as

Fig. 42.
Refining crude silver (After Agricola)

today. We learn of one speculator buying at 6/—with the object of holding till the price reached 17/—. The lead was used commercially for piping, roofing, and metal manufacture generally. Other by-products were red lead κιυυαβαρι, artificial emerald (?), and the medicinal *spodium*.

In some mines in Jugoslavia (Ralja) the slag contains only 7% of lead, but ores less rich in silver, for instance those in Britain, were treated very negligently. Slags from the same period at Mendip contain 20—26% of lead (243). Here possibly old Celtic methods have been used, the Celts understood the production of silver as the fame of British silver had reached the Romans before they conquered Britain. As the smelting technique improved in Antiquity better results were obtained and it was even possible to work slags from older periods. This is what happened at Laurion as Strabo tells us

(244): 'The silver mines of Attica were originally valuable, but they failed. Moreover those who worked them, when the mining yielded only meagre results melted again the old refuse, or dross, and were still able to extract from it pure silver since the workmen of earlier times had been unskillful in heating the ore in the furnaces. But when production stopped at Laurion in the second century it would still have paid to extract another 0.1% of silver from the 2.000.000 tons of ancient slags. Indeed when these mines were reopened in 1864 the

Fig. 43.
Refining silver by cupellation (After Agricola)

old slag, which had already been desilvered in the later period of Laurion was still found to contain $81\frac{1}{2}$ ounces of silver (245).

Wasteful as this ancient smelting process may have been it is clear from the evidence that the essence of the process was the production of a lead-silver alloy, in which all the precious metals were concentrated. Indeed, Biringuccio was right when he said that without lead the extraction of gold and silver would have been impossible.In his days such methods were only used for testing gold and silver, but no longer to produce them. As far as we can judge from archaeological finds lead production did not start long before 3000 B.C. and hence the extraction of silver does not go back beyond the early third millennium.

Agricola's book no longer describes the exact classical methods for in his days considerable specialization had taken root in the metallurgy of silver and lead.

But in Roman and pre-Roman days the only method of producing silver apart from the gold/silver separation from electrum and the (very unlikely) reduction of silver ores consisted of the treatment of galena in two phases: 1)—a combined roasting, reduction and oxidation, and this smelting was followed by 2)—cupellation. The Romans marked their cupelled de-silvered lead Ex Arg. Those ores which contained too little silver were smelted for lead only as there might still remain a small quantity of silver in the lead 'though not enough to make refining of it profitable' (246).

We know very little about the type of furnaces used for the 'smelting process' in the Ancient Near East and research on these furnaces near the ancient mines by experts is urgently needed. But the furnaces described from the Roman world confirm us in the belief that a large variety of types will be found, each type adapted to the special needs of the ore found locally.

In Laurion the furnaces were very high, the upper portion being used for the smelting operation, the lower part being used to oxidize part of the lead previous to further cupellation. The smelting ovens of Spain were provided with chimneys "so that the gas (sulphur dioxide) from the ore may be carried high in the air, for it is heavy and deadly" (247). Gowland describes an oven from Silchester used for the extraction of silver from copper ore with the help of lead. Other furnaces are about 10—12" wide and filled with alternate layers of charcoal and ore. Blümner (248) describes a Roman furnace for smelting lead found at Arles, an immense crucible 3.20 m deep and 2.50 m wide with walls of brickdust and clay 14 cm thick, sunk in the earth. The contents, alternating layers of wood and ore were fired. The molten crude lead and slag flowed into a vessel, after separation of the slag, the lead was poured into a vessel or small crucibles for cupelling. All these furnaces use artifical blast, which is sometimes introduced at the top rim of the hearth (249) (280), they are mostly constructed of stones lined with clay to resist attack from the slag. But the earlier furnaces are often no more than trenches dug in the ground, like those at Siphnos dating from the VIIth century (250). We believe, however, that this is a simplification and that Asia Minor, a country where metallurgy developed at so early a date, will have known good, though perhaps small, furnaces from the smelting of copper and other ores when they started to use them for silver production. After all, when no claim of efficiency is made, any sufficiently heat-resisting construction, either a cavity in the soil, a simple hearth-furnace or a sloping trench will suffice to produce lead from its ores. The fuel is mixed thoroughly with the ore or alternating layers are built up and artificial draft (bellows come very early in metallurgy!) or natural draught supplies the necessary amount of air. The crude lead produced by this primitive smelting contains not only the silver, but also antimony, bismuth, nickel, arsenic and gold which follow the silver. The cupellation of this silver is carried out in a crucible or a furnace (in later stages of metallurgical history) which is dressed with a porous substance such as bone-ash, calcareous clay (marl), magnesia or any other suitable earth that resists corrosion by the oxides of the baser metals formed during the process and is capable of absorbing these oxides. The early Middle Ages possess such cupellation furnaces; Theophilus describes them at some length (III, 23) and Agricola mentions several typs. In the earlier phases of metallurgy the ordinary type of furnace is used and lined with bone-ash, which seems to have been the common material for cupels (or crucibles) and for the lining of these furnaces. Gowland proves that it was used at Laurion, as the slag contains over 2.4% of phosphoric acid together with the litharge derived from cupellation. In the primitive furnaces pre-heating may have been used and after the fire had been lit, the correct temperature obtained and the lead melted, the fire must have been raked towards the sides, the blast introduced and the lead oxidized. The lead-oxide or litharge (plumbago) formed is absorbed by the bone-ash together with the oxides of the other metal impurities and a cake of silver (together with gold and small amounts of lead, copper and other metals) which the alchemists called *regulus* remains behind in the furnace. This primitive method which Gowland saw in Japan is very effective (251), the average from 555 assays was a product containing over 99% of silver. If the silver content is lower than 97% the cupellation was very carelessly executed, but silver contents below 95% point to intentional impurities or the manufacture of an alloy. The blast should impinge on the surface to be effective and the molten litharge floating on top (252) is skimmed off regularly. The litharge slag is of course not lost, it was used for the production of pure lead oxide in Antiquity (253) by washing it with salt to remove impurities, or it was reduced with charcoal to recover the lead. Both Ezech. XXII: 20 and Jerem. VI: 29 contain graphic descriptions of 'trial by fire' and the manner in which the base metals are consumed and 'drossed' while the noble metals pass unscathed through the ordeal. The furnace described by Jeremiah is considerably too hot for cupellation. There are several references to the 'fining pot' (cupel) in the Bible (254) or to the dross obtained in cupellation (255), to cupellation furnaces (256) and to the bellows used (257). If we want to find out when this cupellation was discovered, we must remember that it must antedate considerably all specialization in the smelting process such as liquation, etc. because these refinements were specially introduced to lighten the task of the cupellation furnace and eliminate as much lead as possible before cupellation. It was certainly known at Laurion and practiced at Siphnos in the VIIth and VIIIth centuries. But it must also antedate the salt process and the sulphur process mentioned above, as these are refinements for certain purposes combined with the principle of cupellation to a new complex reaction. Refining gold is mentioned in the Amarna letters but both the Cappadocian tablets and the finds in Troy II mentioned above prove that very pure silver was made in the twenty-fifth century B.C. We must therefore conclude that the cupellation process was invented in Asia Minor in the first half of the third millenium B.C., shortly after the discovery of the manufacture of lead from galena. By the first half of the second millenium cupellation was applied to the refining of natural gold (electrum) with a few additions to eliminate the silver from the gold and recover it from the dross.

5. *Refined silver, its nomenclature and uses*

The use of cupellation for the production of silver can be proved easily by analysis, as Lucas has already argued (258). For the silver produced in this way differs considerably from the silver produced from electrum, the ratio of silver and gold in silver produced from galena is something like 95.4 to 0.3, that is to say there are only traces of gold in the silver together with lead and other metals, but the silver produced from electrum contains much more gold and different metals as impurities. The attention of the analysts should therefore be fixed on the impurities in the silver. The spectrographic analysis introduced by Grassini (259) will help considerably as it requires only minute quantities of material while it supplies all the valuable information desired.

But we need not anticipate the results of further analysis in saying that Lucas' conclusions hold only for silver in Egypt. If he maintains that the earliest silver in Egypt and by inference that of Mesopotamia was the natural gold-silver alloy, electrum, which contained sufficient silver to be mistaken for that metal, he is only partially right as far as Mesopotamia is concerned for that country had ample opportunity to import the refined silver from Asia Minor, and did so as the Cappadocian tablets prove. True, in the earliest periods, for instance at Ur (260) electrum was mainly used, but pure silver appears fairly soon afterwards. Lucas' other conclusions about galena being the primary ore for silver production and the relatively late importance of silver in history remain, of course, intact. Hoover in his edition of the work of Agricola argues that the smelting of silver from ores and refining by cupellation were known before 2000 B.C. but he does not support his conclusions by sufficient evidence from ancient texts and finds. It will be clear from the arguments brought forward in this chapter that Hoover was right and that the conclusion of Lucas holds good only for Egypt, which country took an exceptional place in the history of silver and lead.

There are also many philological arguments that go to prove that silver was obtained by refining at an early date. The Cappadocian tablets call refined silver *kaspum ṣarrupam* (261) and this addition to the word *kaspu* (silver) is derived from a verb *ṣurupu* to refine, smelt (262) (compare also the Arabic *ṣarîf* for pure silver). If the word *ṣarpu* is used as a synonym of *kaspu* it may have been intended to denote "refined metal" (or metal obtained by smelting). The "silver from Kaneš" mentioned in the Cappadocian tablets was an inferior product as is shown by the price, possibly cupellation was repeated in the earliest phases of refining to obtain a purer silver as indicated in the sevenfold purification mentioned in Ps. XII : 6 and also known from gold technology.

The same texts mention Ù-DAR KÙ-BABBAR (crude silver), KÙ-GAZI (possibly "Hacksilber"), KÙ-BABBAR KALGA (strong silver) and KÙ-BABBAR ZA-RI ("brilliant, polished silver"). By doubling the term BABBAR these texts denote high purity (263). Refined silver is denoted by KÙ-LUH-HA (mesu) (lit. "washed silver"), a term used in describing the silver vase of Entemena (264) and used in a Shuruppak tablet and later documents (265).

An old Assyrian text speaks of "five shekels of silver lost in washing" and another one of "four minas of silver washed from ore" (266). An old Egyptian text of the reign of King Sahûrê is also said to mention the "washing of silver" (267). In later periods such words denoting smelting and refining operations but adopted from the kitchen become more and more common, e.g. the verb bašalu (cooking) is used for silver (268) just as the early alchemists of the Leiden-Stockholm papyri use poiésis (preparation) and krasis (mixing) for the compounding of alloys and baphé (colouring) and leukosis (whitening) when they refer to the colouring of metal surfaces by boiling them with chemicals.

Thus in cuneiform texts referring to silver we read the term "murruqu" (cleansed, scoured) applied to currency silver and "patâqu" denoting some kind of smelting process during which the Fire-god "refineth silver and gold" (269). The texts mention not only the "loss in smelting" (NE.KÙ), which is also mentioned when gold is refined, but which in the case of silver seems to mean the first smelting operation for obtaining silver from lead, the second stage being indicated by "eating up by fire" (IZI.KÙ.BI), the cupellation when the remainder of the lead is absorbed by the walls of the cupel and the "button of silver" (ZAG.BAR) remains (270).

In Late Assyrian and Neo-Babylonian times such terms as šaginnu (standardized, pure standard quality) (271), kalû (roasted, purified) (272), pišû (white) or nuchchutu (inferior) (273) are used. Special terms for pure silver (damqu) and specially refined silver (watru), precious (tuhhu), qallalu (medium quality) and gabbu (pure) are used (274).

No such refinements are known to have been applied to lead, the only two qualities the Cappadocian mention are "pure lead" (here the word anaku is wrongly applied to lead) and anak katim which is translated as "loose lead" as the "pure lead" seems to have been shipped (in the form of pigs of lead?) in closed and sealed containers (šuklum). It would therefore appear that some terms referring to the use of refined silver appear early in Sumerian and Accadian documents, later periods creating new terms as the need arose. The terminology of lead is far simpler as no special requirements for the purity of lead arose in these early times.

The Egyptian nomenclature of silver is relatively simple. Apart from the old term ḥd (HWB III. 209.9) we have only a late Hellenistic term 'rḳwr (HWB I. 213), which is evidently taken from the Greek argyros. There are also the terms ḥd 'rf "silver dust" and ḥd n ḳn (HWB V. 49.15) ("best quality silver"). For lead there is only one term, dḥtj (or ḏḥtj) (HWB V. 606.4), a good indication that its metallurgy was of the simplest kind.

The spread of silver technology in the second millenium acted as a stimulus to the development of testing methods, for commerce was impossible as long as no correct estimation of the purity of silver

existed. This testing played an important part in the history of coins
and money. There was of course the test by cupellation which even
in later days continued to be used for the testing of precious metals
apart from its production. The testing of gold is mentioned in the
Amarna letters and we have had occasion to point to many Bible
passages mentioning this 'testing by fire'. A simplification may have
been used as such a method was still current in Egypt in the tenth
century. Qalqashandi mentions that in those days silver was kept
molten (no blast) during 24 hours and weighed to test whether a loss
in weight indicated admixture of base metals which would have been
drossed by that time (275). The 'testers of money' mentioned in
Hellenistic papyri, apart from gold- and silver-smiths, may have used
this test or the specific gravity to ascertain the purity of the metal, as
the touchstone would only indicate the quality of the surface layer,
which is less important in the case of a coin. The specific gravity,
discovered by Archimedes as the story goes, was used by him to test
the purity of the crown of Hiero of Syracuse and this property of
metals played a large part in the early history of assaying. The ancient
Coptic alchemists of the first centuries A.D. tested silver and gold by
the colour of the smelt and by testing it in the '*kaminos*' (cupel). Then
there was of course the touchstone, which still forms part of the
assaying equipement. Pliny mentions some simple tests to discover
the purity of silver (276): 'A filing is placed on a shovel which has
been heated until it glows. If the filing remains bright it is accepted as
pure. Second-rate silver turns red, while that which blackens has no
merit. But deception made its way into this test too. If the shovel is
kept in human urine the filing absorbs some while it is heated and
counterfeits brightness. The other test, if the specimen is polished,
is to breathe on it and observe whether it fogs immediately and easily
shakes off the dew'. One of the peculiar properties of lead is that black
lines can be drawn with it. Pliny (277) comments twice on this property and says that copper and silver give black lines too, but this must
be a mistake for silver gives a silver-white streak and could not
possibly be used for lining. The Latin *plumbum* taken in the meaning
of drawing material passed into the German *Bleistift* and the English
'lead-pencil' though a modern pencil no longer contains lead but a
core of graphite, which makes marks on the paper. The Italian *lapis*
and French *crayon* point to the use of chalk. When the Old Testament
speaks of "graven with an iron pen and *lead* in the rock" we should
read "with and iron pen and a sharp chisel" (278).

Silver-alloys are important in jewelry, an alloy of silver and copper is now used ($7\frac{1}{2}\%$ of copper only in Sterling silver) and in minting. For coins nowadays 10% (or more) of copper is used, an alloy that agrees quite well with the '$\frac{1}{8}$ part of copper added to silver' in Roman

Fig. 44.
Drawing silver wire from a bar of silver

coins since Livius Drusus (279). The precious metals play an important part in the history of coins. In the earliest periods they were used by weight but gradually a special form of ingots arose (rings, bars, etc.) and form and weight of these ingots were more or less regulated (280). Silver remained the standard of currency in the Near East (281) and gold is more or less a commodity used for large values of silver. Silver and gold were passed by weight at marked prices, stamps like 'good gold' or stamps of certain towns were only taken at face value. When Herodotus mentions the coining of pure silver by Aryandes, the Persian satrap of Egypt (282) he makes a mistake, which Milne (283) has explained. The silver coins of Aryandes were probably the ordinary Persian *sigloi* imported into Egypt by Aryandes at their proper value in the Persian Empire where the gold/silver ratio was 13/1, but sold as ingots to the Egyptian goldsmiths for whom a gold/silver ratio of 2/1 held. It is for this abuse of the Royal currency for his private purse that Aryandes was punished, for in other Persian satrapies the governors were allowed to strike their own silver coins without interference of the Persian King of Kings, no adverse gold/silver ratios existing outside Egypt, Analysis of ancient coins reveals much on composition and technique of minting which is important to numismatics and the detection of forgeries (284). Forgeries of Greek coins (285) were found to contain copper and sometimes zinc; they were cast, while the original coins were always stamped between dies (286). Some important modern alloys of gold, silver and lead are tabulated below for comparison with ancient alloys. German silver or Alpaca contains no silver, it is an alloy of 35% copper, 25% zinc and 20% nickel.

Alloy	Gold in %	Silver in %	Copper in %	Lead in %	Other metals in %
Purple gold	79	–	–	–	21 aluminium
Dark red gold	50	–	50	–	
Grey gold	86	0–8.6	–	–	7–17 iron
Green gold	30	70	–	–	–
Blue gold	75	–	–	–	25 iron
White gold	75–85	–	–	–	8–10 nickel, 2–9 zinc
Pale yellow gold	92	0–8.3	–	–	1.7–8 nickel
Silver jewelry	–	76–84	16–24	–	–
Lead shot	–	–	–	99.8	0.2 arsenic
Chemical lead	–	–	0.08	99.93	–
Plumber's solder	–	–	–	50–67	50–33 tin
Silver solder	–	70–75	20–30	–	5–7.5 zinc
Silver solder (best)	–	40	14	–	40 tin, 6 zinc

The composition of such solders should be compared with the many recipes mentioned by Pliny (287). The staining of silver, which played a large part in the early alchemical papyri is also mentioned by him (288).

When discussing gold we remarked that it would be profitable to study the ancient goldsmiths' craft in detail, this applies as well to the silversmith. Only in classical Greece do we hear of a separation of the goldsmith and the silversmith, though the crafts are usually combined like in earlier civilisation. However, the word "ἀργυροχόος" crops up now and then. Still the trade becomes gradually more prominent and in Imperial Rome the Alexandrian silversmiths are famous and Pliny (289) mentions that their work inspired the sculptors of statues in Rome. We also hear of guilds of silversmiths, e.g. at Caesarea (290) and at Carthage (291). By then we have the "ἀργυροκοπος" (silversmith and master of the mint), the "ἀργυρογνωμον" (tester of silver), the chaser of silver (ἀργυρηλάτης), the manufacturer of silver statues (ἀργυροπλάστης) the silver-smelter (ἀργυροποιός), the silver-merchant (ἀργυροπράτης) and of course the banker (ἀργεντάριος) who handled much silver. A papyrus of 300 A.D. informs us (292), that the silversmith bought the crude silver at half the price he sold his finished articles for. In Latin we have the special term "vascularius" for the silversmith who produced vases and cups of silver. Hence it would be important to compare the techniques used in preclassical and classical silverwork (293) with that of other parts of the world (294). Future students are advised to draw upon the valuable information given in a series of lectures published by the Worshipful Company of Goldsmiths (295) where detailed scientific explanations are given of the various phases of the craft and the correct terms for the different techniques and operations are explained.

The lead-worker (μολυβδουργός) is seldom mentioned in classical literature, though lead was of course frequently used in architecture and for lead pipes for water distribution, which has led some (296) to state that chronic lead poisoning not only ravaged the population of Roman cities but even led to the fall of the Roman Empire by sterility! There is no foundation in such theories, the lead pipes are always covered on the inside by a layer of inscrustations from the hard water which the ancients used and the danger of lead poisoning must have been as serious as in our own days.

It has been said that "all gold and silver rather turn to dirt and it's no better reckoned, but of those who worship dirty gods" (Cymbeline, Act III, sc. 6) but even this cloud has its silver lining and the history of silver and lead like that of gold has much to contribute to the better understanding of certain phases in the history of the Ancient Near East.

BIBLIOGRAPHY

Additional information can be obtained from my Bibliographia Antiqua (Leiden, 1950; Supplement I, 1952; Supplement II, 1963)

1. PLINY, *Nat. Hist.* XXXIII. 4
2. AGRICOLA, G. *Zwölf Bücher vom Berg- und Hüttenwesen* (V.D.I. Verlag, Berlin, 1929)
3. BERGSØE, P., *Metallurgy of gold and platinum among the pre-Columbian Indians* (Nature 137, 1936, 29)
   BERGSØE, P., *Recherches métallurgiques et techniques sur l'or des Incas* (Ingeniören, 45, 1936, 68; vi 217—vi 223)
   BERGSØE, P., *The gilding process and the metallurgy of lead and copper among the pre-Columbian Indians.* (Danmarks Vidensk. Samfund, Kopenhagen, 1938)
4. PETRIE, W. FLINDERS, *Naqada and Ballas* (London, 1896, 8, 10, 44, 48, 67)
5. CLINE, W., *Mining and metallurgy in Negro Africa* (Paris, 1937)
6. ADOLPH, W. A., *The beginnings of chemistry in China* (Sci. Monthly XIV, 1922, 441)
   ADOLPH, W. A., *The beginnings of chemistry in China* (Chem. Met. Eng. XXVI, 1922, 914)
   LIPPMANN, E. O. VON, *Entstehung und Ausbreitung der Alchemie* (Berlin, 1919/1954, 3 vols.)
   LI CH'IAO-P'ING, *Chemical Arts in Old China* (Easton (Pa), 1948)
7. FIMMEN, E., *Die kretisch-mykenische Kultur* (Leipzig, 1924)
8. SIRET, *Les premiers âges de métal...*, 231—232
9. CHILDE, V. GORDON, *Man makes himself* (London)
10. BIRINGUCCIO, edit. Johannsen (Braunschweig, 1926)
11. GARLAND, H. and BANNISTER, C., *Ancient Egyptian Metallurgy* (London, 1927)
12. HYGINUS, *Fabulae*; CASSIODORUS, *Variae lect.* 3. 31; PLINY, *Nat. Hist.* VII, 56; CARY, JHS, XLIV, 1924, 169
13. LUCRETIUS V. 1250—1262; STRABO 3. 2. 9. cap. 147; ARISTOTLE, *De Mir. Ausc.* 87; DIODOR V. 35; ATHENAEUS 233
14. NAPIER, *Manufacturing Arts in Ancient Times*, London, 1879, 4
15. ILIAD II. 857
16. STRABO, 12. 3. 19—22. cap. 549—551; 14. 5. 28. cap. 680
17. BURY, *Cambr. Anc. History* II. 492
18. HEHN, O., *Kulturpflanzen und Haustiere des klassischen Altertums* (Berlin, 1887, 499)
    LEAF, W., *Troy* (London, 1912, 291)
    BLÜMNER, P. W., IIIa, 14
    GILES, *Cambr. Anc. History* II, 5

19. DHORME, E., *Les nouvelles tablettes d'El Amarnah* (Rev. Bibl. 33, 1924, 19—32)
20. PLINY, *Nat. Hist.* XXXIII. 58
21. STRABO, 3. 2. 9. cap. 147
22. LEPSIUS, C. R., (Sitzber. Akad. Berlin, 1871, 112)
    LEPSIUS, C. R., *Die Metalle in den ägyptischen Inschriften* (Berlin, 1872)
    LEPSIUS, C. R., *Les métaux dans les inscriptions égyptiennes.* (BEHE fasc. xxx, Paris, 1877, 60 & 62)
23. SCHRADER, O., *Sprachvergleichung und Urgeschichte* (Leipzig, 1883)
24. THOMPSON, R. CAMPBELL, *Dictionary of Assyrian Chemistry and Geology* (Oxford, 1936)
25. PLINY, *Nat. Hist.* XXXIV, 158
26. HAUPT. P., *The Hebrew terms for gold and silver* (JAOS 43, 1923, 116—127)
27. ANDRAE, W., *Altassyrische Bleiplaketten* (Z. f. Numism. XXXIV, 1/2, 1—6)
    GENOUILLAC, H. DE, *Idole de plomb d'une triade cappadocienne* (Syria X, 1929, 1)
    HOFMAN, K. B., *Das Blei bei den Völkern des Altertums* (Berlin, 1885)
    LIPPMANN, E. O. VON, *Entstehung und Ausbreitung der Alchemie* (Berlin, 1919—1954, 3 vols.)
    REITZENSTEIN, R. & SCHAEDER, H., *Studien zur antiken Synkretik in Iran und Griechenland* (Leipzig, 1926)
    ROSE, H. J., *"Fairy gold", an ancient belief* (Class. Rev. 1914, 262)
    ROSSIGNOL, M., *Les métaux dans l'antiquité* (Paris, 1863)
    THORNDIKE, L., *History of Magic and Experimental Sciences* (London, 1929, I)
    JEREMIAS, A., *Handbuch der orientalischen Geisteskultur* (Leipzig, 1913, 238)
28. GRAPOW, H., *Die bildlichen Ausdrücke des Aegyptischen* (Leipzig, 1924, 55, 57)
    LANGE, H. O., *Der Magische Papyrus Harris* (Copenhagen, 1927, 38)
29. DEISSMANN. A., *Licht im Osten*, 1923, 119
    LIDBARSKI, A., *Eine punische tabella devotionis;* (Eph. I, 1900, 26)
    OPITZ, D., *Altorientalische Guszformen, Oppenheim Festschrift*, 1933, 192
    WÜNSCH, R., *Antike Fluchtafeln*, 1907
30. FORBES, *Phil. Mag.* XXX, 1865, 143
31. HILLER, J. E., *Die Minerale der Antike* (Arch. Gesch. Math. Naturw. Technik XIII, 1930, 358)
32. PLINY, *Nat. Hist.* XXXIII. 95
33. PLINY, *Nat. Hist.* XXXIII. 95—98, 111
34. THEOPHRASTUS, *On Stones* (edit. Caley and Richards, Colombus, 1956)
35. DIODOR, III. 13; PLINY, *Nat. Hist.* XXXIII. 66

36. PLINY, *Nat. Hist.* XXXIII. 97
37. RICKARD, T. A., *Notes on ancient and primitive mining methods* (Eng. Min. J. Vol. 122, 1926, 2, 48)
38. AGRICOLA, G., *De Re Metallica* (edit. V.D.I., Berlin, 1929)
    AGRICOLA, G., *Bermannus sive de re metallica* (Basilae, 1546)
39. STRABO, 3. 2. 10. cap. 148
40. FORBES, R. J., *Mining and Geology* (Studies in Ancient Technology vol. VII, Leiden, 1963)
41. BISSING, F. VON, *Zur Geschichte des Silbers und des Elektrons* (Acta Orientalia IV, 1925, 282)
    DIJKMANS, G., *Histoire économique et sociale de l'ancienne Egypte* (Paris, 1936/37, 3 vols., I. 201; II. 142)
42. DIJCKMANS, l.c.
    HUME, W. F., *Geology of Egypt* (Cairo, 1937) vol. II. part 3
43. DIJCKMANS, l.c.
    FITZLER, K., *Steinbrüche und Bergwerke im Ptolemäischen und Römischen Aegypten* (Leipzig, 1910)
44. DIJCKMANS, l.c.
    LUCAS, A., *Silver in ancient times* (JEA 14, 1928, 313)
    LUCAS, A., *Ancient Egyptian Materials and Industries.* (Arnold, London, 1962)
45. GOWLAND, W., *The metals in Antiquity* (R. Anthrop. Inst., London, 1912)
46. FITZLER, K., *Steinbrüche und Bergwerke im Ptolemäischen und Römischen Aegypten* (Leipzig, 1910)
    HUME, W. F., *Geology of Egypt* (Cairo 1937, vol. II, part 3)
    LUCAS, A., *Silver in ancient times* (JEA 14, 1928, 313)
    Mines and Quarries Dept. Report of the Mineral Industry of Egypt, 1922
47. BREASTED, H. J., *Ancient Records of Egypt*
48. GARLAND and BANNISTER, *Ancient Egyptian Metallurgy* (London, 1927)
    BUSCH, Z. f. Angew. Chemie 27, 1914, 512
49. BRUNTON, G., *Qua and Badari* (Vol. I, 1928, 24, 27, 38, 68)
    PETRIE, W. FLINDERS, *Naqada and Ballas* (London, 1896, 8, 10, 44, 48, 67)
    PETRIE, W. FLINDERS, *Royal Tombs* (London, 1900, I, 28; 1901, II, 36)
    PETRIE, W. FLINDERS, *Diospolis Parva* (London, 1901, 25)
    PETRIE, W. FLINDERS, *Arts and Crafts in Ancient Egypt* (Edinburgh 1909)
    PETRIE, W. FLINDERS, *The metals in Ancient Egypt* (Ancient Egypt 1915, 12)
    PETRIE, W. FLINDERS, *Prehistoric Egypt* (London, 1917)
50. MORGAN, J. DE, *Fouilles à Dachour* (Paris, 1895 & 1903)
    SCHÄFER, H., *Aegyptische Goldschmiedearbeiten* (Berlin, 1910)
51. DAVIS, *Tomb of Siptah*, Plate 9 f
52. *Grab des Rechmire*, vol. I, Plate IIa, IIb

53. SETHE, K., Urk. IV, 1101
54. GARSTANG, *Land of the Hittites*, 1910, 322
55. WEIDNER, MDOG, 58, 68; MEISSNER ZMDG 72. 50
56. SCHÄFER, H., *Aegyptische Goldschmiedearbeiten* (Berlin, 1910)
57. BREASTED, *Ancient Records*
58. GARLAND AND BANNISTER, *Ancient Egyptian Metallurgy* (London, 1927)
59. HERODOTUS III. 13
60. RITTER, *Erdkunde, Afrika* vol. II, 1822, 469
61. CLINE, W., *Mining and metallurgy in Negro Africa* (Paris, 1937)
62. FREISE, E., *und Hüttenmännische Unternehmungen in Asien und Afrika während des Altertums* (Z. f. Berg-, Hütten- und Saline-wesen im Preuss. Staat 56, 1908, 347)
63. STRABO, 16. 4. 26. cap. 784
64. STRABO, 16. 4. 18. cap. 778
65. *Gen.* 13. 23
66. *Gen.* 23. 16
67. *Gen.* 37. 28
68. MACALISTER, *Excav. at Gezer*, I. 293, 303
69. *Judges* 17. 4
70. *2. Chron.* 6. 21; *1 Ki.* 10. 22; *Jer.* 10. 9; *2 Chron.* 9. 14
71. *Letter of Aristeas* cap. 90
72. JOSEPHUS, *Wars*, VII. 8. 4
73. *Ezech.* 27. 12
74. *Num.* 31. 22; *Ezech.* 22. 18; 27. 12
75. STRABO, 15. 1. 34. cap. 701
76. STRABO, 15. 1. 30. cap. 700
77. *Indika* cap. 11
78. MACKAY, E., *Early Indus civilisations*, London, 1948, 82
79. SI-YU-KI, edit. Beal, II. 278
80. STAHL, *Chem. Ztg.* XVIII, 1894, 364
81. CURSON, *History of Persia* II, 510, 517
    BOSON, G., *I metalli e le pietri nelli inscrizioni assiro-babylonesi* (Riv. Stud. Or. VII, 1917, 379—420)
82. HERODOTUS V. 49
83. STRABO, 15. 2. 14. cap. 726
84. *Cambr. Anc. History* I, 141
85. MALCOLM, *History of Persia* II, 369
86. MORGAN, J. DE, DP VII, 1905, 72—91
87. DESCH, B. A., *Report* 1931, 271
88. KING, *Sumer and Akkad*, 262
89. WOOLLEY, C. L., *Excavations at Ur* (Ant. J. VIII, 1928, 1—29, 415—447)
90. LUCKENBILL, *Ancient Records* II. 95. 109; I. 130
91. GOWLAND, W., *The metals in Antiquity* (R. Anthrop. Inst., London, 1912)
92. POEBEL UMBS, IV. i. 178, 206
93. SMITH, S., *Early History of Assyria* (London, 1925, 395)

94. MARCO POLO, *Book I*, chapter iv
95. STRABO, 12. 3. 19—22. cap. 549—551
96. MYRES, *Cambr. Anc. History* III, 661
97. LANDSBERGER, B., *AO* XXIV, 1925, no. 4
    BITTEL, K., *Prähistorische Forschungen in Kleinasien* (Istanbul, 1934)
98. MEISSNER, BR., *Woher haben die Assyrer Silber bezogen* (OLZ, XV, 1912, 145—149)
    LEVEY, M., *L'argent dans la littérature ancienne de Mésopotamie* (Rev. Hist. Sci. Fr. X, 1957, 3, 197—204)
99. VON DER OSTEN, OIP, no. 6, 1929, 130
    MEISSNER, OLZ XV, 148
100. LUCKENBILL, *Ancient Records*, I. 206, 244
    KAH XXX, iii, 2
    SMITH, *Early History of Assyria*, 395
101. PLINY, *Nat. Hist.* XXXIV. 18
102. GOWLAND, W., *Silver in Roman and earlier times* (Archaeologia LXIX, 1918, 121—160)
103. RAWLINSON, *Monuments* II, 2941, III. 146, 159
104. SAYCE, JRAS 1920, 68
    SAYCE, A. H., *The lead mines of early Asia Minor* (JRAS, 1921, 54—55)
105. MDAI XXIX, 1904, 268; *see also Bittel*, l.c. and *Freise* l.c.
106. GALEN, IX. 3. 22
107. DAVIES, O., *Bronze Age Mining round the Aegean* (Nature 130, 1932, 985)
108. GOWLAND, *Silver in Roman and earlier times*, see 102
109. PLINY, *Nat. Hist.* XXXIV. 175; DIOSCORIDES V. 103
    HOFMAN, K. B., *Das Blei bei den Völkern des Altertums* (Berlin, 1885)
110. HERODOTUS, V. 49
111. DESCH, B. A. *Report* 1928, 440
112. MEYER, E., *Geschichte des Altertums* (IV edit. Leipzig, 1921, I. 2)
113. CHILDE, V. GORDON, *New Light on the Most Ancient East* (London, 1954, 162)
    PLENDERLEITH, J., *Ur Excavations* (London, 1934, II, 394)
    WOOLLEY, C. L., *Excavations at Ur* (Ant. J. VIII, 1928, 1—29, 415—447)
114. ITT, I, 1388, 24; RA 6, 1907, 148
145. LANDSBERGER, B., JNES XV, 1956, 146—147; UM IV, 178
146. ALBRIGHT, W. F., *the epic of the King of Battle, Sargon of Akkad* (JSOR VII, 1923, 1—20)
    CONTENAU, G., *La civilisations des Hittites et Mitanniens* (Paris, 1934, 53)
    DHORME, E., *Les nouvelles tablettes d'El Amarnah* (Rev. Bibl. 1924, 19—32)
    WEIDNER, E., *Der Zug Sargons von Akkad nach Kleinasien* (Boghaskeui Studien VII, Leipzig, 1922)
147. UET 1928, I. 79

148. KING, *Sumer and Akkad*, 262
149. SMITH, S., *Early History of Assyria* (London, 1925, 395)
    LUCKENBILL, *Ancient Records* I. 246
150. GETTENS, R. J. and WARING CL. L., *The composition of some ancient Persian and other Near Eastern silver objects* (Ars Orient. II, 1957, 83—90)
151. ORTH, P. W., Suppl. IV, 112
    LANDSBERGER, AO XXIV, 21
152. LEVEY, M., *L'argent dans la littérature ancienne de Mésopotamie* (Revue Hist. des Sci. X, 1957, 3, 197—204)
    LEVEY, M., *Chemistry and Chemical Technology in ancient Mesopotamia* (Amsterdam, 1959, 178—184)
153. STRASSMAIER, J., *Inschr. des Nabuchodnosor* (Leipzig, 1889, 38, 1—7)
154. AO, XV, 24
155. POEBEL, UMBS IV, i, 158—206
156. LÚ: amêlu t. 4, col. iii, 264, 266
157. POEBEL, A., *Babylonian Legal and Business Documents* (Philadelphia, 1909, 31)
158. STRASSMAIER, J. N., *Inschr. des Nabonidus* (Leipzig, 1889, 371)
159. LANDSBERGER, *Serie ana ittišu* (Rome, 1937, 138)
160. HARPER, R. F., *Assyrian and Babylonian Letters* (Chicago, 1902, 527)
161. VAB, I, 106; XVI, 21; SAK 16. b. 5. 28 ff
162. HALL AND LANGDON, *Cambr. Anc. History* I, 428, 545, 586
163. VAB I, 120, XXVIII. 14
164. ORTH, PW XII, 112
165. FISH, T., *Aspects of Sumerian Civilisation during the Third Dynasty of Ur*, part IV, Silver (Bull, J. Rylands. Libr., XX, 1936, 121)
166. LIMET, H., *Le travail du métal au pays de Sumer* (Paris, 1960, 54)
167. HEICHELHEIM, FR., *Wirtschaftsgeschichte des Altertums* (Leiden, 1938)
168. *Br. Museum* 19.031
169. LEWY, J., *Some aspects of commercial life in Assyria and Asia Minor in the nineteenth Pre-Christian century* (JAOS 78, 1958, 89—101)
170. KAVI I. 5. 7
171. LEEMANS, W. F., *Foreign Trade in the Old Babylonian Period* (Leiden, 1960)
172. OPPENHEIM, A. L., JAOS 74,8
173. UET, V. 546, 548, 848, 286
174. TCL, X. 13. 15
175. FISH, T., *Manchester Cuneiform Studies* I, 1951, 46—48
176. ANDRAE, MDOG, LIV, 1914, 36
177. KAVI no. 1, II, 81, 102
178. RA, VI, 1907, 142
179. II. R. 51. 10
180. LUCKENBILL, *Ancient Records* I. 130

181. LUCKENBILL, *Ancient Records* I, 144; I. 211, 217; II, 95, 109; II. 9. 96

182. FORBES, R. J., *New evidence on Late Bronze Age Metallurgy* (Sibrium III, 1956/57, 113—121)
WISEMAN, *The Alalakh Tablets* (London, 1953)

183. FRIEND, J. NEWTON & THORNEYCROFT, W. E., *The silver content of ancient and medieval lead* (J. Inst. Metals XLI, 1929, 105—117)

184. ANDRAE, W., *Altassyrische Bleiplaketten* (Z. f. Numismatik XXXIV, 1/2, 1—6)

185. REGLING, PW VII. 979

186. CT. XXVI. 25. 16; SMITH, S., *A pre-Greek coinage in the Near East* (Numism. Chron. Vth. ser. II, 2—11)

187. DOUGHERTY, R. P., *Archives from Erech* (New Haven 1933, 101)

188. CT (1906) 40, 11—13

189. HOEFER, F., *Histoire de la chimie* (Paris, 1842, I, 47)
LAUGHLIN, J. L., *Evolution of money* (Art and Archaeology XXVI, 1928, 3—11, 35)

190. BITTEL, K., *Istanbuler Forschungen* no. 6, Istanbul, 1934

191. OIP, XIX, fig. 65

192. PRZEWORSKI, ST., *Die Metallindustrie Anatoliens zur Zeit von* 1500 *bis* 700 v. Chr. (Leiden, 1937)
SCHMEISSER, C., *Bodenschätze und Bergbau Kleinasiens* (Z. f. prakt. Geol. 161, 1906, 186)

193. HROZNY, B., *Les inscriptions "hittites" hieroglyphiques sur plomb trouvés à Assur* (Archiv Orientalni 1933)
Cambr. Anc. History III, 112

194. DÖRPFELD, TROIA und ILION, 1902, 327, 366

195. GOWLAND, W., *Silver in Roman and earlier times* (Archaeol. LXIX, 1918, 121)

196. GOWLAND, l.c.; FORRER, RL, 78, 737, 750; see also (183)

197. CARY, M., *The sources of silver for the Greek world* (Mélanges Glotz, II, 1932, 133—142)

198. RICHTER, *Kypros*, 339, 368

199. STRABO, 15. 6. 5. cap. 683; DIOSCORIDES V. 100

200. ORTH, PW, suppl. iv

201. OBERHUMMER, *Die Insel Cypern*, 1903, I. 183

202. DAVIES, O., *Bronze Age Mining in the Aegean* (Nature 130, 1932, 985)

203. HERODOTUS, III. 57

204. PAUSANIAS, X. 11. 2; Suidas

205. STRABO, 9. 1. 23. cap. 399

206. ARDAILLON, E., *Les mines du Laurion dans l'Antiquité* (Paris, 1897)
BINDER. I. I., *Laurion* (Paris, 1895)
BINDER, I. I., *Die attischen Bergwerke im Altertum* (Jahresb. K. K. Realschule, Laibach, 1895)
CALHOUN, G. M., *Ancient Athenian Mining* (J. Econ. Bus. Hist. III, 1931, 333)
ERNST, C. VON, *Ueber den Bergbau im Laurion* (Hütten und Bergm. Jahrbuch, Wien, 1902, 476)

FORBES, R. J., *Studies in Ancient Technology* (Leiden, 1963, vol. VII, 145)

GUILLAUME, L., *La métallurgie du plomb au Laurium* (Paris, 1909)

HOFMAN, K. B., *Das Blei bei den Völkern des Altertums* (Berlin, 1885)

MOMIGLIANO, E., *Athenaeum* 1932, 247

MONTANUS, H. H., *Antiker Bergbau in Griechenland* (Mont. Rundschau 1902, 1202—1204)

SAGUI, C. L., *Economic geology and allied sciences in ancient times* (J. Econ. Geology XXV, 1930, 65—86)

207. STRABO, 3. 11. 8—10; 4. 5. 2; 9. 1. 23

PLINY, *Nat. Hist.* XXXIII. 23, 33; XXXIV. 47

HERODOTUS, III. 57

ARISTOTLE, *Polit. Athen.* XLVII

XENOPHON, *Econ. Athen.* IV

208. FIMMEN, E., *Die kretisch-mykenische Kultur* (Leipzig, 1924)

209. EVANS, I. 193, 194

BURROWS, E., *Discoveries in Crete* (London, 1907, 118)

210. SCHLIEMANN, H., *Mycenae und Tiryns* (London, 1878, 372)

211. SCHRADER, RL, 95; FORRER, RL, 94

212. ILIAD, II. 45, 857; XI. 31; XIV. 405; XVI. 135; XVIII. 389; XXII. 41. 807

213. BRONEER, O., *A Mycenaean Fountain on the Athenian Acropolis* (Hesperia, 8, 1939, 416)

214. ILIAD, XI. 237; XXIV. 80; KARO, G., *Die Schachtgräber von Mykenai*, 1930, 312

215. VENTRIS, M. and CHADWICK, J., *Documents in Mycenaean Greek* (London, 1956)

216. BROMEHEAD, C. E. N., *Geology in Embryo* (Proc. Geol. Assoc. London 56, 1945, 89)

217. CALHOUN, G. M., *Ancient Athenian Mining* (J. Econ. Bus. Hist. III, 1931, 333)

CARY, M., *The sources of silver for the Greek world* (Mélanges Glotz, II, 1932, 133—142)

GEORGIDAS, ATH. S., *Mines d'or et d'argent, etc. en Macédonie, Epire et dans les iles exploitées par les anciens* (Arch. Eph. 1915, 88—93)

218. SAGUI, C. L., *The ancient mining works of Cassandra* (J. Econ. Geology XXIII, 1928, 671—680)

219. HERODOTUS, V. 17

220. STRABO, 7. 34; HERODOTUS, VII. 112

221. HERODOTUS, V. 23

222. DAVIES, O., *Ancient Mines in Southern Macedonia* (J. Anthrop. Inst. LXII, 1933, 145—162)

DAVIES, O., *Roman Mines in Europe* (Oxford, 1935)

GAUL, J. H., *Possibilities of prehistoric metallurgy in the East Balkan Peninsula* (AJA, 46, 1942, 400—409)

223. KYRLE, G., *Die Gold-, Silber-, Blei- und Kupfergewinnung in der urgeschichtlichen Zeit in den Alpen* (Bl. z. Gesch. Technik I, 1932, 63)

224. STRABO, 4. 5. 2. cap. 199; PLINY, *Nat. Hist.* XXXIV. 49

CRAWFORD, O. G. S., *Pigs of lead and Roman roads* (Antiquity III, 1929, 217)

CURLE, A. O., *The Treasure of Taprain* (Glasgow, 1923)

FRIEND, J. NEWTON, *Notes on the silver content of Roman lead from Folkestone and Rochborough Castle* (J. Inst. Metals XXXVII, 1927, 73)

GOUGH, J. W., *The mines of Mendip* (London, 1930)

GOWLAND, W., *The early metallurgy of silver and lead* (London, 1901)

METCALFE, J. E., *Early English leadmining* (Sands, Clays, Minerals II, 1935, 3, 51—58)

NORTH, F. J., *Mining for metals in Wales* (Cardiff, 1962)

PATRICK, R. W. C., *Early records relating to mining in Scotland* (Edinburgh, 1878, 34)

RAISTRICK, A., *Notes on lead mining and smelting in West Yorkshire* (Trans. Newcomen Soc. VII, 1926/27, 81—96)

WHITTICK, CL., *Roman mining in Britain* (Trans. Newcomen Soc. XII, 1931/32, 57—84)

WHITTICK, CL., *Notes on some Romano-British pigs of lead* (JHS XXI, 1931, 256—264)

WHITTICK, CL., *The Shropshire Pigs of Roman Lead* (Trans. Shropshire Archaeol. Soc. 46, 1932, 129)

WHITTICK, G. C., *The casting technique of Romano-British lead ingots* (JRS LI, 1961, 105—111)

WOOLER, E., *Roman leadmining in Weardale* (Yorkshire Arch. and Topogr. J. XXVIII, 1926, 93)

TYLECOTE, R. F., *Metallurgy in Archaeology* (London, 1962, 72)

WAY, A., *Notes on Roman pigs of lead* (Arch. J. XXIII, 1866, 285)

225. STRABO, 4. 2. 2. cap. 191

BESNIER, M., *Le commerce du plomb à l'époque romaine d'après les lingots estampillés* (Rev. Archéol. (5) XII, 1920, 211; XIII, 1921, 26; XIV, 1921, 98)

ARMAND-CAILLET, L., *Note sur les saumons de plomb antiques trouvés dans le Chalonnais* (Bull. Archéol. 1936/37, 527—533)

SAUTEL, J., *Note sur l'industrie du plomb et les marques des plombiers à Vaison-la-Romaine* (Latomus V, 1946; 369—371)

ALEXANDER, J. & WRIGHT, T. A., *Lead from an ancient Roman coffin from Arles* (J. Soc. Chem. Ind. 51, 1932, 813)

FIEBER, A., *Über die Untersuchung eines antiken Bleirohres* (Chem. Ztg. 32, 1908, 13)

226. WEILL, A. R., *Analyse de pièces métalliques... en plomb* (Revue de Métall. II, 1954, 459—466)

227. SPERONI, G., *Ricerche su oggetti di piombo dell'Etruria. I. I piombi di Populonia* (Stud. Etr. XIII, 1939, 355—362)

PINZA, G., *L'etnologia Toscano-laziale* (Roma, 1907, 463—492)

SIMON, M. L., *On the lead mines of Bottino* (Ann. des Mines, XIV, 1858, 557)

228. GOUIN, L., *Notice sur les mines de l'île de Sardaigne* (Cagliari, 1869)
   LAUNAY, L. DE, *Histoire de l'industrie minière en Sardaigne* (Ann. des Mines, 1892, I, 520)
   SOLINUS, *Polyhist.* 4
229. GALVEX, CANERO, A., DE, *La metalurgia de la plata y del mercurio* (IX Congr. Int. Quim. Pura y Aplicada, Madrid, 1934, Confér. gén.)
230. STRABO, 3. 2. 8.—10, cap. 146—148; DIODOR, V. 35; POLYBIUS, 34. 9; LIVY, 40. 51. 8; 34, 21. 7; 39. 44. 8; PLUTARCH, *Cato* 19; LIVY 40. 51. 8
231. DAVIES, O., *Roman Mines in Europe* (Oxford, 1935)
   RICKARD, T. A., *Historical Notes on the Patio Industry* (Canad. Min. Metal Bull. no. 285, 1936, 23—48)
   RICKARD, T. A., *The mining of the Romans in Spain* (JRS XVIII, 1928, 129)
   TÄCKHOLM, U. *Studiën über den Bergbau der römischen Kaiserzeit* (Uppsala, 1937)
232. FORBES, R, J., *Studies in Ancient Technology* (Leiden, 1963, vol. VII, 157)
233. PLINY, *Nat. Hist.* XXXIV. 159
234. BARBA, A., *Arte de los metales* (Madrid, 1640)
235. GOWLAND, W., *The art of working metals in Japan* (J. Inst. Metals IV, 1910, 4)
236. PLINY, *Nat. Hist.* XXXIV. 159
237. BAILEY, K. C., *The Elder Pliny's Chapters on Chemical Subjects* (London, 1929/1932, 2 vols.)
238. GRASSINI, R., *Analisi chimica di alcuni relitti antichi* (Stud. Etr. VI, 1932, 561—562)
239. COWAN, W. A., *Note on the composition of old Roman lead* (J. Inst. Metals, XXXIX, 1928, 59—60)
   EBELING, A, und ADAM, H., *Die Bleireinheit zur Zeit um Christi Geburt* (Wiss. Veröff. Siemens Konzern VIII, 1930, 203)
240. *See chapter five*
   RICKARD, T. A., *Historical Notes on the Patio Industry* (Canad. Min. Metal Bull. no. 285, 1936, 23—48)
   BON, I. DE, *Amalgamation des minérais d'or et d'argent* (Vienna, 1786)
241. PLINY, *Nat. Hist.* XXXIII. 95
   GOWLAND, W., *Silver in Roman and earlier times* (Archaeol. LXIX, 1918, 121)
242. LAUNAY, L. DE, *Histoire de l'industrie minière en Sardaigne* (Ann. des mines 1892, I, 520)
243. TÄCKHOLM, U., *Studiën über den Bergbau der römischen Kaiserzeit* (Uppsala, 1937)
244. STRABO, 9. 1. 23. cap. 399
245. WHITE, B., *Silver, its history and romance* (London, 1917)
246. STRABO, 3. 2. 10. cap. 148
247. STRABO, 3. 2. 8. cap. 146

248. BLÜMNER, H., *Technologie und Terminologie der Gewerbe und Künste bei Griechen und Römern* (Leipzig, 1887, IV, 89, 110—141)
249. LEDOUW, P., *Revue des Deux Mondes, févr.* 1875, 599
250. BENT, A., *Researches among the Cyclades* (JHS VI, 1885, 196)
251. GOWLAND, W., *The art of working metals in Japan* (J. Inst. Metals IV, 1910, 4)
252. PLINY, *Nat. Hist.* XXXIII. 95
253. PLINY, *Nat. Hist.* XXXIII. 105—109; XXXIV. 159; DIOSCORIDES V. 101
254. *Prov.* 17. 3; 27. 21; *Mal.* 3. 3
255. *Prov.* 26. 23; *Isa.* 1. 22. 25; *Jer.* 6. 29—30; *Num.* 31. 22
256. *Ezech.* 22. 18; *Ps.* 12. 6
257. *Jer.* 6. 29
258. LUCAS, A., *Silver in ancient times* (JEA XIV, 1928, 313)
259. GRASSINI, R., *Analisi chimici di alcuni relitti antichi* (Stud. Etr. VI, 1932, 561—562)
260. PLENDERLEITH, J., *Ur Excavations* II, 1934, 394
261. LANDSBERGER, AO XXXIV, *Heft* 4; CONTENAU, *TTC* 71
262. *VAB* II, 290, 18; IV *R* 4, 3, 40—41
263. LIMET, H., *Le travail du métal au pays de Sumer* (Paris, 1960, 46)
264. HEUZEY, RA. 1897, 35
265. THUREAU DANGIN RA VI, 1906, 139—145; RA VII, 1907, 149; JOHNS, *Ass. Deeds Documents* II, 277
266. THUREAU DANGIN, *Huitième campagne de Sargon* (Paris, 1912, 36); WISEMAN, *Iraq* XVI, 1954, 42
267. MILNE, JEA XV, 1929, 150
268. HARPER, *Ass. Bab. Letters*, no. 152. rs. 4
269. RAWLINSON CUN. *Inscr.*, London, 1891, 14b; DOUGHERTY, *Arch. f. Erech* 129; CONTENAU, *Contr. Neo-Bab.*, 1927, 46
270. LEGRAIN, L., *UET, Business Doc. Ur* III, 1937, 392, 393, 403
271. JOHNS, ADD, 612; HROZNY BA, 1902, 546
272. DHORME, RA, 1928, 55, 67; HARPER, *Ass. Bab. Letters*, 1902, 1194
273. *NBK* 12, 1; *Dar.* 44, 1
274. MEISSNER, OLZ XV, 1912, 145—149; VAB II, 290, 18
275. QALQASHANDI, *Geography, transl. Wütenfeld*, 1879, 166
276. PLINY, *Nat. Hist.* XXXIII. 127
277. PLINY, *Nat. Hist.* XXXIII. 60 & 98
278. STAMM, J. J., *Versuche zur Erklärung von Hiob* 19. 24 (*Theol. Z.* IV, 1948, 331)
279. PLINY, *Nat. Hist.* XXXIII. 46
280. MORGAN, J. DE, *Les métaux dans l'Asie antérieure* (Rev. Ethn. Soc. II, 1911, 5—9)
281. BLAKE, R. P., *The circulation of silver in the Moslem East down to the Mongol Epoch* (Harvard J. Asiat. Stud. II, 1937, 291—328)
282. HERODOTUS, IV. 166
283. MILNE, J. G., *The currency of Egypt under the Ptolemies* (JEA 24, 1938, 200)

MILNE, J. G., *The silver of Aryandes* (JEA 24, 1938, 245—246)

284. BAUMGARTNER, A., *Die edlen Metalle und ihre hatürliche Rangordnung als Geldstoffe* (Akad. Wien, 1857)

BISSING, F. W. VON, *Das älteste Geld* (Forsch. & Fortschr. V, 1929, 25, 282)

BISSING, F. W. VON, *Zur Geschichte des Silbers* (Acta Orient. 4, 1925, 138)

CREMASCOLI, Rf., *Esami spettografici di monete d'argento romane e degli argenti di Ornavasso* (Sibrium II, 1955, 31—34)

EINZIG, PAUL, *Primitive money* (London, 1949)

GABRICI, E., *Tecnica e cronologica delle monete greche* (Roma, 1951)

GETTENS, R. J. and WARING, C. L., *The composition of some ancient Persian and other Near Eastern silver objects* (Ars Orient. II, 1957, 83)

JENKINS, G. K., *An Egyptian gold coin* (Brit. Mus. Quart. 20, 1955, 10—11)

JONGKEES, J. H., *Athenian coin dies from Egypt* (Numis. Chron. X, 1950, 298)

JUNGFLEISCH, M. & SCHWARZ, J., *Les moules de monnaie impériales romaines* (Suppl. ASAE, cahier no. 19, Cairo, 1952)

KAULLA, R., *Beiträge zur Entstehungsgeschichte des Geldes* (Bern, 1945)

KEMP, W., *Precious metals as money* (London, 1924)

LANTIER, R. *Atelier gallo-romain de monnayeur* (Bull. Mus. France, 1950, 66)

LAUGHLIN, J. L., *Evolution of money* (Art and Archaeol. 26, 1928, 3—11, 35)

MOSS, A. A., *The origin of nickel alloy used in Bactrian coins* (Numism. Chron. 6th ser. X, 1950, 317—318)

SCHUMAN, V. B., *The leaden coinage of Roman Egypt* (CdE XVIII, 2, 1953, 356)

SCHWABAGGER, W., *Geldumlauf und Münzprägung in Syrien im 6. und 5. Jhdt* (Opusc. Archaeol. (Lund) VI, 1950, 139—149)

SPERONI, G. & MORI, L., *Richerche chimiche sulle monete del tesoro di Populonia* (Stud. Etr. XL, 1950, 241—247)

VERMEULE, C., *Minting Greek and Roman coins* (Archaeology X, 2, 1957, 100)

285. ELAM, C. F., *An investigation of the microstructure of fifteen silver Greek coins (500—300 B.C.) and some forgeries* (J. Inst. Metals 45, 1931, 57)

286. HILL, *Ancient methods of coining* (Numism. Chron. II, 1922, nos. 5 & 6)

287. PLINY, *Nat. Hist.* XXXIII. 86; XXXIV. 161

288. PLINY, *Nat. Hist.* XXXIII. 132, 133, 157

289. PLINY, *Nat. Hist.* XXXIII. 131

290. C.I.L. VIII, 9427, 21106

291. AUGUSTINUS, *Confess.* 6. 9. 14

292. RÉMONDON, R., *A propos du papyrus d'Antinoë* no. 38 (CdE XXXII, 1957, 130)

293. ALEXANDER, C., *Jewelry, the art of the goldsmith* (Metrop. Mus. New York, 1928)

CUMONT, FR., *Ancient granulated jewelry* (Mem. Amer. Acad. Rome I, 63)

DIEHL, CH., *L'école artistique d'Antiochie et les trésors d'argenterie syrienne* (Syria 2, 1921, 81)

DIEHL, CH., *Un nouveau trésor d'argenterie syrienne* (Syria 7, 1926, 105; 11, 1930, 209)

DALTON, O. M., *On some Points in the History of Inlaid Jewelry* (London, 1902)

DIMAND, M. S., *Near Eastern Jewelry and Metalwork* (Bull. Metrop. Museum, N.Y., XXXI, 1936, 35)

JERPHANION, G. DE, *Le calice d'Antiochie* (Oriens. Christiana 7, Roma 1926)

IPPEL, A., *Guss- und Treibarbeiten in Silber* (Winckelmannprogramm 97, Berlin, 1937)

KÖSTER, A., *Antikes Tafelsilber* (Berlin, 1924)

LANSING, A., *A silver bottle of the Ptolemaic Pariod* (BMMA 33, 1938, 199)

LAURIE, A. P., *Examination of the gold on the masks of mummified bulls from the Bucheum.* (Techn. Studies Fine Arts, 2, No. 4, 213)

GUMMERUS, H., *Die römische Industrie wirtschaftliche Untersuchungen Bd. I Das Goldschmied- und Juweliersgewerbe* (Greifswald, 1918)

ORBELI, I. A. & TREVER, K. V., *Sasanidskij metal* (Orfèvrie sassanide) (Moskva 1935)

RUBENSOHN, O., *Hellenistisches Silbergerät in antiken Gipsabgüssen* (Ver. Peliz. Museum Hildesheim 1, Berlin, 1911)

SCHÄFER, H., *Die altägyptischen Prunkgefässe* (Leipzig, 1903)

SCHÄFER, H., *Ägyptische Goldschmiedarbeiten* (Berlin, 1910)

STEWARD, W. AUG., *Goldsmith's and Silversmith's work past and present* (JRSA 81, 1933, 837—846; 853—863)

WILLIAMS, C. R., *Catalogue of the Egyptian Antiquities. Gold, Silver, Jewelry and related Objects* (New York Hist. Soc. 1924)

294. JASPER, J. E. & MAS PIRGANDIE, *De inlandsche kunstnijverheid in Nederlandsch Indië. De goud- en zilversmeedkunst* (den Haag, 1927)

ROTH, LING, *Oriental Silverwork, malay and chinese* (London, 1910)

LOTHROP, S. K., *Gold and Silver from Southern Peru and Bolivia.* (JRAI 67, 1937, 305)

LOTHROP, S. K., *Inca Treasure as depicted by Spanish Historians.* (South-Western Museum, Los Angelos, 1938,)

SAVILLE, M. H., *The Goldsmith's art in ancient Mexico* (New York, 1920)

295. GOLDSMITHS, WORSH. CY OF, *The Scientific and Technical Factors of the Production of Gold and Silverwork* (London 1935/36)

PRITZLAFF, J., *Der Goldschmied* (Leipzig, 1920)

ROSENBERG, M., *Ägyptische Einlagen in Gold und Silber* (Frankfurt a. Main 1905)

sidered to be a special metal, not an alloy but a "mock gold" (Konter-feh, Counterfei). Thus Albertus Magnus comments on the calamine from Goslar, which turns copper into gold, but when heated leaves only ashes as the metal evaporates (*De mineralibus*). This failure to perceive the connection between calamine and its metal zinc was not only due to the lack of analytical methods, but also to the peculiar properties of zinc which made it impossible for early metallurgists to prepare this metal on a large scale for many centuries even after its discovery. As brass seems to have been discovered early in the first millennium B.C. there is a difference of more than 2500 years between the manufacture of the copper-zinc alloy, brass, and its metallic con-stituent, zinc. As the preparation of zinc is intimately connected with the evolution of distillation, which started in the first century A.D. only, we may safely conclude that zinc was unknown to the ancients. Of late more attention has been devoted to the history of zinc and its alloy with copper (3).

1.   *The zinc ores*

To understand the history of brass we must look into the *geology of zinc*. Zinc does not occur in the native, metallic state but its com-pounds are widely distributed. Zinc ores are more particularly asso-ciated with the ores of lead, silver, copper, antimony and arsenic, often in the form of complex ores. This fact should be remembered when looking at the map of the zinc deposits where only some of the most important deposits in the history of brass have been indicated, but further localities are to be found on the map of the lead deposits.

At present one of the most important zinc ores is sphalerite or zinc blende (black jack, Zinckblende), a zinc sulphide, forming reddish-brown to black, transparent to translucent, heavy masses of complex crystals. This ore not occurring on the earth's surface was probably treated only when its nature was recognized a few centuries ago.

The following two ores were very important to the early metal-lurgist as they occur in the upper layers of the earth. The true *calamine* (galmei, smithsonite) is a carbonate of zinc which forms heavy crusts of crystals, usually coloured green, blue, yellow, gray or brown by impurities.

A second ore sometimes called electric calamine is a silicate of zinc, *hemimorphite*, forms crusts or masses of glittering crystals or needles.

As these ores were always confused in Antiquity and even modern authors do not always distinguish them clearly, we shall use the term calamine for both of them, as correct distinction in ancient texts is neither feasible nor necessary for our subject. Indeed, the ancients did not only use one word for these two ores, but they used the same term for the white zinc oxide formed in different guises and forms when treating copper, lead or iron ores, thus making it generally impossible to apply the correct term smithsonite, hemimorphite or zinc oxide. Thus the Greeks use the word cadmeia for both the natural and the artificial products, the Arabs use the term *tûtiyâ* (the medieval *tutia* or *totia*) indiscriminately, but if the texts permit us we shall use the proper term zinc oxide for the artificial product. The natural product is often associated with ores of lead, silver, iron and copper and in that case the artificial product, zinc oxyde, is obtained during the treatment of these ores as a by-product, but the zinc ores are also frequently contaminated by large quantities of clay, oxides of iron or calcite and in that case they have an earthy appearance. This latter form was recognized in Antiquity as a special 'earth', which had the property when smelted with copper to give it the colour of gold. In the case of the mixed ores the ancients probably failed to perceive the zinc ore and only knew that the white zinc oxide was formed when smelting some specific silver, copper or iron ore. At present calamine deposits are practically exhausted and the metal is obtained from more complex ores. The zinc deposits are found in America, England (Cornwall), Germany (Rhineland, Westphalia and Harz, Silesia), Italy (Sardinia and Tuscany), Spain, Sweden and Norway, France, Belgium (Vielle Montagne, Moresnet), Carinthia, Styria and Tirol; outside Europe they occur in India, China (Hunan), Japan, Indochina, Altai Mts., Algeria, Tunisia, Nigeria, Rhodesia and Transvaal, but few of these had any importance in Antiquity. In Egypt there are no zinc ore deposits of economic value though calamine is found together with the lead ores at Gebel Rosas and a mixed sulphidic copper and zinc ore is found in the deeper strata at Gebel Abu Hamamid.

The copper ores of Georgia and Caucasia very often bear appreciable quantities of zinc ores. Pontus has several important zinc deposits, they are also found in the Murad valley near Lake Van and in the Qara Dagh, north-east of Tabriz. Southern Iran is particularly rich in zinc ores, the main deposits are situated between Isfahan and Anarek, in the Kuh i-Benan, north of Yezd, and north-east of Kerman, where Marco Polo saw the important *tûtiyâ* factories at Cobinam (the present Shah Dad) which exported their product to India. Many Persian

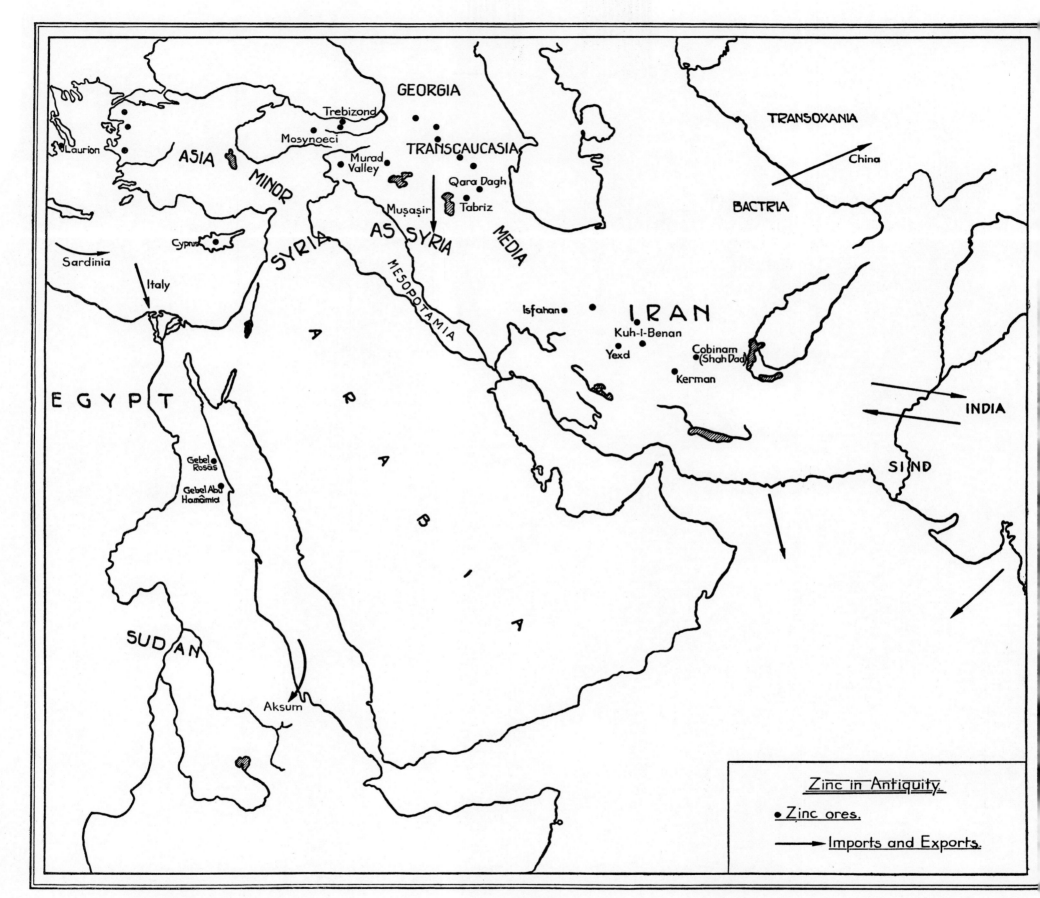

Fig. 45.
Zinc in Antiquity

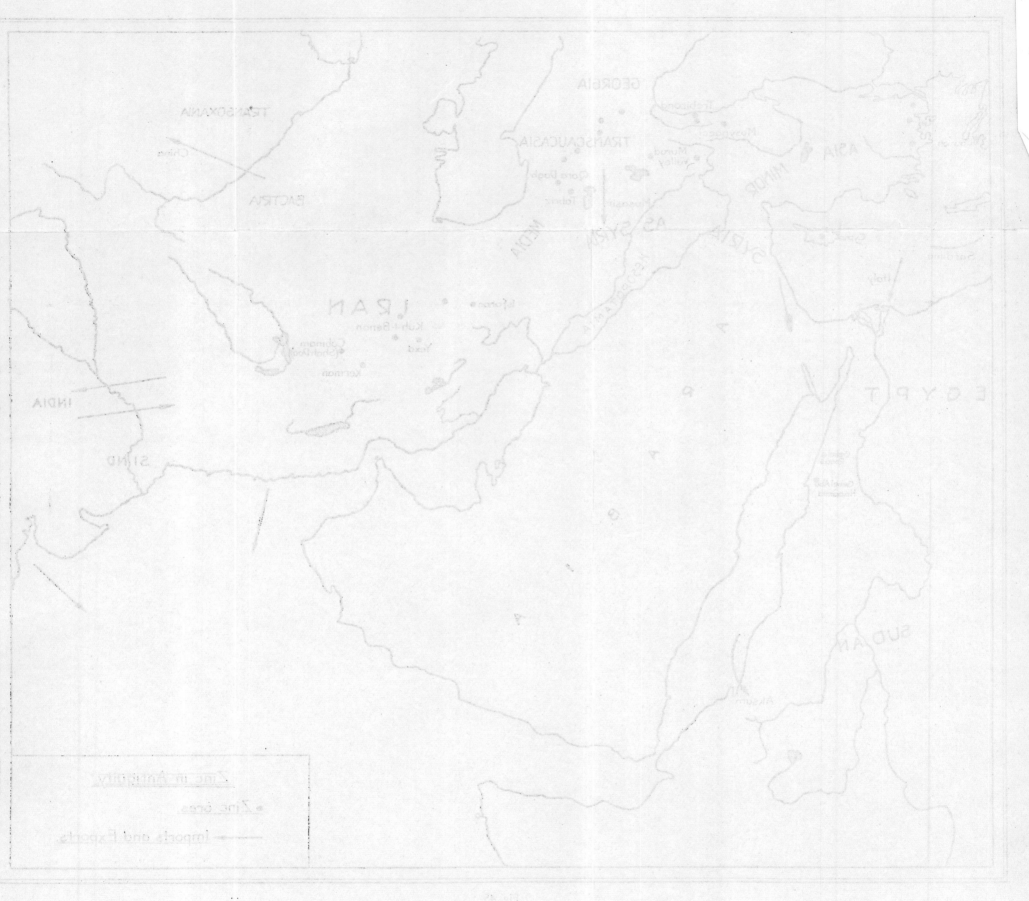

authors mention these deposits apart from those in India and Sind, and even Bontius still knows that there were large quantities of *tutia* in Kerman, though in his time the centre of the brass manufacture was round Isfahan. Pseudo-Aristotle mentions quarries in Sind and India too. The zinc-bearing copper ore of Cyprus is mentioned by Pliny (4), Strabo (5) and Galen (6). The galena of Laurion has an appreciable zinc content, the old slags show beautiful crystals of smithsonite formed by reaction with saline waters, and the treatment of the galena must have yielded zinc oxide as a by-product. Further deposits of cadmea were known to Pliny, especially those in Campania (which however did not exist and must represent a confusion of the cadmea deposits with the Campanian brass industry) and in the country of the Bergomates (7). In the same line he mentions that "a further discovery in the province of Germania is recently reported". This alludes to the calamine deposits of Gessenich near Aachen (8). Arabian authors often allude to the zinc oxyde from Spanish and Sardinian copper ore and these sources may have contributed to the cadmea production of the Imperial Era.

2. *Was zinc produced in Antiquity?*

The calamine can be reduced with charcoal to produce the metal zinc, but easy as this reaction may seem a peculiarity of the metal forces the metallurgist to use a special apparatus for this reduction. Zinc melts at the fairly low temperature of 419° C and molten zinc boils at 918° C, that is below the reduction temperature of its ore calamine. Therefore, when reducing calamine the zinc formed will immediately distill and condense against the roof of the furnace as solid zinc crystals. This sublimation is, however, only possible if there is no air present in the furnace, for if there is, the gaseous zinc will immediately be oxidized and form zinc oxide, which then in its turn will condense on the upper part of the furnace. This is the pompholyx of Dioscorides (9) and the *lana philosophica* of the later alchemists, a white woolly mass of small crystals, part of the zinc oxide being retained in the slag to form the *spodos*, an impure zinc oxide, which looks like pumice-stone. Wyndham Hulme (10) has given a "metallurgists' version" of this passage by Dioscorides, which runs thus:

"Pompholix differs from spodos specifically, but not generically. For spodos is blackish and generally heavier, being full of stalks, hairs and soil as though it were a scraping and flaking of the floors and furnaces of the brassworkers; but pompholix is smooth and white, and withal so light that it can float on the air. And of it there are two kinds, the one sky-blue and fattish, and other very white and extremely light. The white pompholix is produced when in the working and perfecting of brass the workmen sprinkle in more freely crushed cadmeia (= impure oxide of zinc), wishing to improve it, for the ash which is carried off from it being extremely light, results in pompholix; but it is not only from the working of brass and firewood that pompholix is formed but it is also principally produced from cadmeia blown with bellows. It is done thus. A furnace is placed in a two-storied building and in it towards the upper chamber there is a symmetrical aperture which is open to the sky overhead. The wall of the building next to the furnace is perforated with a small hole near the crucible itself for the admission of the draft. It has also a door for entry and departure prepared by the workman. Attached to this building there is another one in which the bellows and the blower work. For the rest fuel is put on the furnace and ignited; then the workman stands by and sprinkles in the finely broken cadmeia from the room over the top of the crucible and this he does by hand at the same time throwing on charcoal until the added mass is used up."

In this passage Dioscorides seems to describe as factory making brass and pompholix with an upper working floor such as persisted throughout the calamine brass industry in England down to its extinction about 1860. As long as the ancients were only preparing this zinc oxyde or cadmeia, they were content to collect the pompholyx and the spodos, but of course they never succeeded in producing zinc in their open furnaces usually working with a plentiful blast of air. Only when furnaces were constructed in the form of retorts connected with a receiving vessel and well shut off from the air, the zinc could be produced by simple reduction of the calamine with charcoal. This is why the production of zinc is intimately connected with the evolution of distillation and why the proper apparatus was only developed in the course of the 18th century. Therefore the ancients could not have produced zinc on a commercial scale and if ever obtained it was produced accidentally.

There is, however, no evidence of metallic zinc in Antiquity, nor was there any term in the ancient languages denoting the metal. Davies believed that zinc was known in Italy in the Iron Age, but the examples which he quoted are very doubtful. Grignon (1774) reports such a sample from a Roman site in Champagne, the date of the zinc(?)

filling of a silver bracelet and rings found by Salzmann in the necropolis of Cameiros on the island of Rhodes (1861) is uncertain; the idol from a Dacian settlement, stated by Helm (1896) to consist of 87.5% zinc, 1% of iron and 11.41% of lead is too vaguely described and it is doubtful whether the Roman cup from Laktaši (11) is really made of zinc. Recently A. W. Parsons (1939) found a fragment of pure zinc with 1.3% of lead and traces of copper and silver (a greater variety of impurities than in any modern grade of zinc!) together with pottery and coins of the fourth century B.C. directly below the cave sanctuary of Pan at the base of the north slope of the Acropolis (12). The metal strip was hammered, not rolled or cast like modern zinc, but it is still a mystery how it remained uncorroded at this very wet spot. It looks very much like the thin hammered zinc used in tea-chests many centuries later and may be an intrusion and not a real Greek product. It seems that the only way in which the zinc-copper alloy which we call "brass" could be produced was not by alloying the two metals but by smelting copper with the ore calamine, which is called "countrefey" in some older texts because of the golden appearance it gave to copper.

3.   *The production of brass*

We must again warn the reader that in books and papers more than a century old bronze is often called brass. In the Middle Ages it was the common term for the metal from which cannon was made and we still find the expression "brass field pieces", when it is quite certain that bronze was meant as brass would be completely unsuitable for such an application. Brass proper was a copper alloy with a low melting point and hence easy to cast and also easy to shape by hammering and embossing. There is no doubt that brass was produced by the Romans on a large scale from 20 B.C. onwards as a coin-alloy, but the origin of such production is much earlier.

It has been claimed that some mixed zinc-copper ores contained sufficient zinc to produce brass on smelting (13) and this statement has often been repeated. To produce brass from mixed ores might be possible in modern metallurgy, but it is doubtful whether this delicate process could have been executed in Antiquity.

It may be that some Spanish mixed ores would give brass on smelting but von Lippmann rightly contended against Sebelien and Witter (14) that the zinc content of the large majority of such ores is far too small and that nowhere large deposits of ores exist which could have given brass on smelting. Indeed the manufacture of brass must have been a deliberate process after a fortuitous discovery in the past. We must not be misled by the accidental zinc content of ancient copper or bronze objects, because many copper ores contain small percentages of zinc ranging from several hundreds of a percent up to 2% and such small percentages in the resultant copper do not make brass. Thus ancient Egyptian copper objects from Naqada and Ballas contain up to 1.5% of zinc, bronzes from the Late Bronze Age from Gandža, Karabağ, Goliat, and Koban in the Caucasus up to 2%, an ancient copper bar from Crete 0.63%, a needle from Thermi 0.29%, copper objects from Portugal up to 3%; but we have to wait until the Graeco-Roman period to find brass spreading all over the ancient world, except for a few exceptions which we will discuss later on. Then only brass occurs in the fringes of the civilized world, then only we find two Romano-British needles with about 14% of zinc (15) and a crucible containing copper with 15.5% of zinc (16). Though Petrie claims that zincblende was used by the prehistoric Egyptians for beads (17) this identification is very doubtful and even if it were correct it would, of course, not infer the knowledge of brass at such an early date. But we need not speculate as to the manufacture of brass in Antiquity for all our texts agree on this point and state that brass was always made from calamine and copper (18). Either the "earthy" natural calamine or the artificially prepared zinc oxyde or *cadmeia* (and all its varieties) were used. Even as late an author as Isidore had no idea of the zinc content of the calamine and thought that it was simply a drug for purifying copper (19). This method of preparing brass remained the only practical one until methods were devised to distill zinc from its ores. The correct term for this process would be the cementation of copper with zinc.

If calamine or zinc ore is finely ground and mixed with powdered charcoal and copper embedded in this mixture in a furnace or crucible, the zinc formed on heating will alloy with the copper giving it the golden yellow colour characteristic of a low zinc brass. It is not even necessary to heat the mixture above the melting point of the copper, but at temperatures of 800° C the zinc will slowly diffuse into the copper to form brass. This is the method mentioned by Biringuccio (20) early in the sixteenth century. He says that "Copper is coloured yellow by calamine and then often resembles gold. There is also an earthy mineral found in Italy in a mountain between Como and Milan and near Fosini in the province of Siena, which also colours copper exactly like the calamine from the German leadmines. This is an heavy, earthy ore of a yellow (zinc ore mixed with clay!).'"

But the process is much older and therefore the frequent statement that is was discovered by Erasmus Ebner in Nürnberg around 1509 is untrue. For in the eleventh century Theophilus describes exactly the same procedure when he indicates how to prepare brass in crucibles suitable for casting (21). It was also known to Avicenna and it was the standard procedure for brass production in that important centre Persia, whence its knowledge spread to China and India. Probably its secret was more or less forgotten in the later Middle Ages when brass was mainly imported from the East and the 'discovery' by Ebner may simply mean a rediscovery, in a period when metallurgy received a new impetus from the Renaissance scientists. Possibly Ebner was the first to make the metal zinc in Europe, though its industrial manufacture did not start until several centuries later.

This cementation-process is also mentioned by 'Geber' in his *Summa perfectionis* and in a work attributed to Zosimos we read the same way of treating Cyprian copper with *tutia* (zinc oxide). It is the standard method of brass manufacture in the Roman Imperial era. Pliny, for instance, says: "Brass (here *aes* is clearly brass!) is also prepared from a coppery mineral called *cadmea*, the most well-known sources of which are across the sea, although it used to be found in Campania (sic)! and is still mined in the territory of the Bergomates" and "Livian copper has the greatest power of alloying with cadmea" (22) and Theophrastus describes the earthy calamine thus: "The strangest kind of earth is that which is mixed with copper, for apart from possessing the faculty of mixing and melting it strikes one by its remarkable lustre" (23). But the process is older than that and its discovery should be sought in Pontus in the beginning of the first millennium B.C.

We have already pointed out that earlier bronzes may contain some zinc, but thus is generally due to contaminations of the copper ore used as in the case of the early Mesopotamian bronzes. Neither are zinc or brass found in *Egypt* before Roman times, the first true brass was found at Karanog (24). There is no term for zinc in Egyptian, and probably the brasses of the Roman period were introduced in a manufactured state. It was 'reexported' in the form of ornaments and vessels to the Abyssinian kingdom of Aksum where it meant an important medium of exchange (*Periplus* cap. CCLXXXII-CCLXXXVI) in the market of Adulis. This statement is confirmed by the many brass finger- and earrings found in late Nubian graves. Nor did brass or zinc come to Egypt from Africa for the negroes never or seldom mine zinc or lead even now (25). All the brass found in Africa must be ascribed to European or Arab trade, which began very early, the same term *nahas* being used for copper, bronze and brass. In the Niger and Guinea regions it was probably introduced by the Arabs and Moors and European coastal-trade and it was brought to the Central Sudan by the Muslim invasion. Kosmas Indikopleutes states that even in the seventh century A.D. the natives of Upper Abyssinia valued brass more than silver! We must therefore look to the north for the discovery of brass. Palestinian bronzes sometimes have a slight zinc content which is more marked at Gezer but can be explained by the impurities of the local copper ores (26), or by imports from the north. These bronzes dating from the Semitic III period (1400—1200 B.C.) contain up to 23.4% of zinc, which probably is a fortitious impurity introduced during the smelting of the copper, for brass is not found in Palestine elsewhere until Roman times, when Josephus reported that the Outer Gates of the Temple were made of brass.

Cyprus was an important centre of brass manufacture in the Roman period and we have Dioscorides' description of a brass-furnace (two-storied) from that island discussed before, but all the information dates from this period and there is no earlier text or find of brass objects.

In Iran brass came into use in the Achaemenian period. Darius is said to have possessed an 'Indian' cup which looked like gold but had a disagreable smell, which points to brass. As zinc-ores were discovered in this country a brass industry grew up here in later times, but this cannot be the country of origin as is proved by the analyses of early bronzes from these regions in which zinc appears only as a minor impurity. Nor is brass common in Mesopotamia and the earliest reference is Sargon II's Khorsabad inscriptions which often mention that he "covered the door-leaves of wood with a sheating of shining bronze" which "shining or white bronze" (*erê pisû*) came from Musasir, from the northern highlands. If this 'white bronze' is really brass, and this is fairly probable, we have here the earliest reference to this alloy in the eighth century B.C.

We have a most interesting text in Pseudo-Aristotle (27) referring to the discovery of brass: "They say that the bronze of the Mossynoeci excells because of its gloss and its extraordinary whiteness. They do not add tin but a special kind of earth, that is smelted with the copper. They say that the inventor did not disclose his secret to anyone, therefore the old bronzes of this region are remarkable for their excellent qualities and the later ones do not show them." This clearly refers to the cementation of copper with 'earthy' calamine, which therefore was the original process. We are inclined on account of the evidence mentioned above to date this discovery in the beginning of the first millennium B.C., somewhat earlier than Przeworski suggested (28). The Mossynoeci were a tribe living in the region south of Trebizond (29) in Pontus where zinc ores abound. Strabo mentions them under their late name of Heptakometai (30), they were possibly of Thracian-Phrygian stock and lived in the many-storied mountain dwellings still used by Ossetic tribes, but not in pile-dwellings as sometimes supposed. As a mountain tribe they were undoubtedly engaged in metal-lurgy as many other in Pontus who brought fame to this region, where so many metallurgical problems were solved.

Can we identify these Mossynoeci with the *Muški*, the redoubtable ennemies of the Assyrians in the early half of the first millennium B.C.? These Muški, Moschi or Meshech appear in power after the fall of the Hittite Empire around 1200 B.C. Though Lehmann-Haupt considers them aborigines of Asia Minor, Sidney Smith and many others agree that they were immigrants of Thraco-Phrygian stock and identical with the Phrygians, possibly speaking an Indo-Germanic language (Goetze) and invaders from the Balkan region. About 1200 they have occupied, together with the *Kaški* the region south of the bend of the Halys. Growing in power, they do not only reign from the Sangarius up to the mountains behind Cilicia, but in the reign of Tiglath Pileser (about 1170 or 1160) they overrun Alzi and Purukuzi, which were within Assyrian dominion and form a state with the Tibareni in the eastern part of the Anti-Taurus range, which the Assyrian forces reach in a campaign from N. E. Cilicia! This Muški state in central and eastern Cilicia probably had Tyana as its capital and the town of Mazaca reminds us of their dominion. Tukulti Ninurta II raids them from Nisibin in 885, and they bring Ašur-nasir-pal tribute including vessels of copper (884/3). They are prob-ably identical with the Meshech (31) who "traded the persons of men and vessels of brass". Allied with tribes of the north Mita (Midas?) of the Muški is the most formidable assailant of Sargon II who only partly subdues them in several campaigns (715—709). In the tenth century a body of Muški is still settled on the foothills near the source of the Tigris, but their state seems to have been destroyed by the Cimmerian invasion which drove part of them in isolated positions,

for instance in Pontus, where the Moschi and Tibareni are included
in the XIXth satrapy of Darius. Other parts of the tribe were subjects
of the Vannic kingdom (700). Herodotus mentions both Mossynoeci
and Moschi in Pontus (32), probably as parts of the original tribe,
they are again mentioned together in the army of Xerxes. Though
some of Xenophon's information (33) must be doubted it is important
that he mentions that they conquered some iron-working Chalybes
to act as their blacksmiths. This seems to prove that the Moschi
themselves were no metallurgists but learnt the craft from the aborigines!

From this centre the manufacture of brass spread west and east. It
was produced by heating metallic copper, charcoal and the zinc ores
calamine (zinc carbonate) at a temperature high enough to melt the
copper at which temperature most of the zinc liberated from the zinc
ore dissolves in the molten copper. The method was gradually improved. It was found that instead of using the earthy calamine this
crude ore should be refined separately by heating it with charcoal. It
was also soon noticed that a similar material was obtained when
smelting certain copper, lead or silver ores. Of course it was not
known that the original material was the natural calamine but that
this new artificial product was zinc oxyde, produced by heating zinc
ores or as a by-product of copper and silver-smelting. Indeed both
products were generally *cadmeia* or *cadmea* and most classical authors
do not distinguish the natural from the artificial product. We have
seen that the natural cadmea or calamine was found in Cyprus (Pliny
and Galen) and that Pliny also mentioned deposits in Campania,
Bergomum and Germania. But Galen knew that a similar, artificial
cadmea came from the silver mines and Dioscorides has a long passage
on both types of cadmea (34). He mentions natural calamine from
Macedonia, Thrace, and Spain which he considers of inferior quality.
The best quality is that produced when smelting copper ores, especially those from Cyprus. When heating them the zinc oxyde subli-
mates against the roof of the furnace and can be collected after cooling
down. The bright, white kind is pure zinc oxyde, which Dioscorides
calls *pompholyx*, while the kind more or less contaminated with soot
and dust in the lower regions of the furnace is called *spodos*. Apart
from this general classification of pure and impure, he mentions several
terms indicating slight varieties of zinc oxyde coloured by impurities
or condensed in peculiar form, such as *botryites, onychitis, placodes,
zonitis, ostracitis*, etc., while Pliny also mentions the kind called *capnitis*.

This zinc oxyde condensed against the furnace-roof is called 'Ofen-bruch' by German metallurgists and Agricola remarked that "when smelting the siliceous lead-ores of Goslar a kind of white liquid flows from the furnace, which is noxious to silver because it burns this metal. Therefore this liquid is drawn off after removing the super-natant slags. The walls of the furnace exude a similar liquid", but he does not seem to recognize this zinc oxide as the well known *tutia*. This *tutia* is described in the widespread medieval treatise on alchemy called *Summa perfectionis* wrongly ascribed to "Geber" and there purification by sublimation from the crude product of the furnaces is recommended (cap. 48). Biringuccio, however, knew it quite well and so did the classical authors, for Dioscorides remarks that the best qualities of pompholyx and spodos are obtained from the Cyprian copper ores and that the degree of whiteness is an indi-cation of the heat of the furnace and the purity. He recommends it for diseases of the eyes and ascribes to it all the healing powers of similar lead-compounds. For this purpose it is further refined with wine, etc. Pliny makes similar remarks and says that the *cadmea* derived from silver ores is inferior to that from copper ores. He also advises refining by heating the crude product with charcoal (35). The reason why the lead furnaces of Laurion were rather high may be found in the observation that these ores contain zinc compounds, which could be won in the upper part of the furnace as fairly pure zinc oxyde and used for brass manufacture. *Cadmeia* thus means both the natural zinc ore and the artificial product and though the only method of brass manufacture consisted in cementation of copper with zinc compounds there was some evolution in this process. The first stage was cemen-tation with the crude natural product calamine, the later stage worked with separately refined zinc oxyde which was then used to obtain a pure brass. This refinement may be a discovery of the Roman period. It was then used all over the world for many centuries later Marco Polo sees it in Persia. This is what he tells us about the tutia manu-facture of Cobinam near Kerman: "Much antimony (zinc) is found in the country, and they procure tutty which makes an excellent collyrium, together with spodium, by the following process. They take the crude ore from a vein that is known to yield such as is fit for the purpose, and put it in a heated furnace. Over the furnace they place an iron grating formed of small bars set close together. The smoke or vapour ascending from the furnace in burning attaches itself to the bars and as it cools becomes hard. This is the tutty; whilst the gross and heavy part, which does not ascend, but remains as a cinder in the furnace, becomes the spodium" (I,20).

The spread of brass manufacture to the west was slow. In Greece neither Homer nor Herodotus know anything of brass, though texts are often wrongly translated and would seem to prove the knowledge of brass. We will revert to this point when discussing the nomen-clature of zinc. Von Bibra (35), whose analyses Desch has recently rightly shoved into the limelight again in the first report of the Sumerian Copper Committee (1928), gives a wealth of material which goes to prove that brass was quite exceptional in Greece until the Augustean Age, the earlier so-called brasses containing only a few percents of zinc and nothing like the usual 30—38% or even 50% of brasses in the true sense of the word.

In Rome some Republican coins contain up to 4% of zinc but the true brass coinage was issued in the Augustean Age. The earliest brass coins contain about 17.3% of zinc, but the percentage gradually grows. Still brass must have been comparatively expensive for the price given during the reign of Diocletianus is still 6 to 8 times that of copper. Manufacture of brass on a large scale began in the west in the first century B.C. and gradually spread. The early Imperial coinage in Greece, Egypt and Asia is always made of alloys of copper with tin or lead, it never contains zinc until much later. It is claimed that this brass industry exploited the ores of Etruria and Achiardi and Grassini (36) may be right though Etruscan exploitation seems very doubtful in view of the rarity of brass among the early archaeological finds, though the exploitation of local lead ores may have led to the discovery of the zin ores.

It is claimed that zinc derived from calamine smelted with copper appears in copper-alloys in France as early as the La Tène period (37). Another important centre of brass production was the province of Germania, where the deposits of Gressenich in the Stollberg district near Aachen were discovered between 74 and 77 A.D. in the neighbour-hood of galena deposits. This centre flourished notably between 150 and 300 A.D. to suffer a decline in the third and fourth century but to be rediscovered in the fifth as brass objects in Aachen prove and to become prominent again in the eleventh century together with the deposits in the Meusevalley (38).

The production of *cadmea* as Ofenbruch from the Laurion ore may also date from the later Graeco-Roman period. It is mentioned by Galen (39) and Pliny (40) who calls this special spodos *lauriotis*. The growth of the Cyprian brass industry is of the same date. In the east little progress was made for many centuries as it seems. We have no data on the Achaemenian brass industry and we do not know whether the local ores were exploited as they were at a later date. It seems that the situation remained rather stagnant here and that the bulk of the brass in Roman times was import from the west as we have seen to be the case in Egypt. Zinc compounds gradually become more prominent in Hellenistic chemical literature. The Leiden-Stockholm papyrus mentions *cadmeia* and *oreichalkos* as ingredients for the preparation of "asem". For the *chrysophanès* and the *xanthosis* of copper Pseudo-Democritos uses *cadmea*, which is also called magnesia or white lead! Zosimos is quite conversant with the manufacture of brass from *cadmea* and copper he says that the preparation of the "yellow or Persian alloy, wholly like natural gold" (brass) and that of the "glittering, light alloy" (bronze) are important secrets invented by a mythical Pabapnidos, son of Sitos. It is remarkable that he calls brass a Persian alloy, which goes to show that there was a brass industry in Iran in his time. Manuscripts of the eight century and later date (for instance the Coptic medical papyrus edited by Chassinat) abound with references to the manufacture of brass, copper and *cadmea*, now more frequently called *tutia*. This 'gold' is only to be distinguished from natural gold by its smell as it will neither rust nor tarnish like true gold, but the *kráma* (krasis: alloy) is a great secret.

In Persia brass production seems to have started on a larger scale in the sixth century A.D. when it was exported to India and some two centuries later passed to China. In Persian legend the feet of Gayômard are said to be of brass, Pollux gives the term *oreichalkos*! Persian scientists like al-Gâhiz (died 869) know that gold can not be made from brass, they call both brass and bronze *sifr* or *sufr*. Ibn al-Faqîh (900) states that brass manufacture was a government monopoly at Mt. Dumbâwand and at Kerman, where the *tutîyâ* was mined, and Ibn Hawqal (950) states that it also comes from Sardan and India, and al-Fâdil knows that the "tûtiyâ of the Sages" or *al-qalamî* comes from many countries, but that Spain has the largest number of varieties. Al-Dimašqî (1300) is the first to mention the metal zinc which comes from China, where its preparation is kept secret, it is white like tin and it does not oxidize but its sound is dull. Finally from the fifteenth century onwards brass and bronze are well distinguished, the first 'birindj' is made from copper and *tûtiyâ*, the second 'sefîdruy' from copper and tin. We do not hear about zinc being made in Persia itself,

this seems to have been done for the first time on an industrial scale
in China. Still in China the earliest reference to the metal zinc is embodied in an encyclopaedia, the Tien King Kai Wu written in 1637,
and there it is stated that it was then known to modern writers only!
Zinc is called *ya-yuen*, that is inferior lead, its industrial manufacture
therefore seems to date from somewhere near 1600, its modern name
is *hsin*[1]. Brass is of course known far earlier, references are found in
sixth century texts, archaeological finds at Kuchâ in Khotan show the
way by which this knowledge penetrated from Persia. It seems that

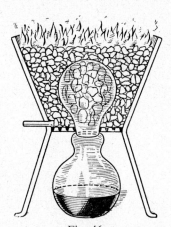

Fig. 46.
The apparatus used by the Hindu metallurgist for the
manufacture of zinc

the earliest term *t'ou shih* may mean both calamine and brass, though
the latter is later called *totan* from *tûtiâ*. Hiuen Tsang, the travelling
monk speaks of brass made from copper and *yu-shih* (calamine?).
Though the value of the old Indian alchemists and their modern
commentators is very doubtful it seems that zinc was prepared by
Indian chemists since the twelfth century, but that this remained a
laboratory experiment and never was applied to industrial production.
This zinc or "the essence of tin" as it is sometimes called was prepared
by distilling calamine with organic substances in an apparatus suitable
for "destillatio per descensum", where a substance could be heated in
an upper flask and the drippings could be collected in a lower one.
    Zinc is also mentioned as the "spirit of *tûtiyâ*" or the "brother of
silver" and perhaps the Tantras around 1100 also mention zinc, which
was the seventh metal known to the Hindus. Brass was of course

known far earlier and brass figurines and ornaments became common from the sixth century A.D. onwards. It was from the East that zinc was introduced by the Portuguese and Dutch traders to Europe, where zinc manufacture started only in the 18th century. Valentin's *Oostindië* mentions *tintenaga* or spelter, the Portuguese name for zink being *tutenago* (the Persian *tûtiyâ* with the suffix *-nak*, this was later corrupted and formed the English tradename "tooth and egg"!)(41). In Akbar's time zinc was produced in India, for we hear from Rogerius (42) that taxes were paid to the temples on the *spiauter* produced. The *calaem* often mentioned in these books on the first contacts with the East was not, as is often supposed, zinc. *calaem* is not a corruption of calamine but it is derived from the Arabic *kala'i*, that is "what hails from Kedah (Qalah) in Malacca" and it means tin! (43).

During the Dark Ages in Europe brass-production stopped in the Stollberg area but not entirely (44) for the Notitia dignitatum and the Codex Theodosius mention "barbaricarii", Syrians who worked under the "praepositi barbaricariorum sive argentariorum" and who were stationed at Arles, Rheims and Trier who used brass for inlay- and other metal work. This craft continued to function from the fifth through the eighth century, the Burgundian law recognizes the "faber argentarius" who makes the same metal-inlay work as his ancestors did under Roman law. But the true revival of the brass industry dates from the eleventh century only.

4. *Nomenclature of zinc alloys*

The *nomenclature* of zinc and its alloys is a difficult chapter of ancient metallurgy, for the ancients did not readily distinguish the alloys of lead, silver, tin, zinc and antimony, they could not analyse the components and chose the names very arbitrarily. This is the reason why they often vary their meaning in the course of the ages. Thus for instance the Sanskrit *nāga* is really lead, but it is used for tin or zinc too!

Strabo tell us in an interesting passage (45): "There is a stone in the neighbourhood of Andeira which when burned becomes iron, and then, when heated in a furnace with a certain earth distils *pseudoargyros* and this with the addition of copper makes the mixture (*kráma*) as it called which by some is called *oreichalkos*." Now this is 'technical nonsense' and Diergart has proposed to leave the *pseudoargyros* untranslated or to say 'mocksilver'. Though zinc-iron ores exist this procedure is impossible. It would seem that Diergart (46) is right here and that this *pseudoargyros* is a silver-like alloy of unknown composition. Though arsenical copper and iron ores abound in the Troad, it is doubtful whether an arsenic-copper or arsenic-iron alloy could be prepared in the way Strabo suggests!

There is a similar doubt about the meaning of *oreichalkos*, which may originally have been an Asianic word. It certainly means a kind of copper and by Late Republican times acquired the meaning "brass" Ancient Greek authors certainly know brass (47) though some of them are not to clear about it and confuse it with electrum (48). Hesychius still calls it a copper resembling gold! Only by the time of Cicero does oreichalcum (49) become aurichalcum and in the passages from Pliny which we mentioned before it is clear that he at first takes it to be a separate metal but later correctly describes as a copper-alloy for the manufacture of aes. Cicero discusses the ethics of selling brass for gold, the value of the latter being a thousandfold of that of the former. We must remember, that the ancients could not possibly know that the zinc ores they smelted with copper contained a metal. If ever they obtained zinc in small quantities by some fortuitious disposition of their smelting furnace or other circumstances, they must have seen it as a freak alloy, which to their mind must hardly have had any connection with the ore used or the copper-alloy they tried to produce. We can not agree with Michell (50) that pseudoargyros was zinc, indeed, it was more probably metallic arsenic or arsenical copper which has this silver-like appearance.

As one would expect from archaeology there is no Egyptian word for brass. The equation *thst*: brass suggested by Budge must be dismissed. There is a curious Coptic term *"chomt n barot"* (ϧⲟⲙⲧ ⲛⲃⲁⲣⲱⲧ), which Crum first called brass (51) but which he translates "a composite metal" in his *Coptic dictionary* (52). Its Greek equivalent is *chalkolibanon*, and it may be brass, though we possess too few texts to fix its true meaning. It is certainly a copper alloy (*chomt*!); *barot*, given by Spiegelberg as "Erz", is derived from the Egyptian *bi3 rwd* (53)

Ebbell's identification of the Egyptian *ḥtm* with calamine (*cadmea*) in the Papyrus Ebers seems very probably as the *ḥtm* figures largely in collyria where we would expect zinc-compounds!

We can not point out an Hebrew term for brass, as *néchôšeth* just like *aes* or *chalkos* may mean brass in late texts, but usually should be translated copper or bronze. The "fine copper" mentioned in Ezra 8 : 27 may well be brass, which alloy was certainly used for cymbals in Hellenistic times.

Campbell Thompson (32) has some interesting suggestions to make on Akkadian terms for brass and zinc compounds. He holds *elmu(e)šu* (sù.ud áG) to be brass and he claims that the text KAR 307 is a symbolic picture of the brass-founder's furnace. Further proof is, however, needed for so early an Assyrian manufacture of brass! He further identifies *tušku* (sù.ʜɛ́) with spodos and *lulu* (kù.ʜɛ́) with pompholyx, but these identifications are of course connected with his reading of the text KAR 307 and his assertion that the manufacture of brass was generally known to the Assyrians.

The sù.ʜɛ́ (Su-gan) can hardly have been spodos, for no trace of a Sumerian brass has ever been found. As the texts say that it is added to copper to improve its casting properties, this was probably antimony (or arsenic?), compare the Hebrew sîghîm (55). Thompson's view that this Assyrian religious text KAR 307 is a symbolic picture of the brass-furnace such as Dioscorides describes would seem to be wrong, when we test his identification of the "zinc-compounds" mentioned therein. The Assyrian Dictionary mentions many passages where the word "elmešu" is used, very few of which could possibly refer to brass. It seems an unknown precious stone or mineral in older times, only in Neo-Babylonian times could it possibly mean brass.

We have already identified the *spodos* and *pompholyx* as forms of zinc oxyde and *kadmeia*, *kadmia* as the general name for zinc ores. The latter term was corrupted by the Arabian alchemists to *kalmeia*, *kalamiya*, *kalimina* and early in the fifteenth century we find the terms *kalmis* or *galmei*.

The origin of the word *messing* is not known. Some claim it descent from the Latin *massa* (lump of metal) and the Greek *maza*, others like Schrader trace it back via an early Slavonic form *mosengjú* to an early Caucasian root *moss* or *mossum*, but this remains to be proved.

Equally doubtful is the etymology of the Turkish *birinj* (brass and bronze!) from the Sanskrit *vrîhi* and the Greek *óryza*, *bryza*, because brass has the gloss of polished rice!

The general Persian term for zinc ores and zinc oxyde is *tûtiyâ*, which occurs frequently in medieval literature as *tutia* or *totia*! Laufer (56) has suggested that the Chinese *t'ou shi* (a metallic product from Sassanian Persia) was brass, but this is not sure, neither is its connection with *tûtiyâ*! The Sanskrit *tuttha* is derived from *tûtiyâ* and it came to mean 'vitriol' (compound of sulphuric acid with different metals) to the great confusion of early translators. There is no Persian term which can be identified with zinc. The term *rozy* (zinc) originally meant 'copper', we find it in the compound term *isfīd-roy* (first 'bronze' then 'brass') which through forms like *sepidruy, isbâdârih* was corrupted to *spelter* or *spiauter*, the sixteenth century term for zinc!

The Persian alchemists use *ruḫ-i-tûtiyâ* (spirit of *tutia*) for zinc. The true Sanskrit term *yašada* (Hindi *jāstā* or *dastā*) may go back on a Persian original (vide the Arabian *jasad*: body) which arose from the same speculations on the connections of zinc and tutia.

Another early European word, occurring side by side with spelter, is *tutenago*. This early word for zinc is usually explained as the Persian *tûtiyâ* followed by the suffix-*nāk*, the whole corrupted by the Portuguese to *tutenago* and still worse by the English tradefirms to '*tooth and egg*'! Further confusion was introduced by the use of *tutenago* to denote *paktong* (*pai-t'un*, a natural Chinese copper-zinc-nickel alloy) and the use of spelter for both *tutenag* and *pewter* (the Chinese *peh-yuen*, a lead-tin-alloy) (57).

The terms *laiton* (Tudor: *latten*), etc. in Romanic languages for brass are derived from the Italian *latta*: sheet brass.

These few lines will go to show that the etymology of zinc and zinc compounds is by no means solved and still remains an intricate, often puzzling, chapter of the history of these metals and alloys, "Yet such as you and I, who are not impractised in the trade, must not suffer ourselves to be imposed upon by hard names or bold assertions". (58)

BIBLIOGRAPHY

For detailed bibliography see my *Bibliographia Antiqua, Philosophia Naturalis* (Leiden, 1942) (Suppl. I, 1952, Suppl. II, 1963)

1. PARACELSUS, *De mineralibus*, edit. Toxites, 1570, 450
2. HOMMEL, W., *Zur Geschichte des Zinkes* (Chem. Ztg. 36, 1912, 905)
3. AGRICOLA, G., *Zwölf Bücher vom Berg- und Hüttenwesen* (Berlin, 1928, 356)
   BAILEY, K. C., *The Elder Pliny's chapters on chemical subjects* (2 vols. London, 1929/1932)
   VON BIBRA, E., *Die Bronzen und Kupferlegierungen der alten und ältesten Völker* (Erlangen, 1869, 17—91)
   BLÜMNER, H., *Technologie und Terminologie der Gewerbe und Künste bei den alten Griechen und Römern* (Vol. IV, Leipzig, 1887, 91, 162, 192, 196, 197)
   DAWKINS, J. M., *Zinc and spelter, notes on the history of zinc from Babylon to the* 18*th century* (Chemistry and Industry, 1949, 515—520)
   DAWKINS, J. M., *Zinc and Spelter* (Zinc Develp. Assoc., Oxford, 1950)
   FLASDIEK, H. M., *Zinn und Zink, Studien zur abendländischen Wortgeschichte* (Tübingen, 1954)
   FRANTZ, H., *Zink und Messing im Altertum* (Berg- und Hüttenm. Ztg. 1881, 231; 1883, 133)
   GARLAND, H. and BANNISTER, C. O., *Ancient Egyptian metallurgy* (London, 1927)
   GOWLAND, W., *Copper and its alloys in early times* (J. St. Inst. 7, 1912, 23)
   HOFMANN, K. B., *Zur Geschichte des Zinkes bei den Alten* (Berg- und Hüttenm. Ztg. 1882, 479)
   HOMMEL, W., *Zur Geschichte des Zinkes* (Chem. Ztg. 36, 1912, 905)
   HOMMEL, W., *Über indisches und chinesisches Zink* (Z. Angew. Chem. 25, 1912, 96)
   MARÉCHAL, J. R., *Petite histoire du laiton et du zinc* (Techniques et Civilisations III, 1954, 109—128)
   MARÉCHAL, J. R., *Petite Histoire du Laiton et du Zinc* (O. Junker G.m.b.H., Gevelsberg) also *Kleine Geschichte von Messing und Zink,* 1957
   LUCAS, A., *Ancient Egyptian materials and industries* (London, 1962)
   MARCO POLO *The travels of —* (edit. Everymans Library No. 306, London, 1918)
   PARTINGTON, J. R., *Origins and development of applied chemistry* (London, 1935)

PRZEWORSKI, ST. *Die Metallindustrie Anatoliens*. (Suppl. to *Intern. Archiv f. Ethnographie* 36, Leiden, 1939)

RICKARD, T. A., *Man and metals* (London, 1932, vol. I)

ROLANDI, G. & SCACCIATI, G., *Ottone e zinco presso gli antichi* (Industr. miner. Nov. 1956)

ROSSIGNOL, J., *Les métaux dans l'Antiquité* (Paris, 1863, 251)

TÄCKHOLM, U., *Studien über den Bergbau der römischen Kaiserzeit* (Uppsala, 1937)

WESTER, WM. REUBEN, *Notes on the History, Manufacture and Properties of wrought brass* (Trans. Amer. Inst. Mining Metall. Eng. 147, 1942, 13—27)

WITTER, W., *Die älteste Erzgewinnung im nordisch-germanischen Lebenskreis* (vol. II, Leipzig, 1938)

ZIPPE, F. X. M., *Die Geschichte der Metalle* (Wien, 1857, 253)

4. PLINY, *Nat. Hist.* 34. 100

5. STRABO, 3. 4. 15. cap. 163

6. GALEN, *De simpl. med.* IX, 9. 11

7. PLINY, *Nat. Hist.* 34. 2

8. DAVIES, O., *Roman Mines in Europe* (Oxford, 1935)

9. DIOSCORIDES V, 85

10. WYNDHAM HULME, E., *Notes and Queries, March* 24, 1945, p. 123

11. KELLNER, *Wiss. Mitt. aus Bosniën und Herzogovina* I, 1893, 254

12. SHEAR, T. LESLIE, *The Campaign of* 1939 (Hesperia IX, 1940, 265)
M. FARNSWORTH, C. S. SMITH & J. L. RODDA, *Metallographic examination of a sample of metallic zinc from ancient Athens* (Hesperia Suppl. Vol. VIII, 1949, 126—129)

13. KIRCHER, *Mundus subterraneus*, 1665, II, 218

14. VON LIPPMANN, E. O., *Entstehung und Ausbreitung der Alchemie* (Leipzig, 2 vols, 1919, 570, 591; 1932, 143)
VON LIPPMANN, E. O., *Zur chemischen Zusammensetzung der vorhistorischen Bronzen* (Chem. Ztg. 56, 1932, 268, 544, 763)

15. CHURCH, A. H., *Analyses of some bronzes found in Great Britain* (J. Chem. Soc. 1865, 215)

16. MOSS, *Proc. R. Irish Acad.* 37, 1927, 175

17. PETRIE, W. FLINDERS, *Prehistoric Egypt*, 1920, 43

18. FESTUS, III, 36

19. ISIDORE, *Etym.* XVI. 20. 3

20. JOHANNSEN, O., *Biringuccios Pirotechnia* (Braunschweig, 1925, 58, 86)

21. THEOBALD, W., *Des Theophilus Presbyter Diversarium Artium Schedula* (Berlin, 1933) III. 64—65

22. PLINY, *Nat. Hist.* XXXIV. 2 & 4

23. THEOPHRASTUS *On Stones* cap. 49

24. WOOLLEY, *Karanog* I. 62, 67

25. CLINE, W., *Metallurgy and mining in Negro Africa* (Paris, 1937)

26. MACALISTER, GEZER, 1912, ii, 265

27. *Pseudo-Aristotle, De mirab. Ausc.* cap. 49 & 62

28. PRZEWORSKI, ST., *Die Metallindustrie Anatoliens* (Leiden, 1939)

29. HALLIDAY, W. R., *Mossynios and Mossynoikoi* (Class. Rev. 37, 1923, 105—107)
30. STRABO, 12. 19. cap. 549
31. *Ezech.* 27. 13
32. HERODOTUS, III. 94 & VII. 78
33. XENOPHON, *Anabasis*, IV. 8. 3; V. 4. 12—13
34. DIOSCORIDES, V. 34—36
35. PLINY, *Nat. Hist.* XXXIV, 100
36. GRASSINI, R., *L'oricalco e gli Etruschi* (Stud. Etr. 7, 1933, 331—334)
37. MARÉCHAL, R., *La présence du zinc dans les bronzes romains, gaulois et germaniques et les débuts de la fabrication du laiton* (OGAM (Rennes), 74/75, 1961, 265—270)
38. CALEY, EARLE R., *On the existence of chronological variations in the composition of Roman brass* (Ohio J. Sci. 55, 1955, 137—140)
    DAWKINS, J. M., *Zinc and Spelter* (Zinc Development Assoc., London, 1950)
    DE LAET, S. J., *Analyse spectrochimique de vases en métal de la nécropole de Samson* (Namurcum (Belgique) 1952, 20—22)
    MICHELL, H., *Oreichalkos* (Class. Review N.S. V, 1955, 21—22)
    SALIN, E., *Copper through the ages* (Cuivre, Laiton, Alliages I, 1953, no. 16, 40—43; no. 17, 36—39; no. 18, 36—39)
    WOOTTON, A., *Brass, A Roman coinage metal* (SEABY's coin and medal Bulletin, June 1960, 223—225)
39. GALEN, *De simpl. med.* IX. 3. 25
40. PLINY, *Nat. Hist.* XXXIV. 13 & 132
41. BONNIN, A., *Tutenag and paktong* (Oxford, 1924)
42. ROGERIUS, *Open deure tot het verborgen heydendom*, (edit. Caland, 1915, 121)
43. LINSCHOTEN, J. VAN, *Eerste Voyagie*, (edit. Kern, I, 1910, 72)
44. SALIN, EDOUARD, *L'emploi du laiton en matière de damasquinure à l'époque gallo-romaine* (Cuivre, Laiton, Alliages 1953, nos. 14 & 15, 34—37, 50—53)
    SALIN, EDOUARD, *Les alliages du cuivre à l'époque mérovingienne* (Cuivre, Laiton, Alliages, 1953/54, nos. 16, 17 & 18, 40—43, 36—39, 36—39)
45. STRABO, 13. 1. 56. cap. 610
46. DIERGART, P., *Oreichalkos and pseudoargyros in chemischer Beleuchtung* (Philologus N.F. 18, 1905, 150—153)
    DAVIES, O., *Oreichalkos* (Man XXIX, 1929, 36)
47. HOMER. *Hymn.* VI. 9; HESIOD, *Scut.* 122
48. PLATO, *Critias* 114e; ARISTOTLE, *De mirab. Ausc.* 58, 834bis; THEOPHRASTUS, *On Stones* 49; POLLUX, *Onom.* VII. 99—100
49. CICERO, *de Off.* iii. 23
50. MICHELL, H., *Oreichalkos* (Class. Review V, 1955, 21—22, 29—30)
51. CRUM, *Coptic ostraca*, London, 1902, 42, no. 459
52. CRUM, *Coptic dictionary* 1939, 44.a
53. GUNN, JEA 3, 1917, 36; WAINWRIGHT, JEA 18, 1932, 6

54. Thompson, R. Campbell, *Dictionary of Assyrian chemistry and geology* (Oxford, 1936, 71, 76)
55. *Ezech*, 22. 18
56. Laufer, B., *Sino-Iranica* (Chicago, 1919, 373, 512, 581)
57. Bonnin, A., *Tutenag and paktong* (Oxford, 1924)
58. Boyle, Robert, *Sceptical Chymist*, (part III)

INDEX